2/89

3000 800013 63471
St. Louis Community College

WITHDRAWN

D0073499

St. Louis Community College

Library

5801 Wilson Avenue
St. Louis, Missouri 63110

Passage from India

St. Louis Community College
at Meramec
Library

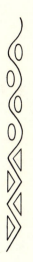

Passage from India

Asian Indian Immigrants in North America

JOAN M. JENSEN

Yale University Press

New Haven and London

Copyright © 1988 by Joan M. Jensen.
All rights reserved.
This book may not be reproduced, in whole or in
part, including illustrations, in any form (beyond
that copying permitted by Sections 107 and 108 of
the U.S. Copyright Law and except by reviewers
for the public press), without written permission
from the publishers.

Designed by Jo Aerne and set in Palatino type by
Rainsford Type, Ridgefield, Connecticut.
Printed in the United States of America by Edwards
Brothers, Inc., Ann Arbor, Michigan.

Library of Congress Cataloging-in-Publication Data
Jensen, Joan M.
Passage from India.
Bibliography: p.
Includes index.
1. East Indian Americans—History.
2. East Indians—Canada—History.
3. Alien labor, East Indian—United States—
History.
4. Alien labor, East Indian—Canada—History.
5. India—Emigration and immigration.
6. United States—Race relations.
7. Canada—Race relations.   I. Title.
E184.E2J46   1988   973'.0491411   87–8316
ISBN 0–300–03846–1 (alk. paper)

The paper in this book meets the guidelines for
permanence and durability of the Committee on
Production Guidelines for Book Longevity of the
Council on Library Resources.

10 9 8 7 6 5 4 3 2 1

Let us run together a new government
Where there will be no one big or small.
All together will be equal,
Everyone will have the same rights.
Let there be no question of high or low.
Let everyone have a job.

—Ghadar protest song

Contents

Preface

This book has its origins in the impact that India had on my family during World War II. During that time, my father was stationed at Ramgarr in Bihar Province in what Americans called the China-Burma-India Theater. There were, first of all, the rugs, silver filigree, and sandalwood objects he purchased and sent home—all carefully sanitized by my mother through scrubbing or dry cleaning. Then there were the hundreds of letters and pictures, all describing the diversity of India with what now seems to me an amazing openness. My father, as an Italian immigrant, seemed to have experienced enough poverty and discrimination in his own life to be able to have a perspective somewhat different from that of many American officers who served in India. On rereading his letters forty years later, I can see an attitude that allowed him to absorb Indian life less with criticism than with appreciation of his own escape into the middle class and its relative economic security. Our familial encounter with India, I am sure, was the basis for my interest at discovering that Indians immigrating to the United States had encountered a great deal more discrimination than my grandfather—also dark-skinned and poor—had met when he came to the West Coast in the first decade of the twentieth century as a construction worker on a railroad in the state of Washington.

When, in the course of my research on internal security in World War I, I discovered that Asian Indians had suffered public discrimination, my own family history provided the motivation to try to explain that discrimination. That was over twenty years ago. My research grew slowly. It became an inexplicable—even unruly—mass of material that I could not quite conquer. What began as a short history of a small group of Asian immigrants grew to encompass British, British India, United States, and German policy. The Sikhs, who made up the majority of Indian immigrants to America in the early twentieth century, turned out to be a socially complex group whose political relations with the four governments were even more complex. A number of years passed before I had enough historical understanding to place this complexity in a framework that made the actions of both the Indians and the governments explicable.

I have tried to explain the role of the people and governments of the West Coast states and provinces in the growing controversy over Indian immigration. In many ways, those players were central to the final United States policy. The West Coast provided the context for Indo-American contact.

This book traces the movement of both workers and political refugees to North America. It also traces the genesis of the 1914 uprising—when thousands of Indians returned from North America to lead a rebellion against British rule in India—and its consequence for the Indians who immigrated to the West Coast during the first part of the twentieth century. The total number of Indian immigrants who came to Canada and the United States during that period could not have numbered over ten thousand. Yet the Indians' search for economic, social, and finally political justice, and the American response to that search, are an important part of early-twentieth-century history. This book analyzes the causes of the Indian emigration from India, the response of Westerners to the new immigrants, and the development of both Canadian and United States policies for their exclusion. Exclusion policies were not reversed in the United States until 1946. Since 1962, Indians have come to this country in large numbers to form a vigorous and important Asian Indian community. The story of how Indian immigrant pioneers settled in a hostile land and struggled to enjoy rights equal to those of Euro-Americans is a part of the history of cultural confrontation in North America. It is a study of why ethnic groups sometimes develop hostilities toward each other and how governments respond to social and economic tensions among diverse ethnic groups. There is much to learn from this study of past ethnic conflict.

I would especially like to thank the Indians who helped me to understand their culture and experiences. Tuly Johl Singh, Bob Baldev Singh, Nand Kaur Singh, and Jane Singh all encouraged and supported me. I have learned much from them.

Passage from India

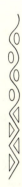

Prologue: Passage from India

One day, oh India, your name was great,
Whether you remember or not.
—Ghadar protest song

Historians of international migration now see the century from 1830 to 1930 as one in which large worker populations on
all continents moved from less economically developed countries (and
areas of countries) to those more highly developed. This migration of
millions of workers—usually from rural areas—was accompanied by
severe social and political dislocation, not only in the sending but also
in the receiving countries. Integrating new workers into the work force—
at first usually as temporary workers in specific jobs for which there was
a demand for their labor, but then as permanent workers with communities, families, and aspirations for full assimilation—was a process
accompanied by great instability. The evolution of public policy to channel and control this great exodus of workers involved a complex interplay
of employers, political parties, trade unions, and ethnic groups.

The millions of Indians who left India during this period were but
one part of a larger movement, and the few thousand who came to
North America but one small part of the Indian diaspora. Telescoped
as it was into a few years, the Indian migration to North America and
the response of various groups to it provide a case study of immense
importance, in which one can see the clash of interests of employer,
immigrant worker, native worker, official, and politician gradually evolv-
ing into public policy.

Among this small group of Indian immigrants was a still smaller group
of political refugees. These men came to North America for political
rather than economic reasons. Although much smaller than the migration of workers, political migration also swelled during the century from
1830 to 1930. Migrants provided potential recruits, and political refugees
potential leaders for more broadly based political movements. Foreign
countries which guaranteed political asylum and also welcomed large
numbers of temporary migrant workers provided fertile ground for revolutionary movements. Irish, Cubans, Mexicans, and Chinese, as well
as Indians, found support in the United States for such movements.
Indians were only one group of political refugees who saw the United

States as a viable base for their revolutionary activities. Because these activities in North America covered a brief period, they provide sharp focus for the study of controversy over the right of political asylum.

Indian immigrants became inextricably involved in the expanding Pacific economy, the economic and social instability that accompanied that expansion, and the political battles that ensued over Asian immigrants. Western anti-Asian campaigns began against the Chinese. As Chinese immigration declined, nativists focused on the Japanese, who were beginning to arrive in larger numbers. The increase of Indian immigration diverted the attention of anti-Asians only briefly and partially. The Japanese remained their central concern throughout the period here studied. Once Indian immigration had been contained, nativists turned to a new group, the Filipinos, who arrived on the Pacific Coast in increasing numbers in the 1920s and 1930s. The history of the first Indians is thus regional history as well as national and immigrant history. The confluence of competing interests and concerns makes it an ideal case study of how national immigration policies took shape in the early twentieth century.

Indian political activities culminated in 1914 when thousands of Indians returned from North America to lead a rebellion against the British in India. The British responded with executions, arrests, trials, surveillance, and reforms. The rebellion was quelled for the moment, but the British believed, and some newspapers proclaimed, that the mutiny had been "hatched in America." There was some truth to the accusation. A number of leaders had been in the United States, where they had raised money and had even attempted one ill-fated shipment of arms to India with the aid of German diplomats.

In 1857 the British subdued the last major revolt against their control of India. During the next two decades, the British India government developed an internal security apparatus to maintain that control. By the 1870s the British felt sure that domestic revolution was an impossibility. So too did foreigners. When the young American army officer Emory Upton arrived in India on an inspection of the armies of Asia in 1878, for example, he was impressed. Upton had gone to India with orders to learn how a colonial power with a small force could maintain control over two hundred million people. The British, with only sixty thousand white troops and a railway system, could, he concluded, hold India almost indefinitely even with the defection of the entire native army.[1]

The British had no fear of domestic insurrection at that time, but they did worry that foreign countries might use domestic discontent as a pretext for invasion. Britain worried first about Napoleon emancipating the Indians; then Russia was feared to have inherited the designs of Napoleon. Finally, after Japan destroyed the Russian fleet at Tsushima in May 1905, it was the Japanese that the British feared. The Russo-Japanese war gave colonial powers notice of the determination of some Asians to end the centuries of European domination in their nations. Britian had to reconsider the power of both the small but independent Japan and the pan-Asian sentiments that Japan's victory had provoked. One speaker in the Japanese diet talked openly of stretching out a helping hand to India, and the Japanese government began welcoming dissident Indian students to its universities. The Anglo-Japanese treaty of 1902 quieted Britain's fear of Japan by defining the special interests of Britain in China and of Japan in China and Korea and by providing for neutrality or assistance in case of war. Because Britain was also concerned about Germany's growing power in Europe, it wished to extend the Japanese alliance to include India as a recognized part of the British Empire, to protect the Empire's Asian flank in case of war. After Japan agreed to extend the treaty in August 1905, the Japanese government opposed all talk of Indian independence. Japan even expelled Indian students who spoke too loudly against British rule in India.[2]

As the threat from Japan receded, a new one appeared in its place, from China. Even in China's impotent days during the 1880s, British India officials had vaguely wondered about Chinese designs on India. But China was not even able to handle its own insurrections, and not until these insurrections threatened to take revolutionary form with the impetus of nationalism did the real threat to British control of India emerge. The 1905 Chinese nationalist boycott of American goods, called to protest unjust United States immigration policies, focused British fears about China. Although the boycott was directed against American goods, much of its motivation was nationalist discontent with the Chinese government for allowing United States officials to mistreat immigrant workers. The activities of Chinese nationalists posed no direct threat to the British Empire in India, but they did symbolize Asian opposition to European domination. Following on the heels of the Japanese defeat of Russia, the Chinese boycott stimulated Indian nationalist sentiment among students.

The student movement rekindled British concern over internal dissent. Almost half a century had passed since the British had crushed the last major revolt, in 1857. In the succeeding years, as British rulers had developed an army to maintain internal security, they had also consolidated their control with efficient administration, improved communication, Western education, and irrigation projects. Westernization of the sons of middle-class Indians and their installation at the bottom of the colonial bureaucracy quieted discontent. In 1885 British rulers allowed Indians to form the Indian National Congress, a moderate political organization designed to channel dissent into a movement for economic reform and for a larger voice in British policy. British liberals rationalized the control of India with vague promises of self-government. As the century ended, however, and educated Indians began to expect a greater role in government, British imperial policies seemed to grow more rigid. Rudyard Kipling perhaps best exemplified the British dilemma in his literary works. He represented the Indian native world as colorful but static and inaccessible, the white world as a set of ordeals by which all Anglo-Indians were tested and most were found wanting. Kipling had no difficulty in accepting the values of the older Indian society, but he excluded the westernized Indians who were beginning to work for self-government.[3]

Young British politicians who would soon be dictating imperial policy had no place for the young westernized Indian either. Take, for example, Winston Churchill, a young junior lieutenant who went to India in 1897 and stayed for three years playing polo, performing military rituals, collecting butterflies, growing roses, and reading British histories of the Roman Empire. He rode with the Bengal Lancers in charges against the tribesmen in one of the continuing frontier wars and wrote of the great work England was doing in India, of her high mission to rule "these primitive but agreeable races for their welfare and our own." The government of India, he felt, could be patient with the natives, because "it knows that if the worst comes to the worst, it can shoot anybody down. Its problem is to avoid such hateful conclusions." Democratic reins, he insisted, were impossible east of the Suez; "India must be governed by old principles."[4]

That was exactly what the government seemed to believe. Queen Victoria's Jubilee took place in London in 1897 amid pomp, pageantry, and promises of an end to racial discrimination. India, meanwhile, was stricken by famine, plagues, and earthquakes. When the English chairman of the plague committee in Poona used dictatorial methods to enforce ineffectual measures, angry Indians assassinated him. Riots broke out in Bombay in 1898, and two years later there were riots in Bihar and Kanpur. Writers, speakers, and groups of protestors began to extol doctrines of nationalism. The British tried to suppress the protest, but young rebels went underground, forming secret societies in which members pledged their lives to liberating India by revolutionary means. In July 1905, viceroy George Curzon refueled discontent by approving a partition of the province of Bengal. The British claimed that the need for administrative reform necessitated the partition, that the province was too large to permit efficient operation. Indian opponents claimed that fear of Indian nationalism caused the British to split Bengal, an area bound by a common language, history, and culture.[5]

Bengali students led opposition to the partition. Feeding their hunger for political independence on revolutionary excerpts from Mazzini and Garibaldi, and on news of the Russian peasant uprising following the Japanese victory, students interpreted the partition as a policy designed to obliterate local independence through centralization. In the fall of 1905, students went to school barefooted to protest the partition and to dramatize the dependence of India on foreign products. School authorities turned the students out of their classes and threatened them with expulsion if they did not return wearing shoes. To encourage a boycott of foreign goods, students braved beatings by police with iron-tipped bamboo sticks. The students' idealism spread to the whole community and inspired others to resist. Cobblers refused to mend English shoes, washermen to wash foreign clothes. Newspapers served as the classrooms for the movement. The Bengali poet Rabindranath Tagore, later a Nobel laureate, wrote songs and plays in support of the protest. The partition and its opposition provoked the first nationalist movement to affect all communities and all classes in northern India. Even members of the Indian National Congress opposed it. "Lord Curzon will convert Bengal into a second Ireland," wrote one Bengali editor.[6]

Seeing an end to student activism as crucial for control of the populace, the government of Bengal punished the students. If opposition continued, students would lose financial support from the government, and university graduates would be declared ineligible for public employment. The "Carlyle circular" of 10 October 1905 ordered teachers to be enrolled as constables and to identify students taking part in the demonstrations. Tagore denounced the circular and promised to stand by the students. There was talk of boycotting examinations, of establishing a new university, and of going to the United States to get technical training. Over all opposition, the partition took place on 16 October 1905.

The British speedily replaced Curzon with a new viceroy, Gilbert Minto. An elderly, ineffectual Conservative whose chief delights in life were horseback riding and hunting, Minto had just come from an undistinguished six years as governor general of Canada. He was appointed in order to give India a rest after the turmoil of the Curzon era. Most careful observers of the politics of the British Empire expected that the new Liberal secretary of state for India, Sir John Morley, would give increased direction from the India Office in London. Minto arrived in November 1905 to face the double Curzonian legacy: a cold, unsympathetic, and subservient bureaucracy that had nothing but contempt for the Indians, and smoldering resentment among the Indians themselves. Nevertheless, Morley announced that the issue was closed. The partition was final.

Students responded by shouting *bande Mataram* (hail Motherland) in the streets of Calcutta. By April 1906, Minto had suspended three hundred students from college and excluded them from government service because of their public shouts. "The British Raj must be a poor sorry affair, if it trembles before a pack of unruly collegians," wrote Morley, as he ordered the pardon of the students. By this time, he had concluded that Minto was "not very clever." Morley underestimated the strength of nationalism, however, for early in August 1906, Indians began a boycott of English manufactured goods, especially cotton. Meanwhile, railroad workers struck for higher wages, better housing, and vacations. Even Muslims supported the boycott, although it was led by Hindus.[7]

Bengali discontent was annoying to the British, but far more serious was the spread of discontent to the Punjab. The British had traditionally relied upon Punjabis to maintain internal security at home as well as to fight abroad. Although the Punjab was not subdued by the British until 1848, Punjabi help had been crucial in suppressing the revolt of 1857, and the Punjab was essential as a supply base. After the revolt was crushed, the British had hurried to complete the Suez Canal and the railway system so that English troops could be landed at Bombay and sent directly to every important part of India. Even so, the British continued to rely on the Punjabis as the mainstay of the native army. The Punjabis were often sent by the British to fight for the Empire abroad—in the Sudan and the Mediterranean, and in the Boxer Rebellion in China—and by the turn of the century the British military tradition among the Punjabis seemed well established. As a precaution, however, Indian officers never received king's commissions, only viceroy's commissions, nor were they allowed to command white troops in India. Possibly as much as half of the native army was Punjabi by the late nineteenth century. There were enough Punjabis that intelligence reports in 1886 noted the possibility that Punjabis might take up arms and fight for the Russians. The number of Punjabi infantry units continued to increase while those of other regions declined. By 1900, over forty-two thousand troops were from the Punjab. Indian recruiters were a common sight in the villages of the northern Punjab.[8]

The Punjabis impressed the British as farmers as well as fighters. Officials considered the Punjabi cultivator easy to manage, a sturdy yeoman, independent and self-willed, yet reasonable and peaceably inclined if left alone. According to Charles Ibbetson, who studied the Punjabis in the 1880s, the Punjabi peasant was "the revenue-payer *par excellence* of the Province." Punjabis provided supplies for the military cantonments in the area, as well as sons for the army. They also increased the population dramatically in the late nineteenth century. A thriving economy relieved population pressure and kept money flowing in, but the basic land problems of the Punjabi were not solved. After making new areas workable through irrigation, the British carefully controlled the distribution of land to provide large holdings to hereditary landowners who were expected to develop the land and to act as natural leaders. Instead, absentee landlordism flourished and tenancy increased. Money flowing into home villages from abroad also had an inflationary effect, driving up the price of land and making it more difficult for families without absent sons to increase their holdings. The British had insured that the village political systems would have difficulty in changing to meet the needs of the villagers by insisting on codifying customary law and fixing village organization as it had existed before 1848.[9]

Punjabi peasants, many of them from the traditional Jat caste, took great pride in working with their hands, considered themselves good farmers, and looked down on debt. Nevertheless, peasants preferred to pay taxes by mortgaging rather than selling their lands. As mortgages in the Punjab increased, so did discontent. Unrest over alienation of land to moneylenders was already growing in the Punjab by 1886, but the British were hesitant to discard their traditional colonial policies to deal with the political realities of the Punjab. By 1893, reports from India agreed that the danger of rural unrest was more significant than the possible repercussions from interfering with the "natural economic process," and, from 1895 on, reports stressed the possibility that debtors might transfer their hostility from moneylenders to the British for not protecting them and warned that "professional agitators" might subvert the peasants from whom the native soldiery was drawn. As money-lenders—usually absentee landlords—replaced the traditional ancestral landlord and middle peasant as landowner, Indian politicians began to argue that the British were incompetent to deal with the situation. In England, Lord Elgin, secretary of state for the colonies, felt compelled to disclaim publicly these accusations and to argue that, in fact, the Indian peasant was prospering under British rule. Moneylenders soon subverted token British reforms, such as an alienation law designed to halt transfer of land, and after 1900 land transfer dramatically increased. Though the period from 1900 to 1906 seemed one of peace and economic prosperity, the British government was concerned about the Punjab. To ensure political support, it summarily crushed signs of rural and urban unrest—thereby sparking further grievances.[10]

The British had traditionally encouraged the Sikh religion, particularly in the army, because they believed Sikh orthodoxy meant loyalty to the sovereign. Being impressed with the supposed martial qualities of the Sikhs and realizing the benefits from dividing those ruled, the British encouraged enrollment. By 1900 Sikh soldiers accounted for a fourth of all Punjabi troops in the Indian army and the same percentage in the armies of the Punjabi states. Separate Sikh regiments were formed and the tenets of Sikhism enforced by British officers. As the Sikh regiments increased and men were assigned to recruit peasants, the army became a means for Sikhs to convert Hindus: Sikh recruiting officers would enlist Hindus on condition that they become Sikhs.[11]

Conversion from Hinduism to Sikhism increased outside the military as well during the first decade of the twentieth century. Between 1901 and 1911, the Sikhs increased by 37 percent in the Punjab—far too much for natural population growth, and an indication that Hindus were converting. The Sikhs, who composed a large minority of the Punjab population, considered themselves members of an ancient and militant religion dating back to the fifteenth century. Sikhs had ruled much of the Punjab for almost a century, and the Sikh religion kept alive a tradition of separatism from British rule among the Jat peasantry. Aiming at reform among the Hindus, the Sikhs opposed the caste system, symbol worship, and other practices they considered corrupt, and preached the unity of god and the brotherhood of man. Accepting both Hindus and Muslims into their sect, Sikhs called themselves "disciples." The increasing conversion to Sikhism began to concern British officials because it coincided with growing political discontent. Religious separatism had the potential for disrupting the military defense of the British raj. The British, who had long depended on the right "outlook" of Sikh soldiers, began to reject recruits from Sikh villages such as Jundialla, where they suspected men of potential disloyalty.[12]

A second reason for conversion was the success of the Sikhs in organizing their communities socially and politically. During the early 1870s, a reform movement, founded by rich landed gentry but emphasizing the unity of the entire Sikh community, began to influence affairs in the Punjab. Reformers established local groups called Singh Sabhas to spread literacy, education, and religious awareness among the Sikhs and to consolidate Sikhs into a single community. *Singh*, which means "lion" in Punjabi, was the name taken by male Sikhs who identified most closely with the warrior-martyr tradition. Singhs expressed their identity publicly by leaving beard and hair unshorn and by wearing a steel bangle and a dagger. In 1902, leaders of the movement formed a chief Khalsa Diwan, a group which was to function as a coordinating body for local Singh Sabhas social and emerging political movements. Both the Singh Sabhas and the chief Khalsa Diwan organized the Sikh community socially and facilitated internal communication. They published newspapers, encouraged literacy, and established educational institutions. The leadership of these Sikh organizations was highly elitist, but the organizations laid a basis for mass political movements by consolidating and representing the entire Sikh community.[13]

From these Sikh communities, men began to leave for the West Coast of America in the first decade of the twentieth century. The Sikh emigrants were part of a larger Indian diaspora that accompanied the development of British colonialism in India. The Indian exodus, in turn, was part of a still larger movement of migrants loosened from their native lands in the late nineteenth and early twentieth centuries by the push of economic dislocation in their own developing countries and by the pull of economic demands in industrializing countries.

The Indian diaspora was already causing crises in the British empire by 1907. The problem dated back to the nineteenth century when, after the abolition of slavery in Britain in 1834, the British began to depend on Indian and Chinese labor. The dual Indian and Chinese migration to British possessions was symbolized by the word *kuli*, which means "bitter strength" in Chinese and "wages" in Tamil, the language of the district from which most of the first Indian laborers were recruited in southern India. Originally desired by the sugar producers to replace slaves, Indian laborers were soon in demand in Mauritius, Guyana, Trinidad, Surinam, Fiji, the Natal, and the Transvaal. Despite criticism in England of the incredibly harsh conditions and the high mortality rates that resulted from importing Indians under contract, the practice continued from 1840 to 1900. The mortality of the Hill Coolies, who went to the West Indies from northern India, was so appalling, however, that the practice of recruiting under contract was virtually abandoned, and migration reached a low point by the 1870s. Migration under contract revived somewhat in the last decade of the century, but was gradually replaced with free migration from new areas such as the Punjab.[14]

By the end of the nineteenth century, enough European settlers had emigrated to Africa and Southeast Asia to react with hostility to Indians and other Asians who sought to remain in settled communities once their indentures had ended. Prejudice against other races probably existed among Europeans of all colonizing groups. When enough Europeans were present to control local governments, the prejudice, once only a state of mind, grew into discriminatory behavior. During the period from 1850 to 1920, attitudes once shifting and flexible began to harden into exclusionary and discriminatory policies. Asian immigrants, as well as native populations, faced increasing hostility from Europeans in the late nineteenth century. The change was worldwide and can be traced in Southeast Asia, North America, and Africa. By the time Indians entered these countries, the battle lines had already been drawn. The very characteristics which made Asian workers attractive to employers— their willingness to remain separate, to maintain their own cultures, and not to assimilate European work attitudes—made them less acceptable to workers and to Europeans less directly interested in their labor. Workers and politicians had an interest in a homogeneous population. To them, foreign workers who maintained their cultural differences were a potential threat. Expulsion was an expedient used by workers confronted with an alien group that had different work standards—that is, worked harder or longer for lower wages and exhibited different cultural behavior (saved more, were less mobile, enjoyed different forms of recreation and entertainment). Restriction was the usual response by that segment of the middle class which feared violent confrontations between migrant and domestic workers.

Literacy tests gradually emerged as one method of restriction. Legal restriction based on a social rather than a racial characteristic was a favorite of moderates who hoped to avoid conflict between the peoples of different cultures attracted to the same areas by the pull of the international labor market. Discussion of restrictive laws based on the ability of an immigrant to read and write English or his or her own language surfaced in the United States in the 1880s. By 1896 a literacy test was being discussed in the Natal as a means of restricting immigration of Indians without adopting an openly racialist policy.

Conflict over Indian immigration in South Africa grew steadily in the 1880s. When Mohandas Gandhi arrived there in 1892 as a young lawyer, he was not only asked to remove his turban to practice in court, he was also discriminated against in hotels and on railways, and was insulted and beaten. When, after a brief return to India, Gandhi arrived back in South Africa in 1896 with his family and several hundred free Indians, a Durban mob attempted to prevent their landing.[15]

At the colonial conference that year, a gathering where colonial leaders discussed imperial policy, the question of Asian exclusion came up. The secretary of state for the colonies, Joseph Chamberlain, declared that the home government was completely in favor of Asian restrictions and agreed that emigration of Asians should be prevented at all costs. He reminded colonial delegates of the Empire's traditions against racial distinctions, however, and said that to exclude Indian subjects or other Asians because of color would be "so offensive to those peoples that it would be most painful" for Queen Victoria to sanction it. He approved a European literacy test as a way to exclude Asians under the guise of education rather than race. The following year, 1897, the Natal followed his suggestion by legalizing a language test devised to eliminate Asian immigration by requiring literacy in a European language.

The Natal solution proved to be an ideal colonial policy. It preserved the legal fiction of impartiality while serving an unabashedly racialist end. There was never any pretense among officials that the law would be applied against white immigrants. From London to India to the Natal, white settlers were the first colonial concern. Liberals in Britain might join outraged Indians in protest, but the British government settled for the appearance of equality and gave in to the practice of discrimination. Thus the practice grew. The Cape Colony imitated the Natal in passing a similar European literacy test, but applied it in such a manner that even Indians literate in their own language and in English were kept out. By 1907, the Natal legislature was debating passage of an immigration restriction bill aimed specifically at Asians, and European colonists were agitating against Indian immigration, a pattern soon repeated in other parts of Africa.[16]

Conflict over Asians was most severe in the Transvaal. In the aftermath of the Boer War, from 1904 to 1906, operators of gold mines had imported over sixty thousand Chinese workers under three-year contracts. The importation of Chinese workers undercut the wages of both African and white workers and led to political pressure from white workers for the repatriation of the Chinese. Some British officials had felt that Indians could simply be substituted as workers where European colonists opposed the Chinese; such a plan was even proposed by the under secretary for the colonies, Winston Churchill, when colonists in the Transvaal began calling for repatriation of the sixty thousand Chinese laborers. The secretary of state for India flatly opposed Churchill's scheme to add to the Indian immigrant population, however, for Gandhi had already mobilized protests by ten thousand Indians in the Transvaal against a European literacy act and an Asian registration act. Gandhi did not demand political equality for the Indians in the Transvaal. As he told a British high commissioner there, Indians wanted only the right to "live side by side with other British subjects in peace and amity, and with dignity and self respect." The Transvaal solution imposed a new system of discrimination there. The British repatriated the Chinese, replaced them with rigidly controlled African workers, and allowed restriction on immigration as well as discrimination against Indians. Despite the protests led by Gandhi, the British approved both the registration and the literacy laws.[17]

The Natal and Transvaal actions opened the way for increased discrimination against Indians in other colonies. East Africa followed South Africa. In 1900, Kenya was known as "the America of the Hindu" because of the opportunities available there, but European settlers arrived in 1903, and within three years the government was refusing Indian applications for land. Although Indians appealed to London, so too did the governor of Kenya, who wrote that Europeans could not compete with the Indian shopkeeper. The British agreed that Kenya should be reserved for Europeans. Events in Africa indicated that the British foreign office would sanction racial dominance by Europeans in future conflicts with Indians. Australia and New Zealand followed South Africa in imposing restrictive literacy tests.[18]

Few Asian Indians came to the United States before 1906. An Indian from Madras who visited Massachusetts in 1790 may have been the first to travel to the United States. During the next decade, as Salem developed its India trade, young Asian Indians sometimes returned with sea captains and worked on the India wharves of Crowinshield or Derby, the two largest shipholders. One captain brought back a tall, black-bearded Sikh who could be seen walking down Derby Street in his blue turban, long white tunic, loose trousers, and red sash. He worked as a family servant and drove the captain to the Unitarian church each Sunday morning. In 1851, half a dozen Asian Indians marched in the East India Marine Society contingent for the Fourth of July parade in Salem. These men left no history, though some stayed in Salem. They were said by New England chroniclers to have married Negro women and become part of the black population of Salem.[19]

There are a few indications that Indians also were brought by early sea captains to other parts of the East Coast and that they fared less well. The line between slavery and indenture was difficult to maintain in areas where dark skin was a presumption of the lack of civil rights. One of the most moving accounts of this tragic racism is a petition filed in the Pennsylvania Abolition Society records and dated "about the 1790's." The petition was by James Dunn, who described how his parents had indentured him in Calcutta, about the age of eight, to the mate of an English vessel, so that he could learn to read and write. The mate had decided to join the army and had left the boy in the care of a widow, who in turn indentured Dunn, now ten, "again to learn to read and write and to learn a trade." After only one month in school, Dunn's new owner was imprisoned for debt and sold Dunn to a man who took him to Georgia. Dunn followed his new owner through various parts of the South until the man died. According to Dunn, the executors of his master's will then took the seals off his indentures and, hiding them in a towel, ordered him to burn them. Dunn was able to determine that they were his papers and, when his time was up, attempted to obtain his freedom through the courts and, when this failed, by shipping out to England. The executor discovered both of Dunn's attempts and punished him. Dunn was then treated simply as a slave and was sold from person to person. There was no indication in the abolition papers whether or not Dunn ever achieved his freedom.

Indians brought to Pennsylvania fared only slightly better. In 1780, the state passed a gradual emancipation bill which provided that all slaves brought into the state had to be indentured. A number of immigrants thereafter indentured their Indian slaves for twelve to fifteen years. Like the Massachusetts Indians, these Indians—if they survived to be freed—probably married black women and became part of the black population. John Ballay, Joseph Green, George Jimor, Thomas Robinson, and several others not mentioned by name were thus among the first Indian immigrants to North America.[20]

The next record of Indians comes from California. John, a forty-year-old cook from the Coramandel in southern India, was in Monterey in

1836. *Hutchings' California Magazine* in 1857 mentioned an Asian Indian adventurer who after three years in the mines was awaiting return passage to India. At least two other Asian Indians also arrived during the California gold rush, probably brought by New England ships. According to later stories, one of these men was killed by American Indians at the instigation of white men, the other was defrauded of his wages as a cook.[21]

After the Civil War, American officials in India did what they could to convince Indians to stay at home. The consul in Bombay told one group of Parsee merchants who wished to migrate to the West that the United States would not be a good place for them. In the 1880s, the United States consul at Calcutta discouraged three Mormon missionaries from taking converts back to Utah. Indians were of no value in the American West, he told the missionaries. This consul also opposed a revision of laws in India to remove racial discrimination because, he explained, it was bad to bring Europeans and Americans down to the level of non-Christian civilizations. Another American consul contented himself with importing jugglers and swamis to exhibit at fairs in the 1890s.[22]

Despite the discouragement of American consuls in India, a few Indian merchants arrived in the United States. When Rudyard Kipling visited Philadelphia in 1889, he met three Parsee merchants and spoke to them in their native language. By the turn of the century, an estimated five hundred Indian traders were in the United States, some in New York and Missouri, some in southern cities. A *National Geographic* photograph from 1907 showed a group of Parsees, probably merchants, being admitted at Ellis Island. Perhaps these traders performed the same function as the *issei* who created mutual confidence and growing acceptance of Japanese trade during that period. If so, their story has yet to be told. The Indian merchants imported silks, linens, and other goods from India and kept quiet.[23]

Along with wanderers and merchants, a few religious leaders visited the United States. American intellectuals had discovered Indian religions in the early nineteenth century, at the same time that American merchants were developing Indian trade. Those were the days when Boston seemed enthralled by the romance of India. The Boston Theatre performed *The Rajah's Daughter* and *Cataract of the Ganges* while people sang "The Hindu Girl." The Boston elite read books on India and bought Bengal ginghams and Calcutta goatskins along India Street while ships tied up along the India Wharf. Ralph Waldo Emerson and particularly

Henry David Thoreau enthusiastically studied Indian religions. Though most Americans dismissed Asian religions as having little relevance for their own lives, the interest still continued. When Walt Whitman wrote the poem "Passage to India" in 1868, the idea that the wisdom and art of India could act as a mirror for Americans was strong. The Suez Canal and the transcontinental railroad, India and California, became linked in Whitman's imagination, and he planned to write a book about a journey of the soul to God, called *Passage to India*. By the 1870s, therefore, a literary tradition of interest in India had taken root, particularly in the Northeast. There, new Asian religious reform movements, such as the Brahmo Somaj, and European religious reform movements, such as theosophy, led to an active scholarship on Hinduism and a receptive audience for traveling Indian teachers who began arriving in the 1880s. In 1893, Phillips Brooks, minister of Trinity Church in Boston, wrote in a letter from India that his pilgrimage there was necessitated by the fact that "a larger part of Boston prefers to consider itself Buddhist rather than Christian." The term *Boston Brahmin* was born of this interest. Bostonians even appointed an Asian Indian who had received his medical training in England as a port physician. Later, the Boston Museum of Fine Arts would install the Asian scholar Ananda Kentish Coomaraswamy as curator of its Indian art collection.[24]

Evidence of the popularity of Indian religions and their teachers was evident in many ways by 1893. In that year, Americans enthusiastically welcomed the visiting Vedantist Swami Vivekananda to the World's Parliament of Religions. Vivekananda dressed in the orange robes of the *sannyasin* (monk) but spoke fluent English. Having, as one commentator said, an impressive stage manner and a gift for the memorable phrase— he pronounced Whitman an American sannyasin—Vivekananda became a celebrity at the parliament. His success paved the way for an increasing number of Indian swamis who established Vedanta centers and preached to what Christian missionaries considered disturbing numbers of interested Americans.

Though Christian missionaries imagined Asian religious leaders to be a threat, most Americans saw no reason to be concerned. Neither merchants nor swamis provoked much negative comment. Their numbers were small enough for Americans to enjoy them as exotic curiosities. The census of 1900 reported 2050 people from India in the United States, but this number included Anglo-Indians and members of any race born in India. Only 20 Indians entered in 1903, 258 in 1904, and 145 in 1905. During 1906, however, 600 applied for admission, mostly from Vancouver. Since no laws excluded Indians, American immigration officials simply gave them a stringent physical examination before permitting them to enter the United States. Several hundred were rejected, but many were admitted by immigration inspectors, and the men began to move south in small groups.[25]

Several hundred Indian workers appeared in the lumber mills and logging camps of Oregon and Washington and as far south as Chico, California. When, at the beginning of November 1906, the American consul at Vancouver received his first complaint about the influx of Indian immigrants from a man in Chico, he wrote from Vancouver to the state department: "Decided steps are being taken by the local labor unions, to stop this immigration, but of course the matter is much complicated as most of these men are British subjects, and many of them have served in the British Army." The almost four hundred Indians who had arrived on the *Tartar* in November 1906 had been admitted to the United States. The men were strong and would easily find employment in lumber camps, the consul wrote to the state department on 22 November 1906. "Unfortunately, there is a long frontier here, and without much more extensive protection these people could easily cross into the United States," he warned. He urged that immigration officials be alerted.[26]

Among the workers arriving on the Pacific Coast were also the first of the political refugees. The arrival of these men gave rise to concern by the British that the refugees might be able to enlist American sympathizers in the cause of Indian independence. From the time that the first American trading ship arrived in Calcutta in 1784, British officials were concerned about American political influence in India. George Baldwin, the British consul in Egypt, had warned his government of the dangers of unrestricted American trade: "The Americans arrive among them free, exhulting, broke loose from all restraints." Such concerns led the British to refuse to recognize the Newburyport, Massachusetts, merchant appointed first American consul to India in 1788. The East India Company confined the Yankees to seaports and the carrying trade, and made them use Indian brokers. The Yankees, however, proved uninterested in politics. They concentrated on profits, sometimes making 700 percent profit on those early voyages and gladly carrying the profits of British officials back to Britain as well.[27]

When American missionaries arrived in India in the early nineteenth century, the British were also suspicious at first. British East India authorities ordered the first two Congregational missionaries out, suspected the next three of being spies, and only reluctantly allowed them to stay. By the second half of the century, the British were encouraging the Presbyterians, Baptists, Lutherans, and Methodists to spread more orthodox forms of Christianity to India. There was little criticism in the United States of British colonialism in the nineteenth century. When the British suppressed the Indian rebellion of 1857, missionary magazines defended British rule and only a few journals took up the Indian cause.

As for Indian self-government, even the most advanced political thinkers discounted it. Writing for the New York *Tribune* in 1853, Karl Marx commented that obvious and terrible as were the destructive effects of British rule in India, this bourgeois period of history would create the material basis for a new world. The drain of men and money caused by the rebellion of 1857 and its suppression prompted Marx to write to Friedrich Engels that "India is now our best ally," but he was primarily concerned with how the burden of keeping the Empire intact might loosen the foundations of capitalism in England and divert the English from suppressing socialism on the continent. Ulysses S. Grant, who visited India on his world tour in 1878, declared that there was "no despotism more absolute than the government of India," but his was a lone criticism not echoed by Americans. For the most part, Americans, like Europeans, did not oppose British colonialism in India.[28]

There were, however, increasing numbers of reformers at the turn of the century, especially in New England, who were critical of United States policy toward the indigenous Indian population. During his visit to the World's Parliament of Religions in 1893, Vivekananda had denounced Christians for their demand that Asia accept Christianity and attain prosperity. "We look about us and we see England the most prosperous Christian nation in the world, with her foot on the neck of 250,000,000 Asiatics," he told the parliament. "Christianity wins its prosperity by cutting the throats of its fellow men. At such a price the Hindoos will not have prosperity." Americans shipped large quantities of food to India during the famine of 1897, and magazines sent special correspondents to report the depressing scenes firsthand. A few even began to question imperial policies. An article in *Cosmopolitan* denounced England for arguing that India was given to England because England had made the greatest effort to preserve the Christian religion; the author declared that Britain's true goal was economic exploitation rather than Christianity. *Cosmopolitan* editors juxtaposed a picture of the Queen's Jubilee statue in Bombay with a picture of gaunt Indians over a caption saying that the British government was prepared to spend a hundred million dollars on the jubilee ceremonies while millions starved in India.[29]

Such criticism alarmed the British. British ambassador Julian Paunceforte nervously collected articles to send to the British secretary for foreign affairs in London, warning him about possible conflict with Britain's new diplomatic policy of seeking the United States as an ally.[30]

American expansion into the Caribbean and the South Pacific in 1898 came as a blessing to Britons who feared American criticism of their Asian policy. Kipling sent Theodore Roosevelt a poem called "The White Man's Burden," urging him to take the Philippines. Winston Churchill, after being elected to parliament as a Conservative in 1900, came to the United States to compare notes on imperialism with President McKinley and with Roosevelt, then governor of New York and vice-president-elect. Roosevelt, the British hoped, would be a strong supporter of their Asian policy, for he had already elaborated a theory of American history that emphasized the similarities between expansion into the American West and expansion by other Western nations into Africa and Asia. For Roosevelt, western expansion had been part of the process of wresting areas from their aboriginal owners, something for which all civilization should be in debt to the conquerors.[31]

While the British gained much support from the imperialists in the United States, anti-imperialists did little to oppose British rule or to argue that Asians were competent to manage their own countries. On the contrary, most anti-imperialists shared a belief in the inferiority and incapacity of non-Europeans, and many based their criticism of American policy primarily on the argument that control of colonial areas would enlarge the military and civilian bureaucracy, thus threatening traditional American democracy for the Euro-American population. Some leaders of the Anti-Imperialist League, such as Charles William Eliot, privately thought the English colonial system a good model for the United States. Anti-imperialists William Dean Howells and Samuel Clemens did criticize both British and American imperialism, however. Howells responded to Kipling's poem "The White Man's Burden" with a critique of imperialism, and Clemens associated war in the Philippines with the Boxer Rebellion and the Boer War. Although members of the Anti-Imperialist League sometimes pointed to America's bad record with American Indians, Negroes, and Chinese, most emphasized that free government in the United States would be destroyed by ruling another people without their consent. Many other Americans who opposed overseas expansion hoped to exploit colonies through more indirect means than actual occupation.[32]

Anti-imperialists in the United States fought and lost the election of 1900 on issues of race and republican government with little reference to British India. Then Anti-Imperialist League chapters across the country vanished, leaving only the original parent league in Boston, while Roosevelt preached expansionism from the White House. By 1903, Roosevelt was calling the conquest of the Philippines by the "dominant race" an "inevitable march of events" at a time so opportune it might be considered providential. In his message to Congress in 1904, he compared American rule in the Philippines to British rule in India.[33]

Despite Roosevelt's pro-British pronouncements, Britain had good reason to watch the United States as Indian nationalists took their case abroad. In the autumn of 1905, Lala Lajpat Rai, an Indian nationalist from the Punjab, visited the Boston Anti-Imperialist League to establish relations and to arrange for subsequent visits by other delegates from the Indian National Congress. The nationalists were primarily interested in informing the English people of the needs of India, Rai told the League, but he also enlightened Americans about the "unspeakable blessings of British rule." The Anti-Imperialist League had dwindled to a few members in Massachusetts who, under new president Moorfield Storey, were only beginning to explore the link between racialism at home and imperialism abroad. Storey was committed to racial egalitarianism and believed in agitation as a means of achieving social reform. He broadened his critique of American imperialism to include British imperialism in India and wrote a letter to the editor of the Boston *Evening Transcript* criticizing the conditions of British rule in India. When the newspaper printed a reply from London, Jabez Sunderland, secretary for the league, countered British claims with a twenty-two page critique of British colonialism.[34]

Indian nationalists soon spread their anti-British dissent to New York. They contacted the *Gaelic American*, which published an article in December 1905 titled "India and Ireland Working Together." Another issue carried a tract in which Indians declared openly for a republic and described the new national flag of India. Bengalis passed these treasured copies of the *Gaelic American* around, and one student in Oregon sent a copy to a fellow student in Calcutta. In 1906, Asian Indians in New York founded the Pan Aryan Association and the Indo-American Association. The British consul general in New York was soon writing home that

Indians in New York were sending revolutionary literature to India. He sent extracts from the *Gaelic American* to Viceroy Minto along with rumors that one Indian was said to have been in touch with Sinn Fein, the Irish Home Rule Party, and the Clan-na-Gael, a secret society of Irish revolutionaries. Opposition in India had been quelled through repressive measures, arrests, and imprisonment of nationalist speakers and newspaper editors. The only Indians allowed to speak freely were moderates who counseled slow constitutional reform. Now it appeared to the British that young Indians were transferring their nationalist activities to the United States.[35]

During 1907, plague took half a million lives in the Punjab, and opposition to the government's change in land tenure spread. During March and April of that year, twenty-eight protest meetings were held at which nationalists, such as Lala Lajpat Rai and Agit Singh, told peasants that petitions were useless, that they must resist by withholding taxes on their heavily mortgaged land and, if necessary, stop cultivation. Gopal Gokhale, a moderate in the Indian National Congress, warned Viceroy Minto that the whole younger generation of India was going over to the extremists' side and was much attracted by the idea of getting rid of British rule. No longer were the young fascinated by the glamor of the British raj. The British would need more than such superficial prestige to rule unchallenged.[36]

By May 1907, unrest was widespread in the Punjab. At Khalsa College in Amritsar, students staged a hostile demonstration at the farewell visit of outgoing lieutenant governor Sir Charles Rivaz. At Rawalpindi, one of the largest military outposts in the Punjab, people observed a complete *hartal* (strike), closing all stores; workers in the government arsenal, the railway shop, and some private shops also struck. When the government insisted on proceeding with its land tenure plans, a crowd destroyed government property. In the course of the flareup, the American Presbyterian Mission was also attacked, the homes of the missionaries broken into, and Europeans assaulted.[37]

Rather than use military force, British rulers in India chose to suppress the political activities of students and nationalist leaders whom they considered the cause of opposition to British policies. The new policy was well expressed by a newspaper at Simla, where many Anglo-Indians summered to escape the heat of Calcutta, in an article titled "Students and Politics." Colleges exist for the purpose of education, the article began, and the conversion of institutions of learning into centers for the dissemination of political doctrines could not be regarded with indifference. If students became involved in political activities, the local government should have them expelled. As for professors, if one "abuses his position by diverting the minds of the students to political agitation, if he encourages them to attend political meetings or personally conducts them to such meetings or if while avoiding open propagandism he adopts a line of action which disturbs and disorganizes the life and work of the college at which he is employed," the university—and if not the university, then the government—must check the abuse. Although Minto vetoed the proposed land tenure act for the Punjab, reports of sedition being preached to the Sikhs so alarmed the lieutenant governor of the province that he had the nationalist leaders Lala Lajpat Rai and Ajit Singh summarily arrested and deported without trial to Mandalay under an 1818 law. Then he hastily approved the Seditious Meetings Act to put an end to political gatherings and had a number of editors imprisoned for publishing seditious material.[38]

At first the American consul general at Calcutta, Ohio Civil War veteran William Michael, ignored the juncture of nationalism and student protest. Michael had been one of the few American consuls to encourage the gradual increase in Indian students going to the United States. The first Asian Indian student had arrived on the Pacific Coast sometime in the winter of 1901–1902, and the next year a Lahore mathematics professor arrived from Japan. By 1905, this professor had secured three scholarships for Indian graduate students at an agricultural college in Oregon, and an association in Calcutta soon began to send students to the United States. Between May and October 1906, Michael wrote twenty-five letters of introduction for students and wrote optimistically to the State Department that with encouragement the number should increase.

With the spread of nationalism, however, Michael began to take note of the growing student unrest. In mid–1907 he reassured U.S. secretary of state Elihu Root that the British government had the power to suppress any uprising but wanted to avoid using that power. He clipped a copy of the "Students and Politics" article and sent it to Root, together with his approval of British methods. He hoped the arrest of the "traitor" Rai would cut short organizing and quiet dissent, but he admitted to Root that the mutiny had gone further than the British government had thought possible. An immense amount of money was available to back sedition, attempts were being made to buy the native soldiers, and according to Michael, rich Hindus, princes, rajas, and maharajas were supporting the movement. Moderates, Michael reported, were using the threat of an armed uprising to get the support of the Liberal Party in Britain. But, he predicted, the British had too much capital invested in India to allow any political change. The British had come to stay and, as far as Michael was concerned, the longer they stayed the better it would be for India.[39]

Arrests did not quiet dissent as Michael hoped. Even moderate Indian politicians were outraged by the arrests, and events in the Punjab fired the imagination of student expatriots still more. Several years earlier, Shyamaji Krishnavarma, an Indian educated at Oxford and admitted to the British bar, had started the first India Home Rule Society in London. The society established six lectureships, began publishing a penny monthly called the *Indian Sociologist*, and preached freedom through passive resistance. Boycotts, members thought, would achieve independence; the British would not force Indians to resort to the use of arms, although members did not rule out violence if necessary. India House soon became the headquarters for the India Home Rule Society, the meeting place for Indian students who challenged British imperialism in India and discrimination against Indians abroad. London officials pronounced India House "notorious as a center of sedition," placed it under surveillance, and began opening the mail of all Indian students. By July 1907 members of parliament were asking whether or not the government intended to stop the society.[40]

Increasing harassment by British officials soon drove Krishnavarma to Paris, where another group of nationalists were organizing around a Parsee from Bombay, Madame Bihaiji Rustamji Cama. During 1907, Cama suggested noncooperation with the government as a protest against the arrests in the Punjab, and in August she went with students from Paris to the Socialist International Conference in Stuttgart to ask for moral support. There, Cama delivered a fiery speech against the evils of British rule, unfurled the Indian flag, and demanded a resolution against the British. Socialists were already divided by questions of nationalism, questions that would soon lead to complete fragmentation of the international socialist movement. With a single exception, the British delegation opposed the resolution, and other members refused to support the Indians. The conference merely condemned restriction of immigration on the basis of race. Not ready to give up, however, Cama announced she would leave immediately for the United States to gather support for the nationalists there.[41]

Thus the stage was set in North America by 1907 for a joining of two major historical trends. Economic conditions in India and the British

Empire were leading thousands of Indian migratory workers to look for new areas in which to sell their labor. Political conditions in India and the Empire were leading a much smaller group of Indian revolutionaries to seek political asylum and an audience for their grievances against the British raj. The arrival of these two groups in America provoked a crisis of public policy that would take over a decade to resolve.

1

By Ship, by Train, by Dusty Road: The New Immigrants

We who engaged in world-wide trade,
having lost that must starve.
—Ghadar protest song

Ships of the Canadian Pacific Line docked at Vancouver with loads of the new immigrants. The men wore white, yellow, pink, and blue turbans, loose white pants or western suits. Some still dressed in the regimental uniforms of the British Empire, some wore medals won in foreign campaigns. A few of the Akali group, known for their strict and devout religious practice, wore black suits with black turbans. Men carried umbrellas and cotton bags slung across their backs. With dark skin, black hair, and angular features, they might have passed for immigrants from southern Italy or Portugal rather than from Asia, had it not been for their strange dress. A few of the immigrants were Muslim or Hindu but most were turbaned Sikhs from the Punjab.[1]

Called the land of the five rivers, the Punjab was a great alluvial plain adjacent to the Himalayas and situated in the northwestern corner of India. Three million Indo-Aryan peasants farmed small irrigated land holdings there, living in villages of several hundred persons. Although holdings were small, intensive cultivation allowed the Punjabis to go beyond subsistence farming, making their province the granary of northern India and producing a surplus of butter and milk. During the last decades of the nineteenth century and into the early twentieth century, economic conditions worsened in the Punjab. There was a population explosion followed by droughts, famines, and severe epidemics. Irrigation canals helped to increase crop yields after 1900, and the railroad distributed the surplus, but migration also became an important factor in maintaining prosperity. As conditions became worse, younger sons were increasingly encouraged by their families to migrate so that the villages would not become impoverished. Absent sons did not have to be fed, and their absence reduced births at home. Moreover, they were expected to send money home to maintain the extended family households.

Several alternatives to migration existed. The army was one. Enlistments increased as times became more difficult at the end of the century. Sikh soldiers began to appear in Southeast Asia and the Far East, particularly in Singapore and Hong Kong, where many stayed on to become car drivers and municipal policemen. Settlement in arid areas of the Punjab that are now part of Pakistan was another alternative, for the British offered land to settlers who helped to construct irrigation canals there. Large numbers of Punjabis also worked as contractors and laborers on railroad construction. A last alternative was migration directly over-seas in search of work. By the turn of the century, Punjabis had already ventured to Australia and were sending their savings home. They also helped to build the Uganda Railway in Africa. As opportunities in South-east Asia and Africa lessened, Sikhs began to look to the Pacific Coast of America for jobs. In North America wages were higher, and men could emigrate as free workers rather than as contract laborers.

Migrants to the Pacific Coast came mainly from the districts of Jul-lundur and Hoshiapur, north of the Sutlej River and east of the Beas River, from a region known as the Doaba. Following a pattern of emi-gration already established in that area, younger sons ventured out to find jobs that would allow them to send money back to stop the frag-mentation of land and, perhaps, to increase the land base of their families.

Most of these men were in their early twenties. A few were married and had left wives and children with their father's family. Households were patrilineal and patrilocal, with older brothers sharing responsibil-ities on the farm and wives joining the extended family at marriage. Sikh women had no tradition of staying single if widowed and could remarry if their husbands died overseas. But separation was difficult for wives, some of whom spent most of their lives apart from their hus-bands. Separation was also hard on sisters, for close relations between brothers and sisters were common and were even honored by a special protection rite called *Rakhri*. One of the spinning songs young girls sang spoke of the importance of brothers. A husband you have for a while, they sang, but a brother always. While personal relationships suffered, emigration caused no basic change in the extended family. Although few men knew how long the separation might last, they expected to rejoin their family when they had earned enough to ensure that the family land would be maintained. All sons inherited the land equally, so each would have a share of the family patrimony when he returned—if the moneylenders had not foreclosed.[2]

Sikh veterans of the British India army played a key role in the original immigration to the Pacific Coast. A number of Punjabi Sikhs were be-coming disillusioned with the British army, and a few refused to reenlist after their first three-year tour of duty. Some of the first Indian immigrants to Canada were overseas veterans who settled in Canada rather than return to army life in the Punjab. Veterans were also dissatisfied with the treatment they received in the international army that gathered in the sweltering summer of 1900 to lay siege to Peking. One writer said that after the white army officers refused to recognize Indian officers in any way, some Indian officers resigned, and many soldiers secured discharges after the Boxer Rebellion had been crushed. When news reached them from those who had already immigrated that Canada was a land of opportunity, they chose it as an alternative to returning to hard times in the Punjab. Sikh veterans kept in close touch with each other by letter and through the Sikh temples, or *gurdwaras*, that most overseas colonies established.[3]

Veterans, who wrote Punjabi and spoke some English, were the natural leaders of the groups of men who immigrated to Canada, and in fact formed the majority of all early immigrants. Usually a group of four of five villagers would plan the trip together. Occasionally uncles would ask young nephews from nearby villages to join them. Village and kinship ties, together with planning and experience, gave the men the best chance of succeeding.

Money was essential, too, as the voyage to Vancouver cost at least three hundred rupees. Raising such a large sum for the trip was not a simple matter. Veterans might have saved enough cash, but village men had more difficulty. One young immigrant was lucky enough to inherit jewelry from his mother, who had recently died. Another received money from brothers in Australia. But perhaps as many as 80 percent of the Sikhs who left for America mortgaged their share of the family lands to obtain passage money. The risks of land mortgage were high, and great agonizing must have been involved in the family councils where decisions to follow this method were made. Emigration was costly, not only in terms of separation from loved ones and culture, but also in terms of joint family responsibility.[4]

Once the decision had been made, passage money secured, and farewells said, the trip began by rail. Villages from which most emigrants came were not far from the railway. Jullundur, for example, was on the main line from Amritsar, and trains went through many other small villages on the way to Delhi. From there, the wanderers took another train to Calcutta, paid thirty-five rupees for the boat to Hong Kong, and then fifty dollars in gold for steerage to Vancouver. Most immigrants went directly from India to North America; a few went by way of Fiji or Australia.[5]

The voyage was easier for Sikh peasants than for other Punjabi peasants because of the network of Sikh temples, established wherever Sikhs had settled in groups. The Sikh temple in Hong Kong was especially important, for emigrants sometimes had to remain there as long as a month before they could book passage. As a principle, Sikh temples maintained free lodging for wayfarers and usually provided one free meal a day. Non-Sikhs were also welcome to use the temple as a hostel, but the Sikh had a great advantage over members of other religions: he knew he could depend on these facilities, he often had already established communication with members of the temple, and he could be a part of the temple services as well. The weeks of crossing from Hong Kong to Vancouver must have been the hardest of the voyage. The conditions on ship were crowded and uncomfortable. The food for those who had not brought their own was so alien that even the men who were not sick could not eat it. The new immigrants had heard that the climate of Puget Sound would be similar to that of the Punjab in the winter, and they looked forward to landing.

The immigrants disembarked into a boom town perched precariously between the sea and the forest. After 1885, when the railroad first linked Vancouver to the rest of Canada, the town became an important terminus. Soon the largest town in western Canada, Vancouver also became the chief Pacific port because the mild winter climate allowed year-round activity. On the boardwalks of this town of immigrants, Indians jostled with American lumberjacks, Cornish miners, declassé Oxford graduates, Irish nationalists, British railway workers and printers, and Chinese and Japanese laborers. Most of the new immigrants went right through Vancouver—then a jumble of shanties and grand modern buildings—into the lumber mills and railroad camps of Port Townsend, New Westminster, and Port Moody, where labor was scarce and unions had not yet organized to keep Asians out. Men could make between $1.35 and $2.00 a day working in the sawmills or clearing land. For those who could speak English, there were jobs as foremen for as much as $2.50 or $3.00 a day. The luckiest were those whose countrymen had already arranged for them to be employed at a lumber mill and who could start work the day after their arrival.

Later, Sikh immigrants in Great Britain preferred to settle on the land but would try anything to make money. The same was true of the early immigrants to the Pacific Coast. Normally, some of the Sikhs might have become electricians, printers, car drivers or conductors, policemen, or artisans in the building trades. In British Columbia, however, methods of work differed from those in India, and the newly formed Canadian labor unions discriminated against Asians, keeping them from learning the necessary skills and practicing these types of employment. Some Sikhs met old friends in Vancouver and stayed in town to work in gardens, to engage in selling, or to clear land for the expanding population. They were not interested in working as domestics but were willing to undertake any other jobs.[6]

British Columbia lumbermen hired Asians in their mills because workers of European descent were organizing and because there was a relative shortage of men willing to work more than a few days for the wages offered. From the employer's point of view, the European immigrants stayed just long enough to get broken in and then moved on. Asians were willing to stay. Employers often built bunkhouses that Asians rented, and if, after a long stretch of work an Asian wished to get away for a while, he would arrange for someone else to take his place. To the employer, this showed consideration of his interests. Mill owners had no problem finding skilled workers to fill high-paying positions but often could not retain less skilled workers because the work was hard, seasonal, and low paid. Punjabis had been accustomed to working in the fields from sunrise to sunset, seven days a week, for nine months a year. During the other three months they had had almost no work at all. They were therefore quite willing to work long, hard hours at seasonal work in Canada.[7]

Within a few weeks after arrival, the most adventurous among the Indian immigrants had adopted Western dress—Panama hats, blue jeans, and work jackets. Most, however, adhered to the tenets of the Sikh religion and refused to shave their beards, cut their hair, or abandon their turbans. A few spoke English, and the rest soon acquired a working use of broken English. The new immigrant may have been surprised by the extent of commercialized vice in Vancouver, but some Punjabis probably indulged themselves on occasion. The peasant in India was well known for his capacity to drink, and new immigrants often engaged in this pastime. Undoubtedly, however, their favorite and most common leisure activity was talking. In India, men had gathered at the local temple to talk about farming and village politics, to gossip and to listen to passages recited by the priest from the *Granth*, the holy book. Money, savings, work, and relations with coworkers became the topics of endless conversation among immigrants. By 1907, Sikhs in Vancouver had already organized and were talking of establishing a gurdwara. Wherever a group settled together, the men did their own cooking, trying to reproduce in simple form the food they had eaten at home, mainly lentils, dairy products, and vegetable curries fried in butter. Occasionally the Sikhs would have a lamb or chicken curry, and they always had a round, pancakelike unleavened bread called *roti*.[8]

Housing proved more difficult to obtain than food. Those who did not live in mill or railroad towns found it difficult to obtain housing anywhere except in the Asian ghettos of Vancouver. The housing there was seldom adequate or sanitary, but usually the rents were cheap, enabling the immigrants to save money. The wages for one week often fed and housed an immigrant for a month. Those who had just come off the broad plains of the Punjab wanted only to save a few hundred dollars to maintain or extend family land holdings. Those who had lived in Vancouver longer sometimes thought of owning land in the New World and of bringing their wives from India. They saved to purchase houses and lots. Dreams of a better future made all willing to endure disheartening conditions.

One immigrant from this period, Tuly Singh Johl, gave an account of that early migration.[9] Born in Jundialla in the 1880s, the youngest of four brothers, Tuly was four when two of his older brothers immigrated to Australia to work in the sugarcane fields. As Tuly grew older, he helped to farm the family acres and, because he was strong and healthy, took up wrestling as a favorite pastime. Jundialla people had such a history of insubordination to the British that the village was blacklisted, and young men could not enlist in the Indian army. With this avenue of mobility removed, Tuly remained in his village and, when he was about twenty, married. He and his wife had one son; then his brothers sent him three hundred rupees from Australia. Village men told Tuly about Sikhs who had immigrated to Canada to make money to send back to their families, and so, leaving his wife and ten-month-old son behind, he went to Hong Kong and from there booked passage for Vancouver. The morning after he arrived in Vancouver, he went to work in a lumber mill. Four months later, friends came to visit from Bellingham, Washington, and convinced Tuly and three other men to go back with them to work in a lumber mill there.

Lumbering was a good prospect. By the fall of 1907, several hundred Indians had arrived in the Bellingham area, and most mills had employed a few of the new immigrants by that time. They lived in barracks in Old

Town, in the South Bellingham Rookery on Donovan Street, in tenements on Forest Street, and in shacks near Larson's Mill at Lake Whatcom. Eighty-five worked at the Bellingham Bay Lumber Mill, forty-three at the Morrison Mill, and nearly fifty at Larson's Mill.

Mill owners did not care what color Indians were or whether they wore turbans. The owners were interested in a steady labor supply and felt that Euro-American men were not steady workers, were too transient, and would save their money, then disappear on a spree. Indians could be depended upon to show up every morning. Since the Indians were inexperienced, employers paid them $2.00 a day rather than the $2.22 paid to white workers. The Indians quickly learned their jobs and stayed on. Employers asked them to work double shifts and began to replace Euro-American workers with the new immigrants while continuing to pay the Indians lower wages than they had the whites. The attitude of mill owners was well summed up later by the president of one lumber company: "You find a lot of people who kick because some of us hire orientals but I can't see any reason why we shouldn't because they are good men and mind their own business. It's mostly only floaters and agitators who complain, anyway."[10]

For seven months Tuly Singh Johl worked at a mill outside Bellingham. Then Euro-American workers began to complain because they were being replaced by Indian workers; they attacked some of the immigrants, driving them out of the mills. The next day, the manager at Tuly's mill told the Indians they would have to leave because he feared that his mill would be burned by angry white workers. Tuly and about twenty other Sikhs went south to California.

Tuly remembered going from Bellingham to Chico by train. The men, he said, knew no one there, but the ticket seller told them they could purchase a ticket for either San Francisco or Chico, a small town about 150 miles northeast of San Francisco. The men chose Chico, rested in an orchard after arriving that evening, and then went on to Marysville, where they had heard that the railroad was employing men.[11]

A small number of Indians had been working on railroad construction in the West since 1904, but it was not until 1907 that relatively large numbers of men found work with the Western Pacific Railway in northern California. That railway, the last transcontinental line to be built across the Sierra and the one with the lowest grade (1 percent), began with the ambition of financier Jay Gould's son George to have rails coast to coast. Local companies had been formed earlier to construct a railroad along the Feather River, but despite the enthusiasm of Walter Keddie, the Scottish surveyor who first charted the route, local capital had been insufficient to complete the difficult task. Secretly at first and openly after the spring of 1905, Gould poured money into two railroad corporations that completed surveying work for the seven-hundred-mile road from Oakland to Salt Lake City, and let contracts for construction in the fall of 1905.[12]

Contractors immediately began hiring thousands of laborers for the job—usually ethnic gangs, each with a head boss responsible for managing the gang and transmitting orders from the contractors. Forty years earlier, the Central Pacific, which had abandoned the idea of using the Feather River route because of the heavy character of the work, had used Chinese workers, but the Western Pacific had a large pool of new European immigrants to choose from and began hiring Italians, Austrians, Swedes, and Norwegians, as well as Chinese, Japanese, and Koreans. By 1907, the Western Pacific had perhaps as many as two thousand Indians at work. One newspaper reported that the railway put three hundred Indians to work as section hands in 1907. Other reports claimed that as many as seventeen hundred worked on the three-mile Spring Garden Tunnel (the longest of the forty-four tunnels constructed) at the divide between the Middle and North forks of the Feather River.

From the beginning, construction work proved far more difficult than either the contractors or most of the European immigrants expected. A trail had to be blazed along the river, then small camps supplied by pack animals established as bases for building a wagon road. As the difficulties of the work became known and other jobs became available during 1906, many of the Europeans quit. Finally, the chief engineer, believing that outside agitators were stirring up trouble, had private detectives infiltrate the work camps. The detectives reported that difficult work conditions were the sole reason for workers quitting. Floods during the spring of 1907 halted much of the work in the mountains.

Work in the valleys went on. During the winter of 1907, Tuly Singh Johl was in a gang of Indians that helped level land for the Marysville station. In the spring he moved up to the mountains near Portola, where about sixty Indians worked as a section gang replacing rails on old sections of track for $1.60 a day. Other Indians got work at a lumber company in nearby Palermo, sawing ties for the railroad. Greek gangs continued to work with the Indians, and farther along the line were Chinese gangs. Tuly remembered that a few of the Greeks and Indians who knew English would talk together and that the Greek workers were friendly to them. Although the Indians had less contact with the Chinese gang, they too had good relations. Tuly eventually moved down to work on the Sacramento Northern electric line between Oakland and Chico. He had no difficulty with Euro-American workers there.

Fewer Indians worked on the railroads after 1908. According to an Immigration Commission report of 1909, there were only seventy-three Indians employed in the West on railroads. This report claimed that the men were not strong enough to be employed, but Tuly's experiences and the amount of work done by the men during the previous two years clearly contradict this statement. Indians were responsible for the construction of a large number of bridges, tunnels, and section work in northern California between 1907 and 1909, and although the work lasted a short time, many immigrants remembered well their employment on the railroad.[13]

On 1 November 1909 the work gangs from east and west met at Spanish Creek, California, and there, without fanfare, the track foreman drove the last spike. It had cost twice the estimated thirty-nine million dollars to construct the line, both of the railways involved in the corporation had gone bankrupt, and there was no money left to construct the feeder lines intended to tap the new agricultural areas. Almost 45 percent of the new road's business in the first years of operation was in unprofitable passenger traffic. It took the economic boom of World War I to make the railroad solvent again. Despite the disappointment of capitalists with the costs of the Western Pacific, the growing network of interstate railroad lines did bring increased agricultural activity to large areas of northern California as ranchers began to develop crops they could send to the Chicago market by fast trains. Agricultural development opened up new jobs at wages comparable to those earned on the railroad. Previously, many Indians had preferred the $1.60 a day earned at railroad work over the seventy-five cents a day to be earned in field work. Now Indians began to move into agricultural jobs. Tuly and four of his village friends went to Fresno to work harvesting grapes. For over six years, he worked for the same farmer in the vineyards and sent money home to India. The men worked on contract, sometimes making four dollars a day.

By 1910, agribusiness was expanding rapidly in California, bringing with it a demand for more workers. Like Euro-American workers, Asian immigrants were already exhibiting a willingness to use their bargaining power—especially at picking time—to demand higher wages. There is no doubt that the Punjabi enjoyed farm work and that the choice became more common as other sources of day labor disappeared or were available only to white workers. But in Canada, where conditions were different, Sikhs did not turn to agriculture. They remained primarily in the lumber industry. Later, in Great Britain, Sikhs went into textile mills and transportation. The decision of Punjabis in California to enter into agricultural activities was based in part on their experience and confidence in agriculture, and in part on their evaluation of the prospects of success in a large-scale, highly complex industry in which they would have to create new social arrangements in order to survive and prosper.[14]

From its early beginnings in the nineteenth century, California agriculture was affected by a scarcity of labor. Only a small percentage of the land was suitable for farming—mainly a small strip running through the center of the state—and only a small percentage of the people chose to be farmers. Since most of the first Americans in California came to secure a fortune in the mines and then leave, they preferred to import staples from Chile and vegetables from Hawaii. Even after farmers could feed Californians, they had no export trade. After 1861, however, with the first cargo of wheat to Liverpool, farming fever replaced mining fever in many California counties. Native American Indians helped in the plowing and harvesting, but as soon as possible, Euro-American immigrant farmers replaced these first agricultural workers with elaborate machinery. By 1875, farming in the San Joaquin Valley had already become highly mechanized; by the first decade of the twentieth century, most of the large Mexican land grants had passed from the hands of their original owners into the hands of Euro-Americans interested in agribusiness. In southern California, irrigation projects laid the basis for expansion into new areas. Throughout the state, specialized large-scale vegetable and fruit ranches were developed at a time when local Euro-American workers and business people were driving out the main agricultural labor supply—the Chinese. The Japanese, who replaced the Chinese as a farm labor force, were too few to fill the demand for labor.[15]

Expansion brought increased competition for wage labor and increased wages. The men from the Punjab turned from lumber and railroad construction to agricultural work as it became better paid. Although agricultural wages in California attracted few Euro-American workers, they now compared favorably with wages made by the new immigrants in other forms of day labor. Punjabis also found the agricultural lands of California similar to those at home. The central California alluvial plain, irrigation projects, and crop specialization were all familiar elements of Punjabi agriculture. Two techniques, already tried by other immigrant groups, were soon adopted and developed by the Indians: cooperative land leasing and work by gangs. Both techniques were worked out during the early years of the Indians' agricultural work. Indian settlement began both in the older agricultural lands in the Sacramento and San Joaquin valleys of central California and in the newly developed Imperial Valley. In these valleys, together less than three hundred miles long and approximately forty miles wide, most of the Indians worked for the next few years, and some, eventually, established permanent homes.

During the summer of 1908, a few of the men who had originally worked in construction near Chico began to work in the fields. Three hundred were at work in Vaca Valley orchards, most at $1.25 a day. Five hundred Indians were reported to be living east of Sacramento, at Newcastle, picking and hoeing in the orchards. Most of the Newcastle men were gone by the next fall, but a few remained to cut wood and clear land, usually making $1.20 to $1.50 a day. In 1909, over four hundred Indians worked in the beet fields at Hamilton, where growers found it difficult to get workers. Others worked in the beet fields at Oxnard and Visalia because of a shortage of Japanese. Some became teamsters and worked hauling sugar beets. A few men were hired their first season for as little as fifty cents a day—much less than Japanese workers were demanding—but Indians were soon bargaining for higher wages. By 1909, their earnings almost equaled those of Japanese workers, but where they could, growers continued to bring in Indians specifically to check the power of the Japanese. It was, said the United States Immigration Commission report of 1909, "practically universal to discriminate against the East Indian in wages."

There is some evidence that Indian workers countered this type of exploitation by refusing to work at the pace employers wished. A student who worked with his countrymen one summer described a group of Muslims who worked eleven hours a day in the fields. These men took their religion into the fields, having one man act as imam by perching atop a pile of bales of hay to read from the Koran five times a day. The workers took fifteen minutes for each reading. The next place, said the student, offered the men fifteen cents a day more if they would pray only three times a day.[16]

Other Indians used more direct methods of pacing their work. During the spring and summer of 1909, Indians appeared near Holt, two miles west of Stockton in the delta area, where they began to work in the celery, potato, and bean fields. White owners in the area hired Indians at the usual discriminatory wages. In at least one case, Indians equalized wages by slowdowns, and when the white owner tried to pace them at hoeing beans, workers threatened violence to the pacer if he did not slow down. A similar case of worker control comes from an account of work in the celery fields, where Indians performed the tiring work of transplanting celery seedlings. As long as their Italian boss shouted at them, they worked steadily, a student worker recalled, but when he stopped, they would work more slowly, eventually wearing him out so that they were able to work at a reasonable rate during the rest of the day.

Indians, like other workers, were more likely to go along with intense speedups when working by the piece. In the vast asparagus flats near Isleton, men worked from 4:30 A.M. to 7:00 P.M. cutting and boxing asparagus for ten cents a box. Here, some Indians worked so hard that drinking became the only way to forget their fatigue in the evening. In the vineyards near Fresno, men were sometimes hired to pull up old plants at two cents a piece and worked incredibly hard for the extra money their efforts would bring.

We know little about the Indians who moved farther south. A few Muslims worked in the orange groves of southern California in 1909. One Sikh policeman from Hong Kong worked from 1910 to 1916 on lemon ranches near Pomona. Some men picked lemons near Claremont and Upland and cleared land. A man named Inder Singh, who came originally to do missionary work, worked on ranches near Los Angeles. Employers usually kept Indians isolated on the farms, and few received any encouragement to move into Los Angeles. Although the sheriff refused to arrest them for vagrancy, they found employers unwilling to hire them for anything but porters' jobs. A researcher in the early 1920s could find no Asian Indian colony in Los Angeles, only about eight workers, all of them bitter at the discrimination they encountered there.[17]

Day laborers no doubt fared best when they hired on in groups under a boss of their own choosing who negotiated the terms of their contract and looked after their interests. Talet Singh, for many years a Fresno work boss, is a good example of the kind of man the Indians selected for these jobs. Though he had a propensity to drink—and when the police picked him up on the streets of Fresno and locked him up to curse them out in English and Punjabi—Talet Singh kept his men working hard and steadily. (As often as he was locked up, they would bail him out.) In Fresno, ranchers and townspeople considered the Indians good workers who were reliable in their financial dealings.[18]

It is difficult to trace the settlement patterns of these early immigrants precisely. There is no doubt, however, that most eventually settled in the Sacramento, Imperial, and San Joaquin valleys. Two measures of this concentration are available. The first is a 1919 census of land occupancy published by the state of California. At that time, Asian Indians occupied over eighty-eight thousand acres of land in California, 52 percent of it in the Sacramento Valley. They also occupied over thirty-two thousand acres in the Imperial Valley. Another rough indicator of their settlement patterns is the death index published by the California Department of Public Health. Between 1905 and 1929, the deaths of 258 Singhs were recorded. Since most Sikhs took the name of Singh, this figure may be taken as a close approximation of the total deaths of Indian immigrants. Sikhs died in twenty-nine counties, indicating that many men went their own way in the 1920s and lived away from the majority of their countrymen. Three-quarters of the deaths during these twenty-four years, however, took place in eleven counties in the San Joaquin, the Sacramento, and the Imperial valleys.[19]

In some ways, the Imperial Valley offered the most opportunities, for it was just becoming an agricultural area when the Indians arrived in 1909 to pick melons and cotton and to clear ditches. Attempts to build a canal from the Colorado River had resulted in disastrous floods in 1905, and for two years the land had remained inundated. After 1907, when canals finally did bring water to the valley, many Euro-Americans believed that the area was suitable only for Asian workers. "I do not believe the Imperial Valley is a white man's country and I am willing to hand it over to the Hindus and the Japanese," wrote E. E. Chandler, a professor of chemistry at Occidental College who purchased a ranch near Brawley in 1909, rented it to Euro-American tenants to raise barley, and lost money.

Chandler believed that Euro-American tenants were not willing to do the hard work needed in the Imperial Valley. On the other hand, he was very much impressed with the work of the Indians. Those who leased land amazed Chandler with their industry. "When it comes to work," he wrote, "they are the original 'men with the hoe.' In the heat of summer they get up at 4 o'clock, work with their teams until about 10 A.M., then with the hoe until say 4 P.M., and then with their teams until 9 o'clock in the evening." An Indian who had to haul cotton more than ten miles into town might get up at one o'clock in the morning, hitch his four-horse team, and be there before the American who lived nearer town.[20]

Other absentee landlords also preferred Asian to Euro-American workers. Because of high irrigation costs, the hot climate, and a political and legal structure that favored large landholders, about 60 percent of the Imperial Valley was owned by nonresidents by 1924, and 88 percent of all the ranches were operated by tenant farmers. Middle-class owners like Chandler, as well as judges and other landowners, preferred lessees and tenant farmers who could bring them a regular profit from the land without their supervision. Large corporations, like the American Fruit Growers Corporation, which owned almost three thousand acres, hired some wage labor but were also dependent on tenants. A few blacks had farmed the valley, but they tended not to like the isolation and, except for a few teamsters, soon left for the city. The first poor Euro-American tenants who had come from Texas did not bring in enough profits, and so they were soon eased out of leasing by the owners and replaced with other ethnic groups. Discrimination kept Asians from mingling publicly. At Brawley, for example, Indians were not allowed in "white" restaurants.

To avoid trouble, Indians, like other Asians, accepted the town taboos and concentrated on their work. When the first Indians arrived in the valley in 1909, there were already Chinese and Japanese working in the fields, but they tended to be engaged in intensive agriculture. A few Chinese landowners around Brawley were successful with as little as one acre of strawberries; the Japanese also raised berries and canta-loupes near the towns. The Indians, however, preferred raising cotton, a crop for which they needed at least 160 acres to be competitive.

While Indians were regular workers and often were preferred by growers to Euro-Americans who refused to work permanently for the low wages offered, they were quick to exchange day labor for tenant farming when they could. Once they had secured some capital by day labor and their reputation as hard workers was established, Indians apparently sought loans. Their experience with moneylenders in India made this a familiar process, and there was money available for spec-ulation in agriculture, especially after World War I began in 1914. In the Imperial Valley all the cotton gins were owned by one man who secured his capital in Los Angeles and lent it to cotton producers at 10 percent interest, taking a mortgage on crops as security. Banks also considered Indians thrifty and hardworking and were willing to lend them money. In the Fresno area, the response of white bankers was similar. They considered the Indians good workers and reliable borrowers.

The Sacramento Valley was also relatively open to Indian settlement.

In Butte, Colusa, and Sutter counties, Muslim Indians were particularly successful in becoming land tenants and leasing land to grow rice. Before 1911, no rice was grown in Colusa County, but by 1914, large companies were leasing or subleasing land to rice growers. Growers introduced new strains of rice and hired Indians to harvest it. Indians helped to harvest a record crop of 121,000 sacks in 1914. The following year they began leasing land, and during the next few years Indians made enough money to earn the title of "Rice Kings of Colusa County." In self-defense, white growers created the Rice Growers Association of California, to maintain favorable price levels and to compete with the Japanese and Indians through increased use of machinery for harvesting. Because of the highly successful crops from 1917 to 1919, bankers extended credit to almost anyone planting rice. Heavy rains in 1920 (for twenty-two days straight) caught the rice crop before harvest, however, and many Indians went bankrupt. Bankers accused Indians of changing their names and refusing responsibility for indebtedness. The losses of 1920 drove a number of men out of the rice industry, but Indians and Japanese still held a third of the total rice acreage in 1923. One California farm woman remembered how skilled Indians were at rice irrigation and how they would shock rice after family workers had bound it. They lived in what she called "Hindu Camp."[21]

The experiences of three Muslim immigrants are a good example of a successful pattern of Indian settlement of the Sacramento Valley. Imam Bakhash Khan, his son, Kalu Khan, and another youth, Aha Muhammed, arrived in Vancouver in 1906. The following year they moved south to work on a railroad gang between Sacramento and Woodland, the two youths serving as water boys. Then they went into ranch work and rice farming near Willows. These men prospered in rice, leased, and eventually owned a thousand acres of land. After the older man died in the 1930s, the younger men continued on as partners. Another Muslim, Fazal Mohamed Khan, who arrived in the United States in 1923, also settled near Willows and began raising rice in 1929. By 1946, he owned an estimated twenty-five hundred acres of land.[22]

While Indians were establishing communities in the Imperial and Sacramento valleys, they were also beginning to settle in the San Joaquin Valley delta. South of Stockton was a particularly attractive area, and Indians started working in the celery and asparagus fields as day laborers. The delta lands were a swampy area at the confluence of the San Joaquin and Sacramento rivers, a region originally ridden with malaria and typhoid. The air was filled with peat dust, and the delta lacked roads, bridges, and drinking water. Euro-Americans considered it an undesirable place to live, but Asians took risks that other people would not. Chinese and Japanese workers recognized the land as potentially fertile and, like farmers in Holland, patiently began to reclaim the delta areas by creating islands here and there, digging drainage ditches, installing pumps, and building levees. More than 250,000 acres were soon arable, and the land values of nearby Euro-Americans owners increased as a result. As in the Imperial Valley, Indians in the San Joaquin Valley were seldom content to remain laborers, and by 1912 they had begun to pool their money to lease land. Indians who leased land discussed business propositions collectively, appointed a spokesman to handle transactions, and shared the costs and profits of the venture. They soon earned a reputation as keen competitors. In this respect, said Chandler, "the Hindu resembles us except that he is black—and we are shocked to see a black white man."[23]

A few men began working together as tenant farmers in peach orchards around Selma and Hanford, where Euro-American owners considered the Punjabis efficient at irrigation and picking. Within a few years, Indians were using the profits of these joint ventures to buy land. Land was usually purchased by an individual or in partnership, but money was often lent by fellow countrymen, without notes or interest, after collective discussion. If money was borrowed from the bank, the men cosigned notes. By 1914, Indians had created the main community economic organizations that would make them successful landowners in the New World. Many Indians were still day laborers, but the economic possibilities were already apparent.

Before 1914, these possibilities were exploited by only a few Indians who bought land with their profits from leasing ventures. Most saved their money and accumulated capital quickly. Men often lived together, hired one man as cook, and were able to save as much as two-thirds of their wages to send home. Although a few men who lived together worked separately, each contributing his share to group expenses, the most common arrangement was to form labor partnerships in which the men lived in common, worked as a unit, and divided earnings equally. The purchase of an orchard or a small farm usually did not disturb this household, for the men continued to work as day laborers or to farm on leases, tending their own ranches or farms in the evenings and during off-seasons. Kinship, village relationships, and even regional origin formed the basis for living groups and for the trust upon which their business relationships developed. By using the social and economic relationships of the old village community, Indians were able to prosper in a highly competitive agricultural market.

A few were satisfied with success and returned to India. Haji Muhammad Sharif Khan, for example, arrived in 1903, worked on the railroad, did farm work in the Sacramento Valley, then in 1914 leased land in Petaluma and started a poultry farm. With fourteen thousand chickens, hard work, and heavy demand for poultry during World War I, Khan prospered. In 1920, he sold out and went back to India. There, he married, raised a family, and lived well as a result of his American sojourn.[24]

Many, however, chose to remain in California. Indians were willing to work hard, were proud of their self-sufficiency, could use common sense and initiative to achieve a foothold in California agricultural communities, and were anxious to educate themselves. Moreover, although they were considered social outcasts by many urban Californians, they were indispensable as laborers, often were paid well for their work, and were by no means at the bottom of the rural social scale. At a time when Californians were already divided ethnically, Indians were sometimes placed above blacks and Mexicans because of their willingness to undergo social isolation and their competence in dealing with the American economic institutions. When, for example, Indians in the Imperial Valley and other areas decided to stay in California, Mexican women considered them to be highly eligible husbands; after 1917, many Indians married and settled down, forming stable and accepted community ties. Almost no Indian women immigrated to the United States, which may have been one of the reasons why Indian men were accepted in some areas more readily than Japanese with families. It was expected that the men would return to India, die without establishing families, or intermarry and raise their children within the American culture. Indians thus presented less of a cultural threat to middle-class whites, who feared that Japanese men would marry without returning to Japan, have their so-called picture brides join them in California, and raise their children as Japanese.[25]

The price for economic acceptance was cultural and geographical isolation. Indians did not mingle with the Japanese communities already established in California, and some cultural conflict appears to have accompanied the economic competition of the early days. Tuly Singh Johl remembered the Japanese taunting Indians as "English slaves" and, because of their height, calling them "poles." Indians either kept to themselves or joined Mexican-American or black communities. Some

Indians who had difficulty finding jobs in cities claimed to be Mexican or black, believing the prejudice to be greater against Indians. A few stayed in San Francisco, for example, where they abandoned their turbans and passed as Mexicans, peddling tamales, enchiladas, and peanuts from horse-drawn carts. Most, however, lived simply in rural areas, preferring to sleep in screened porches or outdoors in the summer and keeping few personal belongings. Floors often served as beds, fields as toilets. The immigrants washed clothing regularly and bathed daily whenever possible, but their clothing was often ragged and unconventional. They took turns cooking or hired a cook to buy supplies and prepare meals. Local merchants found that they bought the best quality and wondered at the huge quantities of butter they used. Vegetables and fruit remained their favorite foods, with occasional chicken curry.

Like many of the new immigrants, Tuly Singh Johl thought America was better than India. There were jobs and the economy was good. Most of the farmers were good to him, and, except for young toughs who provoked fights, life was not difficult for a young and healthy man. Usually, fights began on the Fourth of July, with the Americans toppling off the turbans of the Sikhs. Tuly took an active part in these battles and with his training as a wrestler often bested his tormenters. He lived with men from his village, who shared cooking and divided their wages equally at the end of the month.

A few Indian students who had come to study at the University of California usually joined their countrymen in the summer to act as translators and to do the same hard field work. Students told workers of the prejudice evoked by turbans and recommended that they be abandoned. The tendency of the workers to drink and spit seemed the worst of their offenses, although one student betrayed class and caste prejudice by commenting that the Indians' love of work disgusted him.

In 1909, Sikhs had discussed organizing a Khalsa Diwan and establishing a Gurdwara in Berkeley to function as those in other ports had functioned, providing a hostel for traveling workers and students. But Berkeley was not to become the center for the Indian workers in the United States. Instead, Sikhs established their first Gurdwara in Stockton in 1912. By that time, the worker population had moved inland, clustered in the ranches around Stockton and Fresno, and had become an accepted part of the ethnic communities south of the Stockton business area.[26] The shift resulted from the beginning of successful adaptation to California agriculture, as well as from the use of force by Euro-American workers to keep Indians out of urban jobs and communities.

2

The White Man's Last Frontier: Expulsions

Some push us around, some curse us.
Where is your splendor and prestige today?
—Ghadar protest song

As Indians moved into Washington state to work in lumber mills and on the railroads, they came into contact with Euro-American workers already locked in combat with employers over issues of wages and working conditions. The employers welcomed the new group of Asians, who could be used to undercut these organizing efforts. The presence of even a small number of Asian workers increased the high level of tension already present in the Pacific Northwest. First at Bellingham, then at Vancouver, and later in a series of smaller towns as far up and down the coast as Juneau, Alaska, and Live Oak, California, groups of Euro-American workers responded to Indians by organizing to drive them away. These expulsions eventually pushed Indians out of many areas and jobs in Washington, Oregon, and much of northern California, forcing their retreat into agricultural regions of central California where other Indians had already settled, Euro-American workers had not yet organized, and growers were expanding their operations.

The expulsions—in fact small riots directed against the presence of Indians in communities in the Northwest—fit well into the typology of riot developed by the sociologist Otto Dalke, who found that there are certain prerequisites for the occurrence of a riot. First, the community usually must be in transition. The subordinate group—in this case Asians—must have a history of being victims of violence, must be regarded as undesirable competitors, and must exhibit some trait or characteristic that can serve as a focal point for negative assessments. Established authorities usually must tacitly support violence or refuse to assume responsibility for riot control. An association devoted to propaganda or advocating violence against the minority group usually must exist, with a press that enforces the association's negative assessments. Finally, the upper and middle classes must either stand by or encourage violence. All these situations were present in 1907, when the major riots and expulsions of Indians took place in the Pacific Northwest.[1]

The communities in which these riots occurred were in an extreme period of economic and social transition when the first Indians arrived.

Bellingham, a frontier town fifty miles south of Vancouver and linked to it by the Great Northern Railway, had a burst of population in the first years of the century similar to that of Vancouver. Salmon, trees, and coal brought men to Bellingham Bay in the late nineteenth century. In 1903, four clapboard villages along the sea joined to form a town, which in the next three years shot up to a population of over thirty thousand. The new town served as a distribution center for Whatcom County and an industrial center of mines, canneries, and mills. A park with a roller coaster and an opera house made the town a social center as well. "Our community is composed of men who accomplish results," boasted Mayor Alfred L. Black. "There is plenty of room for more of that class." The Pacific Northwest brought quick profits for some, dis-illusionment for others. Railroads and lumbering provided much the same incentive for young men to go west as had the gold rush fifty years earlier. Boom conditions in the summer of 1907 brought hordes of young men, most under age twenty-five, to the mill camps bordering the rail-road. Overcrowded, buggy, and unsanitary, the camps bred disillu-sionment. The men, often migrants, were discontented and frustrated, outcasts of the working class who nevertheless considered themselves protectors of the frontier tradition of white supremacy.[2]

These Euro-American newcomers had the potential for hostility to Asians, and they were entering a West that already had a tradition of violence against Asian immigrants, particularly the Chinese. Hostility toward Chinese had already been growing for more than a decade when, in 1873, Euro-American workers joined race and class antagonisms in a violent outbreak against Chinese workers. Many of the fifty thousand Euro-Americans who had been enticed west by low railway fares and an economic depression on the East Coast became convinced by nativists that Chinese immigrants were unfairly competing for the jobs they them-selves sought. Sporadic violence against the Chinese continued for the next twenty years, culminating in the Chinese Exclusion Act of 1882, which began a century-long policy restricting Asian immigration.

National legislation did not halt the violence, however. In 1885, white workers chased Chinese workers out of thirty-five small California com-munities, such as Chico and Eureka. White miners massacred Chinese miners in Wyoming, and mobs in Tacoma, Seattle, and Bellingham drove Chinese immigrants out of Washington. Anti-Chinese riots occurred throughout the Puget Sound area in 1886. Chinese were driven from camps and terrorized in Vancouver. By 1907, Chinese were allowed into Bellingham only during fishing season, when their labor was needed in the salmon canneries. Violence against Japanese workers was much less widespread, in part because Japanese officials were more active in defending their nationals, and in part because Japanese immigrants were more militant in defending themselves. When white mill hands at Bellingham attempted to expel Japanese lumbermen, the Japanese armed themselves and threatened retaliation. Rather than risk open warfare, the whites acquiesced, and by 1907, Japanese workers constituted about 5 percent of lumbermen in the Bellingham area.[3]

By 1907, there was also an association dedicated to organizing opposition to Asian immigration. At first called the Japanese and Korean Exclusion League, the organization was soon renamed the Asiatic Exclusion League (AEL) to include Indians among its targets. The stated goals of the league were not to encourage violence but rather to create and focus hostility against Asians in order to influence officials to exclude Asians. However, the actual tactics of the AEL, especially arranging parades to bring together hostile workers, were calculated to motivate people to act on their hostility toward Asians. Many of the leaders of the AEL were also leaders in the organized labor movement and thus had access to networks through which they could spread anti-Asian arguments, goals, and plans. The combination was a volatile one.

Moreover, neither the police nor their middle-class employers in the Northwest were convinced that Asians should remain. While there is no evidence that police joined anti-Asian mobs, they did allow mobs to expel Asians from several areas. Policemen no doubt protected some individual Asians from beatings, but they did not protect them from harassment and expulsion. Added to police inaction was the attitude of the middle class in Northwestern communities. Holding a precarious position at best in a sea of working-class men, the middle class was unsure not only of its own sentiments toward Asians but also of what opposition to Asian exclusion might mean for business and political careers. When owners needed Asian labor badly and Euro-American labor was difficult to find, employers lauded Asian workers. When Euro-American workers organized against owners who employed Asians, the employers were more hesitant. Political leaders valued workers' votes. Social leaders feared workers' potential for violence in western boom towns.

Perhaps the most important physical characteristic that helped exclusionists focus hostility on Indians was the turban. Chinese had become "Chinks" in exclusionist rhetoric; Japanese had become "Japs." Indians became "rag-heads." Because most Indians were Caucasians, their features were less likely to distinguish them even with brown skins. Some Indians, in fact, found that they could discard their turbans and pass as southern Italians or Portuguese. But for Sikhs and other men trying to maintain their religious and cultural identity, the turban was an essential symbol. They would not abandon it. Much of the animosity thus came to be focused on the turban and on a cluster of complaints about cultural patterns that exclusionists associated with the turban. Much of the hostility, however, was an outgrowth of deep-seated and long-standing animosities already in place against Chinese and Japanese. The Indian was labeled an "Asiatic," one of the hordes of potential competitors in a job market already depressed, volatile, and difficult to organize.[4]

The attitudes of white workers were bitter and would remain so into the 1920s. "One of these days, by God," swore one disgruntled lumber piler interviewed later, "the whites are going to chase all of them out of camp and they won't come back either. We'll drive them all down the line with a two-by-four. If the whites only knew enough to stick together and organize we wouldn't need to work with those damned Orientals."[5]

Union representatives championed workers' opposition to the employment of Indians, arguing that the shortage of American labor was only temporary. If Indians established themselves in the mills, the union men argued, they would provide strong competition for white workers. Late in August 1907, mill workers warned all owners that they must not employ Indians after Labor Day, September 2. On Labor Day, a thousand unionists paraded down the main streets of Bellingham to show their solidarity.[6] It is difficult to see how the subsequent riots in Bellingham could have been avoided, given all the elements that presaged violent conflict.

The day before the Bellingham parade, Indians congregated in one of the main streets. Workers later claimed that women were crowded off the streets. After the parade several Indians were beaten, ostensibly in defense of "white womanhood." Nevertheless, on Tuesday morning the Indians showed up for work as usual. All day, white mill workers continued to complain. That night five instances of violence against Indians were reported to the police. Windows in two Indians' houses were smashed. The police chief ignored the evidence of growing violence; he assigned no extra deputies and made no special report to the mayor. The Bellingham police force was understaffed, with only nine men for a population of more than thirty thousand.[7]

On Wednesday, mill hands circulated an informal notice: meet to "drive out the Hindus." That evening, two Indians walking along C Street were attacked, knocked down, and beaten. One attempted to escape onto a streetcar but was dragged off. Both men managed to flee into the water of nearby tidal flats, where two young men pelted them with stones. Meanwhile, workmen collected to encourage the harassment. Speakers fanned the indignation of the crowd with impromptu speeches urging them to "help drive out the cheap labor." By the time the police chief and a patrolman arrived, the mob had grown to several hundred workers and townspeople. The police arrested and handcuffed the two youths who were stoning the Indians. The mob surrounded the police and demanded that the boys be released. Four more policemen arrived. Two-thirds of the entire force was now on the scene. Later the chief said he feared that bloodshed would have followed arrests. He released the two youths. Stepping back, he simply cautioned the rioters against violence.

Assured of the acquiesence of the police, the mob—now five hundred strong—swept down to the waterfront barracks where many of the Indians lived. Battering down the doors, the mob threw belongings into the street, pocketed money and jewelry, and dragged Indians from their beds. The Indians fled, some injuring themselves by jumping from buildings in an attempt to escape. Those who did not move fast enough were beaten. One landlord turned out four Indians to protect his boarding house from damage. Rioters attacked a tenement on Forest Street, roused the occupants, and forced them into the street. Fifty men stormed the surrounding mills, pulled Indians from their bunks, and began to burn bunkhouses. To avoid further physical violence, the police chief turned over the red-roofed, turreted city hall to the rioters to hold Indians. By morning over two hundred Indians were jammed into the city hall. At dawn, the tired revelers dispersed. From that time on, as one reporter wryly commented, "the police had the situation well in hand." Police held the Indians in custody as the city council arrived to hold a special session. Three Sikhs—Nand Singh, Attar Singh, and Sergent Singh— were allowed to appear before the council in the morning.

Mayor Black, conspicuously absent the evening before, now assured the three tall bearded men who solemnly stated their grievances that they would be protected. Black lectured his council. "They have the legal right to be in this city so long as they do not infringe upon the laws thereof. I do not think that there is any charge that these men have broken any law of our state or city, and therefore they have a legal right to remain in this city and perform any occupation that they see fit. They have a right to the protection of the laws of this state and city, so long as they do not break those laws." Then turning to the Sikhs, he assured them: "The entire force of this city and of the state, if necessary, will be called on to protect you in doing anything that you may see fit in this city, so long as you abide by the laws of the state and of the city." The mayor asked Thomas to swear in fifty deputies to prevent further rioting, and the police chief promised to arrest some of the rioters that he could identify himself. The council seemed most concerned about the mill owners, but promised to investigate the cause of the riots and to report at a meeting the following Monday evening.

The mill owners all vowed to protect their property and to defend their employees from the mill hands. A few owners said that they did not want the Indians in town, openly calling them undesirable citizens and laborers. One owner told the council that the problem would be eliminated if "white" men could be secured for the low-paying jobs instead of Indians. Larson's Mill, one of the largest in the country, announced that it would shut down anyway because the eastern market was closing up as a result of a financial panic. Another large employer of Indians outside of town discharged them all because, he said, he feared his mill would be burned. Even though some mill owners offered them wages equal to the whites', the Indians were ready to leave town. Many had already gathered together what they could find of their meager possessions—little brass lamps, brass kettles, coffee pots, clothes, blankets—and started up the railroad tracks that led back to British Columbia. Others waited until police escorted them to collect back pay from the mills and to withdraw savings from the bank before trudging down to the station to wait for the next northbound train. Crowds of townspeople jeered them off on the Great Northern.

Despite promises of protection by the mayor, there was a growing undercurrent of approval in the white community for the sentiment behind the actions of the mob, if not for the riot itself. The Bellingham *Herald* carried an editorial, titled "A Public Disgrace," condemning the riot but supporting the ideology of white supremacy. "It is simply a question of whether the people of this city are to deal with all questions that arise in a dignified manner, in keeping with the restriction placed upon them by law, or whether they shall, whenever the whim strikes them, convert this into a lawless frontier settlement," wrote the editor. One reporter even condemned the police force. "The turning over of the jail to the men is regarded as the strangest piece of work ever performed in any city in the country." Police could simply have closed the doors and had most of the mob in jail, he observed. These journalists felt that although the method had been wrong, the sentiment had been right. It was not bitter racial hatred that motivated the crowd but a "half-humorous spirit," wrote the editor. "The Hindu is not a good citizen," he concluded. "It would require centuries to assimilate him, and this country need not take the trouble. Our racial burdens are already heavy enough to bear. . . . Our cloak of brotherly love is not large enough to include him as a member of the body politic."

Such criticism of the current action but support of the tradition of a "white" West Coast was echoed by other editors. The cause for the outbreaks had been "general uneasiness of the whites," said the Sunday San Francisco *Chronicle*. California, wrote the editor of the San Francisco *Call*, "even in the days of Kearney, never went after her Asiatics as savagely as this. [He was wrong; there had been more violence in California.] It was here the sentiment was born that this favored land must be maintained as a white man's country, and we are resolved that this principle shall be established as fundamental and vital." He called on the Northwest to quit talking about California hoodlumism and to join in using constitutional and legal means to keep the West Coast white.[8]

Sentiment began to shift from support for the rights of the Indians to support for exclusion. Newspapers reported rumors that Indians had been bold and insolent, had insulted women in streetcars and pushed them into gutters. Indar Singh, spokesman for the Bellingham Indian community, announced on Friday that all his countrymen would be gone before Saturday morning. Once the Indians had decided to leave, the police chief proclaimed the troubles over. Five alleged rioters were arrested on Friday, including one hack driver and one shingle-weaver, but there were no prosecutions. The riot had been successful, even if, as some still thought, regrettable.

This was the sentiment expressed by A. E. Fowler, secretary of the Seattle Exclusion League, when he arrived in Bellingham on Friday evening en route to Vancouver for a big anti-Asian parade scheduled for the next day. Fowler had been the driving force in organizing the anti-Asian movement in the Northwest. Fifteen years on the Pacific Coast had given him a feeling for the temper of the Euro-American laborer. During those years he had worked as a cook, traveled to Japan, and spent thirteen months in the army. He liked to boast that he had been discharged from the army as unfit for service by character and temperament because he had refused to sweep the carpet of his commanding officer. Settling in Seattle sometime after 1901, he tried his hand again as a cook, then worked as a cartoonist, launching a magazine called *The Yellow Peril* in 1906. After the first issue, he began lecturing against Asian immigration, organized the Seattle Exclusion League, and began preparing a series of anti-Japanese pamphlets.

When the Bellingham riot began, Fowler was making careful plans to lead his own movement to exclude Asians. The Central Labor Council and various unions at Bellingham were affiliated with the exclusion league, but mill men refused to wait for orders from Fowler. Fowler told a reporter: "While we do not attempt to disguise our satisfaction at seeing the Hindus leave Bellingham, we look upon the riot as a very regrettable thing." He encouraged the labor unions to keep working to exclude Indians and went on to Vancouver. By Saturday, the British consul was in Bellingham to investigate. Mayor Black hosted the diplomat, assuring him that the disturbance had not in fact been a "riot" at all, merely a "tumult." No physical harm had been done, he claimed, and no money taken. Although Bellingham ministers took the opportunity on Sunday morning to condemn the inaction of the police and the action of the mob as unpatriotic, un-American, un-Christian, and cowardly, the undercurrent of approval of the Bellingham riot spread along the West Coast.[9]

The conflict spread south along Puget Sound to Seattle. The first Bellingham refugees to arrive in Seattle booked passage for Valdez. When they boarded the steamship, however, passengers seized the men and pushed them down the gangplank, threw one over the rail onto the pier, and left them all there to spend the night in the cold. Other Indians became involved in a brawl with twenty Swedes and had to be rescued by police, who took them to a nearby lodging house for safety. One Seattle paper proudly claimed credit for the Bellingham riot, and the exclusion league, anxious to continue its work, demanded that police disarm Chinese and Japanese who were arming in self-defense. The Seattle *Post-Intelligencer*, however, attacked the exclusion league: "If anybody is to be excluded from this city and State, it will be the meddling busybodies, who persistently seek to stir up passion, prejudice, and violence against peaceful and non-offending aliens who are here under the sacred pledges of the Federal government." Seattle officers needed no help from the league, it continued, or from any other "un-American" organization. All that exclusion agitators were expected to do was to obey the law, and they would not be begged to do so, they would be forced to do so, the article concluded. Probably the presence of an active Japanese consul was the most important factor in keeping Seattle cool.

As soon as he heard of the riots, the consul appealed to the chief of police to prevent any kind of demonstration by the exclusion league. He insisted that the Japanese were not arming themselves but were depending on the police for protection. The chief announced that he would pay no more attention to arms stored in foreign homes than in American homes but that he would arrest anyone found carrying a gun.[10]

Indian immigration had added a third dimension to the ongoing conflict on the Pacific Coast over Japanese and Chinese immigration. Anti-Asian feeling seemed the same on both sides of the border, in Seattle and in Vancouver. West Coast Americans and Canadians were beginning to sound much like white colonists in Africa and Australia, who were demanding that their governments discriminate against Asians. Race and economics seemed to be joined.

Some fought against this rising racial conflict by trying to emphasize its economic basis. Oscar Straus, the United States secretary of commerce and labor, was among them. Straus had decided to spend the summer of 1907 traveling along the Canadian border from Montreal to Vancouver, then down the Pacific Coast and to Hawaii, to test attitudes toward immigration. His immediate concern in planning the trip was the growing incidence of violence against the Japanese. Straus lectured Japanese in Hawaii, then half of the entire population, on their duty to the United States, conferred with Japanese diplomats, and returned convinced that Japanese were entering through Hawaii. Nonetheless, Straus wanted to dampen the anti-Asian rhetoric of Californians and placate Japanese officials who were concerned about the growing racialism in the immigration controversy. Therefore, when Straus returned to Washington, D.C., on 14 September, he announced that problems on the Pacific Coast were not racial but economic. Asians were wanted, especially in the fruit and beet industries, he maintained, because they worked better than Euro-Americans and seemed fitted by habit and custom for field labor. He assured reporters that Japanese and United States officials understood each other and advised labor unions to study the racial situation in Hawaii, where, he claimed, there was no racial prejudice. Straus, scoffed union leader Samuel Gompers, "apparently wants to pull down the barriers against Oriental labor." Gompers hinted that Straus was collaborating with the National Association of Manufacturers. The Denver *Post* agreed with Straus that the riots were economic, even though that newspaper sympathized with the Indians. "So they've pushed the colored brother a little harder against the wall at Bellingham. And the colored brother must be getting accustomed to it in his patient way."

But, the editor concluded, "it is not a question of color at all. It is a bread and butter affair."[11]

Other journalists dismissed the undeniably economic reasons for the dispute and concentrated on convincing their readers that Indians were simply undesirable immigrants. "The Hindu," said one, was "dirty and gaunt and with a roll of pagan dry-goods wrapped around his head" but was still to be regarded with complacency alongside the Japanese. The Japanese, said another, had gone into the scrap with a relish, the Chinamen fled at the first sign of danger, and the Hindus, were "the most craven, crying in their flight like children." Werter Dodd in *World Today* also emphasized culture; the Indian, he said, was not a desirable citizen, did not fit in, and was a poor workman.[12] Even such irresponsible journalism could not hide the truth. The problem was that the Indians were good workmen who came from a country where the living standards were lower; they thus provided a cheaper, more disciplined labor force for employers. The arrival of the Indians touched off a wave of solidarity among Euro-American workers in the face of what they considered unfair competition from Asian workers.

The Bellingham riot led to opposition to Indian workers in other parts of Washington. At Blaine, across the border from Vancouver, a Bellingham missionary spread the rumor that Indians were responsible for an outbreak of spinal meningitis the previous spring. At Anacortes, mill owners received threats when the rumor spread that they planned to hire 150 Indians. Workers demanded that landlords not rent to Indians. A mill at Robe, east of Everett, closed because it could not obtain Euro-American labor and owners apparently were afraid to hire Indians. White workers obtained a virtual free hand in imposing their standards in Washington after the riots and recaptured their monopoly on available jobs in the lumber industry. The hold of Euro-American workers over lumbering would not be broken until World War I, when the United States government established a large internal security system to control spruce production and a federal union to curb the independent organizing of workers.[13]

In Bellingham, meanwhile, the actions of the mob were being approved. When the city council met on the Monday after the riot, it condemned not the mob but the mill owners for hiring the Indians. The Socialist council member opposed a resolution to this effect only because it did not go far enough; he wanted to condemn the landowners for renting to Indians as well. The council admitted that the Indians had as a rule been peaceful and quiet, but it concluded that their manner of living was demoralizing to the laborers employed before their arrival. The spirit of the mob had been primarily one of self-preservation. "While we deplore the action of the mob in molesting an innocent people, we condemn the millowners for introducing into this city a class whom they publicly state are undesirable and to whom they would not grant the right of citizenship." The chief of police swore in more deputies. "The people of Bellingham have had one little taste of mob rule," the Bellingham *Reveille* warned, "and that is quite sufficient to last them for some time to come. . . . Any attempt to start another mob in this city will be attended with dire consequences to the mob."[14]

Most Asians had already cleared out of Bellingham by this time, but fifty Japanese had decided to remain and arm themselves. Afraid they too would be "Hindued," the Japanese finally decided to leave town also. Five lone Indians who had refused to leave town although they had no work were finally evicted by their landlord, and on 17 September they left the city by boat. Bellingham no longer had an Asian problem. Mayor Black released the five rioters who had been arrested, denounced newspapers for exaggerating the riot, and prepared to run for reelection as a defender of law and order.[15]

At Everett, a lumbering town on Puget Sound, sixty miles south of Bellingham, Indians sought new jobs. Although a lack of orders was causing some mills in the Northwest to lay off skilled workers, mill owners continued to hire Indians for some unskilled labor. The Bellingham *Herald* quoted one unidentified labor leader as saying, "I always advocate peaceful methods, but there always comes a time when some of the workers most seriously affected are hard to keep down when the pressure gets hard. Judging from history, if the millmen will not dispose of the Hindus as the places can be filled [with whites], I would advise the Hindus to go away." On 5 November, five hundred armed men invaded Indians' lodgings and rifled their belongings. Because police turned their backs, Indians left Everett and crossed the border into Canada. Violence was working. Ten Indians crossed the border at Danville, Washington, and rented a cabin. A mob of men and boys surrounded the cabin, threw stones, broke windows, and injured the Indians. The next morning the immigrants recrossed the border into Canada.[16]

In Canada, where a riot was triggered by the anti-Indian Bellingham riot but was directed primarily against Japanese and Chinese, Indians remained in the mills. White workers in Canada did not have strong labor unions, there was less conflict over Indian workers, and workers and the government did attempt to control the violence. Eventually, a few Indians bought timberlands and became wealthy landowners. But in Washington, where neither the federal government nor the British consul took active steps to curb the violence, most Indians soon disappeared from the lumber industry, and even the number of Japanese employed was drastically reduced. A few Indians did remain in the mills of Washington. One immigrant who arrived in Aberdeen, Washington, in 1906 continued to work and eventually became a foreman at the Bay City Lumber Company there. Others maintained jobs at a lumber mill in Rochester, Washington, a place that worker graffiti identified as "a cheap outfit," "a hell of a camp," and "a place for scabs." As late as 1924, however, out of over 57,000 lumber workers in Washington, only 94 were Indians, and they worked in 6 of 873 lumber mills. Indians were learning that the West had its own system to decree that they would be free to choose their occupations only within certain limits set by the dominant race.[17]

The violence followed Indians north to Alaska. Indians arriving at Oakland from Bellingham booked passage to Wrangell, Alaska. When they arrived at the port of Wrangell, a mob prevented them from landing. The steamship lines refused to allow them to stay on board because they had not booked return passage. Finally, a United States official stepped in and unofficially paid for their return passage to Seattle. Indians who tried to disembark at Douglas Island and at Juneau were greeted in the same way. Mobs forced them back onto the ships. The panic of 1907 ensured that Indians would not be needed urgently in the mills. The boom in the Pacific Northwest was collapsing. It was a hard winter for workers of all races.[18]

Hostility also followed Indians south to California. There was distrust of Indians in the Chico area as early as 1906, when one resident wrote to the United States consul at Vancouver that steps were being taken by local authorities, especially the local labor unions, to stop Indian immigration. There was little complaint from workers during the summer of 1907, when many Indians became section hands on the Southern Pacific and Northwestern railroads in the Sacramento Valley. Trouble came rather from townspeople after a group of eighty Indians had finished one job in January 1908 and were waiting for more work at Live Oak, ten miles north of Marysville.[19]

According to newspaper accounts, the Indians had leased houses in Marysville while they awaited employment. Several landowners, including the wife of the constable, rented to the men. Exactly what caused the townspeople to take the law into their own hands is not clear.

Newspapers said that the Indians did not dress properly and did not observe the laws of decency, and that they were guilty of indecent exposure in the presence of women and children—an excuse often used for discrimination against nonwhite males. There was, however, no effort to have the Indians arrested for violations of any law. Townsmen simply formed a vigilante group to run the Asians out of town in the traditional manner. At the vigilantes' request, several linemen from the Southern Pacific joined the crowd, but the main impetus came from the townspeople themselves. The mob rounded up the Indians, threatened them with weapons, robbed them of almost two thousand dollars according to the Indians, and drove them out of town. The governor, in what was by now a familiar ritual, asked the district attorney for an investigation. The district attorney called upon the sheriff at Yuba to protect the Indians. Yet when the Indians attempted to have two men whom they positively identified prosecuted for theft, there were dozens of witnesses to swear that the men did not steal any money. The accused were released with an admonition by the judge that they had done wrong to join the mob; the judge added that the Indians could have been arrested for overcrowding their houses. The Sacramento *Bee* summed up the incident thus: "All is quiet today and there will be no more trouble if the Hindus keep away."[20]

Indians tried to obtain work at the New Idria Mines in San Benito County and at the Judson Mills in Oakland; a colony of Indians appeared at Stege, in the mountains south of San Francisco, to work at the California Cap Company plant. At Stege, white men immediately protested with volleys of rocks at the bunkhouse where the new immigrants lodged and with bodily attacks. By mid-November 1907, townspeople feared racial war as Indians moved into other factories and lumber camps. Talk of driving the Indians out began to be heard. In 1910, Indians buying groceries near Woodland were stoned, and when police refused to protect them, they resorted to using ax handles to beat their attackers.

Where the men did not resist, they were driven out of communities. At the Fair Oaks Fruit Packing Company, late in 1911, fourteen white men arrived with guns, pistols, and wagon spokes to march on an old house where eleven Indians were living. Claiming that the Indians had been annoying young women in the neighborhood, the vigilantes drove the men from their home. The next day, the head man from the Indian group had warrants sworn out against the vigilantes. Three sons of wealthy farmers were arrested and jailed in Sacramento, then all were released. The San Francisco *Examiner* reported that almost everyone had sided with the young men and had declared that the Indians should have been driven out of the country.[21]

The dimensions of force are difficult to measure. It seems likely, however, that the force used to keep Indians out of certain jobs and towns, the failure of the local courts and police to protect the Indians' rights, and the failure of the British government to press for damages and the federal government to strongly condemn the force used against the men, affected the patterns of settlement. The economic and racial patterns of the dominant culture partly explain the actions of economically, racially, and culturally oppressed groups. As Indians found themselves confronted by white workers in jobs for which the two groups competed, and as violence continued against Indians in urban areas, it was natural that they began to drift more and more into agricultural work, where they competed with no white workers, could live in small, isolated groups, and had the support of anti-union growers.

A dominant group never completely determines the actions of a subordinate group, however. The process of interaction determines the result. The Indians played an active role in determining what their lives would be like in California in the face of these patterns of discrimination. The movement of the Punjabi peasants into agricultural work was more than just the acting out of a natural affinity. It is true that most of the men were accustomed to hard agricultural labor in the Punjab, but their primary purpose in coming to the United States in the early twentieth century was to work at jobs that paid well so that they could send savings back to their families. Most of the Indians who first came to the United States worked in lumber mills, then at construction; although a few worked at agriculture from the beginning, most preferred day labor that paid better. After 1909, however, railroad work was decreasing, anti-Asian sentiment in urban areas was growing, and new opportunities seemed to be opening up in agriculture.

The years from 1907 to 1909 were turbulent ones for Indian immigrants. Harassment and the threat of violence were always present, but lack of competition from Euro-American workers in agriculture allowed Indians to settle in rural areas of California and establish small but relatively stable communities there. This was only one factor in their struggle, however. The other was that Californians would mount an intense political battle to obtain exclusion of Indians in 1910. While riots could keep Indians out of individual communities, only exclusion could halt other Indians from joining their countrymen in the search for economic well-being. Diplomats, then politicians, had to deal with the troublesome problem of how to exclude Indians from North American shores.

3

White Canada Forever: Canadian Exclusion

The whole world calls us black thieves,
the whole world calls us "coolie."
—Ghadar protest song

Expulsions of Indians on the West Coast in 1907 were more than a local issue. Antagonism of westerners toward Asian immigrants and the resulting riots were symptoms of political unrest on the West Coast and, as politicians knew, were likely to be the precursor of demands for exclusion. Both the United States and Canada had already dealt with the Chinese by excluding them. Attempts to exclude the Japanese had provoked diplomatic responses, and the Japanese had insisted on diplomatic agreements, "gentleman's agreements" that would allow Japan to restrict its own workers and those of Korea. Many Euro-American workers on the West Coast distrusted diplomacy as a solution, however, because they thought the Japanese government would not keep its promises.

Asian immigration posed peculiar problems for Canada and for the British Empire. The British foreign office had an interest in keeping Japan pacified because it wanted no foreign meddling in India. The India office hoped to avoid discrimination against Indians because it would have to deal with the resulting negative repercussions within British India. On the other hand, western Canada was a colonial outpost which eastern Canadians and the British foreign office feared might lose its allegiance to the Empire should its own peculiar interests not be accommodated by the Canadian government. The problem for the British government resulted in great measure from its efforts to maintain a commonwealth that included a homeland, colonies governed by Europeans, and the governed, an indigenous majority population. The Canadian premier had little to fear from indigenous peoples, but he did have to balance both Canadian and imperial interests, and watch a nation to the south that could not fully be trusted.

Although the trouble began with Asian immigration, it did not end there. Soon after the Canadians concluded their gentlemen's agreement with Japan in 1900, the British Columbia legislature insisted on passing a literacy act that the British, fearing a Japanese protest, asked the Canadian premier to disallow. The premier did so, but he knew that there was separatist sentiment along the West Coast and that political parties in the United States might be willing to exploit anti-Asian sentiment to their advantage. As late as 1896, the Republican party platform in the United States had a plank calling for annexation of Canada. Republicans dropped that plank in 1900, and in the East the election was fought on economic issues. In the West, however, the main issues were race and expansion. Theodore Roosevelt, the Republican vice-presidential candidate, told westerners that American expansion in Asia was a continuation of the old westward expansion, a new stage in the winning of the West for the white man. In the 1900 campaign, Roosevelt maintained that Asians should not be allowed to migrate to "white" lands such as Australia or the American West. Roosevelt used the Boxer Rebellion, which had just occurred in China, to justify taking the Philippines. William James called Roosevelt's followers the "party of red blood," but the commitment of Republicans to expansionism in the West did help turn a narrow victory for Republicans in California in 1896 into an easy win in 1900.[1]

With the Republicans in control of the federal government for four more years and anti-imperialist sentiments smothered by growing prosperity in the United States, Canadian officials had cause for concern. Male immigrants could be enfranchised in Canada after three years of residence. Between 1900 and 1903, 150,000 United States citizens immigrated to western Canada, and by 1903, these men were beginning to vote in large numbers in the British Columbia elections. Conservative eastern Canadians claimed that the loyalty of these new Canadians could not be relied upon and that such liberal voting rights would mean ultimate annexation of western Canada to the United States. Publicly, the premier and his Liberal Party insisted that the Americans were loyal. Privately, they worried that American ruffians on the farthest frontier might provoke an incident to test the loyalties of United States immigrants.[2]

Canadians had some evidence that the United States government might do nothing to discourage separatist movements along the coast. Roosevelt did not openly encourage insurrection in the Klondike as he did later in Panama; he did, however, manipulate the judicial system in a territorial dispute to get a larger chunk of Alaskan territory than Canadians thought the United States was entitled to. Three of Roosevelt's appointments to the tribunal that was to decide how much of the territory should go to Canada and how much to the United States were men who had denounced Canada's claims; these appointments naturally provoked suspicions among Canadians. Although both the United States and Great Britian maintained publicly that war was increasingly improbable along the Canadian frontier, the United States regularly sent army officers on secret reconnaissance tours to Canada to map military installations. Imperial defense schemes for Canada drawn up in 1903 still assumed that war with the United States was possible.[3]

While the Canadians watched both Japanese and Americans, the Chinese opened the issue of Asian immigration again in 1903. After British Columbia joined the dominion in 1871, anti-Chinese sentiment had taken the form of a head tax on Chinese immigrants. Despite an increase from fifty dollars in 1885 to a hundred dollars in 1902, the Chinese kept coming. Boom times brought prosperity, and Chinese already in Canada could lend immigrants the money necessary to enter. The dominion government raised the tax to five hundred dollars in 1903, but despite a brief drop in the immigration figures, neither Chinese immigrants nor anti-Asian sentiment disappeared. That year Robert McBride, a Conservative, became premier of British Columbia, and the legislature passed another literacy act. The dominion government disallowed the second literacy act at the suggestion of the British colonial authorities, claiming that it was in the national interest to do so.

One irony of the immigration from Asia was that the Canadian and British governments had subsidized the Canadian Pacific Railroad to develop ship service between Hong Kong and Canada. Ships were to be built under the supervision of the admiralty and converted to transports or warships if necessary. At first the ships carried mail and passengers. British Columbians were confident that Asians would soon be importing Canadian wheat as well. But Asians did not learn to eat Canadian wheat for another sixty years, and the increase in trade was disappointingly slow. Meanwhile, the Japanese merchant marine flourished, bringing competition to the Canadian Pacific. After the Russo-Japanese war in 1905, wheat exports declined, and, with immigration from China curtailed because of the increased head tax, shipowners looked for new immigrants to fill the steerage. In the Punjab, advertisements began to appear touting the work opportunities in Canada.[4]

Before 1903, only a trickle of Indians had entered British Columbia. A few English-speaking Sikh soldiers returning through Canada from service in the Mediterranean and from the Queen's Jubilee in 1897 settled on the Pacific Coast of Canada. In 1902 six Indian policemen from Hong Kong joined their compatriots in British Columbia and obtained good wages of $1.50 a day. The natural increase in immigration to Canada that resulted from the enthusiastic accounts of the first pioneers was compounded by the efforts of the steamship companies. By the end of 1903, there were almost twenty-five hundred Indians in British Columbia. The following year, Canada opened the Dominion Immigration Office to keep account of the Asians drifting in from the East. Probably because of the Russo-Japanese War, only forty-five Indians entered Canada in 1904. The next year, however, the trickle of Indians into the province began to grow, and almost six hundred immigrants from India entered Canada during 1906. The legislature passed yet another literacy act, and the premier once more disallowed it.[5]

British govenor general Sir Albert Grey, the imperial representative in Canada, was annoyed at the actions of the British Columbians and frustrated by the restraints placed upon him by his office. He felt that development in British Columbia, the richest and most attractive province in Canada in his opinion, was being hindered by an absence of cheap labor that allowed laborers to form unions and strike for better wages. Like many eastern Canadians, he was impatient with westerners who blocked economic development with anti-Asian agitation. Such activities were more evidence of the appalling decentralization of the Empire. Grey, who with his friend Sir Cecil Rhodes had advocated a federal parliament to solve the imperial labor crises, considered the anti-Asian agitation in British Columbia a form of anti-imperial dissent and a threat to imperial unity. To show imperial disfavor with the attitudes of British Columbians, he cancelled an official visit to the Pacific Coast late in 1905.[6]

At first Canadian premier Wilfred Laurier hoped to ignore the Asian immigration issue that intruded into his pattern of leisurely politics. Laurier, the first French-Canadian premier, was an outgoing man who preferred to handle politics informally. The keys to his administration were unity, caution in changes, and reluctance to submit to the centralizing demands of imperialists. Subordinates full of nervous reform energy, such as the young deputy minister of labor William Mackenzie King, disapproved of Laurier's caution. "As a politician Sir W. sometimes waited for the events themselves," King once complained to Grey. Laurier's main policy had been to develop western territories, build up the railroads, encourage immigration, and work for control of Canada's defense. The British began to withdraw their troops from Canada in 1904, and in 1906 the last English soldiers were transferred to the rolls of the Canadian army. Laurier was still negotiating for the transfer of several naval ships and the withdrawal of the British navy from Canadian waters.[7]

By 1906 Laurier had realized the necessity of support from trade unionists and the working class to keep his Liberal Party in power. He had come to this view slowly. Most distressing to him was the control that labor unions in the United States seemed to exert in British Columbia. When British Columbian coal miners struck, for example, Laurier had to send King to negotiate with John Mitchell, president of the United Mine Workers of America. The Laurier administration was watching British Columbia carefully.

British Columbians had taken little notice of the possible implications of an alliance of August 1905 between Great Britain and Japan. For the British government, the alliance brought a freer hand in India and the prospect of trade advantages. In January 1906, with lingering hopes of profits from trade in wheat to Japan, the Canadian government quietly joined the British-Japanese treaty on commerce and navigation, which allowed free entry, residence, and movement of Japanese immigrants in Canada. That spring, with little opposition, the Canadian legislature sanctioned this treaty, to go into effect on 30 January 1907.[8]

The growing number of Indian immigrants began to trigger anti-Asian hostility among British Columbians during the autumn of 1906. Indian immigrants complained that Sikh soldiers were harassed by retired English officers and reported that one Indian had been shot. More often, however, antagonism took the form of economic and social discrimination. Because of the already overcrowded housing conditions in Vancouver, many Indians lived in temporary shelters or in tents. Even Indians who had money could not always buy what they needed. Some begged. One lived entirely on potatoes. Said Alexander Munro, the dominion immigration inspector at Vancouver: "It is a shame these Hindus are treated as they have been. They all have money in their pockets to pay for whatever they get, but the trouble is they can't get it." Citizens accused the Indians of being poorly dressed and poorly fed, of being dirty and having a standard of living that proved their inferiority. Opposition to employment of Indians in towns reached such a level that soon many could find no jobs. Five hundred were unemployed in Vancouver alone. "It is a daily sight to see them wandering, here, there, and everywhere," reported one commentator, "half-starved, half-naked, hording in wretched hovels, ordered here, excluded there and despised everywhere." One Indian rented a shack in Cedar Cove to provide shelter for some ninety men. An abandoned cannery on the Fraser River became a home for another three hundred homeless Indians. In Vancouver, one charitable organization purchased a tent to provide a partial shelter called the Maple Leaf Refuge. Late in August 1906, 150 more Indians landed in Vancouver and were admitted. Public discussions and meetings followed. Almost two thousand of the new immigrants had arrived that year.[9]

No one knew exactly how many Asians were in British Columbia by the end of 1906. About twenty-five thousand Chinese were in the province, and perhaps as many as eight thousand Japanese had entered. Some labor leaders claimed that there were only seventy-five thousand white adult males in the province and that thus a third of the adult male population was already Asian. Unless something was done quickly, they argued, the province would soon become an Asian outpost. At their 1906 convention in Victoria, the Trades and Labor Congress asked that "Hindus" and all "Asiatic" people be excluded, and that only Anglo-Saxons be allowed to participate in the country's empire building. After a visit to the coast, J. T. Clark wrote in the Toronto *Saturday Night*: "Organized labour in the Pacific Provinces wants the Chinese excluded, the Japanese excluded, and the Hindus excluded and no white labor imported from Europe." On the streets of Vancouver, belligerent exclusionists were soon singing "White Canada Forever:"

> For white man's land we fight.
> To Oriental grasp and greed
> We'll surrender, no, never.
> Our watchword be "God save the King,"
> White Canada for ever.[10]

Grey was listening with alarm to news of the growing anti-Asian feeling in British Columbia. In the fall of 1906, he proceeded with plans to visit British Columbia, hoping to head off the growing anti-Asian agitation. He arrived in Vancouver late in September, and the populace turned out to cheer. He was pleased with the bared heads and popular demonstrations of loyalty to the crown, but at the Canadian Club in Vancouver, he warned provincial leaders that they should not jeopardize chances for Asian trade by antagonizing the Japanese with exclusion activities. "At present," Grey wrote to Canadian premier Laurier when he returned east, "British Columbia is being tyrannized over by American trade unions and nobody that I have met with the exception of Dunsmuir [lieutenant governor of the province] and Mrs. Ralph Smith [wife of a member of British Columbia's parliament] has the courage to say Boo to them." Grey referred to the premier of British Columbia, Robert McBride, as "that picturesque buffalo." But for the newly appointed lieutenant governor, James Dunsmuir, he had nothing but praise: Dunsmuir was "a rough diamond but a stout and excellent big hearted fellow" who was spending money generously for development in the province. Dunsmuir was a millionaire mine owner and the largest employer of Asian labor in British Columbia. Grey wrote to Sir Victor Elgin, the secretary of state for the colonies, that the trade unions were being controlled from the United States. "I confess I feel like an Elizabethan in the face of Papal Domination," he complained.[11]

Although Vancouverites lined the roads to cheer the king's representative, they were not ready to take his advice on the Orient or to stand by while Indians walked down the gangplanks. When the *Empress of Japan* docked in October 1906, a week after the departure of the governor general, and Indians marched into the immigration sheds to be cleared by dominion officials for entrance into Canada, exclusionists protested. Before the Indians could be released, Vancouver mayor Fred Buscombe intervened, threw a cordon of city police around the sheds, and held the immigrants prisoner, demanding that the general superintendent of the steamship company detain and deport them. The superintendent replied that the passengers had complied with immigration laws and had passed the inspection of government officials, and that the company therefore had no right to detain them. That evening the city council met in an emergency session to decide on a course of action. One alderman suggested that the immigrants be shipped to Ottawa, but after more thoughtful consideration, it was decided that the mayor should send telegrams to the offices of the colonial secretaries at London and Hong Kong. The messages read: "East Indians being shipped to British Columbia in large numbers under misrepresentation respecting state of labor market. Feeling very acute against people responsible, as liable to be large mortality among destitutes. Please take such action as you deem necessary to prevent further shipments." The colonial secretary at Hong Kong replied that the mayor must ask Laurier to request that the government of India do something. The mayor wired Laurier: "City of Vancouver will not stand for any further dumping of East Indians here. Mass meeting called to consider active preventive measures unless definite authoritative assurance received that Government has prohibited importation of these undesirable immigrants."[12]

The mayor's telegram was a clue to Laurier about the changing attitudes in Vancouver. As the president of the Pacific Coast Lumber Mills, the mayor might have been expected to favor Asian immigration as a source of cheap labor. Although a native of England, he had lived over forty years in Canada, fifteen years of that time in Vancouver, and had a good ear for local politics. The attitudes of Euro-American Vancouverites made his stand a political necessity. Typically, however, Laurier stalled and replied: "Government not prepared this moment to take action. Will wait for further communication on the matter."

Exclusionists would not wait. At a mass meeting on 18 October, the mayor and other city leaders spoke out strongly against allowing the immigrants to land. One defender of the Indians, a retired colonel, was howled down by shouts of "Canada is a white man's country." One alderman said that the best way to solve the problem was to let the Indians wander the streets until they died of cold and hunger, as that would be a good way to discourage others from coming. The angry crowd passed a resolution that the dominion government take immediate action to stop immigration. Imperialists tried to argue that as long as the British Empire contained three hundred million Indian subjects, it could not be a white man's empire. One called the harangues of the mayor's meeting the "height of frenzied folly." After three days, dominion officials released the Indians, but the minister of the interior warned Laurier about the growing opposition to Indian immigration, and for the first time the premier began to look for ways to discourage immigration.[13]

Actually, the hostility in Vancouver had already begun to divert the stream of migrants southward. On 13 November 1906, when the *Tartar* landed at Victoria and almost four hundred Indians disembarked, most applied for admittance to the United States rather than face opposition in British Columbia. But the Asian issue would not die. Conservative leader Robert Borden raised the question of Japanese immigration in parliament and warned that Canada had no control over the situation; Borden offered a resolution against the policy "under which our wage earning population cannot be protected from destructive invading competition except by entreating the forbearance and aid of a foreign country." Two months later, McBride, also a Conservative, campaigned for reelection on an anti-Asian platform and defeated the Liberals.[14]

Then the attorney general of the province launched a doubled-edged campaign. First he alarmed labor organizations by announcing that Liberals had allowed Japanese labor contracts to be signed by employers in Vancouver, and then he reassured workers that the Conservatives would protect them with a new immigration bill that contained a literacy test.[15] Contracts were, in fact, being signed, but by the very company for which the attorney general was a solicitor. This firm, the Canadian Nippon Supply Company, had arranged for the Japanese foreign office to issue passports to workers with certification of the consul in Vancouver that they would be employed on valid contracts from reputable firms requesting workers. The total number of workers under contract was only nine hundred, and these men had not yet arrived. Most of the Japanese who had already arrived were immigrants in transit to the United States.[16]

The controversy in the spring of 1907 took the form of a fight over the literacy test. That April, British Columbians again voted to introduce the test, and officials in Ottawa again refused to assent, explaining that the act interfered with federal interests and international agreements. McBride supported the disallowance but managed to give the impression to British Columbians that Ottawa was responsible for it. Liberal politicians in Vancouver began to denounce the Japanese government for allowing a Japanese invasion, Socialists held capitalists responsible, and Conservatives campaigned on a platform of exclusion of all Asians, promising to denounce the trade treaty with Japan if elected.[17]

In British Columbia, meanwhile, the head tax placed on Chinese immigrants had again resulted in making labor scarce, forcing up wages, and enabling Chinese to earn enough money to bring in countrymen. Fifteen hundred entered in 1907. Japan kept its promise to issue no more passports (with the exception already mentioned), but still over 8000 Japanese entered before winter, 3600 of them en route to the United States. Almost a thousand Indians had already entered that year. Employers insisted that they needed the immigrants to develop the resources of the area and even promised to increase wages of the Asians, but Euro-American workers opposed Asian competition at any price. Politicians believed that Indians posed a menace because, after a declaration of intention to make British Columbia their home, the new immigrants needed only one month's residence in the district before they could vote. Liberals were concerned that Conservatives would have mill owners deliver the votes of the new immigrants to defeat them; Conservatives fully expected the Liberals to buy the immigrants' votes. Neither party wanted the immigrant Asian to be added to the already complicated political picture. That year, Indians were disfranchised from the provincial elections.[18]

This was the situation when Indians began to straggle back into Van-

couver after the Bellingham expulsion. Early in August, Vancouver exclusionists had called in Olaf Tveitmoe, president of the San Francisco–
based Japanese and Korean Exclusion League, to help them establish a
Vancouver league. Tveitmoe's visit was more a symptom than a cause,
but from that time on, tensions in Vancouver began to grow. Rumors
spread that the Japanese were buying arms. There were complaints
about a parade that the Japanese held in honor of Prince Fushimi, who
had stopped in British Columbia on his return trip to Japan after visiting
England as envoy to King Edward. By the time the *Athenian* arrived from
Hong Kong in August with 145 Indians on board, sentiment against
Japanese in particular, and all Asians in general, was strong. The Japanese and Korean Exclusion League called a large meeting, attended by
four hundred men and representatives from both the Liberal and Conservative parties. The meeting passed unanimously a resolution declaring that the Japanese must be checked because otherwise they would
"ultimately control this part of Canada," would prove dangerous in time
of war, and would be difficult to dislodge without a rupture of peaceful
relations with Japan. R. G. Macpherson, a member of parliament, appealed for support at Ottawa to prevent the Pacific Coast from being
"flooded with Asiatics."

Then exclusionists discovered that the director of the commercial bureau of the Japanese foreign office, Aikujiro Ishii, was in the United
States to investigate anti-Japanese riots in San Francisco and had decided
to extend his tour to investigate charges of discrimination in Seattle and
Vancouver. They planned a huge anti-Japanese demonstration for the
day Ishii was to arrive in Seattle. Forewarned, Ishii cancelled his visit
to Seattle and announced that he would go straight to Vancouver. On
23 August, the Vancouver exclusion league called an emergency meeting
attended by two hundred members, who shouted that they would meet
the next boatload of Japanese with guns. They settled for a parade in
Vancouver on Saturday, 7 September, with a band to attract attention
to their protest.[19]

With open approval, the Vancouver *Daily Province* billed the parade
as a "bumper anti-brownie parade." The *Charmer* was due to dock Saturday evening at 7:00 P.M. with four hundred Japanese. The paper announced that the *Monteagle* would also soon arrive with more "oriental
hordes"—nine hundred Sikhs, eleven hundred Chinese, and a few
Japanese.[20]

That Saturday was a sultry day; tempers grew short as rumors of the
arrival of the Bellingham refugees and the new Asian immigrants spread

through town. Thousands of laborers from the outlying lumber camps filled Vancouver for an evening of excitement. Japanese also crowded into town, gathering in "Little Yokohama," where most Japanese immigrants lived, to watch the parade. A delegation from Seattle arrived to join in the protest against Asian immigration: Frank Cotterill, president of the Washington State Federation of Labor; Grant Hamilton and C. O. Young, organizers of the Seattle branch of the American Federation of Labor; George P. Listman and J. W. Blaine of the Seattle Central Labor Council; John Campbell, international secretary of the Shingle Weavers Union of Everett, Washington; and Fowler, secretary of the Seattle Exclusion League.

An estimated ten thousand gathered in Vancouver on Saturday evening to follow the parade to the city hall. At the front of the line, marchers carried a straw dummy labeled "to be burned before city hall." Fraternal orders and unions carried banners proclaiming: "White Canada—Patronize your own race and Canada"; "Stand for a white Canada"; "A white Canada and no cheap Asiatic labor"; and "Steamer Monteagle will arrive here shortly with 900 Hindus, 1100 Chinamen and a bunch of Japs." Some protestors carried small flags emblazoned, "A white Canada for us."[21]

Noisily, the crowd moved to the city hall. There, the paraders shouted themselves hoarse. Moving to the nearby town hall, thousands squeezed in to pass resolutions condemning the governor general for his inaction and demanding that the premier of British Columbia resign. Fowler delivered a flaming attack on Asian immigration with a detailed review of how Americans had dealt with the problem of Indian immigrants in Bellingham. Outside, the thousands who could not get in milled around. About 9:00 P.M., Fowler proposed a march through Chinatown. As the mob crowded around Fowler, the sound of broken glass was heard in the nearby Chinese quarter. Someone had thrown the first stone. The crowd needed little incentive to become a mob. As in Bellingham, police attempted to make arrests, but the mob forced them to free most of the men. Only the quick work of the fire brigade prevented buildings in Chinatown from being burned. Not until 3:00 A.M. were the last of the rowdies scattered. By dawn on Sunday the city was quiet.[22]

On Tuesday, the *Monteagle* arrived in Vancouver with over twelve hundred Asians. When the mayor warned the captain that he could not guarantee a safe landing for the 914 Indians, 114 Japanese, and 149 Chinese eligible to land, the captain put back to Victoria, where he landed the Japanese. Returning to Vancouver on Wednesday, he asked to land the Indians. Over the protests of the mayor, dominion officials ordered that the Indians be landed, saying that the city must protect the immigrants. The militia was alerted, and police roped off the wharves and marched with the Indians to the hill at the approach to Granville Street in front of the Canadian Pacific Railroad. There, a crowd refused to yield possession of the street, and the police could not force a passage through. The Indians marched back to the ship.

The mayor called the city council into emergency session to discuss plans for restoring peace to the city. Businessmen started a petition to charter a train to send the Indians to Ottawa to impress officials with their attitude toward Asian immigrants. First to sign the petition was Vancouver mayor Alexander Bethune, who pledged a hundred dollars. The editor of the Vancouver *World* pledge a second hundred. When the businessmen discovered that the railroad would not give excursion or charter rates for this forced deportation to Ottawa, however, they dropped the whole scheme. No one wanted to spend thirty thousand dollars to be rid of the Asian problem. A second scheme, to send the Indians across the border, also was abandoned as too expensive. American officials wanted four dollars a head for every immigrant who entered, which would have cost the exclusionists over \$3,700.[23]

Late on Wednesday evening a hundred Indians were allowed ashore, and the next morning officials permitted the rest to land. Then they could find no lodging. Several hundred finally went to neighboring mills, and some to tents on Canadian Pacific Railroad land. They would probably stay in the tent city until they either obtained work or contracted pneumonia, remarked one Vancouver reporter. Two former officials of the British India government volunteered to look after them. Conditions in Vancouver now seemed less critical concerning the Japanese and Chinese than the Indians. Chinese had returned to work, and the police were adequately defending them. Morikawa Hideshiro, the Japanese consul in Vancouver, had used his influence to calm the Japanese and had started negotiations for reparations. On Thursday, a thunderstorm and heavy rain dampened the last embers of the Canadian violence.[24]

The riots in Vancouver in the summer of 1907 were thus the culmination of several years of growing hostility toward Asians on the part of British Columbians. The riots also marked the beginning of action by the British, Canadian, and Indian governments to exclude Indians from Canada. There was little doubt that the most visible and publicized attitude in British Columbia was virulently anti-Indian. Major Vancouver newspapers, such as the *World* and the *Daily Province*, outdid themselves in condemning the Indians after the riots. The *World* compared them to cattle. The *Daily Province* headlined: "Hindu eclipse of the brownie moon; Japanese forgotten in the rush of men from northwest Bengal."[25]

Exclusionists in British Columbia considered the property damage a small cost for the publicity their cause received. Said one prominent exclusion league member: "I feel very sorry that the mob broke loose, but as no lives were lost and no damage done beyond a few thousand dollars worth of broken glass I cannot but feel that the attention of the provincial, federal and imperial authorities will now be so attracted that they will be forced to recognize the fact that British Columbia people will not permit this country to be made the dumping ground of yellow cheap labor. . . . Now I expect that Ottawa and the Imperial authorities will realize that the people here are not fooling and will take steps to prevent a recurrence of trouble." The Vancouver *World* echoed his comments. "Had the foreign element been dragged from their beds, had any considerable portion of the adult white population harried and hunted the Asiatics as was done in Bellingham, it would be another matter. As it is, practically only whites have been hurt, and a few thousand dollars' worth of glass has been smashed." Attention would now be paid to legitimate grievances without bloodshed or murder or the calling out of the militia. The riot had focused the attention of the Empire on the "Asiatic issue." The *World* repeated the by then commonplace attitude that "white" races were the true guardians of the frontier and said that the Vancouver riot was only one phase of the "white man's" need to predominate over economic competition of the Asian.[26]

Finding public opinion favorable, organized exclusionists redoubled their efforts. The exclusion league in Vancouver met to claim the riot a victory. Members decided to send representatives both to Victoria, to "arouse the city," and into mining areas, to edit a news sheet to be called *The Exclusionist*, and to send demands to Laurier that the Japanese be stopped. A few days later the Trade and Labor Congress met in an emergency session to decide whether a general strike should be called all over Canada to express opposition to the Asians. Instead, the congress served notice to employers to replace all Asian help with "white" workers within thirty days. Ribbon boutonnieres began to appear bearing the words "White Canada."[27]

Members of parliament from British Columbia rushed to support the spreading exclusion movement. One Liberal parliament member from Vancouver told reporters: "If the Federal Government does not step in and put a stop to the already humiliating condition of affairs, regarding

Asian immigration, there will be another episode like the one which occurred in Boston Harbor when the tea was thrown overboard." The Bellingham *Herald* responded: "When British Columbia begins to talk of another Boston tea party it begins to look as if the Bellingham incident might have far reaching consequences."[28]

At first, the Canadians and British attempted to blame Americans for the Vancouver riot. A former Canadian minister told reporters at Ottawa: "There can be no question that this particular labor element came from the south and that it consisted of foreigners practically exclusively." The Toronto *Globe* picked up the theme and reported that the riot had been caused by a gang of thirty Bellingham men who had come over to organize the parade with the intention of causing trouble. British newspapers, which habitually criticized American violence, now quickly reported that the violence in Canada had been caused by Americans. The *British Colonist* drew a close comparison with the Bellingham riots. The Manchester *Guardian* flatly declared that the riot had been arranged by American leaders. The London *Morning Post* blamed American rowdies. The London *Times* editorialized boldly that San Francisco intriguers had organized the riot. The possibility of American responsibility seemed attractive to the harried Canadian officials. "I hope the result of the investigation into the causes of this abominable outbreak," Grey wrote to Laurier, "may be to show that it was not spontaneous but the work of Seattle and other American organizations."[29]

To find out whether Americans had instigated the riot and to gauge the seriousness of the situation, Ottawa sent a secret agent, Thomas McInnes, to Vancouver to investigate. Under an assumed name and with the help of an interpreter, McInnes interviewed more than a half dozen Indians and talked to members of the exclusion league. After two weeks in Vancouver, he made a "very confidential" report of his findings.

In his report, worth summarizing at length because of its detailed analysis of the situation, McInnes described the three streams of Asian immigration and the reactions of British Columbians to each. While Chinese were being brought in by the *Tongs* (associations formed to take care of Chinese immigrants), there was no "Chinese question" according to McInnes. British Columbians did not feel threatened by the Chinese because Chinese immigrants did not assert their equality, were usually employed in subordinate positions (mainly as servants), did not compete with Canadian merchants, and bought peace at any price. Indians, on the other hand, were not considered by British Columbians to be as "adaptive" as the Chinese. Indians were "remarkably inoffensive and peaceable" and seldom in trouble with the police, said McInnes, but Canadians considered them physically unfit for the culture and handicapped by their religious customs and practices.

McInnes believed that the immigration movement by the Indians had been induced by agents of the Canadian Pacific Railroad at Hong Kong sometime in 1905. He was convinced that the movement was now spontaneous and came directly from India. Conditions were bad for the Indians; five hundred were unemployed, and even many with money were living in tents. Discontent was beginning to take the form of organization; a "Hindu Liberation League" was being planned to promote the Indians' interests. McInnes suggested that the Indian government should set up an examination office in India on the theory that many men were not physically fit to immigrate to British Columbia and would die of consumption. If future Indian immigration was not checked in India, McInnes went on, "in order to prevent the steamship companies dumping the more squalid misery of India in increasing proportion on our Coast," the Canadians should set up a very rigid physical examination for all Indians. Otherwise, in the winter, "premeditated riots" would probably occur, or a "slight incident" might lead to an outbreak which local authorities assured him the militia could not suppress.

McInnes's real concern over Indian immigration was that it might exacerbate feelings toward the Japanese, whom British Columbians considered more aggressive than either the Chinese or the Indians. "There is an uneasiness in British Columbia today," McInnes confided, "that would not be felt if the Asiatic immigration were confined to Chinese and Hindus, who are looked upon by the whites as greatly inferior races. The danger in the situation, and there is danger, is caused by the presence of Japanese in numbers that were never anticipated. The attitude of the people of the Province toward the Japanese is one of fear—the whites are afraid of what the near future threatens from these people. The Japanese do not confine themselves to certain limited and subordinate occupations as do the Chinese and Hindus." In the nearby town of Steveson, McInnes went on to report, three thousand "white" fishermen had been replaced by Japanese. The town had become a Japanese town. The Vancouver Japanese had threatened to call in all their fellow countrymen in the province if another anti-Asian parade was held, and American sympathizers eagerly anticipated such an event, according to McInnes.[30]

McInnes recommended several actions to Canadian officials. The first was a new treaty with Japan before winter and an effort to impress the Japanese government with "the danger that the Americans to their own obvious advantage may egg on and secretly increase the anti-Japanese feeling now becoming rampant in the Province till that feeling reaches a stage where the British Columbians forget they are British and look upon their highest interests as identical with those of California, Oregon, and Washington." McInnes had become convinced that the Vancouver Exclusion League had been the handiwork of men from Seattle and San Francisco, and that the league, headed by an American citizen, was not to be trusted. It had two thousand paid members, 15 percent of whom were in the professional and mercantile classes; new members were being recruited, and a newspaper was to be started soon. Major city officials, both Liberals and Conservatives, were joining the league. The next meeting would discuss Indian immigration. Canadian land, McInnes concluded, "should be reserved for our own race, and races capable of assimilating with us." Somehow immigration must be stemmed and trade relations with Asians fostered at the same time.

McInnes suggested that the minister of labor meet with the head of the exclusion league to discuss Indian as well as Japanese immigrants. "I know that there is an element in Vancouver working to bring about a renewal of violence," McInnes warned. The Seattle Exclusion League would encourage Canadian anti-Asian attitudes, and to end the conflict, according to McInnes, it was absolutely essential to replace the current hostility toward the federal government with a friendly attitude. This could best be done, he emphasized, by giving the league assurances that Indians would be restricted.[31]

The McInnes report was probably an accurate reflection of the prejudices of the British Columbians toward Asians and Americans. What they wanted was docile workers. Indian immigrants and American exclusionists seemed to be disrupting that plan. The cause of the problem, by implication, was external to Canada. Officials had to stop Indian immigration in order to stop the outside agitators from the south. The report thus made Indians appear to be the pivotal element in the situation.

The report reinforced Laurier's concern about the effect of Indian immigration on the Japanese. Before receiving the McInnes report, Laurier had been pleased to hear that the Japanese had repulsed the Vancouver rioters. "The Rowdies got a well deserved licking," he wrote. But he thought the success of the Japanese might make them "very saucy." Laurier also feared that enmity toward the Indians would extend

to the Japanese, who would defend themselves, that subsequent contending forces might prove stronger than the police, and that much
bloodshed might ensue. With the secret McInnes report in hand, he was
even more concerned.

Laurier dispatched King to Vancouver to inquire into the Japanese
and Chinese claims and into the causes of Indian immigration.[32] King
was to play a major role in subsequent diplomatic negotiations in London, Washington, and India. Eight years before, he had entered the
Canadian civil service, full of reforming zeal. The grandson of a Canadian
rebel who had organized an invasion of Canada from the United States
and had once been imprisoned in the United States for violation of
neutrality laws, King saw reform as the logical continuation of revolutionary fervor. At first he had considered the ministry as a career. "There
is nothing in the world I like better than a good sermon," he had written
in his diary. But after a few years at Harvard, he decided that public
life was more attractive than the ministry and reluctantly turned down
an instructorship at Harvard to accept a position in the labor department
at Ottawa. Social welfare work in Boston and a visit to Hull House in
Chicago had given him an insight into the distress of workers, and he
saw the labor department as a new avenue of reform. Eight years in the
Canadian government had not lessened King's religious impulses. He
often knelt down by the desk in his office to pray, sometimes for the
premier when he was impatient with Laurier's procrastination. Laurier
had offered encouragement to King and had promised to appoint him
minister of labor, but had stalled until King despaired of the "hand of
destiny" to which he ordinarily entrusted his affairs. The Asian crisis
seemed to provide him with an opportunity to work out his own
destiny.[33]

When he arrived in Vancouver, King went to the Canadian Nippon
Supply Company to seize the papers of the Japanese immigration agent,
who had his office there. Then King coerced the employee of another
Japanese firm into translating the documents for him. The Japanese
government was deliberately "Japanesing" the Pacific, King told Grey
when he returned to the East Coast. The Japanese were not abiding by
their promises. Actually, as one historian has explained, the papers
confiscated by King did not indicate an intentional breach of Japan's
legal commitments. The Japanese government observed its agreement
as far as ordinary immigrants were concerned but had not been able to
stop the influx of 2,775 Japanese from Hawaii. Because of the influence
of the Canadian Nippon Supply Company, an immigration company

that was determined to exploit the desire of Japanese workers to emigrate, the Japanese foreign office had also issued nine hundred passports after the company had given Japanese officials the impression that jobs were already available for them and that British Columbian officials had approved the arrangement.[34]

King painted the Japanese in a much more hostile light in his report, however. His picture of the complicity of the Japanese government had a drastic effect on the governor general. "The inevitable tussle between the White and Yellow races may come before we are ready for it," Grey wrote to Laurier after he had talked to King. Canada would have to steer between the danger of a "yellow invasion" and that of a "yellow boycott." Invasion was by far the more serious to Grey, and although he did not want to risk "too yellow a complexion" in British Columbia, neither did he want to risk Japan closing its doors against trade in retaliation for exclusion of its people. There was evidence that Japan wanted to avoid any controversy that might spread the "anti-Asiatic rot" over all of Canada and into Europe, Grey thought, but if no agreement were reached and a Japanese boycott were to follow, the result might be "a growing feeling of enmity which will burst into active war as soon as the times are ripe."[35]

Grey warned Laurier about Canada's security. Canada had only the Japanese-Anglo alliance, the British navy, and the Monroe Doctrine, which Grey felt applied to Asia as well as Europe. To extend the Monroe Doctrine to the Pacific Coast, a poorly maintained United States fleet would have to travel fourteen thousand miles to the Pacific. "I have thought it desirable to try to stiffen the back of Sir W. Laurier," Grey wrote to London.[36]

London was not eager to add Canada to its growing list of commonwealth nations that were resisting Asian immigration. The issue of European opposition to Indians in the Transvaal had just been resolved in London by the passage of a bill prohibiting even limited immigration of educated Indians and forcing all Indians to register with the government. "England might have to choose between India and the Colonies," Gandhi had told a crowd in the Transvaal. That choice did not have to be made in 1907, however, because the Congress party in India was split and there was a lull in opposition to British rule. Discussions about action over Canadian immigration thus continued to proceed at the somewhat leisurely pace to which the Laurier government was accustomed.[37]

The Japanese problem seemed easily solved. Laurier and a special commissioner from Japan agreed that immigration to British Columbia should be quietly decreased. "The effect," Laurier reported to Grey, "will be that the incident will be speedily forgotten but for the rushing in of Hindoos—an element to which the people of B.C. have a still greater aversion than to the Japs." Grey consoled Laurier, adding that he realized the need for a larger agricultural vote before Laurier could counteract the labor unions. If India could regulate emigration as Japan had, Grey advised, Canada might be able to buy time until the political climate changed.[38]

In his report, King emphasized that Indian immigration was not spontaneous. Glowing accounts of the fortunes to be made in British Columbia had been distributed in rural areas of India by steamship company agents who saw an opportunity for quick profit selling tickets. Peasants were so attracted by the reports that they were mortgaging family homesteads to come to America, and Indians in British Columbia were inducing others to leave India under "actual or virtual" agreements to work for hire. Only a few men had emigrated to Canada of their own accord, according to King. King also provided the Canadian ministers with an idea for stopping Indian immigration. In his report, he had noted that most of the Indians had to change ships in Hong Kong or Shanghai, as no ships came directly from Calcutta. In January 1908, therefore, the Canadian cabinet issued an order-in-council temporarily prohibiting immigrants who had not come on a continuous voyage from their native country from entering Canada. The order, carefully worded to avoid express discrimination against British Indian subjects, gave the Canadian government time to negotiate an agreement with the viceroy in India, such as the one being worked out with Japan, to stop emigration through passport control.

Indian immigration was more complicated than Japanese immigration precisely because the interests of the Canadian and the British governments were not identical. At the time of the outbreak in Bellingham, Grey had adopted an active interest in assisting the Indian refugees. He had sent a letter to the mayor of Vancouver expressing his "sincere regret" at the outrage upon Asians and a telegram to the British ambassador in Washington, D.C., asking about the Indians across the border, and had even dispatched his secretary for military affairs to Laurier with a personal request to take care of the Indian refugees fleeing from "American persecution to the holy sanctuary of Canadian soil." As British subjects, Grey reminded Laurier, Indians were entitled to protection, to be housed in comfortable camps, and to be cared for "in safety and dignity" if they could find no employment. Always mindful of the Briton in India, Grey lectured Laurier on his imperial obligations. "At this time of emotional unrest and excitement in India, it is doubly important that these poor Indian refugees should, as soon as they arrive on British soil, experience the advantages of being subjects of the King." Perhaps the Victoria *Colonist* summed up best the concerns of Grey: "A blow struck at a Hindu in Canada may be felt by a white man in India."[39]

Unlike Grey, Laurier voiced no public regret at the outbreak, and his silence was taken as tacit endorsement of the anti-Asian sentiment on the Pacific Coast. Laurier told the governor general that the dominion government could do little to assist the Indian refugees. He had no money to take care of refugees and could see no way to get any from parliament without serious difficulty. Laurier even refused to allow the Indians to use the Vancouver drill hall as a refuge and told the mayor of Vancouver that the more than five hundred Indians expected to arrive on the the *Tartar* in October should be deported as paupers, as they probably had no money.

The Indians aboard the *Tartar* did have money, however—thirty thousand dollars in gold among them—and therefore could not be deported as paupers. Laurier ordered them deported anyway. "The situation with regard to the Hindoos is far more serious and to speak frankly I see no solution for it, except quietly checking the exodus from India," Laurier wrote to Grey immediately after the Vancouver riot. After excluding the Indians aboard the *Tartar*, Laurier wrote to Grey that while he had imposed an exceptional disability on His Majesty's subjects, there was no other means open. He asked Grey to wire London for advice. "Sir Wilfred is genuinely alarmed," Grey wrote to Lord Elgin, "and fears the result of a new batch of Hindu arrivals at Vancouver may be the putting of a lighted match to a lot of explosive material—mainly of American manufacture, knocking about Vancouver."[40]

When no answer came from London, Laurier sent a copy of the McInnes report to Grey, saying again that he did not have the power to prevent an outbreak. Grey felt that the report, which had emphasized the inability of Indians to weather the climate in British Columbia, would give the British an excuse for prohibiting immigration. He was now convinced that the influx of Indians, like that of other Asians, had to be regulated to avert serious trouble. Even with a new agreement with Japan, the cry for Asian exclusion might not be dropped if immigration was "reinforced by another and to the people of B.C. an uglier flood from India," Grey wrote to the secretary of state for the colonies in London. "In B.C. the people appear to have lost their heads."[41]

Both Liberals and Conservatives used "white Canada" slogans in the next elections. While Conservative contenders were demanding open exclusion to achieve a white Canada, Liberals appealed to patriotism and responsibility to the Empire, and to diplomacy rather than insult, as a means of achieving the same end. Liberals lost seats in the British Columbia election. More seats were probably lost because of scandals over public land sales and fishing privileges, an issue that the Conservatives used adroitly in eastern cities, but even so, the losses were not substantial enough to dislodge Laurier from power. Liberals maintained their majority. The British Columbia legislature had, meanwhile, passed an Asian exclusion act. To keep Vancouver cool, Grey ordered the lieutenant governor of British Columbia to approve the act and to send it on to Ottawa, to shift the scene of the struggle away from the Pacific Coast. When the situation seemed calmer, the dominion government could disallow the act.[42]

As Canadian and imperial officials stalled in Canada, the Indian government refused to act. Under the Indian Immigration Act of 1883, the passport proposal would not be legal and would be severely criticized in India, the Indian government informed London. India's government had already publicized the continuous voyage order and warned Indians of hostility in Canada, but it wanted no action to be taken expressly discriminating against Indians.[43]

The continuous voyage order of January 1908 had given Canadian officials only a partial respite from the issue, for Indians continued to trickle into Vancouver. In March, fifteen Indians arrived on the *Empress of Japan*, requested admission, and were declared eligible to land by dominion officials. At the immigration sheds, however, the provincial inspector announced that they had failed to pass the literacy test prescribed by law and ordered their deportation. When constables of the Canadian Pacific Railroad refused to allow the Indians to return to the ship, provincial police arrested and jailed the immigrants. The men filed suit and obtained release on habeas corpus proceedings for not being informed why they were detained. The British Columbia authorities rearrested them, and the men were sentenced to fines and imprisonment for violating immigration laws. The men again applied for habeas corpus proceedings, and again the courts released them, holding that the literacy test was repugnant to the British North America Act. British Columbia authorities appealed the case to the privy council. Authorities expected another two hundred Indians to dock soon in Vancouver, and Laurier had ordered the group deported under the January order-in-

council. Officials were not sure whether they could successfully use
the continuous voyage law to exclude the Indians.[44]

To buttress the January order, the privy council hurriedly approved
a report emphasizing that Indians' difficulty surviving in the harsh climate of British Columbia was the basis for exclusion. The report stressed
that immigrants from tropical climates were "wholly unsuited to this
country" and therefore were suffering. As a minor point, the report also
mentioned that such immigration was causing serious disturbance to
industrial and economic conditions in British Columbia. Laurier ordered
King to go to London to discuss the crisis, and on 5 March 1908, King
boarded the *Empress of Ireland*, bound for Liverpool. The next day the
Canadian senate held heated debates on a motion to restrict immigration
of Indians but finally decided to wait until King had returned. In Vancouver, meanwhile, the Indians kept arriving. Eleven who came from
the Fiji islands were arrested and detained by the dominion authorities
for not coming directly from their land of birth or citizenship.[45]

To prove that the January order was being applied to Europeans as
well as to Indians, officials also detained a German from Australia and
excluded a Russian and a Frenchman. Certainly, McInnes complained,
"this new regulation was not intended to be enforced in this absurd
manner." He felt that the situation involving the Canadian branches of
the Asiatic Exclusion League was not so serious now that the group was
using constitutional methods of agitation and the new officers were
opposing cooperation with the Americans. Most white men now had
steady employment, and there seemed to be no ready "material" for a
mob, as there had been in the autumn and winter. There were still over
fifteen hundred Indians without regular employment, however, and
McInnes recommended that officers "stretch" the continuous voyage
regulation as far as possible to keep more Indians out.[46]

During March, boats continued to land with more Indians. One
brought seventy-eight who had been unable to board an earlier steamer
and who had been waiting for a month in Hong Kong for passage.
Another hundred men arrived on a ship all the way from Calcutta, thus
complying with the continuous voyage regulation. Dominion officials
refused to let either group land, however, the first because they had
not come on a continuous voyage, the second because the men could
not prove that they had come directly from Calcutta. Rejecting each
man, the government ordered their deportation.[47]

The response to this decision was immediate. Indians called a protest
meeting, and five hundred gathered to voice their discontent with the

treatment their countrymen had received. They dispatched a cable to the British secretary of state for India, John Morley, claiming protection as British subjects. "If our interests are overlooked, brothers in India must necessarily resent your Government's neglect."[48]

Indians were testing the theory of empire. The British Empire, spread over a fifth of the globe, depended on the assistance of the native populations for its functioning. To the Indian, the double standard was now becoming clear. As one editorial put it: "That the white man should enter the territory of an Asiatic nation is regarded as perfectly right and proper thing. . . . But when a few hundreds or thousands of these Asiatics go to a white man's country, not as conquerors, or monopolists, or concessionaires, but simply as humble labourers offering labour for wages which satisfy their frugal requirements, there is wild excitement, political agitation, and mob violence." One Indian wrote in the Toronto *Globe*, "This is of deep Imperial significance and our people will be greatly disappointed if Canada will not meet us halfway in settling the difficulties."[49]

Despite the justice of the demands, the British in London could do little to force Euro-Americans to accept the Indians; just as the Empire depended upon the indigenous population for labor, it depended upon European colonists for administration. Disputes between the Transvaal authorities and the colonial office over Indian immigration there had proved that the Empire could do little more than fret over exclusion. It did not seem likely that the British foreign office would attempt to restrain exclusionists in Canada any more than it had done so in the Transvaal.

When King arrived in London, he thoroughly reviewed Canada's immigration problems with British officials. Secret conferences continued for a month with the secretary of state for the colonies, the secretary of state for India, and the secretary of state for foreign affairs. King emphasized that the presence of Asians was causing an increase in socialism among laborers who had no desire to invest in property because they were being driven out by Asians. He also mentioned the danger of allowing people along the Pacific Coast to make a common cause of the exclusion issue and pointed out that police authorities had said they could not be responsible for law and order if Asians were allowed to enter. King presented the climate theory—that Indians could not survive in British Columbia anyway—and told of steamship lines distributing enticing literature.

The London officials reassured King that they appreciated Canada's position on Asian immigration and that a "satisfactory understanding" of the situation could be reached. Morley told King that matters in India were only at the beginning of what might become an even more serious situation. Morley agreed, however, that Canada would have to protect itself if the Indian government did not restrict emigration, and he joined Grey and Elgin in cabling Viceroy Minto to ask that some action be taken to restrict emigration because Indians were unsuited to the Canadian climate. Minto still objected to any permit system, but he agreed to prohibit distribution of all literature giving accounts of opportunities in Canada and to issue warnings of the risks involved in emigration. Steamship companies were informed that authorities in Great Britain, Canada, and India did not "view with favor" their transportation of Indians to Canada. Finally, the officials agreed that the Indian Immigration Act of 1883, originally aimed at controlling emigration of indentured laborers, would henceforth be interpreted to prevent laborers from leaving for Canada even with a prearranged employment agreement.

King was back in Ottawa by 25 April and made his official report to Grey a week later. Because of immigration difficulties in other parts of the British Empire, King reported, Canada had an advantage in the issue. British officials regarded Canadian desires to restrict immigration as natural and felt it desirable for economic and social reasons, and highly necessary on political and national grounds, that Canada remain a "white man's country." The British had placed no restrictions on the right of the dominion to legislate on immigration matters. They clearly recognized, he told Grey, that a native of India was not suited to Canada and could not readily adapt, and that competition among workmen would be dangerous if left unrestricted. King reassured Grey that exclusion would prevent hardships to Indians, who needed to be protected from the false representations of business interests and steamship companies, and that exclusion would help to avoid friction between the races and to protect Canadian workmen. The policies of Great Britain and Canada would thus dovetail to protect native races of India and white Canadians, according to King. He justified this arrangement on humanitarian and economic grounds while maintaining that it would "safeguard" the "liberty of British subjects in India."[50]

Canada gained much more than independence in excluding British subjects of certain races from its territory. King also worked out an arrangement on Japanese immigration during his visit. In return for British concessions allowing restrictions on Japanese and Indian immigration, Canada agreed to pay the full Chinese claims from the Vancouver riot. King held a last series of hearings in Vancouver on Chinese claims on 26 May. The previous December, Japanese claimants had quietly accepted nine thousand dollars despite earlier claims for over thirty-five thousand in damages plus costs for lost business. The Chinese had claimed about five thousand dollars in actual damages and over nineteen thousand in lost business, but they expected to receive very little because so little had been given to the diplomatically powerful Japanese. To their amazement, Canada gave all the Chinese asked, plus an extra thousand dollars for counsel and court costs. The Chinese ambassador was so surprised that he asked whether the amount was really correct.[51]

From Vancouver, King went to India to arrange for an understanding there. By the time he arrived, Indian criticism had been stifled, and there seemed to be no reason to make any further immigration agreements. Indian migration to Canada had ceased for the moment, and there was little open dissatisfaction with restriction. None of the British indicated any interest in an international immigration conference, something King thought might be a good idea for all the nations of the Empire. King's visit was thus largely a goodwill tour, giving him time to witness the social discrimination practiced against the Indians in India and to be properly shocked by the "badge of inferiority" placed by whites on Indians. Then he returned to take up his portfolio as the new minister of labor.[52]

Minto wrote to Laurier that the crisis seemed to be over. "We have published the conditions imposed by Canada widely in India, with the result that immigration has ceased altogether, and we consider there is practically no chance of its being reopened." Further action on India's part was "out of the question," he told Laurier, but he had no objection to Canadian methods, and "a solution has been found which we believe will be a lasting one, without involving us in any of the troublesome controversies which have arisen out of Indian immigration in some other places." Laurier too was satisfied. "The Hindu question," he replied to Minto, "has been very troublesome in British Columbia for some time, but thanks to the excellent disposition taken by your administration, things are now easy. . . . Strange to say, the Hindu and all people coming from India, are looked upon by our people in British Columbia with still more disfavor than the Chinese. They seem to be less adaptable to our ways and manners than all the other Oriental races that come to us."[53]

Canada could now arrange immigration matters as it wished. At Grey's urging, a new order-in-council allowed non-Asians to enter from countries other than their own, so that Scandinavians and Germans could enter the western provinces from the United States. Another order raised the amount of money an immigrant had to have at the time of arrival from twenty-five to two hundred dollars—an amount calculated to eliminate any Indian who might slip through the other legal nets. A new Vancouver act depriving Indians already in Canada of municipal suffrage was added to provincial disfranchisement. Indians were restricted from entering the province and from making their presence felt politically.[54]

Canada had no further problems concerning immigration. In his annual report for 1909, the deputy minister of labor concluded: "The inflamed state of public feeling noticeable a year ago, appears to have wholly disappeared." Restrictive legislation successfully kept out new immigrants. In 1907–1908, 2,623 Indians entered Canada. In 1908–1909, only six entered. During the following two years, fifteen entered.[55] Canada had stopped the "Hindu invasion." The question now was what the United States would do about the men from India who were moving south along the coast, looking for work.

4

The White Man's Burden: Diplomacy

Beware of these sinners;
they are not friends, they earn deceit.
They never work with their hands.
—Ghadar protest song

The Indians who moved south from Canada brought with them larger issues than just the right to work. The issues of fair treatment mingled with those of politics and diplomacy as they had in Canada. The status of Indians in the United States, however, was different from their status in Canada. Now they were colonial subjects in a foreign land, precariously dependent upon both the British and the American governments for protection. Their journey south thus linked immigration policy and foreign policy.

American foreign policy had traditionally been concerned with questions of war and peace between sovereign states. Immigration was usually part of domestic policy. During the period from 1900 to 1920, however, it was difficult for the United States to consider immigration a solely domestic matter, for Asian countries sending laborers had become increasingly concerned about the laws under which their nationals would be admitted and about the working conditions for immigrants. American presidents often wanted to control immigration without risking the political issues that congressional discussion of immigration laws might provoke. No regular machinery existed within the state department for studying and advising presidents on immigration policy, however. Hence, immigration policy frequently fell into a gray zone, being handled as an ad hoc foreign policy with special diplomats dealing with specific issues.[1]

During the late nineteenth century, immigration issues began to intrude into diplomacy. Trade agreements with China began to include clauses regarding immigrants. Although Congress excluded most Chinese workers during the 1890s, the executive branch had to handle the complaints of the Chinese government regarding the implementation of legislation passed by Congress. The 1905 Chinese boycott of American goods signaled the new diplomatic dimension of immigration policy.

President Theodore Roosevelt chose personal diplomacy as a response to the growing complexity of the immigration problem. Rather than expanding the traditional diplomatic functions of the state department and ambassadors, he depended primarily on personal emissaries to ne-gotiate special agreements. While American consuls and the state de-partment became increasingly active in monitoring the involvement of Asian governments and peoples in immigration issues, Roosevelt at-tempted to gather his own information at home and abroad to make policy decisions regarding immigration. The tradition of regarding im-migration as part of domestic rather than foreign policy made it difficult to separate it from politics in quite the same way that issues of war and peace had been separated in the past. The Constitution offered little guidance. While the growing controversies over Asian immigration were pulling Congress toward legislation, the lack of consensus on Asian restriction and the strong sentiment for continued free European im-migration made Congress unable to take the lead in formulating policy. Roosevelt, and then Taft and Wilson, assumed by default the burden of dealing with a wide range of immigration policy issues during the first two decades of the twentieth century. These years formed a tran-sition between the open immigration of the nineteenth century and the restrictive legislative period that followed. The handling of Indian im-migration thus became a part of diplomatic history.

Because of the informal restrictions imposed on Indian immigrants at the border in 1906, Japanese rather than Indian immigration became the primary foreign policy concern of the American government during 1906 and early 1907. The Japanese had restricted passports in July 1900, but during 1904 Japanese immigration again increased, and in February 1905, the San Francisco *Chronicle* printed a series of flaming exclusionist arti-cles. That March the California legislature had passed a resolution asking that federal representatives take the matter up with the president and the state department, and in May San Franciscans had formed the Jap-anese and Korean Exclusion League, dedicated to perpetuating the Chinese exclusion policy and extending that policy to Japanese and Koreans. The earthquake of April 1906 slowed the movement, but Jap-anese scientists inspecting earthquake damage in June were stoned and assaulted. A boycott of Japanese restaurants followed, and assaults on Japanese were widespread by September. Under mounting pressure from the exclusion league, the board of education ordered Japanese and Korean children into segregated Asian schools with the Chinese in early October.[2]

The attacks on Japanese immigrants were particularly troublesome to President Roosevelt because he believed that the Japanese might use them as a pretext to attack the Philippines. Roosevelt's military advisers expected such an attack in case of war, but they had not yet been able to agree where to build the naval base needed to ward off the expected attack. Since his advisers could not work out a defense against "orange," as Japan was later to be color coded, Roosevelt quieted the San Franciscans by stationing troops near their city, with orders to put down a riot should one break out and should city authorities be unwilling or unable to suppress it. He also sent his new secretary of commerce and labor, Oscar Straus, to the Pacific Coast to assure agricultural employers that the administration sympathized with their labor problems. While Straus was on the West Coast in the early summer of 1907, San Francisco officials informed him that Japanese immigration was increasing again. Although Roosevelt had stationed enough troops near the city to quell rioting should it break out, he decided to send the American navy to Pacific waters.[3]

As the crisis deepened, Roosevelt also decided to send his secretary of war, Howard Taft, to Japan. Taft had orders to sound out officials on an agreement to further restrict laborers, perhaps in exchange for naturalization of Japanese already in the United States. In 1905, Roosevelt had asked Taft merely to exchange views on the Pacific situation with officials in Japan. Since that time, the president had become convinced that the United States could not defend the Philippines should Japan attack. Roosevelt was also determined to support Japanese restriction now, for he believed "that the convictions of the great mass of our people on the Pacific Slope were unalterable."[4]

While negotiations with Japan held the attention of diplomats, the number of Indians entering the United States continued to increase. By the summer of 1907, that number had already exceeded six hundred— the total for all of 1906. In July and August alone, over two hundred Indians crossed the Canadian border at Vancouver to seek mill jobs. The Bellingham riots followed.

The riots first brought Indian immigrants to the attention of British and American diplomats. The American state department, accustomed to hearing complaints from Chinese and Japanese diplomats in response to violent treatment accorded their nationals, braced itself for another diplomatic encounter. The British took pride in protecting the lives and property of their subjects, and American secretary of state Elihu Root expected to hear from the British ambassador, James Bryce. Reporters predicted that the state department might complain to the governor of Washington in the name of the president and request him to take action to prevent a recurrence of the violence. Claims would probably be brought in local courts, as the Japanese had done after rioting in San Francisco. It was expected that a report of the riot, when sent to Bryce, would result in a sharp diplomatic protest.[5]

Bryce had been appointed ambassador to the United States early in 1907. "A worthy and dull old person" was First Lady Edith Roosevelt's description of the genial, sixty-nine-year-old Scotch-Irish scholar whom Roosevelt had wanted as ambassador, and whose appointment had indicated that the British favored cooperation with the United States. After moving into the unsightly old embassy building on Connecticut Avenue, Bryce went to Canada to visit his old friend Grey and to reassure Canadians that his appointment did not mean that their interests would be sacrificed to those of the United States. Britain no longer considered the dominions as colonies, Bryce told Canadians, but as sister states. Bryce had favored home rule in Ireland and in the Transvaal. Now he talked to Canadians of equality and partnership. Back in Washington, he wrote an article explaining to Americans the difference between self-governing colonies such as Canada, where Europeans could be allowed freedom, and crown colonies, such as India, where the natives were unqualified, by "racial characteristics," education, and enlightenment, to govern themselves. He assured Americans that "perfect order" was being maintained in India and that an efficient police force was able to quell quickly any disturbance from riot or sedition. After a round of speech making, Bryce went to his summer home in Intervale, New Hampshire, where he received news of the Bellingham riot. As predicted by reporters, he ordered an immediate investigation by the British consul in Seattle and sent a note to the state department requesting information on the outbreak.[6]

The Vancouver riot slowed the diplomatic assertiveness of Bryce, however. A Washington, D.C., news story announced that the Vancouver riot would dramatically alter the diplomatic situation with regard to the Bellingham riot. One reporter commented, "If Great Britain makes any demand on us for reparation for the outrages committed by Americans on the Sikhs, she will thereby be conceding in advance, anything Japan may claim from her for the Vancouver outrage; for the two cases are precisely similar, in fact, are two parts of the same case."[7]

The Vancouver riot did not go unnoticed by President Roosevelt. On 8 September, he dictated a letter to a British friend, John St. Loe Strachey, to offer complete agreement on an article in which Strachey had argued that the attitude of Americans on the Pacific Coast was no different from the attitude of Australians and British Columbians, and that it was basically a proper attitude, but that its expression in riots was wickedness and folly. After dictating the letter, Roosevelt heard of the Vancouver race riots and added in a postscript: "This shows again how like the problems are that our two countries have to meet—and incidentally, like the San Francisco affair, it gives the chance for narrow-minded people of both countries to indulge in pharisaical self-glorification, each at the expense of the other." Roosevelt concluded that the "English-speaking commonwealths" of the Pacific seacoasts would not submit to unchecked immigration of "Asiatics," that they "ought not to be asked to submit to it, and that if asked they will refuse."[8]

Americans seemed pleased that the Canadians also had anti-Asian problems. Senator Henry Cabot Lodge rushed an exultant letter off to Roosevelt, self-righteous about Canadian mob violence. "It is a demonstration of the fact that the white peoples will not suffer Asiatic competition in their own country and I think it will perhaps make England a little less inclined to preach in a patronizing way at us about San Francisco," he wrote. Roosevelt replied, agreeing that the Vancouver outbreak was indeed worse than anything that had occurred in San Francisco. The riot would inform both the Japanese and the British public that the attitude in the Canadian provinces along the Pacific was precisely the same as that in the American states along the Pacific, he wrote to Lodge. Mob action was indefensible, but the attitude behind the movement was sound, Roosevelt maintained. He gave himself a pat on the back for preventing such "outrages" against the Japanese by taking preventative steps. Californians in Washington, D.C., predicted that the Japanese would not complain against their Canadian allies as they had against the United States. They claimed that Japan's real grievance was the United States' possession of the Philippines, which was the only reason that Japanese diplomats had protested the assaults in San Francisco.[9]

Shortly after the riots, Taft arrived in Seattle on his way to Japan. He expressed virtually the same opinion as Lodge and Roosevelt when he talked to exclusionists. "We agree the Asiatic laborer does not amalgamate with the laborers of this country," he wrote to California representative Everis Anson Hayes. In a public speech on 9 September, Taft took an exceptionally prolabor stand without mentioning Asians. He went "rather far on the labor question but it was the thing needed" commented Benjamin I. Wheeler, president of the University of California at Berkeley and Roosevelt's political adviser on the Pacific Coast. Lumbermen in California were also falling into line in support of the Republicans.[10]

The diplomats continued their slow inquiries. On 12 September, Bryce sent a letter to Alvey A. Adee, British acting secretary of state. "The local authorities," wrote Bryce, "profess to be quite competent to protect life and property in these localities and say they are doing their best to prevent a recurrence of disorder. If the Federal Government were to instruct its representatives on the spot to take every possible opportunity of strengthening the hands of the local authorities in the task of restoring order and confidence, the possibility of another outbreak would be materially decreased." He hoped that fuller reports from the consuls would show that newspaper accounts contained "some element of exaggeration." Undoubtedly relieved at this mild inquiry, Adee sent it on to Washington governor Albert E. Mead, asking for a report on the situation. Mead asked the mayor of Bellingham and the police chief of Everett for reports. "Hindus have largely left here," Mayor Black reported to Mead when he received the query about the riot. "There is no danger of trouble under present conditions. No force has ever been used, they were ordered out of town by a crowd of men and boys. I immediately swore in sufficient officers to protect them and so notified the Interpreter; also caused the arrest and prosecution of rioters. Press reports are largely exaggerated. Hindus are receiving and will receive full protection." The police chief at Everett gave similar reassurances. Elihu Root sent a copy of Mead's report to Bryce. No one was sure whether the British would accept this slipshod dismissal of the whole affair. The British consul at Tacoma told reporters that he was still investigating attacks in Bellingham and other cities. The Sikhs were good soldiers, he said, and could be fierce when aroused. They had a right to be in the United States and a right to expect the same protection as other working men, he warned. The British government may or may not proceed further, announced the Bellingham *Reveille*.[11]

Despite the promises of officials, racial violence encouraged the Japanese government to back off from its defense of Japanese immigrants. The riots did put Japan and her ally Great Britain in a difficult position because they could not raise the issue openly with the United States unless they also did so with Canada. Root was delighted with the new events. He wrote jokingly to the president that Roosevelt's secretary must have sent someone to make a demonstration to relieve the Japanese situation. "It is not logical, but it is certain that the strain is off," he told

Roosevelt. Bryce accepted a copy of Mead's telegram to the state department as the final word. On 27 September he sent the state department his formal thanks for the information. He then informed London.[12]

The efforts of the British government probably did discourage future violence against Indians, but the slow actions of officials also indicated to exclusionists that the British would not vigorously defend the right of Indians to immigrate or to receive the same rights as did other British subjects in the United States. Indians from Everett, who had waited in Seattle to hear from the consul, asked him to find out what Britain was doing to obtain reparation for damages. They would have to wait until he received a report from the mayor of Everett, the consul replied. Indians driven out of Alaska also appealed to the British consul at Seattle. It was too late now, the consul told them, and besides, they should have contacted the consul at Portland, whose jurisdiction included Alaska. Finally, realizing that the British diplomats intended to do nothing, these refugees recrossed the border into Vancouver.[13]

The inaction of the British diplomats allowed Roosevelt to concentrate on Japanese immigration rather than dealing with the issue of Indian immigration. He still wanted some sort of formal agreement, for he asked Root in November 1907 to point out to Japan that their ally, Great Britain, was in the same position concerning the feeling on the Pacific Coast and that it was an economic question. "Cannot we put this formally on record?" he asked. Roosevelt did not think Japan would attack the fleet that he expected to send to the Pacific, but he was not sure. Violence against the Japanese was a major concern to diplomats. On 14 October, another outburst against the Japanese occurred in San Francisco. Like Laurier, however, Roosevelt knew of no way to stop the violence without endangering his own political position. When no diplomatic protest from Japan followed the October outbreak, Roosevelt was convinced that his theory about the riots was correct, that Japan did not plan to protest to the United States because it would then have to protest to its Canadian ally as well.[14]

The Japanese were not willing to sign an immigration treaty, however, and were quick to point out the facts of the situation to Taft when he reached Japan to conclude such a treaty. No American laborers wished to immigrate to Japan, and therefore the United States was not really making a bargain. The Japanese nevertheless agreed once more to limit emigration administratively and gave no indication that they would retaliate by seizing the Philippines. Taft felt that they were more concerned with China than with the United States. From Japan, Taft wrote Roosevelt that the Japanese had no desire for a formal treaty but were willing to reach another informal agreement on immigration. "I hope this statement may assist you in making plain to California congressmen the necessity for stopping agitation and accepting the present satisfactory *status quo*," wrote Taft.[15]

Roosevelt, meanwhile, had heard that Canada and Japan were conducting negotiations. He made inquiries through a lawyer friend who knew Grey. The lawyer met King at Grey's residence, was impressed with the confidence Grey had in King, and suggested that Roosevelt invite King to the White House. Because the visit was decidedly outside the normal diplomatic channels, King cleared it with Laurier before he left for Washington. Bryce had asked Laurier to be informed of talks with Japan, too, but King planned to talk only to Roosevelt. King arrived in Washington late in January 1908. Roosevelt liked King at once, later describing him as "a very capable, reliable fellow" and their talk as "very full and pleasant." King reported to the governor general that, for his part, he mainly answered questions put to him by Roosevelt and added information about the Japanese situation in Canada.[16]

Roosevelt and King gave different versions of their conversation later, but they agreed that it had revolved mainly around Japanese immigration. King said he told Roosevelt that he had documents (but did not mention that they were stolen) proving that the Japanese were issuing two or three times the number of passports they claimed to be issuing. He and Roosevelt discussed the sentiment toward secession on the Pacific Coast of both countries and the need for the people on the East Coast to be made aware of that sentiment. They discussed the American fleet that had been sent to the Pacific. Roosevelt later claimed that King had also asked about the advisability of going to England to inform the imperial government about the sentiment in western Canada and the Pacific states and to discuss the desirability of the United States and Britain working together on the matter. King wrote in his diary, however, that Roosevelt had suggested the trip to England and had said to tell Laurier that if the United States and Great Britain were indifferent to agitation on the Pacific Coast, it would lead to the formation of a new republic west of the Rocky Mountains, and to ask Laurier for Canada's assistance.

While in Washington, King also attended the annual dinner of the Gridiron Club as Roosevelt's guest. Dinners at the Gridiron were an established custom where presidents talked off the cuff to members of the press in exchange for a tacit agreement not to publish what was said. Roosevelt, according to King, said that the time was approaching when it might be desirable to substitute the "big stick" for politeness in dealing with Japan and that the fleet had been sent around to the Pacific for a purpose. He thought it highly probable that Japan and the United States would drift into war.[17]

When King returned to Ottawa on 28 January, he went immediately to Laurier to discuss his extraordinary visit. Laurier was convinced that Roosevelt had read about the Canadian-Japanese agreement and that he was put out that Canada had so satisfactory an arrangement. But Laurier could not understand what Roosevelt meant by asking for Canada's assistance. Laurier did not attach much significance to the meeting or to the Gridiron speech, which he considered "all flame"—impulsive and not to be taken seriously. Nor did he feel that Bryce need be involved. Laurier decided to send King back to ask Roosevelt what he meant by assistance and to tell him that Canada would assist in any way it could to prevent war, but that the governor general would have to be consulted. Roosevelt could not be serious, Laurier wrote to Grey. King asked Roosevelt for a second meeting on 31 January, and Laurier wrote a formal letter offering to cooperate.[18]

Grey was disturbed that Laurier was ready to engage in such irregular diplomatic maneuvering without consulting the British ambassador. "*Make sure* King sees Bryce," Grey wired Laurier immediately and dashed off a letter telling Bryce of King's report. When King returned to Washington, Roosevelt brushed off his own exclusion of Bryce from the discussion with the remark that Bryce was a "fine old boy" but was fonder of books than of active politics and viewed the Japanese question as academic. "It is necessary that the British statemen should feel that it is a practical and immediate question," Roosevelt told King, but he promised to include both Bryce and Root at a luncheon meeting the following day. At lunch, Roosevelt lectured Bryce and King on the significance of the Vancouver outbreak, saying that it showed Japan it could not play the United States against Great Britain. Roosevelt talked about Australia, where the white birth rate was declining, and said that Australians had to defend against the "blackbird" and the "yellowskin." Eventually, the United States would have to give up the Philippines for the same reason, he said, although it would be generations before the Filipinos learned to govern themselves. He had now lost confidence in Japan, however, and the time had come to stop further influx of Japanese into America because the race could not be assimilated. On this question all races must stand together, Roosevelt exclaimed, and for that reason he wanted King to discuss the issue in London. Assuring Bryce and King that the request was not official, Roosevelt went on to say that he wanted a friendly word from Britain to Japan about the attitude of the United States. King went back to Canada still unsure what Roosevelt was up to.[19]

What assistance could a small power like Canada give to the United States? Laurier and Grey were puzzled, too. Grey was distressed that King had discussed Japan with the United States because the Japanese had never mentioned their difficulties with the United States to Canada. It seemed like dangerous amateur diplomacy to Grey. Laurier brushed the matter aside, however, telling Grey that it had helped to show Roosevelt that Canada was friendly; he added that the incident was probably closed. The situation was odd, Bryce said, and had every possible irregularity, but he concluded that Roosevelt had acted "all in good faith and good humour and with good intentions." Japan had promised to restrict emigration and, despite Roosevelt's Gridiron speech, neither side seemed to want war.

Roosevelt refused to let the incident close. The day King left for Ottawa, Roosevelt drafted a letter to Laurier saying that Bryce agreed that it would be a good thing to have King go to England to explain matters fully to the imperial government. When Laurier received the letter, on 7 February, he termed Roosevelt's dealings a "yankee trick." King, who had started the negotiations feeling flattered by Roosevelt's attention and hopeful of obtaining the long-awaited promotion, was distressed. That night he wrote in his diary, "Every sentence in the letter had the twist of a smart politician, who asks questions with a view of receiving an affirmative reply, and then twists the statement as though it had been offered in the first instance by the person to whom it had been addressed."[20]

Roosevelt seemed determined to use Canadian affairs to blackmail Japan into an agreement. Three days later, when four Canadian members of parliament arrived in Washington, Roosevelt invited them to the White House. According to this surprised delegation, which kept careful notes of the interview, Roosevelt asked if the Asian question in Canada was settled; when they replied that it was, Roosevelt gave them his views. "Well," the Canadians reported him saying, "I hope so, because as you know, we have the same kind of an arrangement as you have, and if it is settled for Canada it is settled for us. Our interests are identical in the matter." He continued, "Gentlemen, we have got to protect our workingmen. We have got to build up our western country with our white civilization, and"—here, the Canadians noted, he spoke vehemently—"we must retain the power to say who shall or shall not come to our country. Now, it may be that Japan will adopt a different attitude, will demand that her people be permitted to go where they think fit, so I THOUGHT IT WISE TO SEND THAT FLEET AROUND TO THE PACIFIC TO BE READY TO MAINTAIN OUR RIGHTS."[21]

The fleet, Roosevelt insisted, was there to protect the whole Pacific Coast—British Columbia as well as California, and even Australia. One member of parliament inquired whether this meant that the Monroe Doctrine applied to the entire Pacific Coast, to which Roosevelt replied: "Yes, and to Australia as well—if it doesn't I'll make it apply." Roosevelt concluded by mentioning that he understood that British interests in India were a factor that had influenced the imperial authorities to enter into a convention with Japan; although the United States also wished to have friendly relations with Japan, he said, self-preservation was the first law of nature. "I have my troubles here, but I am going to have peace, IF I HAVE TO FIGHT FOR IT."

Still agitated about the question, Roosevelt next called in Bryce to discuss Asian immigration. If the situation became critical, he told Bryce, he hoped the British would tell the Japanese that emigration must stop and that a crisis might otherwise arise in three months, at the beginning of June, if Congress passed an exclusion law. Roosevelt felt sure that in the event of war between the United States and Japan, British Columbia would "rush into the fray." Still, he did not expect war now and intended to send the fleet through the Indian Ocean, the Suez Canal, and home again to the East Coast instead of keeping it on the Pacific Coast.[22]

What was Roosevelt trying to do? Grey thought that Roosevelt was convinced either that war with Japan was inevitable and that the right time to have it was the present, or that the only way to avert war was to allow the whole world to know that America was prepared to go to war if Japan did not keep its promises. Grey was convinced that Roosevelt had "lured" King down to Washington to embroil Canada in a quarrel with Japan. Laurier told King that he should not go to London, that it seemed to be "a deep-laid plot" and that he was sorry they had been drawn into it. King now saw all his hopes for glory fading. It might show "bad faith," he told Laurier, not to go to London; he offered to return to Washington with a reply from Laurier and to obtain from Roosevelt a statement that the controversial letter in which Roosevelt had asked for assistance had been confidential, although it had not been marked so. Correspondence and interviews would thus be safe from parliamentary scrutiny. Laurier agreed to King's proposal and sent him back to Washington with a letter marked confidential.[23]

In the letter to Roosevelt, Laurier wrote that they both knew from experience "that wherever on this continent, as well as in other lands, labourers of Asiatic races come in competition with labourers of the Caucasian races, serious troubles immediately arise, and that for many years and perhaps many generations the only way of preventing those troubles is to restrict, to the narrowest limits possible, the contact of those races in the labor market of our continent." Laurier went on to explain that Canada had to consider the relations of the dominion not only with foreign powers but also with fellow British subjects in India. Imperial authorities were therefore concerned, and Laurier planned to send King to England.

Upon receiving Laurier's letter, Roosevelt assured King that the seriousness of the situation could not be underestimated, that peace depended upon Japan's taking a sane and commonsense view, and that England could help to prevent war by explaining to Japan that the United States, while not unfriendly to Japan, would not stand for any further "trifling." He suggested that King propose a convention to reach an agreement among English-speaking peoples to exclude Asians and to disallow immigration of whites to Asian countries. Roosevelt had little choice but to depend on diplomacy, for on 26 February the secretary of the navy informed him that there were no facilities to maintain the American fleet in the Pacific. Roosevelt decided that the fleet would go to the Pacific only for a goodwill tour, then would return to the Atlantic.[24]

Although Indians certainly believed that Bryce entered into an unofficial agreement with Roosevelt to exclude Indians from the United States, there is no evidence that he did so. A circular was distributed in India in late February saying that industrial conditions were unfavorable for British Indian immigrants in the United States as well as in Canada. American consul general William Michael was convinced that the United States government had arranged this circular through Bryce. It is likely that the government of India would have approved of this method, since it had followed similar action regarding Indian immigration to Canada. Just what part each diplomat had in exclusion seems less important than the fact that there was a growing sentiment among the white diplomats that Asians must be kept out. Bryce was concerned about reports that Indians in the United States were beginning to make known the grievances of their countrymen in India and were using those grievances as an argument for self-government. Early in April 1908, Bryce warned the

India office about a group of Americans "sympathizing with the Natives" and asked that Indian students be kept at home or trained in England, for the atmosphere in America would "encourage their political delusion." Morley forwarded Bryce's information to Minto with the comment that "Hindu anti-British propaganda has not produced any sensitive effect so far on United States opinion." For the moment, the question of Indian workers and students immigrating to the United States came to rest.[25]

Diplomats were satisfied with discouraging Indians rather than excluding them. In Calcutta, Michael refused to grant visas to Indians who requested them and suggested that they migrate to western Australia rather than to the United States. He even proposed that western Australia be set aside especially for Punjabi farmers who, he thought, might be induced to settle there. America, Michael said, had too many immigrants; "America should be given a rest." The U.S. state department commended his efforts.[26]

Reports sent from India by Michael revealed that the fear of growing anarchy there was leading to increased demands by English colonists for protection. The situation, as Morley had predicted, was becoming increasingly serious. On 30 April 1908, someone threw a bomb at the house of a British judge; the bomb landed in the carriage of a British woman and her daughter, killing them both. Two students were arrested. One confessed and was hanged, the other committed suicide. Unrest was again sweeping Bengal. The Indian government responded by arresting a leader of the Bengal nationalists for editorials he had written and sentencing him to six years' imprisonment for sedition. Following his conviction, striking mill hands and police clashed, and the police fired on the workers.

The activities of Indians in North America were only one part of the mosaic of Indian discontent. The Canadian minister of labor had informed Grey of King's investigations of Indian nationalists—an additional reason to supervise carefully all immigration, he noted. Copies of King's reports, sent by the Canadian government to the new secretary of state for the colonies, reached that office along with reports of renewed civil disobedience in the Transvaal. Led by Mohandas Gandhi, Indians there had protested compulsory registration and increased immigration restriction by building huge bonfires, throwing their certificates of registration into cauldrons, saturating them with kerosene, setting them ablaze, and cheering. British agents informed Grey that seditious printed matter was being forwarded from Vancouver to Indians in different parts of South Africa to encourage a feeling of discontent with British rule. Again the reports were forwarded to London.[27]

The growing discontent of Indians made the British more anxious than ever to court American diplomats favorable to colonialism. When Democrats nominated William Jennings Bryan in 1908, domestic politics were again coupled with immigration issues. Bryan, who had had the support of the Anti-Imperialist League in the election of 1900, had made a trip to India early in April 1906 to study England's colonial system. Upon his return he had announced: "British rule is far worse, far more burdensome to the people, and far more unjust—if I understand the meaning of the word—than I had supposed." It was, he argued, worse than Russian despotism because it was exercised over an alien people and drained a large part of the wealth of the country. "Let no one cite India as an argument in defense of colonialism," he concluded; the Briton had demonstrated on the Ganges and the Indus "man's inability to exercise with wisdom and justice, irresponsible power over helpless people" and had impoverished the country through "legalized pillage." India, he said, should be given back to the Indians. Bryan may simply have wanted more trade for the United States, but his words brought home to the British the potential harm of American anti-imperialists. When Bryan's views were reprinted in the 20 July 1906 issue of *India* in London, the British government labeled them "seditious." That fall, other anti-imperialists echoed Bryan's criticism. Andrew Carnegie joined in condemning Great Britain, which he said had troops poised against the people of India; in New York, Samuel Clemens criticized British rule in India as being similar to boss rule in the cities of the United States.[28]

The British in India were thus much relieved when Taft defeated Bryan in November 1908. It was not surprising that British merchants in India believed that Republican policies in the United States coincided with the best interests of the Empire, whereas Democrats under Bryan might increase anticolonial rhetoric even if they did not adopt an anti-colonial policy. The Calcutta Board of Trade was so delighted when Taft was elected president that it borrowed a United States flag from Michael, raised it beside the British flag, and allowed it to fly all day. The chamber of commerce, not to be outdone, did the same. Never had such a thing happened in the history of India, Michael wrote in a note of appreciation. By electing Taft, he said, the American people "proclaimed to the world that they are in favor of sound business principles and economic theories that make for the widening of the spirit of brotherhood, the peace of the world, and the enlargement of trade."[29]

Roosevelt's final assistance to the British Empire came just before he left office in 1909. He had been following the growing unrest in India and considered it likely to upset the balance of power in Asia that he had nurtured so carefully. He had already acknowledged to American Ambassador Whitelaw Reid in London that the difficulty of controlling thickly peopled tropical regions by self-governing constituencies was "very intricate" and that the English encouraged agitation by educating Indians but then not giving them enough public offices. Roosevelt had hinted to English friends in September that he would like to visit India but, receiving no encouragement from London, had settled on Africa for a postpresidential tour. Sidney Brooks, editor of the British *Saturday Review*, was appointed by the colonial office to act as liaison with Roosevelt in arranging the trip to Africa.[30]

Brooks was to play an important role in the attempts of the British to build up support in the United States for restriction of Asian immigration and for continued British control of India. Anti-imperialist sentiment in the United States was a disturbing development that the British hoped to have American help in quelling. The London correspondent for *Harper's Weekly*, Brooks had summed up the "Pacific Question" as it was beginning to look to diplomats in October 1907. "There is no more urgent need than that the problem of Asiatic immigration into English-speaking countries should be taken out of the hands of mobs and vested in those of statesmen," he wrote. Brooks had earlier warned the British against placing blacks and whites on an equal level in South Africa—a policy he compared with giving suffrage to blacks in southern states after the Civil War, and one he called "unbalanced and egotistical philanthropy." Brooks ingratiated himself with Roosevelt by defending him against British critics and by predicting a Republican victory in the 1908 election. Soon after Taft's victory, Brooks warned Roosevelt of the increasing number of attacks on British rule in American newspapers. "I'm sorry to learn it," Roosevelt replied, assuring Brooks that he and Taft both felt that British rule had been "one of the mighty feats of civilization, one of the mighty feats to the credit of the white race during the past centuries." Roosevelt promised that he would speak very strongly on the subject if he had a chance.[31]

Roosevelt wrote to Reid in London that he was concerned about the "very ugly feeling" growing in India. "How do the British authorities feel about it? Are they confident that they can hold down any revolt?" he asked. Roosevelt had dinner with Bryce, then wrote directly to Morley asking for more information. "I grow concerned now and then at what

I hear about the unrest in India. I know very little about it save that I realize the immensity of the burden which England has to bear in India." Roosevelt asked Morley, Reid, Brooks, and Bryce to furnish material for a speech that would put an end to talk in the United States for Indian independence. Each of the four men replied by sending copies of recent articles and speeches defending British rule in India. When Roosevelt had finished the draft of his speech, Bryce went over it carefully and told Roosevelt he liked it.[32]

Roosevelt chose to present his defense of British rule in India in an address to a group of Methodist Episcopal church members in January 1909. India, Roosevelt told the group, was the most colossal example history afforded of the successful administration by men of European blood of a thickly populated region in another continent. He went further, saying that British rule in India was "the greatest feat of the kind that has been performed since the break up of the Roman Empire"—a greater feat, in fact, than that performed by the Roman Empire, and one of the most admirable achievements of the white race during the past two centuries. Were England to withdraw, Roosevelt predicted, India would become a chaos of bloodshed and violence.[33]

British officials were delighted. "A splendid vindication," Morley wrote as soon as he had read the speech. "Friendlier words have never been spoken by an American in connection with British achievements anywhere," Brooks wrote. Edward Gray, James Bryce, Arthur Lee—all expressed their gratitude. "I am glad you like what I said about India," Roosevelt replied to Lee. "I have had it in mind to say ever since Bryan made his silly and hysterical pronunciamento which, so far as by flattery one can say it meant anything, meant that he thought there should be a kind of Indian republic established out of hand. . . . If I did any good, I am pleased." Roosevelt's speech also delighted the British press. It came as proof of the happy change in relations between Great Britain and the United States because "none of his predecessors could have ventured on such a step," announced the London *Times*. A "timely eulogy," added the London *Daily Mail*. A "generous panegyric," noted the London *Standard*—and one that was merited, of course.[34]

Not everyone was so pleased. Opposition came primarily from the newly formed Society for the Advancement of India. Myron Phelps, a wealthy New York lawyer, had set up India House as a hostel where Indian students and Americans could meet on common ground and had created the new society from remnants of the Anti-Imperialist League and from a group of pro-India reformers. The society's purpose was to take up the cause of Indian independence. Reformers, such as Paul S. Reinsch of the University of Wisconsin, editor Louis F. Post, and Jabez T. Sunderland, an English-American Unitarian who had been active in the Boston Anti-Imperialist League, joined the group. As secretary of the society, Sunderland composed a twenty-nine page open letter to Roosevelt. A hundred Indian editors and leaders were in jail and several had been deported, he wrote; freedom had been greatly restricted in India. "Is this method of governing a people, one which the President of a Republic should praise?"

Brooks prepared a series of counterblasts for Roosevelt, labeling the Sunderland letter "a masterpiece of mendacity or ignorance." Phelps defended the society's position in a number of papers, but each time Brooks followed with a more virulent denunciation. Finally, a New York law firm complained that Phelps had been using bar association club rooms for meetings and had the society evicted. Unable to take the public denunciations, Phelps soon resigned from the society and left for a tour of India. The group quietly folded in 1910. By that time, Roosevelt had packed his guns and gone off to Africa, leaving Taft with the problem of Indian immigration and exclusionist sentiment in the West.[35]

Roosevelt's immigration policy was thus absorbed into his personal diplomacy. On the surface, not much seemed to change between the Bellingham riot in 1907 and Roosevelt's departure from office in 1909. Diplomacy by the dominant race had put off more than answered the question of Indian immigration. While the immigration gates remained open legally, diplomatically they were being closed to Asians. Immigration made several things evident. While political refugees might be tolerated or even welcomed by some Americans, large numbers of Indian workers migrating to the Pacific shores were helping to make American officials more sympathetic to British colonialism than they had been at any time since before the American Revolution. Diplomats, still restricted to certain issues, could not shut the gates permanently, but they could help shape the way in which immigrants would be treated by the host government and predict how the American executive branch might develop its domestic immigration policy.

Despite Roosevelt's anti-Asian, procolonial rhetoric, he had not stopped Indians from entering the United States during 1908. They continued to arrive. By the end of 1908, 1,710 Indians had been admitted to the United States—more than in any other single year. In the two previous years almost a thousand had been excluded by the normal process of examination, but now, with the ports of Canada closed, the men were turning south to San Francisco in ever greater numbers and demanding the right to be admitted on the same basis as other non-Asian immigrants. Declaring that no rules specifically excluded Indians, the San Francisco immigration inspector continued to admit them. The stage was now set in San Francisco for a showdown on the issue of exclusion.

5

Sahib North:
Executive Restriction

They have sold their self-respect;
now they sell the dear country to live on.
—Ghadar protest song

Indians who embarked at San Francisco between 1908 and 1910 did so at a port embroiled in the politics of Asian immigration. On one side stood immigration inspector Hart North, already controversial for his handling of immigration issues and his determination to admit Indians. On the other side raged the San Francisco Japanese and Korean Exclusion League, which had changed its name to the Asiatic Exclusion League (AEL) to include Indians among its targets following the Bellingham riot in the fall of 1907. In the middle were the politicians, caught by the growing anti-Asian stance of the white workers of San Francisco.

Early in 1908, the Asiatic Exclusion League had begun to beat the drum for exclusion of Indians by announcing that almost three thousand of the new immigrants had arrived in California by the end of 1907. Taking up the complaints of the Canadian exclusionists against James Dunsmuir, British Columbia's lieutenant governor, leaguers called him a "persistant and vindictive opponent of all forms of organized labor" for allowing unrestricted immigration into British Columbia. The AEL damned the steamships of the Pacific Railroad for transporting laborers from Hong Kong to British Columbia and told its members that plans to divert Indians from Vancouver to Hawaii had not succeeded because Hawaiian plantation owners did not want Asians either. Newspapers picked up and followed the league's lead on extending exclusion to cover the Indians. On 19 January 1908, the San Francisco *Call* published a series of six pictures of turbaned immigrants landing at San Francisco with the caption "The Hindu Invasion." The league announced that it was calling an "Asiatic exclusion convention to meet in Seattle on February 3." Canadian officials managed to keep all but one of their exclusionists away from this meeting, but 163 American delegates flocked to hear AEL president Olaf Tveitmoe make an address on the dangers of Oriental immigration.[1]

At the Seattle meeting, reported in full to Canadian officials by their agents, Tveitmoe used his most aggressive rhetoric. He talked of an impending race war in which labor unions were to be organized into armed military bodies to counteract armed Japanese. Western America had to act as a unit if war came, he warned, because "the map of the Pacific coast might be changed in forty-eight hours." He hinted that American occupation of British Columbia might be necessary because there was no British fleet in British Columbia and no military forces in Canada, and the Japanese in British Columbia were armed. Delegates decided to form an international organization with headquarters in San Francisco, pledging themselves to shape and influence the immigration policies of Mexico, the United States, and Canada. In the United States alone, the AEL estimated that it represented 750,000 voters who would support the Democrats if the Republicans did not pass an Asiatic exclusion act before the next election. The next meeting was scheduled for March 1908 in Vancouver. It was rumored that the one delegate from British Columbia had promised to "deliver a riot," and Tveitmoe had offered to pay eighty dollars a month to the secretary of the Vancouver league to maintain affiliation with the American organization.[2]

The Asiatic Exclusion League exaggerated its own influence. Still, a group such as the AEL, feeding the fears and unrest of workers, had a potential for influencing politicians if not for determining elections. Once portrayed as a specific menace by exclusionists, Asians were less important as direct economic competitors than as a focus for the anxieties of workers about the economic structure and their place in it. Republican politicians generally did not wish to feed these insecurities, but neither did they wish to restrict the Asian immigration that many economic developers wanted at the time. Democratic politicians were more likely to see the AEL as an opportunity to embarrass the Republicans and to court the support of workers.

Republicans tried to avoid the immigration issue in the election of 1908. Although Republican senator Frank P. Flint of California promised specifically to take a stand against Indian immigration, neither he nor Republican senator George C. Perkins, also of California, ever did so in Congress. In December 1907, Republican representative Everis Anson Hayes of California had introduced a bill to regulate Japanese, Chinese, and Korean immigration, but Republicans generally avoided the issue as long as they could, and Congress made only minor changes in the law. It agreed to enlarge the class of immigrants excluded for physical and moral reasons and to raise the head tax from two to four dollars. Roosevelt was able to avoid confrontation with westerners and to obtain the Republican nomination for Taft.

As soon as the conventions were over, Republican officials in San Francisco revised their immigration policies to exclude Indians, arguing that Indian immigrants would not be able to obtain work, would become public charges, and might as well be excluded on that basis immediately. Oscar Straus, the secretary of commerce and labor, was on vacation when the revisions were made, and the acting secretary, William R. Wheeler, a Republican exclusionist from San Francisco, immediately sustained the action. When Straus returned from his vacation, however, he ordered the officers to resume the old policies.[3]

Democrats came out strongly in favor of restrictions on Asian immigration and naturalization in 1908. When California voters proved responsive to anti-Japanese rhetoric, Democrats began to court the Asiatic Exclusion League. The AEL had previously maintained a bipartisan stance while boasting that it could, if necessary, use its 110,000 members to defeat Republicans who did not support exclusion. At a crucial fall meeting, Andrew Furuseth, a Swedish AEL leader, proposed a resolution to support the Democrats, while Tveitmoe attempted to push the resolution through by refusing to recognize objections from the floor. Republicans on the floor raised a furious clamor. Tveitmoe ordered league secretary A. E. Yoell, a taciturn German who was extremely popular with the workers, to sit down when he objected vehemently. Gaining the floor, other Republicans shouted that Bryan had educated and reared a Japanese in his household; these dissenters offered a resolution supporting Taft. The meeting broke up among angry shouting. No resolutions were passed, but the political situation in California remained volatile. The Republicans made just enough clamor about opposing Asian immigration to win the election with a safe margin. Taft carried California, winning the support of middle-class voters and almost 50 percent of the labor vote. In the East, he had no difficulty defeating Bryan on economic issues.[4]

The AEL quieted down after the election of 1908. Then, late in 1909, members once again began publicly to oppose immigration. Moving with the cycle of elections, the league began to attack Hart North for his refusal to exclude Indian workers at San Francisco. Members derisively dubbed him Sahib North.

North had held his job as immigration inspector for almost twelve years when the AEL began to attack him. He was a native Californian, born in Marysville, who had grown up in Oakland, studied law, and then left his practice in 1894 to serve as a Republican state representative from Alameda County. In exchange for marshaling legislative support for the election of Perkins, North was appointed in 1898 to the position of immigration inspector for the states of California and Nevada. During the next few years he dealt with the first influx of Japanese immigrants, both directly from Japan and through the territory of Hawaii. He supported Roosevelt's negotiations to restrict emigration from Japan and from Hawaii and opposed admission of Japanese picture brides. There seems to have been little controversy over North's handling of Japanese immigrants, but he had gained a controversial reputation for his handling of Chinese immigrants. During inspections of the immigration bureau in 1904, North was criticized by the press for delaying decisions, showing favoritism to friends and cronies, and practicing a policy of secrecy. Constant bickering between North and his subordinates arose. Finally, the commissioner general of immigration, Daniel J. Keefe, ordered an investigation, told North to remove the secrecy ban, and placed the Chinese bureau under an inspector who reported directly to the Washington office.[5]

Throughout 1905, there were accusations that North was sheltering men involved in the trafficking of Chinese prostitutes. Rumors spread that women could be bought for three thousand dollars each in San Francisco. In 1907, the dapper young inspector with his needle mustache reluctantly testified against San Francisco political boss Abe Ruef in an investigation of the trade. The Chinese, however, still considered North their friend, and the Chinese consul general Hsu Chen Ping sent him two scrolls as a token of appreciation for his treatment of the Chinese. One poem read:

> With the clear zephyrs filling your bosom,
> Your anxieties, be they ever so numerous,
> will all subside,
> So that the state of tranquillity reached
> will be as when
> Not one grain of dust or sand is raised.

There was much dust and some sand raised when the San Francisco exclusion league took up the issue of Asian immigration with North.[6]

Late in 1909, the Asian Exclusion League took its complaints about North to Washington. League members protested to secretary of commerce and labor Charles Nagel that other ports had excluded Asians and maintained that the previous secretary had upheld their exclusion. Leaguers saw no reason why Indians should be allowed entrance, since Chinese and Japanese had already been excluded. Nagel, a former corporation lawyer and the son of a German immigrant himself, simply referred the letter to Keefe. Keefe replied politely to the league that special legislation would be necessary before Indians could be excluded because of their race. Few were being admitted, he maintained, but each case had to be decided as the alien applied for admission at the port.[7]

The league's next move was typical of its tactics: it issued a report that Indians were being admitted with exotic Oriental diseases, were sending all their earnings out of the country, and were becoming public charges. The same laws enforced in the northern ports, the league claimed, had resulted in total exclusion. Why, it demanded, were the laws not being enforced in all ports? In the name of organized labor in California, the league protested the Hindu invasion and promised to back California politicians who would join the battle.[8]

Mention of exotic diseases was calculated to play on San Franciscans' fear of the plague, a recent political issue there. In the spring of 1900, a Chinese who kept a woodlot was found dead of the bubonic plague in the basement of a small hotel in the slums of San Francisco. The board of health roped off Chinatown and the Japanese areas, but within sixty hours the quarantine was lifted because of pressure from newsmen and doctors who scoffed that there was no plague and that the whole affair was a hoax to sully the reputation of the city. For three years, physicians, businessmen, politicians, and news editors raged loudly while the plague quietly carried away its victims. The last person died in February 1904, the same year that Congress enacted the permanent Chinese Exclusion Act. Another outbreak occurred in 1907, and the city launched a giant crusade against rats. Newspapers also reported that a plague in India had killed a million people in the first six months of 1907. The plague in San Francisco was probably caused by infected wildlife rather than by any Asian carrying it to the white man's land. There was no threat of disease as long as the health authorities were allowed to carry out their jobs unhampered. But the league had a ready issue at hand.[9]

One of the first consequences of anti-Asian agitation was the removal of the immigration station from San Francisco to Angel Island in January 1910. The old station was destroyed by the earthquake of 1906, but the federal government never rebuilt it. During 1909 the immigration bureau negotiated with the war department to lease the offshore island for use as a detention center for immigrants. A new immigration station was set up on the northeastern shore of the peaceful and quiet island. Buildings were temporary, however, with only large bunkhouses and a crude hospital. The result was hardly homey, as the department of labor and commerce claimed it should be, and the costs of fuel and ferry service were high. Moreover, from its inauguration as an immigration station in early 1909, Angel Island was a symbol of repression rather than of freedom for many Asian immigrants. While Ellis Island and the Statue of Liberty in the East were still symbols of freedom, Angel Island had no glorious past rooted in the ideology of the open gate. The island stood as a sentinel of exclusion for the Asian immigrants who sought entry there. The move to Angel Island made North's immigration officials less visible but no less controversial.[10]

As it had done two years earlier, the San Francisco *Call* gave prominent publicity to the anti-Asian crusade of the league. On 31 January 1910 the front page carried a picture of Indians disembarking from the *Manchuria* with the caption "Coming to California at rate of 200 a month"; the accompanying article was headlined "Orientals flock to state, arrive in steady stream." Every China liner, the newspaper informed its readers, who were predominantly laborers, was depositing up to a hundred Indian workers. Almost two hundred of these men, bringing "caste prejudices" and "said to be indifferent laborers," had arrived on the *Manchuria*. According to the league, the article concluded, ten thousand Indians were already in California and two hundred more were arriving every month. Since the men did not come under contract, the article said, they could not be excluded unless diseased or disabled.[11]

When the election of 1910 rolled around, politicians, especially Republicans like Julius Kahn, took another look at the politics of prejudice. A Bavarian Jew known for his dramatic appearance—soft black hat, flaring black cravat, flowing salt-and-pepper hair, and a cigar perpetually in hand—Kahn had been a loyal Roosevelt man and a Taft supporter. Until 1908 he had kept aloof from the Asian question, but the narrow escape of the Republicans in the 1908 election apparently caused him to have second thoughts. In 1902, Kahn had been defeated by the combined support of the Union Labor Party and the Democrats, and he did not like the taste of defeat. Early in 1910, he wrote a letter to Keefe. Some Indians had found employment, he admitted, but in the long run they would become burdens to the community. He asked for more rigorous physical examinations. "Our government ought at least to protect its laborers on the Pacific Coast against this threatened invasion of undesirable Asiatic immigrants," he demanded.[12]

In the House of Representatives, meanwhile, other Californians were active, too. John Pomeroy of San Francisco advocated extension of Chinese exclusion to all Asians, and during discussion in the House in the spring of 1910, Californians introduced a number of letters from the South condemning Asian immigration. The American Federation of Labor opposed Asian immigration, and the United States minister to Persia took time to write that the Asian races had no clear notion of self-government.

Exclusionists were gaining enough attention that the editors of *Collier's Weekly*, then one of the largest popular magazines in the country, decided to run a scare article on the "Hindu invasion" in their March 1910 issue. Two pictures of turbaned immigrants accompanied the article and carried the captions "They are as a whole inferior workmen" and "They manifest no interest in the country or its customs; and they differ from the unobtrusive Chinaman by being sullen and uncompromising." The league might not be representative of sentiment in California, the author concluded, but popular sentiment in California was behind the league's appeal to Washington for exclusion.[13]

When more immigrants arrived on the *Siberia* in April 1910, the inquiry board first ruled that they should not be admitted. Then North said that railroad contractors needed the men for completion of the California Northwestern extension and that there was no reason to exclude them. The league declared open warfare on North, announcing that it would seek the support of organized labor in a protest to Congress, charging North with not enforcing the immigration laws. Local officials had disregarded the "tacit understanding" with the immigration bureau to exclude all Indians, the league complained. It demanded an investigation of North. The Indians, according to the league, had been the victims of "unscrupulous labor buyers." The next evening, Tveitmoe appeared before the Building Trades Council to denounce North for admitting Indians in violation of law and evasion of orders from Washington. He reminded the workers of the danger from the plague. The council replied with a resolution denouncing the immigrants as "unspeakably filthy" and in almost every instance suffering from "dangerous and incurable diseases." The resolution passed without a dissenting voice. On 23 April the San Francisco *Call* announced that thirty Sikhs had arrived on the *Chiyo Maru*; the next day the newspaper published pictures of the same Sikhs, with the headline "Hindu horde joins 10,000 countrymen in California." The men who employed the Indians said they were dirty, lazy, shiftless, and lacking in initiative, the *Call* insisted.[14]

By this time exclusionists had been able to establish a contact within North's office who was willing to work with them. Immigration inspector Frank H. Ainsworth, who had been transferred from Ellis Island to Angel

Island late in 1909, told exclusionists that he believed Indians could be turned away on the basis of antagonism in the community; if there was prejudice, he argued, the Indians would be unable to find jobs and hence would become public charges. North insisted that there was insufficient proof that Indians could not find employment. He also allowed the Indians to be represented by legal counsel at the immigration board meetings held at Angel Island to determine whether each immigrant should be admitted. Ainsworth brushed past North and appealed directly to Keefe to endorse a restrictive policy.

This time Keefe could not avoid making a more drastic interpretation of the law. He told North that although no law excluded Indians as a race and that the bureau did not advocate exclusion of any race, there were nevertheless ways to exclude Indians. The bureau had received information on the poor physical condition of all the Indians, Keefe told North, and this, added to the fact that Indians were "not desirable additions to the community," made Keefe conclude that Ainsworth was correct. As Ainsworth said, Indians were likely to become public charges—a sufficient ground for exclusion. Furthermore, Keefe told North not to consider whether they could obtain employment but only to consider their physical condition, on the theory that Indians could not retain jobs even if they found them and that prejudice must be recognized as a factor. Finally, Indians should not have counsel at their hearings. A lawyer could review the written case just as well for the purpose of appeal. Keefe thus committed the immigration bureau to a policy of restriction based not on law but on the prejudices of the community. But North was still in office, and exclusionists continued to watch the immigration figures at Angel Island with dismay. Ninety-five Indians entered in January, 377 in February, 47 in March, and 169 in April.[15]

The San Francisco *Call* raged openly against North for admitting Indians, who, the newspaper contended, were the most undesirable of all Asians. Not only was North allowing exploitation of a weak and helpless people, but he was also demoralizing the labor market and lowering the American standard of living. "The process of dumping human derelicts on these shores will not be tolerated," warned the editor. North struck back at Ainsworth through the Oakland *Enquirer*. "Ainsworth is responsible for all this," he told reporters. "Go to him if you want to find out anything. He's a dirty dog and he's dirty enough to do anything." After reading the article, Ainsworth filed formal charges against North, asking for an investigation. This wanton attack by North, he told a San Francisco *Call* reporter, had moved him to action.[16]

While Ainsworth and North exchanged insults, more ships from Asia docked. The *Mongolia* arrived with thirty-two Sikhs and three Afghans. The Sikhs were "unassimilable," and the Afghans were from a tribe known for their "treacherous cunning," said the *Call*. Even worse, one Sikh brought his wife, bringing the total of Indian women in California to four. "Hindu women next to swarm to California," ran the *Call* head-line, though the article admitted, in smaller print, that the Indian women already in California were thrifty housekeepers and said to be morally beyond reproach. Exclusionists were beginning to be alarmed over the increase in Japanese women and the prospect of Asians producing native-born Americans. Between 1900 and 1910, the number of Japanese women over age 15 increased from less than a thousand to over nine thousand. The arrival of Indian woman thus received special attention. Even when no women arrived on the *Tenyo Maru*, which brought seventy-two Sikh veterans and farm laborers, the *Call* predicted that the immigrants would later import their wives to the United States. By the end of May, 231 more Indians had been admitted at Angel Island. When still more immigrants were admitted in early June, exclusionists mobilized the press and pressure groups into an organized outburst against the indignity of Asian immigration. When their cries reached Washington, Keefe called North to the capital for a conference.[17]

"Everything is in a muddle just now," North announced to reporters when he returned. He claimed that the Chinese were behind it all, and that those who were agitating against the landing of Hindus were being used, innocently perhaps, by the Chinese who wanted to embarrass him because he was enforcing the law. North convinced no one, however; exclusionists did not believe that North was enforcing the law or that the Chinese were using them as dupes. Hayes announced in the House of Representatives that the law was being violated in San Francisco and demanded that the officers of the immigration bureau see that the "man-date" of the law be carried out. He claimed that during 1909 and early 1910, North had allowed 293 immigrants—mostly Asians—to land with trachoma.

Though disease was discussed, everyone knew that it was not the issue. North may have been condoning or winking at irregularities in his office, but he was simply interpreting the law strictly. "I stand by my previous statement," he affirmed, "that no government official has a right to refuse entrance to this country to any man entitled under the law to land." No law excluded the Indians; they had the same legal standing as any European immigrant, and North could not impose illegal restrictions. Most Indians were strong, could get jobs, and had money. They were not desirable as citizens, North agreed, but the remedy was a general Asian exclusion law. Exclusionists continued to insist that North do as immigration inspectors in other ports had done—exclude Indians without a law. They continued to refer to the immigration inspector as Sahib North.[18]

Again the *Call* damned North on its editorial page. Exclusionist opposition was based on principle, and strict enforcement of the law would solve the problem, said the editor. Moreover, organized revolution was rife in India. The India office had announced that it maintained secret service agents in Vancouver who had determined that Indians were raising money for the purchase of arms. It was almost certain, said the editor of the *Call*, that Vancouver had become the headquarters of a movement for the overthrow of British rule in India. "We may assume that revolutionaries are also organized in the United States and that a treaty with Great Britain for exclusion of East Indians is underway." The treaty might be facilitated if the British discovered that United States Indians were sending home money, the editor concluded. North seemed to be vacillating. He reversed an earlier decision and ordered forty-five East Indians deported, but then he allowed fifty-four men from the *Nipon Maru* and eighty from the *Siberia* to enter.[19]

It was difficult to reject men on the basis of health because few who left India were unhealthy. Only 10 percent of the Indians who wished to come to the United States were able to book passage, for steamship lines rejected most of them. Since 1906, when an immigration act held steamship lines responsible for paying the return fare of any rejected immigrant, the lines had instituted a strict medical examination before issuing tickets. Michael also openly explained his examination policy. When Indians applied to his office for visas, he told a reporter from the English newspaper *Calcutta*, "I give them a thorough examination. I find out their character, question them regarding their sentiment with regard to the government, determine whether they are in favor of sedition in India, qualifications as farmers, artisans, etc., and lastly their educational and financial condition. After these examinations I turn down practically all of them." Men who came to San Francisco were thus in excellent health, either young farmers or veterans hardened by military discipline and experience. Unless something else could be charged against the men, according to law, even strictly applied, they should have been admitted.[20]

When the figure for admissions in June reached 183, Tveitmoe and Yoell were determined to wait no longer. They wired Nagel, asking for an immediate investigation. On 17 June they also sent a letter to President Taft, complaining that North was "not in harmony with public sentiment in California nor is he enforcing the law without fear or favor." Keefe ordered an investigation on 28 June. Then he and Nagel left Washington for their summer vacations.[21]

With only a brief pause for exultation, the exclusionists continued the fight. They publicized twenty-one new arrivals on the *Manchuria* on July 2 and broadcast a claim by a Vallejo sheriff that embittered Indians discharged from railroad work had attempted to derail trains. Other inspectors, exclusionists continued to argue, were not letting in Indians.

The Seattle immigration inspector had, in fact, managed exclusion with no complaint from Nagel. Indians were Muhammadans, he claimed, who believed in polygamy. Polygamy was illegal in the United States. Therefore, although the immigrants had come without wives, he would not permit them to land. He never revealed how he had discovered the Indians were Muhammadans. Perhaps he had used the method suggested by W. Stanley Hollis, an American consul in Africa, who had written to the state department after the 1907 riots to recommend that immigrants be inspected to see if they were circumcised: "Whenever you find a circumcised colored man who is not a Christian, you can be absolutely sure that, at heart, he is a polygamist, no matter how much he may deny it." A number of Indians had applied for admission in 1910, the Seattle inspector reported to his chief in Washington. But all had been rejected by a special board of inquiry on the grounds of either belief in polygamy, likelihood of becoming a public charge, poor health (as confirmed by a doctor's certificate), or status as an assisted (contract) immigrant. These laborers were not fit to enter the country anyway, the inspector added, for they were physically unfit to compete with American labor, came without their families or any intention of becoming permanent residents, and had "filthy and unsanitary" habits. Besides, he complained, the Indians' practice of eating only food that they themselves had prepared made it difficult to care for them at the immigration station. "We have enough race problems of our own without permitting the Hindus to invade our shores," he concluded.[22]

When the San Francisco exclusion league heard that immigrants were being turned away at Seattle on the basis that they were Muhammadans and believed in polygamy, Yoell rushed another letter off to Keefe, asking if this rationale could be used at San Francisco and adding that many Indians were also vagrants. The *Call* announced triumphantly that sixteen Indians had been excluded at Seattle and ordered to be deported. They were illiterate, could not speak English, had poor physiques and little money, and had said they believed in polygamy.

Meanwhile, one recently excluded immigrant, Nika Han, obtained a writ of habeas corpus from federal judge William C. Van Fleet on a claim that his examination had been unfair because he had been deprived of right of counsel. Van Fleet ordered North to show cause why Han should be deported. When North could not do so, the exclusionists damned him again. "Horde of Hindus here to enjoy welcome extended by North," the *Call* proclaimed when 110 Indians arrived in August on the *Mongolia* and the newspaper learned that more were scheduled to arrive on the *Tenyo Maru*. "Their habits are objectionable and their customs a constant source of trouble," wrote the *Call*. The turban seemed particularly offensive to exclusionists. "The outside is usually rather clean," the *Call* admitted, but "it would take a bacteriologist to write the story of the inside." Having insinuated a health menace, the article concluded ominously, "All of yesterday's arrivals wore turbans."[23]

Thoroughly alarmed now, citizens bombarded Washington with petitions and letters demanding exclusion. "The Pacific Coast is fast becoming the dumping ground of the most undesirable people whose morals and customs make an assimilation with our citizens an impossibility," wrote a group from the Glen Park and Mission districts of San Francisco, requesting North's dismissal. This group sent along a copy of the August issue of *The White Man* with a vicious lead article titled "The Filth of Asia."[24]

The chairman of the immigration committee of the state council of California, Frederick C. Pattison, went straight to President Taft, calling North's attitude "unwarranted" and including copies of the exclusionist magazine and press propaganda. William R. Wheeler, former under secretary to Straus, now back in San Francisco working for the chamber of commerce, wrote indignantly to Charles P. Neill, the federal commissioner of labor: "It appears that Hindus are being landed in San Francisco provided they can fulfill the requirements exacted of Europeans. It seems to me that the Administration is justified in adopting any policy which will keep these undesirables out." The Goodfellowship Club of San Francisco demanded that North be recalled for allowing "obnoxious" aliens to land on their shores. "59 undesirable Asiatics arrive," the *Call* announced. Seventy-five Indians had been deported on the grounds of polygamy and likelihood of becoming public charges. In Arizona, four Indians had been arrested on the grounds that they were likely to become public charges. "Them nigger kind of fellers won't eat," the *Call* quoted the prison keeper as saying when the prisoners refused to accept their noonday meal of beans and coffee and asked for uncut bread and hard-boiled eggs.[25]

In India, meanwhile, Michael had discovered that despite his efforts, Indians were leaving for San Francisco in ever greater numbers. On 10 August, he cabled the secretary of state in alarm: "Five hundred sailed this week Calcutta for San Francisco. Undesirable. Refuse admission." In a letter following the cable, Michael explained that after he had turned down almost all who applied, Indians began to avoid his office. He had arranged for steamships not to sell tickets to the United States, but then lines began to sell tickets to Hong Kong. Michael was sure that the lines had hired sharp Bengalis to spread exaggerated stories of opportunity. Immigrants were "undesirable," he repeated, undesirables who would overrun California. Before the state department could notify the department of labor, Michael's reports reached California and received prominent attention in the newspapers, which announced that fifteen hundred Indians had sailed for California in July after having been turned down by the Calcutta office, that the state department had been warned, and that Washington was expected to make representation to Great Britain on the subject.[26]

Despite Michael's sense of alarm, executive restriction of Indians was already having an effect. Late in August, a shipload of 150 Sikhs returned to India after having been turned away from California. Tired, ragged, and broke, they straggled through Calcutta, looking for transportation back to the Punjab. The number returning from San Francisco had reached almost a thousand. Each had spent about four hundred rupees on his trip, and together they provided the best possible discouragement to future immigrants. "We have been ruined by greed," one said to a reporter in Calcutta, "and we must suffer for our sin." Others were not so philosophical. They spoke of their hatred for America and demanded that all Americans be excluded from India. Many would-be emigrants waiting in Calcutta for ships gave up and went home. Two hundred ready to depart from Hong Kong asked that their tickets be refunded. Only twenty-two of the remaining three hundred passed the ship's medical exam.[27]

By 1 September 1910, Michael could report to the state department with satisfaction that the attempt to emigrate seemed to be over. "There is plenty of room in India for all Indians and they are better off here than they would be in the United States, so that, as a matter of fact, their exclusion from the United States is really a kindness and benefit to them," he wrote. Agricultural wages in India were very low, he admitted, but that was a problem for the British India government, not for the United States. All patriotic Americans should be concerned with keeping up wages in the United States through exclusion, he concluded.[28]

When Keefe returned from his vacation at the beginning of September, petitions and letters covered his desk. He answered most of them, assuring the petitioners that boards of special inquiry in San Francisco had been instructed about the "characteristics" of the Indians and notified of the bureau's conclusion that Indian immigrants were likely to become public charges. Upon his return from vacation, Nagel left on an extended tour of the Pacific Coast and Alaska to investigate exclusionist sentiment himself. Election time was dangerously near.[29]

The gains that Democrats had made through anti-Asian campaigns were beginning to worry Republicans seriously by 1910. A. E. Fowler, out of the Washington sanatorium and back in San Francisco as an active AEL member and editor of *The White Man*, had circularized the candidates for governor to get statements on their attitudes toward Asian immigration. The progressive Democratic candidate Theodore A. Bell replied promptly in favor of exclusion. Although progressive Republican Hiram Johnson refused to speak before the league, he wrote to Fowler, "I am in favor of Asiatic Exclusion." Only Philip A. Stanton, former speaker of the assembly and now the conservative candidate for the badly split Republicans, failed to reply. Harrison Gray Otis, the owner and editor of the Los Angeles *Times*, who favored Asian immigration because of his business associations, telegraphed Taft to express his indignation at the new exclusion campaign. Stanton, he said, was the only candidate not committed to the "lawless" demands of the league. When the votes were counted, Stanton received only 18,000 to Johnson's 101,000 in the August 16 primary. Stanton polled virtually no votes in northern California.[30]

North, still attempting to distract exclusionists from their campaign against Indians and oblivious of the Republicans' waning political fortunes, issued some press releases of his own. He accused a Chinese scholar attached to the Chinese bureau of turning his back while a

Chinese caterer passed out fortune cookies stuffed with notes giving immigrants the right answers to questions posed by officials. North removed two other inspectors. Still, the immigration figures at San Francisco hovered uncertainly. Sixty-five Indians had entered in July and sixty-seven were excluded. In August, 189 had entered and 183 were excluded.[31]

The league increased its pressure, writing a second letter to Keefe and replying to his inquiry for facts with a file of charges against North. On 12 September, the league wrote again to Taft. Keefe replied that the letter he had received would get careful attention. Publicly, the league boasted that it had awakened the government to the acute situation and hinted that Sahib North might be axed. As the election neared, the debate became more acrimonious. The league accused North of having removed four inspectors from Chinese fraud investigations and thus allowing Chinese immigration to swell to "unusual proportions," and of being friendly to the Japanese and "shortsighted" in regard to the Indians. The league also charged that North had postponed hearings on Indians and started petitions from Chinese residents to counter those of the league, and it reported that the matter would be discussed at a cabinet meeting. Another investigation would be ordered as soon as Taft received Nagel's recommendations, the league predicted. From Washington came rumors that North's days were numbered—three or four days at most. The department of commerce and labor hinted that his dismissal might come within the week. During September, only forty-five Indians were admitted, and 183 were excluded.[32]

Ignoring the decreasing number of entrants, newspapers chose to report numbers of immigrants who had already been admitted or numbers of those arriving rather than those admitted. The *Chronicle* took up the exclusionists' banner, saying that over three hundred Indians were arriving each month and listing three ships that arrived in August, bringing almost 250 migrants. Indians were beginning to send for wives, and fifteen hundred more men were on the way, warned the newspaper. A doctor had discovered that Indians were infected with "dred hookworm," the article continued, and would all have to be excluded on that basis. A treaty with Great Britain would be necessary to keep out the anemic and weak, who were otherwise eligible for admission. Nagel returned from the Pacific Coast dissatisfied with affairs. Something "radical" had to be done, he told Keefe. Nagel asked that the justice department make a secret investigation and wrote to secretary of state

Philander Chase Knox that rigid inspection was likely to result in discontinuance of all immigration movement of Indians. Knox passed the glad news on to Michael in Calcutta.[33]

One serious loophole remained in the informal system of exclusion. Under the Immigration Act of 1907, immigrants who entered American possessions could obtain certificates allowing them to go on to the mainland without a second examination by immigration officials. Statistics kept by the bureau of immigration did not include Indians who arrived from insular possessions. Immigration officials in the possessions tended to apply more lenient standards than those on the mainland, so that it was possible for immigrants to enter the possessions, spend a few months, and then go on to the United States. Since 1900, some Japanese and Chinese had entered the United States in this way, after a stay in Hawaii. One Indian writer published an article in the *Calcutta Modern Review*, encouraging men to go to Hawaii as a temporary stop and in this way gain entry onto the continent. Although Hawaiian plantations paid only eighteen dollars a month, jobs there provided an opportunity to learn English, to study American customs, and to acquire a skill. After a year or so, the Indian immigrant could take a boat from Honolulu to San Diego, where, the writer claimed, prejudices were not so great.[34]

Immigration authorities soon discovered this unguarded border when Indians began to arrive from Hawaii. At first, all Indians arriving from Hawaii were arbitrarily held at San Francisco and denied entry upon some pretext. Later, however, some from Honolulu were admitted. In September 1910, in the midst of the battle over exclusion, twenty-five Indians were admitted. The next day, Yoell mailed a letter to Keefe advising him of the situation and offering the league's services in spying on the activities of the immigration inspectors. Keefe immediately nailed shut the door from Hawaii by revising immigration regulations to force all immigrants to undergo a second examination before they could obtain new certificates and leave Honolulu. The war department, which was in charge of immigration in Hawaii, strictly enforced the regulation. None of the Indians was given a new certificate, on the theory that they were likely to become public charges.[35]

Two inspectors sent to the West Coast to do a quick investigation returned to tell Keefe that the best interests of the department would not be met by retaining North. He had completely lost control of the situation and was totally unfit for the position. His records were in chaotic condition, many were incomplete, he did not give sufficient time to his duties, he chose inefficient subordinates who had allowed many fraudulent entries, and his domineering manner and lack of executive ability had led to dissension. Furthermore, North had used his official position to influence boards of special inquiry to allow the landing of Indians, thus encouraging "the unusually large influx of undesirable alien Hindus"; he allowed an attorney to interview Indians before their official examination and allowed them to use an Indian interpreter. The inspectors recommended that the bureau replace North and make another thorough investigation. The *Call* announced that North would probably be replaced by Ainsworth, who had made the first charges against him. On 27 October 1910 Taft suspended North and ordered another investigation.[36]

It was a historic day for the exclusionists when North turned over his yellow jacket, the combination to the safe, and the key to the card index to the new temporary inspector, Luther C. Steward. That same day the *Korea* brought a load of Chinese and six Indians into port. But the flow of Indians had already been almost stopped at its source by the news that immigrants would no longer be admitted. To turn away those few who persisted, exclusionists now pinned their hopes on the hookworm test.[37]

Progressive candidate Hiram Johnson made few anti-Asian statements during the gubernatorial campaign. Progressive papers, however, battling for Johnson and for a ticket of middle-class and labor reforms, identified North with Republican forces of reaction. The Republican administration had to choose between being defeated by accusations of being soft on Asian immigration because it maintained the letter of the law, or changing the law to conform to exclusionists' demands. The politics of the election gave them little choice. On 8 November, the *Call* proudly bore a banner headline urging its readers to vote for Hiram Johnson, "your champion fighting for your freedom." Voter, it demanded, "free yourself from political serfdom." Beneath the banner was news from Washington. Keefe was on his way to help with the San Francisco investigation. "Affairs in the San Francisco immigration office have presented such a bad appearance to Steward's superficial investigation," the article announced, "that the appearance of the commissioner general of immigration himself was requested." Johnson and the progressive Republicans carried California, cutting deeply into the old margins previously held among labor districts by the Democrats and gaining enough votes in the San Joaquin Valley and in lumbering regions to offset losses in southern California and in some Catholic and northern coast areas. Middle-class reformers could now begin unabashedly wooing the labor machine that had controlled San Francisco and the northern part of the state.

Restriction by executive action was, naturally, not as satisfactory to California exclusionists as exclusion by congressional legislation or diplomatic agreement would have been. This type of restriction necessitated constant vigilance over immigration inspectors. Eugene E. Schmitz, the mayor of San Francisco, wrote to Nagel, urging congressional or diplomatic action. "This is no narrow sectional feeling or narrow prejudice against Hindus as a people any more than it is against other Asiatics," he argued; the Indians were "servile, enervated members of a degenerated race," and no technical quibble over the law should interfere with the welfare of the commonwealth. The AEL finally decided to support an executive agreement between Taft and Great Britain, similar to that signed between Roosevelt and the Japanese government. Yoell wrote to Taft, asking him to act.[38]

A few token revelations of irregularities in North's term followed, such as claims that he had forced immigrants to pay steamship companies for board during their detention, which, by law, the companies themselves should have paid. But once the election was over and Indian immigration had been restricted, public interest waned.[39]

No one knew exactly how many Indians actually entered the United States in 1910. Several sources reported that over five thousand had entered the port of San Francisco alone, but it seems more likely that the figure of the local exclusionists, 1,403, is more accurate. A total of only 1,783 is given in the official estimates for that year. In November and December of 1910, only two Indians entered at San Francisco, and 289 were turned back at Angel Island. The figure for 1909 was 337, and the figure for 1911, after the crisis had subsided, was 517. During the height of the campaign, wild guesses, sometimes consciously falsified, were circulated, but after the battle had ended in victory for the exclusionists, the estimates dropped to more realistic figures.[40]

By 1910, exclusion had become the policy choice of most middle-class reformers along the coast. Bred in the traditions of frontier racism, they were ready to extend that racism to Asians. The attempt to admit blacks to politics, it seemed to reformers, had already failed, and they had no intention of making the same mistake with Asians. Progressive reformers had a commitment to "equality," but for most that commitment extended only to the white person. In the days when railroad moguls had ruled the coast, it had been a question of labor versus capital, and the railroad owners had kept the Pacific gates open to Asians. By the time the Indians arrived, however, the days of the Pacific moguls were almost at an end. Their influence could still be seen in philanthropy and in the conspicuous consumption practiced atop Nob Hill, but succession to their political empire was being quarreled over by labor and middle-class reformers. Republicans could no longer ignore the Democrats' appeal to race and were forced to act to neutralize it.

Keefe had told the league the year before that special legislation was necessary to exclude Indians on the basis of race. The league's efforts had not forced legislation to be enacted, but it had fostered alarm among politically powerful constituencies. Pressure at the proper political points moved the executive branch to action. Officials in Washington, with the approval of the president, put the policy of restriction into practice without law. By April 1911, the AEL could report immigration of the previous four months with satisfaction: two farmers, three farm laborers, four students, one merchant, one mason, and one Indian listing no occupation—a total of eleven—had entered since December.[41]

During his first six months in office, Steward gained the support of Nagel, who recommended that he be made the permanent appointee at San Francisco. Four typewritten volumes of investigation into immigration affairs at Angel Island had been forwarded to Washington, and the new rules were being enforced. The two Republican senators, however, wanted a political appointee. The senators' choice had no qualifications or training, Nagel protested to Taft's secretary, Charles Hilles. "I can only say that San Francisco is about as troublesome a post as Ellis Island. The conflict between the different forces is constant and intense, and the Commissioner has anything but an easy time. He must be a man of experience and discretion, willing to take punishment; and able to keep his head."[42]

Taft chose to listen to the senators and picked Samuel Backus, a sixty-seven-year-old Civil War veteran and former California adjutant general. Successful as the owner of the San Francisco *Post* and of the *Wasp*, the first color cartoon magazine in the United States, as well as at various other business enterprises, Backus had been postmaster of San Francisco under Benjamin Harrison and had moved into the progressive wing of the Republican party and worked to elect Johnson governor. The AEL objected to Backus as "incompetent, inexperienced and aged." But Taft needed support from progressives in California, who promised that Backus would enforce the laws "to the letter and the spirit."[43]

The end of Indian immigration did not end administrative problems at Angel Island. For many years, as one official later noted, "endless scandals and cliques" continued. The separation of immigration inspection from the mainland only compounded problems. No boats left Angel Island after 4:35 P.M., so swamped officials who wished to work overtime could not do so. Dishonest officials flourished. Assistant secretary of labor J. B. Dinsmore estimated in 1917 that there was over $100,000 in graft each year. One Chinese immigration superior, an honest official, confided in his diary when he left in 1918: "It is not a safe place to be connected with and I feel I will have to be pretty desperate to return to it."[44]

Executive restriction was thus enforced amid a welter of political considerations. As in India, American officials had to deal with dishonesty and political intrigue while they tried to establish discriminatory policies based on race. Not surprisingly, such deviousness drove officials to resort to ever more extreme measures to achieve control of Indians, who claimed the right to work as equals alongside white men in the West.

6
Komagata Maru:
Challenging Exclusion

Why doesn't our flag fly anywhere?
—Ghadar protest song

Since the beginning of exclusionist organizing in 1907, Indians had organized in response. They had attempted to bring Indians together in broad protest groups to defend systematically their interests in both North America and India. Like other groups of Asian immigrants, they used the courts to achieve equality with non-Asian immigrants. Finally, in 1914, Gurdit Singh, a Sikh peasant from Amritsar who had become a wealthy contractor from overseas investments, decided to hire a boat to challenge the Canadian laws. Indians were challenging laws all over the Empire during the winter of 1913–1914. The sailing of the *Komagata Maru*, the boat chartered by Gurdit Singh, brought to a climax seven years of protest in both the United States and Canada over the treatment of Indians. Attempts by Indians to obtain entry into Canada were watched with concern by United States officials, who feared that success there might lead to attempts to challenge administrative restriction in the United States.

The first response of Canadian officials to Indian immigrants in 1907 had been not only to keep them out but also to attempt to expel those who had already been allowed in. But the growing unrest in the Punjab made it unwise to expel the Indians, especially Sikh veterans, and attempt to send them back to the Punjab. An alternative plan was then broached: to arrange for the Indians to migrate to Hawaii, where sugar plantations had long welcomed Asians to perform arduous field labor. Late in 1907, Canadian officials questioned the Alexander and Baldwin Company, which controlled twenty sugar plantations in Hawaii, to see whether it was interested in having Indians as employees. A representative of the sugar interests visited Vancouver in December to look over the unemployed who were being turned out of camps and gathering in the city. A few weeks later an official of Alexander and Baldwin arrived in San Francisco to talk with the leader of an Indian colony there. The San Francisco *Call* announced that three hundred men would probably leave the city for Oahu and that others would be leaving Vancouver as well. "The frosty weather in the North completely paralyzed their energies," wrote one reporter, predicting that Indians would surely trade northern California for the warmer climate of Hawaii.[1]

After investigation, however, planters decided that they did not want the Indians. They did not publicly say why, but they probably feared that the men would not be satisfied with the Hawaiian conditions. A representative of Alexander and Baldwin offered his condolences to the San Francisco exclusion league: "The problem confronting the Anglo-Saxon race (and why not say Celtic also) in British Columbia is a serious one. We believe the American continent should be preserved as the exclusive heritage of the whites. Hence the sympathetic interest we take and the warm hopes we entertain that Oriental immigration will be prohibited."[2]

Although the Hawaiian proposal died, the British authorities became more concerned when agitation against Sikhs still in Canada persisted. In September 1908, secretary of state for the colonies Robert Crewe mentioned his continuing concern about the Sikhs in Canada to brigadier general Eric Swayne, governor of British Honduras, who was then in London to discuss Honduran development problems. Swayne, who had commanded Sikh troops in India for sixteen years before assuming his colonial post in Honduras, mentioned that perhaps the Sikhs might be moved to Honduras, where labor was scarce. Crewe passed the suggestion on to Grey, who proposed it to Laurier as a method for decreasing the Indian population in British Columbia. The Canadian privy council considered the Swayne proposal early in October 1908 and decided that "in view of the fact that many are of the soldier class and that their enforced return to India by a British colonial Government might in the present state of India prove detrimental to Imperial interests," efforts should be made to remove the Indians to Honduras. The Canadian government agreed to pay the expenses of an Indian delegation to Honduras to determine whether conditions were favorable. The San Francisco *Call* announced joyfully that the department of the interior in Canada had solved the "Hindu" problem. The entire colony was to be moved to British Honduras as soon as plans could be worked out between Laurier, British officials, and Swayne, who was on his way to Canada.[3]

When Swayne arrived in Montreal, he went first to discuss the proposal with Grey. Grey took the old soldier to visit Laurier, who, impressed by Swayne's devotion to the Empire and to the Sikhs, encouraged Swayne to visit Vancouver. In Vancouver, Swayne was alarmed over the high wages that Indians commanded there—over four times the current Punjab wages—and feared that the difference would cause trouble in the Punjab if the men returned. "The terms of close familiarity which competition with white labour has brought about, do not make for British prestige," he reported to Grey. "It must be recognized that it is by prestige alone that India is held and not by force. The importance of a circulation of labour between Vancouver and India as affecting that prestige is such, I submit, as cannot be wisely overlooked."[4]

Swayne was concerned that Indians had been exposed to American radicals in Vancouver as well as to high wages—a volatile combination. Indians had already made contact with the left wing of the West Coast labor movement. Primarily socialists and anarchists, these radicals saw the Indian struggle as part of an international labor movement that would eventually bring the working class to power in all countries. Emma Goldman, the fiery anarchist leader of Industrial Workers of the World (IWW), had already lectured to Indians in British Columbia before Swayne arrived; Goldman had obtained letters of introduction to leaders of the Indian nationalist movement, whom she planned to visit while on a lecture tour in India. Socialists, according to Swayne, had also "tampered" with Indians, and Bengali immigrants were in touch with nationalist leaders in Bengal. At Swayne's suggestion an undercover agent, William Hopkinson, was appointed to conduct investigations and to communicate with the Calcutta police; Swayne redoubled efforts to arrange for the Sikhs to move to Honduras.

By the time Swayne arrived in Vancouver, the Indian community was already well organized enough to consider his offer as a group. They selected two men, Nagin Singh and Sham Singh, to go to Honduras to investigate Swayne's offer. The Canadian interior department hired an interpreter to accompany them, and the group left immediately. As soon as the two Sikh delegates returned, the entire Indian community held a closed meeting at the Sikh temple to discuss the emigration plan.

The Sikhs who had gone to Honduras were not impressed. They reported that they had found thirty Indians in the Central American colony, the only remaining workers of a group of contract laborers who had immigrated to the colony over a generation before. All thirty men wanted to return to India. Yet it was difficult for the Indians in Canada to turn down an offer that seemed to be a solution to their problems. They were demoralized but now ready to face the reality that, as one Sikh later wrote, "the white man has two standards, one for his own use and the other for the man with the brown skin."[5]

At this point Teja Singh, a tall young Sikh with a long beard who had just arrived from New York, came forward with a new suggestion. The son of a physician, he had studied law and had then abandoned the legal profession after one week of practice in favor of teaching and government service. Under the guidance of his Sikh mother, he had studied Sikh scriptures and had become an orthodox Sikh. After traveling to England in 1906 and 1907, he had entered Columbia University Teachers College in July 1908. Canadian Sikhs heard of Teja Singh through lectures, invited him to visit, and asked him to move to Canada to work with his fellow countrymen. He had promised to join their cause and had just settled in Vancouver with his family when the Honduran delegation returned.[6]

Teja Singh had a better plan than emigration. He urged Sikhs to band together to form agricultural communities where they could live independently and devote some of their earnings to educational and missionary purposes. They should foster Oriental philosophy and art, engage in business, real estate, mining, logging, and shipping, and establish a mining and trust company to purchase several hundred acres of land to establish "United India homes." There, men of all races, castes, and creeds might gain admission with only a promise to refrain from smoking and drinking. The company would plan such colonies in Europe and the United States. Men could also build Sikh temples in Canada and the United States and help students. Teja Singh's utopian scheme gave the poorer Sikhs hope for the future in Canada. Wealthy Sikhs, fearing that if the poorer Sikhs accepted the offer to emigrate, the movement for deportation might gain support and all Indians be forced to give up their land and leave, also lent support to the scheme. On 23 November, Teja Singh made a public speech announcing the decision of the Indians to remain in Canada. He also claimed that the department of interior interpreter had offered a bribe of three thousand dollars to the delegation to give a favorable report on Honduras. "No empire can exist if held together by ties of mistrust," he warned. Indians were treated badly in Australia, South Africa, and India; Queen Victoria's proclamation of equal treatment irrespective of color was not being maintained, and if Indian's just rights were not granted, a leader would arise to direct Indians' cause in open warfare.[7]

Immigration officials were dismayed. Not only had Teja Singh discouraged the Honduras proposition, he had also been able to use unfair treatment as a rallying point to unite Punjabi Muslims, Hindus, and Sikhs with Bengali Brahmans in a way they had never been united in

India. The Canadian agent, Hopkinson, reported that Indian agitators in Seattle and Chicago were responsible for the decision, for the delegates had been pleased with Honduras and he had offered no bribe. He had no doubt that the Vancouver Indians were working with the revolutionists in India, for an employee of the Indian government railway had told him that Teja Singh was wanted for sedition in India and had come from New York expressly to block the Honduras proposal. Whether or not Teja Singh had come for this purpose is certainly not clear. At first, the India office reassured the Canadian government that Teja Singh was not wanted for sedition in India and that his political views, rather than being dangerous, were "fairly moderate." Later, British government officials would reverse that view, warning that he had written a seditious pamphlet in India and was a dangerous revolutionary.[8]

Regardless of Teja Singh's political past, the terms of work in Honduras could hardly have been attractive to the Indians. According to a man named Nand Singh Sihra, the men were offered only eight dollars a month plus four dollars' worth of rations—little more than they could have earned at home in the Punjab. Moreover, some Indians were beginning to lease land with the prospect of becoming landowners. Nevertheless, Grey wrote to Laurier in December 1908 that he suspected the allegations of bribery to be "deliberately concocted calumnies" to work mischief in India and that vigilant watch must be maintained, for statements and newspaper reports, if repeated in India, might "inflame the minds of those who are the tools and victims of sedition." Grey asked that the minister of the interior regularly supply him with information on Indian immigrants. Laurier had already received alarming reports from Vancouver that Indians had established an "infernal machine manufactory" at Millside and that they were using support of "mutineers in India" as a pretext to collect money. The consequence of beneficent rule in India, Laurier concluded, was the rise of agitators and agitation. Laurier ordered officials in British Columbia to watch Teja Singh and to arrest him if his "misconduct provided them with a legitimate excuse." Grey also sent his military intelligence agent, Rowland Brittain, to report on a meeting called on 6 December to reconsider the Honduras proposal.[9]

Brittain reported back that the Sikh temple was a "hotbed of sedition." The meeting had turned into a demonstration against immigration officers, and Brittain recommended more espionage to see whether the Indians were really disloyal. "I have no fear that the Hindus will give

any trouble here if properly treated and firmly handled," Brittain concluded, but went on to say that they should be carefully watched to see
that they did not encourage the "mutinous party in India."[10]

Exclusionists were now demanding that Indians be deported.
Swayne, still insisting to reporters that his offer was "too tempting to
be refused," nevertheless firmly insisted that if the Indians did refuse
to go to Honduras, they should be allowed to remain unmolested. Driving the Indians out of Canada would aggravate the situation in India,
he argued, and since no more could immigrate, those already in Canada
would return after a few years, when they had earned some money.
Their presence in British Columbia "or in any other white colony" was
"politically inexpedient," however, for they acquired "familiarity with
the whites." An instance of this, Swayne said, "was the speedy elimi-
nation of caste in this Province as shown by the way all castes help each
other. These men go back to India and preach ideas of emancipation
which if brought about would upset the machinery of law and order.
While this emancipation may be a good thing at some future date, the
present time is too premature for the emancipation of caste."[11]

Viceroy Minto soon added his veto to the Honduras plan. He had
grave doubts about the transfer, for the men were of the soldier class
and were less likely to settle as agriculturalists than to become policemen
or messengers or go into industry. Similar men had been recruited for
sugar plantations, and trouble was developing. The Colonial Sugar Re-
fining Company in Hawaii had asked Minto to tell recruiting agents not
to send Punjabis, discharged soldiers, or high-caste people who could
read or write English, as they tended to spread dissatisfaction.[12]

Swayne himself delivered the final blow to the scheme after he had
arrived back in Vancouver to talk to the Indians. He found that hostility
from the whites had decreased because labor conditions were improving
and because half the Sikh population—about twenty-five hundred of
five thousand—had gone to the United States. The depression had
ended, mills had reopened, and work was available. The stories about
Indians not being able to stand the climate, he said, were false. Indians
probably suffered less than whites under similar conditions. Swayne
thought that anti-Asian politicians were using the Indians to get votes;
in fact, politicians had promised the white electorate that they would
deport a thousand of the new immigrants. Indians feared that they
would all be forcibly deported and had formed a labor union to prevent
deportation. There was little unemployment among the Indians. Those
still not employed were being taken care of with funds supplied by the

rest. During the summer all of the immigrants had found work, and Swayne could find only three out of work that winter. Mill owners seemed to prefer Sikhs to Euro-Americans because they were more permanent. As long as exclusion kept out further immigrants, exclusionist sentiment would subside. The Sikhs seemed destined now to remain in Canada.

The Canadian Sikhs might have become a small, forgotten colony of expatriates but for their determination to obtain equal rights with other Canadian immigrants. During the next two years, Vancouver Sikhs worked hard, saved their money, and did very little protesting over exclusion. Teja Singh remained the most outspoken and visible leader, but after 1910 he was joined by other Sikhs in attempts to open Canadian gates.

Many immigrants were now prosperous, propertied, and anxious to be reunited with their families. Canadian Indians took complaints about Canadian immigration laws to the imperial council and petitioned the government at Ottawa to allow their families to be admitted. When complaints and petitions brought no response, they talked of appealing directly to King George and of chartering a special steamer to bring their wives and children. Hira Singh, a veteran who had lived in Vancouver for more than four years, sent for his wife and their daughter, who arrived aboard the *Monteagle* on 21 July 1911. Officials promptly ordered the family deported, but Hira Singh demanded a hearing and posted a one thousand dollar bond; after much debate, the woman and child were allowed to remain "as an act of grace."[13]

In September 1911, Laurier went down to a hard defeat at the polls. Canadian interests, Conservative critics claimed, were not being given sufficient attention. Attempts by Liberals to work out commercial agreements with the United States also came under fire by Conservatives, who spread rumors that Laurier wanted Canada to secede from the British Empire and become part of the United States. A Conservative might be less influenced by labor and more influenced by imperial concerns, the Sikhs reasoned, so soon after the election of Robert Borden, a shy Nova Scotia lawyer, they held a mass meeting at the Sikh temple in Vancouver to discuss sending a delegation to Ottawa.

The Indians chose Teja Singh to lead the delegation in November. The men planned to claim British citizenship, ask that families of Indians be allowed to come to Canada, and request that restrictions on students, merchants, and tourists be removed. They promised to give bond that no Indian would become a public charge. "All Indians' interests are bound up indirectly in the decisions that may follow on the matters presented by the delegation," wrote one Indian. "There will either be one standard, or two, within the Empire of British subjects, interests and privileges. If the latter then it must be based on race privileges, or race superiority. Hence India is looking to Canada most anxiously as to her own present and future status."[14]

To gain support for entrance of Indian immigrants' families, the Vancouver leader Sundar Singh began a speaking tour in eastern Canada. He lectured his audiences on the unfairness of keeping families apart by a policy of subterfuge: "It does not savor of justice and it is neither straightforward nor humanitarian." He found some sympathy among Canadian missionaries, but the Toronto labor council immediately threatened to withdraw from the church if it supported the claims of the Indians. A member of parliament from British Columbia, H. H. Stevens, began a campaign against admission of Indian families. The argument for and against Indian admission, when taken to the East, thus spread the hostility once confined mainly to British Columbia. The Conservative government acted no differently than the Liberal government had: it refused to revise the policy.[15]

Early in 1912, the Indians tried again. Balwant Singh, a young priest of the Vancouver Sikh temple, and Bhag Singh, president of the Vancouver Khalsa Diwan, had returned to India to bring their wives and children. Immigration officials promptly ordered that the wives and children be deported when they arrived in Vancouver, but the Sikhs appealed to the courts for a writ of habeas corpus, and the judge ordered the release of the prisoners. Indians pointed out that other Asians were being allowed to enter. During 1911, more than eleven thousand Chinese and almost three thousand Japanese—a third of them women—had entered Canada. After a bitter, three-month controversy, the government finally dropped its case, and the families were allowed to remain "as an act of grace without establishing precedent."[16]

Late in 1912, members of the Vancouver Sikh temple selected delegates to speak again to the premier, to go to London, and then to proceed to India to plead their case. This time Teja Singh and Sundar Singh were joined by Bhag Singh and Balwant Singh, the men who had just had their families admitted. At Ottawa and London, the delegation was refused recognition. Sikhs, one Indian told reporters, were throwing their war medals into the harbors and were assuming that the adoption of a self-assertive attitude was the only way to secure justice. "Unless something is done, and quickly," he warned, "I am afraid the 6,000

Hindus of British Columbia and their landed wealth of nearly three million dollars may try to make their existence felt in a very disagreeable manner."[17]

The Canadian delegation arrived in the Punjab in the summer of 1913 to describe the situation of Indian immigrants in Canada. In the *Indian Review*, the delegates said that Sikhs and other Indians had invested millions of dollars in real estate and buildings in Vancouver but that they could not vote or bring their families to join them. Neither British subjects nor immigrants, they were without rights. The Japanese paid a tax of fifty dollars to enter, the Chinese five hundred dollars, but the Indians could not enter at all. The delegation also presented its case to the viceroy of India and to the Indian National Congress. Protest meetings quickly turned into general criticism of British rule, and the lieutenant governor of the Punjab first ordered the men arrested, then had them released. Although Teja Singh, who was already having difficulty retaining his leadership in Canada, decided to remain in India, the others returned to Vancouver, taking forty-three of their countrymen, thirty-nine of whom had never been admitted to Canada before.[18]

Immigration officials naturally ordered the men deported. This time, however, the men appealed to the supreme court of British Columbia for a writ of habeas corpus. Chief justice Gordon Hunter ordered all the men released and held that the continuous voyage clause was inconsistent with the Immigration Act. He also ordered another Indian being held by the immigration inspectors to be released. Other Indians appealed to the court for further protection and were also ordered to be admitted. The Hunter decision precipitated a crisis in British Columbia. Officials met in secret sessions for long hours and emerged haggard to make guarded statements about what would be done to meet the national emergency. The Hunter decision, the premier of British Columbia admitted, had caused "a critical state of affairs."[19]

Other officials were less circumspect. One said that thousands of Indians would soon be on their way and that the only way to deal with them was to have an army of working men sufficient to force them back and stop them from landing. He predicted more riots. The Toronto *Globe* reissued its statement that Indians were not desirable settlers for Canada.[20]

The battle of Canadian Sikhs was a part of the larger battle going on within the Empire for equality for Indians. That November, Gandhi led striking Indian mine workers and their families across the Natal border into the Transvaal to a communal farm to protest legislation and to launch his program of *satyagraha* (soul-force or nonviolent resistance) there. Officials arrested the workers and forced them back into the mines as prisoners. Charles Hardinge, the new viceroy of India, was outraged by the action of the South African government, asked for an investigation, and supported civil disobedience of unjust legislation. His pressure brought a compromise settlement early in 1914. Had it not been for the struggle in South Africa, Gandhi wrote in his reflections on using satyagraha in South Africa, Indians would have been hounded out of the country. Victory there had served as a shield for Indian emigrants in other parts of the British Empire. Unless Indians employed satyagraha, their rights would be suppressed.[21]

Events in South Africa certainly caused the India office additional concern about the Canadian Sikhs. "The situation produced in India by events in South Africa is . . . already so grave, that any decision which may extend and exacerbate Indian popular feeling against other portions of the Empire must add to the anxiety caused by the existing position," T. W. Holderness of the India office wrote of the Canadian difficulty. Despite the growing international dimensions of the Indian protest, however, the Canadian government issued a new order-in-council reasserting the continuous voyage doctrine along with an order requiring all Asian immigrants to have two hundred dollars. Although immigration officials at Vancouver said that the order-in-council was actually directed at Indians, it was worded to appear to include all nationalities. The order-in-council quieted the Sikh immigration issue for about three months—the period that the order was in effect. It expired on 31 March 1914.[22]

Vancouver was in the throes of one of its periodic financial panics when, in April 1914, rumors began to circulate that a ship had left Hong Kong with a load of Sikhs determined to test the continuous voyage law. Borden favored a nonaggressive response to the challenge and one that would not involve Ottawa directly. The government hurriedly extended for another six months the order excluding Asian artisans and laborers that had lapsed on March 31. The minister of the interior stated categorically that the Indians would not be allowed to land. Ottawa left to Vancouver officials the responsibility of carrying out that promise.

While Vancouver officials braced themselves for the arrival, the *Komagata Maru* steamed across the Pacific, bringing almost four hundred Punjabis. The project was not arranged directly by Canadian Sikhs. Gurdit Singh, concerned about the Canadian Sikhs he had seen in Hong Kong who wanted to go to Vancouver but who could not obtain passage, conceived of the idea of chartering a boat that would arrive after the order-in-council expired on 31 March. He had already challenged laws in other parts of the Empire, and he planned to challenge Canadian laws as well if the men were not allowed to enter. Beyond that, Singh apparently had only commercial motives. He hoped to start a ship line that would bring immigrants to the West Coast. There seemed to be no other direct political reason for his chartering of the *Komagata Maru*, although later historians noted that his grandfather had fought against the British in the Sikh Wars of the early nineteenth century and that Gurdit Singh himself had protested against the British practice of forcing poor villagers to perform labor on public works. Indians challenged laws in many parts of the Empire during the winter of 1913–1914, and the Sikh temple in Hong Kong, where the men who had been refused admittance to Canada gathered that winter, would have heard news of many of the challenges from Sikh travelers.[23]

Gurdit Singh promised to act as manager of an expedition, and the men collected enough money for him to charter the *Komagata Maru* for $66,000. Renamed the *Guru Nanak Jahaj*, the 2900-ton freighter sailed in April with a cargo of coal, a crew of 40 Japanese, and 165 Sikhs. At Shanghai, the ship picked up another 111 passengers; by the time it left Kobe and Yokohama, the ship carried 376 Indians—340 Sikhs, 24 Muslims, and 12 Hindus—all Punjabis.

At one point Canadian officials thought that the sailing of the *Komagata Maru* might be a "Japanese-Indian conspiracy" to challenge the immigration laws. Japanese involvement in the voyage is still unexplained; for example, Japanese coal dealers agreed to take a lien for coal even though they knew that the ship might be turned back and that Gurdit Singh might be unable to sell the unused coal in British Columbia. The Japanese consul in Vancouver later met with the Japanese captain at the behest of Canadian officials but failed to convince him to leave. No evidence was uncovered then or later to prove any attempt by the Japanese to test Canadian immigration laws, however. The challenge apparently came solely from the Indians. British officials might have stopped the ship from sailing, but they did not. The responsibility for responding to the challenge thus rested with Canada.[24]

Canadian officials hoped to turn the ship back at the mouth of Victoria Bay when the captain asked for clearance to proceed to Vancouver. When the Japanese captain presented his papers, however, officials cleared the ship for Vancouver. After the quarantine officer had inspected the ship and each Indian had been vaccinated, the ship was allowed to proceed. Reporters interviewed Gurdit Singh at the quarantine station, where he stated his case briefly: "We are British citizens and we consider we have a right to visit any part of the Empire. We are determined to make this a test case and if we are refused entrance into your country, the matter will not end there. Other boats will be chartered and my people will continue to cross the Pacific until we secure what we consider to be our rights." All Indians had the necessary amount of money, and none had made the trip directly from India. When the ship arrived in Vancouver, immigration officials ordered it to anchor in the harbor rather than to dock. Launches patrolled the shore so that no Indians could leave the ship; Vancouver city police guarded the landward side. Thus began a three-month battle to test Canadian exclusion of Indians.[25]

Events during that three-month controversy were incredibly complicated. Vancouver Sikhs raised money to help take the case to court, shouted encouragement from the docks, and attempted to provision the ship. Gurdit Singh and his secretary meanwhile negotiated with the Sikhs on land, as well as with dominion, British Columbia, and Vancouver officials.[26]

The plan evolved by officials was to try to get Indians to bring a test case to a board of inquiry, then to one judge of the supreme court of British Columbia, and finally to the court of appeals. This path would circumvent Hunter, who the officials feared would allow the men to enter. Officials were sure the court of appeals would not allow the Indians to land. Apparently, the attorney for the Indians did not realize the significance of the maneuver; officials assured him that all rights of appeal would be preserved by this procedure. Gurdit Singh wanted the men to apply directly for a writ of habeas corpus instead of going before a board of inquiry, but immigration officials refused; they did not want to risk judicial admittance of Indians with no legal avenue of appeal for the government. So the negotiations dragged on into June.[27]

Meanwhile, rations were running low on the ship. Gurdit Singh saw this situation as a possible way to move negotiations to a new course. He refused provisions sent out by local Indians but appealed to the governor general of Canada and to King George to come to the assistance of the starving men. Immigration officials sent undercover agents on board to find out whether the men were eating food secretly cached away at night and then feigning hunger during the day.[28]

The delay in the decision allowed exclusionists in Vancouver, who had been relatively quiet since the 1907 riot, to reassert their arguments against Indian migration. The Vancouver *Sun* depicted what it considered to be the feelings of its white readers in a cartoon captioned "Will the dyke hold?" The cartoon showed a small home flying the Canadian flag; behind it were garden plots labeled "Content," "Living wage," and "Organization" and a sign reading "Population of eight million." The dyke was labeled Immigration laws" and the ocean "300,000,000 Oriental laborers." The *Sun*, backer of the Liberal Party, insisted that under Laurier the ship would not even have been permitted to enter a Canadian harbor. It accused the Conservative government of hoping that the courts would open the doors to Asian immigrants. The *Sun* also accused Vancouver Indians of preaching sedition and treason. The magazine *Academy* presented the case in more theoretical terms, opposing cultural pluralism: "Human progress and happiness cannot be furthered by implanting aliens with divergent social customs, ethical conceptions, and economic status." Exclusion must replace restriction, the editor argued, for by the laws of the pioneer, the land belonged only to the white Canadian.[29]

White Canadians held their own meeting of twenty-five hundred people; the mayor presided, and members of parliament H. H. Stevens and Ralph Smith argued that white men must have no degrading competition. Said Smith: "Canada has no responsibility with regard to the management of business in India—that is entirely an Imperial Question." To him, empire meant self-government for men from Europe. Asians must be kept out. The crowd responded with shouts of "Hear, hear," then passed a resolution asking that the Indians on the *Komagata Maru* be deported and that legislation explicitly excluding Indians be passed. Feelings ran so high at the meeting, the United States immigration inspector in Vancouver reported to his chief, that it would have taken very little to start another riot.[30]

The Canadian department of labor, meanwhile, had asked Hopkinson to report on the crisis. Immigration officials allowed Hopkinson's Indian informants to board the ship to discuss conditions with the men on board; other Indians were carefully kept away from the ship. Disguised as a Sikh, Hopkinson attended meetings at the temple, then warned that the men were becoming bolder and talking openly against the British government. He advised emulating the South African government and removing or expelling all the agitators. The Indian community now suspected an extensive spy network, and one Indian was said to have advised assassination, the punishment meted out to police informers in Bengal. Plainclothesmen began guarding Hopkinson.[31]

At an impasse, with the Vancouver populace daily growing more hostile, the Indians finally agreed to the immigration officials' procedure. The board of inquiry proceedings were waived, the case was speedily brought before a supreme court justice sympathetic to exclusion who refused a writ of habeas corpus, and the case went to the court of appeals as arranged. On 6 July, a unanimous court decided that it had no jurisdiction to intervene. The refusal of the writ stood, and the Indians could now be legally deported.[32]

Three days later, Hopkinson went on board with immigration officials and the Indians' attorney to negotiate the deportation of the men. The angry men threatened to hold immigration official Robie Reid hostage if they did not receive food. Hopkinson advised Reid to give the men a small quantity of food and water—enough to last twenty-four to thirty-six hours—and then to order the ship out of the harbor. It would have taken little to incite a general outbreak among the passengers, Hopkinson reported to Ottawa, to overpower the crew, and to attempt a landing.

Food was loaded on board that evening and final arrangements made for the deportation. On 18 July, Canadian officials ordered the captain of the *Komagata Maru* to leave the harbor. The passengers mutinied, refusing to allow the crew to get under way. Officials felt they could wait no longer. Making plans to transfer the Indians forcibly to the British steamer *Empress of India* and return them to Hong Kong, officials approached the *Komagata Maru* with city police in a tug named the *Sea Lion*. The militia, meanwhile, stood guard over food on the wharf that was to be loaded onto the *Empress of India* after the men had been transferred on board. The *Sea Lion* would then escort the ship out of the harbor.[33]

The Indians on board had other plans. They armed themselves with bamboo poles, stoking irons, axes, swords, wooden clogs, and a few firearms. They gathered coal, stacks of bricks, and piles of concrete and scrap on the deck. As the *Sea Lion* came alongside the *Komagata Maru* and police attempted to board, Indians cut the grappling ropes. Police then turned a water hose on them. The Indians, in return, began to hurl lumps of coal and bricks. Since the deck of the *Sea Lion* was fifteen feet below that of the *Komagata Maru*, the police had difficulty getting out of range. Several were bruised and cut, one was knocked down, and another was knocked overboard; according to Hopkinson who was on board, three shots came from the ship, one passing between him and Reid as they stood on the bridge. After fifteen minutes of battle, the tug retreated with its injured to the wharf. For three days, the battle-scarred *Sea Lion* and armed picket boats patrolled the ship while city officials tried to decide what to do. Finally they appealed to Ottawa. H. H. Stevens requested that a naval cruiser be dispatched to Vancouver.[34]

When the *Komagata Maru* had arrived in Vancouver in May, the entire Canadian navy had consisted of two cruisers that had been purchased from the royal navy in 1910. One, the *Niobe*, was stationed in Halifax. The other, the 3600-ton *Rainbow*, was out of commission at Esquimalt, near Victoria. As soon as the Indians had arrived, Stevens had talked to Borden about refitting and manning the *Rainbow* in case it should be needed to repulse the Indians by force. By 11 July, the *Rainbow* had hurriedly been refitted and a hundred men ordered on board. On the evening of 20 July it steamed out of Esquimalt toward Vancouver. It anchored near the *Komagata Maru* the next morning. Immigration officials announced to reporters that it had been authorized to secure control of the ship.[35]

The morning the *Rainbow* anchored in the harbor near the *Komagata Maru*, the minister of agriculture, Martin Burrell, arrived from Ottawa to make one more attempt at a peaceful solution. Burrell offered to ask the premier to appoint a commissioner to investigate the claims of the temple committee, whose members said they had invested seven thousand dollars and had taken over the charter, and therefore had a right to land the cargo and make arrangements for a return cargo to defray the cost. If the passengers would give control of the ship back to the captain and peaceably return to Hong Kong, Burrell would urge that "full and sympathetic consideration be given to those who deserve generous treatment." The situation was "acutely critical," Burrell wired the premier. All day the negotiations continued. Finally, at 5 P.M., the Indians agreed to accept the terms. The government would provision the ship, and the Indians would return to Hong Kong.

Tensions were still high as fifteen men from the Sikh temple committee arrived on the wharf to inspect the provisions. They were forced to pass between troops with bayonets to inspect the provisions: curry powder, flour, cayenne pepper, ginger, tea, pickles, hair oil, tobacco, toilet paper, and other stores. The provisions were loaded, and at 5 A.M. on 23 July 1914, exactly two months after its arrival in Vancouver, the *Komagata Maru* weighed anchor. Thousands of Canadians crowded the shore and housetops, and troops still lined the wharves as the *Rainbow* fell in behind to escort the Indian ship out to sea. Meant to be a symbol of unity for the Empire, the new Canadian navy was thus first used to prevent the landing of British subjects in the Empire. "What if it had been a real invasion?" asked an editor in the Vancouver *Saturday Sunset* two days later. Canada must have coast defenses, the writer demanded. Residents of British Columbia insisted that guns be installed on the *Rainbow* to protect them from further danger of invasion.[36]

While the *Komagata Maru* was in the Vancouver harbor and negotiations went on openly, undercover work was also occurring. Hopkinson warned Borden that the resistance by the Indians aboard the *Komagata Maru* was the result of a conspiracy headed by educated Indians living in the United States. Borden then wrote to Grey that he was "more and more convinced that the attempt to have these Hindus enter Canada is but one incident of a deliberate plot to foment sedition." After the *Komagata Maru* left Vancouver harbor, Hopkinson reiterated his claims of conspiracy. He suggested that an investigation be made in the United States and Canada, and newspapers soon announced that revolutionists had been on board. The India office was so alarmed by the reports that it wired Grey on 29 July to ask: "Do your Ministers attach any importance to press reports that some passengers intend to initiate in India agitation against the Government?" Grey replied that the trip was believed to have been financed by political agitators who would use the refusal of admittance as a ground for agitation against British rule in India. Early in August 1914, a printed circular titled "Open Letter to the British Public by the Hindustanees of North America" and signed by nine prominent Indians was circulated in Portland and Seattle. It hinted that England might regret deportation, for the men on the *Komagata Maru* would induce their Sikh relatives serving in the British army at Hong Kong to desert. The British government ordered the men to be arrested if they landed at Hong Kong.

There is no evidence that the men had planned the trip as a political challenge to British India. The voyage had been organized primarily to test Canadian laws and perhaps to begin a profitable enterprise—not to challenge the British in India. But the two months of waiting, the treatment by Canadian officials, the presence of undercover spies and legal manipulation, combined with the fact that a few of the passengers were in touch with nationalists, left the men in a hostile mood. They had already endured much. Many of them were Sikh veterans who were reaching the limit of their peaceful challenge.[37]

Other events conspired to make the men's return to India less than peaceful. When they reached Yokohama, they heard that Germany had invaded Belgium and that England had declared war on Germany, as well as that they would be arrested as vagrants if they landed at Hong Kong. Gurdit Singh appealed to the British consul at Yokohama to provision the ship so that it could return to India; the consul refused. The ship steamed on to Kobe, where Gurdit Singh appealed to the British consul, this time threatening demonstrations if the provisions were not supplied. The British furnished funds for the rest of the trip, with the proviso that the ship not discharge passengers at Singapore but sail directly from Kobe to India. On 27 September, six months after leaving for Canada, the ship arrived at the mouth of the Hooghly River and moored at Budge Budge, about ten miles from Calcutta.[38]

The British had made special provision for the arrival of the men because they wanted to return them directly to the Punjab before they could spread their discontent to other Sikhs. Before boarding the special train that was to transport the men to the Punjab, however, the British gave the Sikhs permission to make a religious procession to the Hooghly. With the Sikh flag flying, the men marched out peaceably, escorted by police. When they asked to proceed to Calcutta, British troops barred the way, and the men turned back. The government promised to have a representative meet with the men at the railway station. On the way back, however, many Sikhs started to go into byways for drinks of water. Fearing the loss of their charges, the police apparently started hustling stragglers. When angry Sikhs protested, police called out Gurdit Singh to discuss the situation, and his followers, assuming that he was being arrested, became belligerent. The police and the Sikhs exchanged shots and when the smoke cleared, an estimated twenty-six people were dead, mostly Sikhs but also two Europeans and two Indian policemen. Gurdit Singh and twenty-nine passengers had disappeared. Almost all of the remaining Sikh passengers were arrested and imprisoned under the new wartime Ingress of India Ordinance, passed on 5 September to allow suspected subversives to be summarily arrested and held without trial. The Bengal government claimed that the Sikhs had opened fire with revolvers and that the troops had been compelled to fire to check the rush of the rioters. The majority of the men arrested were held until January 1915, when thirty-one were released.

Gurdit Singh wandered as a fugitive until 1921, when, on Gandhi's advice, he finally surrendered to the government. Always maintaining that he had no intention of revolt, Gurdit Singh denied having arms, making seditious speeches, or working with the revolutionary party in Vancouver or in Germany. Historians have tended to agree that there was no evidence of his complicity with revolutionists, even though some of the passengers on the ship had copies of revolutionary newspapers. To later Indian historians, Gurdit Singh was a "benefactor of his community." Jawaharlal Nehru wrote, "The whole *Komagata Maru* incident was resented all over India." It was also resented by Indians in North America. Using force to remove the *Komagata Maru* from Canada so embittered the Sikh workers that they needed little encouragement to mobilize against the British. They took action against the British in both Canada and the United States.[39]

Actually, the sailing of the *Komagata Maru* was both the last peacetime resistance to exclusion and the first wartime resistance to British rule in India. It also marked the beginning of the final drive in the United States for legislative exclusion of Indians.

7

The Wrong Side of A Red Line: Legislative Exclusion

Why is there no respect for us
in the whole world?
—Ghadar protest song

The question of congressional exclusion increasingly divided the American public after 1900. Before the 1880s, Congress had seldom discussed exclusion, and Chinese exclusion did not provoke much debate despite its significance as the first exception to a generally open immigration policy. Employers continued to want migrant workers, and Euro-American workers who complained of job competition could safely be ignored. Executive restriction of Japanese, Korean, and Indian workers by 1910 signaled the increased political power of workers on the West Coast to obtain a selective regional response from presidents, but Congress was anxious to avoid dealing with such potentially explosive legislation. The problem was how and where to draw the line, if such a line needed to be drawn. Open immigration had the support of business interests as well as European immigrants.

Exclusionists existed in many parts of the country, but they formed no political block before 1917. East Coast exclusionists, who were most concerned about southern Europeans, saw no unity of interest with West Coast exclusionists, who worried about Asians. The Japanese government actively opposed congressional exclusion of their nationals, and although colonialism made the British hostage to a policy of inactivity in protecting Indians, Congress seemed reluctant to legislate at the national level on the basis of ethnicity. Despite the arguments of exclusionists based on economics, race, health, religion, and almost anything else they could find about Indians that might not please Americans in other regions, Congress stood fast. Only the approaching war with Germany and the activities of Indian radicals—in short, political issues—finally prompted a majority in Congress to favor limiting immigration. Even then, exclusion was couched in terms of geography rather than race or politics, an indication of the extent to which Congress was willing to go to avoid overt discrimination. It took another seven years, until 1924, for Congress openly to restrict all Asians and most southern European immigrants.

During Theodore Roosevelt's administration, the issue of further restriction of Asian immigration was raised by exclusionists but deftly put off by the Republicans. Debate began in February 1907 with discussion of legislation requiring immigrants to pass a literacy test. Designed to keep out southern Europeans as well as Asians, such legislation had been the exclusionists' dream for many years. A literacy act had first been passed by Congress in 1897, but it had been vetoed by Grover Cleveland, who had called it "a radical departure from our national policy relating to immigration." Such a provision could not save America from violence and disorder, he lectured Congress; it was "a misleading test of contented industry" and provided "unsatisfactory evidence of desireable citizenship or proper apprehension of the benefits of our institutions." Congress did not overturn Cleveland's veto.

By 1907 congressional opinion was still divided. Some exclusionist congressmen in the East wanted open restriction of immigration from southern Europe, but many southern European immigrants had already been enfranchised and were thus able to hold the balance of power in congressional elections. Other congressmen feared that a reversal of free immigration policy toward the Japanese might lead to increasing restrictions on southern Europeans. A few could not see why the United States should risk antagonizing a strong military power in Asia to satisfy a few workers along the Pacific Coast. Roosevelt thought that white laborers on the coast had a right to be free from competition with Asians, but he had to consider both the political and the diplomatic consequences of discriminatory legislation. When he added his opposition to the literacy bill, congressmen decided to drop the scheme. Congress did agree to raise the head tax from two to four dollars and to add to the classes excluded because of physical or moral reasons—such as prostitutes and anarchists—to prove that it really had done something about immigration. It also established an immigration commission to study immigration and make recommendations, thus putting off any action.[1]

Californians managed to obtain good representation on the immigration commission. Although there were no Californians among the six congressional members, two of the three other members were Californians: Charles P. Neill, the commissioner of labor, and William R. Wheeler, the assistant secretary of commerce and labor. Meanwhile, California congressmen began openly to advocate exclusion of Indians. Senator Frank Flint, who had worked his way up the Republican political ladder in Los Angeles with the help of the Southern Pacific Railroad, first raised the issue of legislation to exclude Indians. "We don't want these Hindus," he told reporters in 1907, "and they should be barred out just as the Chinese are excluded. When Congress meets I expect to take the matter up, and will do my best to protect the Pacific coast from the brown horde. . . . There is plenty of room for good citizens, but there is no room at all for fakirs and mendicants."[2]

These delaying tactics also prodded angry exclusionists to obtain support for segregation of Japanese in San Francisco schools and to introduce anti-Japanese bills into the California state legislature. Roosevelt wrote with some concern to secretary of state Elihu Root early in March 1907 that delay might cause problems; he asked James Norris Gillett, the Republican governor of California, to work against the bills and promised federal action if the city would rescind the segregation order and if the legislature would drop the pending bills. The Japanese agreed once more to withhold passports from laborers, and Congress passed legislation allowing the president to exclude any Japanese laborers who did not have passports, including Japanese attempting to enter from Mexico, Canada, and Hawaii. Roosevelt subsequently used an executive order to exclude these workers, and California legislators agreed in return to drop proposed segregationist legislation.

When the immigration commission finally issued its report in 1910, the Angel Island controversy was in full swing. The commission devoted forty-two volumes to reviewing the facts and concluding that there were differences between the old and new immigration and that new immigrants from southern Europe were definitely inferior to old immigrants from northern Europe. The commission also released its report of a special investigation of Indian immigrants. After an exhaustive study of a sample group of 474 Indians—a number estimated to be 15 percent of the total Indian population in the country—the commission concluded that the men would probably wish to stay in the United States but that they were almost "universally regarded as the least desirable race of immigrants thus far admitted to the United States." The head of the special investigation thought that Indians were unassimilable and that they wanted only to exploit the resources of the United States. The commission recommended congressional exclusion and a temporary gentleman's agreement with the British government to prevent Indian laborers from coming to the United States. The commission's overall recommendation was that a literacy test be used to keep out unwanted immigrants.[3]

The commission's report only angered West Coast exclusionists. Since a literacy test had been suggested before the commission was appointed, exclusionists felt that the commission had been used only to delay action that should have been taken three years earlier. Secretary of commerce and labor Charles Nagel opposed the literacy bill. The real objection to the Indian immigrants, he wrote to Taft in November 1910, was not their illiteracy but their "character and physical condition." Because of Nagel's opposition, a literacy test was not even included in the first immigration bill Senator William P. Dillingham introduced into the Senate. The bill did include a citizenship test, however.[4]

The citizenship test, while narrower than the literacy test, also had severe problems, as exclusionists soon discovered. Congress had already explicitly barred Chinese from citizenship, but the supreme court had not yet defined precisely which other Asians could become citizens, nor would it do so for another fourteen years. The problems were reviewed in a legal opinion drawn up for Nagel in April 1912 by his department. According to this opinion, exclusion on the basis of citizenship would confuse the executive and judicial functions, for executive officers would be given the authority to decide who was eligible for citizenship—and that was a judicial prerogative. One proposed plan had called for United States immigration officials to board ships before they left foreign lands to exclude persons ineligible for citizenship—a plan that amounted to the right of search—and to question, arrest, and deport any unqualified immigrant found in the United States, with no limit on the time of apprehension. The department of labor and commerce rejected this plan for both its domestic and its foreign effects, as a law more drastic than that of any free country, and one likely to cause "international unpleasantness."[5]

Despite the problems with literacy and citizenship tests, a bill with both provisions passed Congress just before Taft left office in 1913. Taft vetoed the bill, sending to Congress a copy of Nagel's arguments against the literacy test. The Senate repassed the bill over Taft's veto, but the bill narrowly failed repassage in the House, following a vigorous debate. The literacy clause continued to be included in various bills and was finally passed again early in 1917, when President Wilson vetoed it again. By this time, however, the literacy test had been paired with a barred zone provision that excluded immigrants from an area roughly equivalent to Asia. This act, finally passed over Wilson's veto in 1917, officially barred Indians from immigration into the United States.[6]

The barred zone act, although it excluded Indians, was actually a compromise between the most rabid exclusionists, who wanted a bill openly excluding all Asians or at least all "Hindus," and the Wilson administration, which was still hoping to avoid an open confrontation with the Japanese over immigration. The controversy with Japan threaded its way through all the debates. Held hostage by exclusionists on the question of Japanese immigration, the executive finally lost the battle on both the literacy test and Indian exclusion.

Probably no two people were more instrumental in achieving the desired exclusion of Indians than John Raker, a progressive Democrat from California, and Anthony W. Caminetti, a second-generation Italian Democrat from California, who became Wilson's commissioner of immigration. Together, these men spearheaded the drive for exclusion that finally culminated in the barred zone provision.

Raker was elected to Congress in 1910 from northern California. Born in Illinois, he was a progressive lawyer and superior court justice who championed women for political office, supported municipal ownership of utilities, and favored Asian exclusion. As soon as Raker took his seat in the House, he introduced a bill excluding all Asians. He also demanded correspondence from Taft regarding Japanese immigration, and when Taft refused, Raker revised his bill to make it more restrictive and reintroduced it. The second bill called for registration, thumbprinting, and photographing of Asian laborers, and deportation of any found without certificates. The idea was reminiscent of the Geary law passed in the 1880s to control Chinese immigrants. Raker's bill applied to Japanese as well as to Indians.[7]

Raker's Asian bills did not get very far in the House, but they did give him something to campaign on during the 1912 election. That campaign was one of the most vicious fought by exclusionists. Woodrow Wilson, the Democratic candidate, was baited relentlessly as soft on Asians because of a statement he had made earlier comparing the "new" southern Europeans unfavorably to Chinese immigrants. Wilson finally approved a statement, written by Democratic senator James Phelan of California, that he opposed Asian immigrants as a "serious industrial menace" and as unassimilable because of race. Exclusionists also baited Roosevelt, who had bolted the Republican Party and convinced Hiram Johnson to be his running mate on the Progressive ticket. Roosevelt had earlier favored Japanese naturalization, and although by 1912 he viewed Asian immigrants as a menace, the Democrats were able to cite his earlier view as an indication of pro-Asian sympathy.[8]

Taft, whom exclusionists also attacked, could not, as president, make equally racist comments without causing diplomatic problems with the Japanese and British governments. Furthermore, exclusionists could hold his administration responsible for any increase in Asian immigration. The executive restriction of 1910 had quieted exclusionists temporarily, but they hoped to use the election of 1912 to extort support for an exclusion bill from Taft.

Taft's first inclination was to work through an executive agreement with the British as Roosevelt had with the Japanese. In a December 1911 letter to Taft, Massachusetts senator Henry Cabot Lodge suggested such a move as the best route to avoid further problems with Indian immigration. Taft's commissioner of immigration, Daniel Keefe, also favored such an agreement when Philander Knox sought his opinion on Lodge's suggestion. Keefe warned that most Indians were being excluded under "a rather drastic application of the exclusion laws." An agreement with Britain would thus be welcome. The best solution, he volunteered, was for the British to pass a law requiring Indians to carry passports, as the Japanese had done. It would then be a simple matter to refuse passports to laborers. Keefe recommended such an arrangement. The British, he was sure, would recognize the reasonableness of this request, since Indians were already being excluded from Canada and the United States.[9]

Keefe was also enthusiastic about the tough Raker bill, however. After Raker introduced his bill in May, Keefe recommended to the state department that all Asians be excluded. The department of labor also endorsed the legislation, arguing that an 1815 treaty with Great Britain providing for immigration of British subjects was neither explicit nor inclusive. Furthermore, Australia, Canada, and other colonies of the British Empire had already excluded Indians, an indication that Great Britain would be unwilling to oppose exclusion by the United States. Regardless of the support of immigration officials and representatives from the South and West for a new immigration bill, the House rules committee refused to release any of the bills onto the floor of the House until after the election. In the East, immigration restriction was too hot an issue for politicians to risk any debate before an election. In the West, Democrats wanted to use the Asian peril and supposed Republican inaction as a campaign issue.[10]

In the absence of clear-cut guidance from Washington, Taft's appointees in California could not decide how to handle the new immigration crisis when it came. In July, immigration officials in Manila predicted that six or seven thousand Indians would soon arrive in San Francisco, using their admission to the territory of the Philippines to gain admittance to the United States. Since immigration officials had already admitted a few Indians from the Philippines, the way now seemed open for the thousands of Indians already in the Philippines to enter the United States. San Francisco authorities immediately issued warrants for the arrest of a few Indians who had already arrived; then they canceled the warrants, appealed to the immigration bureau for help, and waited. The bureau's delay made Taft even less popular in California. Taft saw the California Progressives as his main enemies and considered them pseudo-reformers who were practicing a bunco game on Californians, as he once grumbled to a friend. On 3 October the California supreme court held that the electors of Progressives Roosevelt and Johnson could appear on the official ballot but that Taft's electors could not.[11]

The Progressive record on exclusion could not match the promises of hungry Democrats long out of the White House, however. With Indian immigration as a minor theme, politicians fully exploited Californians' fear of Japanese immigration. The working men "responded splendidly" to the Asian issue, Phelan later wrote to Wilson's campaign manager, William F. McCombs. Taft was not on the ballot in California, and write-ins were difficult. He received only 3,914 votes. Eugene V. Debs, the Socialist candidate, received 79,201 votes. Roosevelt won 283,610 votes to Wilson's 283,436. Johnson estimated that he and Roosevelt lost at least ten thousand votes on the Asian issue alone. It was a great triumph for Democratic exclusionists in California, despite the fact that Wilson won only two of the thirteen electoral votes in California. Nationally, he won the election, giving Democratic exclusionists from California renewed enthusiasm for their crusade.[12]

When Taft left the White House in April 1913, executive restriction was still in force, although no legislation legitimized that restriction—either directly by excluding Indians or indirectly by excluding persons not eligible for citizenship—because courts had not decided whether "white" included "brown." Wilson's backers in California had presented him as a Southerner who would understand West Coast racial attitudes. Many voters who left the Republican Party for the Democratic Party expected Wilson to take a strong stand against Asian immigration. The first Southerner in the White House since Reconstruction, Wilson might look differently at racial issues nationwide than had his northern predecessors. His actions depended on more than the views he had expressed as a candidate, however; even Roosevelt's campaign rhetoric had faded before the realities of office. It was possible that Wilson's actions would not confirm exclusionists' expectations.[13]

California exclusionists had already set the stage for Wilson's first test. An alien land act was pending in the California legislature when

Wilson was inaugurated in April 1913. Prior to 1913, aliens in California, whether or not they were eligible for citizenship, had the same rights to personal and real property as citizens. The land law of 1913 radically altered this policy by restricting the right of aliens to hold land to those aliens eligible to become citizens. The main purpose of the act was not to exclude aliens ineligible for citizenship but to exclude Japanese from land ownership in California. As one California lawyer said later, "Of course, the Japanese were not mentioned in the act. Whenever we want to do anything very drastic, we never mention the fellow we are going to hit." A 1911 treaty with Japan stated explicitly that the Japanese must be allowed to acquire land for commercial and residential purposes. The California law turned this provision around, restricting landowning except for these purposes and thus violating the spirit of the treaty. *Commercial* was interpreted to exclude agricultural production. While exclusionists may have had Japanese immigrants in mind, the proposed law would exclude from holding land any immigrant the courts held ineligible for citizenship.[14]

Two days after Wilson's inaugural, the Japanese ambassador protested the pending California law. Wilson wrote to Johnson implying that the legislation violated Japanese treaty rights, warned him of litigation if the law passed, and indirectly suggested that aliens who had filed their first naturalization papers should be allowed to own land. Because the bill had the overwhelming support of the California legislature, however, Johnson did nothing. Wilson then sent the new secretary of state, William Jennings Bryan, to California to ask personally that the legislation not be passed.

Bryan was met in Sacramento by Anthony Caminetti, the man who was to join Raker in working for exclusion of Indians during the next four years. Caminetti was a state senator from Amador County who had campaigned as a native son and had become the first non-Hispanic native-born person elected to the California senate. Caminetti had begun activities aimed at Asian exclusion as early as the 1870s. In 1907, he had challenged the Roosevelt administration by introducing anti-Japanese bills in the California legislature; when Roosevelt criticized Californians for this proposed legislation in a message to Congress, Caminetti had retorted that Roosevelt's message was a "criminal absurdity." In the election of 1908, Caminetti had denounced Republican congressman Everis Anson Hayes for standing by quietly until "the whole matter was worn threadbare before he followed the example of lovers of liberty on the Atlantic seaboard and raised his voice for the people of California."

The Democratic candidate, Bryan, had a sterling record in his fight to help California exclude the Chinese, Caminetti had argued. In 1910, Caminetti had helped Democrats in their unsuccessful attempt to capture the votes of Asian Exclusion League members by delivering a fierce tirade against the Republican administration and attacking representative Julius Kahn for "not daring to raise a voice in Congress in favor of Asiatic exclusion."

By 1912 Caminetti was chairman of the Democratic state executive committee and had campaigned vigorously for Wilson. Defeated in the primaries in a bid for the California senate, he had turned his efforts to tarring Roosevelt and Taft with the brush of pro-Asian sentiment. Caminetti's support for Wilson gained him appointment as commissioner of immigration. Bryan personally requested the appointment, and the entire Democratic congressional delegation supported the choice. At Wilson's request, Caminetti stayed in California to help with the crisis. He voted to postpone action on the California bill until the next legislative session, and he stopped open anti-Asian agitation. He was hardly convincing as an opponent of such legislation, however, and he voted with the majority to pass the bill. After the Japanese lodged a formal protest, Bryan urged the governor to veto the bill, but after only a slight delay Johnson signed it into law on 17 May.[15]

Caminetti came out of the affair without blame. Progressive Democrats lauded him as a student of sociological problems who had devoted much time to special study of immigration. Late in May, Caminetti moved to Washington to take up his post as commissioner of immigration.

One of Caminetti's first moves after taking office was to ask the secretary of labor, William B. Wilson, to request officially that all steamship lines voluntarily stop carrying Indian laborers as passengers. Although the secretary thought the request should be unofficial, he endorsed the idea, and early in June, representatives of the steamship lines met with Caminetti in Tacoma, where they discussed the possibility of halting service for Indian immigrants. The Great Northern and Northern Pacific railways had already indicated to Caminetti that they were willing to agree to his request. When smaller Canadian and Japanese steamship companies heard the representatives of the largest companies volunteer to refuse passengers, they quickly fell in line and offered to discontinue their services to Indians. The shipping lines put the agreement into effect immediately, ordering their agents to refuse to sell tickets to any Indian laborers. Men who put their money down to purchase tickets were simply turned away without explanation. For Caminetti, this solution seemed to ensure that the policy of executive restriction worked out during the Taft administration would not be challenged. Private companies could do the work of immigration officials. Men already on the way would be locked up as soon as they arrived.[16]

Caminetti also revised the rules applying to immigration from the Philippines. In the past, the government had not required a second examination of Indians when they reached the mainland, but on 16 June, with the approval of William Wilson, Caminetti amended this rule to allow aliens bound for the continent to be inspected a second time. Indians were now permitted to land only if they were not members of excluded classes or likely to become public charges. The war department was to enforce the new restrictions for the labor department through its officials in the Philippines. The only remaining problem for Caminetti was how to deal with the several hundred Indians already on their way from the Philippines with certificates issued before the change of rules. If the men were turned away, the Great Northern steamship line would have to pay for the return passage of two hundred Indians already on their way to Seattle on the steamer *Minnesota*. When the Indians arrived in Seattle, the immigration inspector detained them, scheduled a hearing, and ordered seventy-seven of the men to be deported on the ground that they were likely to become public charges. A group of thirty-five Indians arrived in San Francisco shortly after the Seattle group. William Wilson also ordered that these men be deported, on the same ground. But the men refused to leave quietly; they contacted countrymen in Canada who were actively fighting exclusion and asked for assistance.[17]

Vancouver Indians hired a representative to go to Seattle to offer the support of the Khalsa Diwan Society to immigrants there. Indians also gathered at the Sikh temple in Victoria to protest the exclusion bills being considered in the United States and the detention of Indians in Seattle and San Francisco. Members pledged thirty-five thousand dollars so that the Seattle immigrants might be released on bond while they appealed their case. Vancouver Sikhs also telegraphed President Wilson, protesting the unfair exclusion bill that would violate British treaty rights. "Protest against our discrimination as unfair inhuman and unjust," said the telegram. "Protect our rights." The protest went to the state department, which simply sent it on to the bureau of immigration and naturalization for a report. Despite Caminetti's precautions, over a hundred Indians being held in Seattle were released because they had certificates qualifying them for admission. R. S. Miller of the division of

Far Eastern affairs wrote J. B. Moore, the counselor of the state department, that there was considerable anxiety over the arrival of the Indians
because they were physically unfit and generally unwelcome and undesirable. Like other officials, however, Miller believed that the new
order would control the flow of Indians from the Philippines in the
future.[18]

In September, a United States federal court heard the appeal of the
Indians detained in Seattle. The Indians argued that they had not been
given a fair trial. The court responded that it had no jurisdiction to see
that the men had had a fair trial, only to guarantee that they had been
given a hearing. The court would not examine or consider the sufficiency
of the evidence upon which the immigration officers acted as long as
the defendants had had counsel and had presented all the facts bearing
on their qualifications to be admitted. According to the judge, the action
of the secretary of labor in ordering their deportation was res judicata,
not open to review. The Seattle Indians, along with those in San Francisco, nevertheless appealed their cases.[19]

From petitions that reached Caminetti in the fall of 1913, it was clear
that exclusionists in California were now escalating their attack on Indians. Influential businessmen promoting the San Francisco Exposition
of 1913 and planning an exposition in San Diego for 1915 actively opposed any legislation against the Japanese, whose trade they wished to
cultivate. From the summer of 1913 until after World War I, agitation
for Japanese exclusion, while still the major focus of exclusionists,
seemed to receive less support from high officials. Strident demands for
the exclusion of Indians continued. Between September and November,
Pacific Coast labor groups flooded Caminetti with resolutions. The Central Labor Council of San Joaquin County declared that Indians were
driving out white men with their competition and had become a menace
to the whole community. That group promised the votes of its three
thousand members in support of Indian exclusion. The Central Labor
Council of Alameda promised the support of its twenty-five thousand
members as well. The Washington state Federation of Labor telegraphed
to protest the claims of employers who hired Indians and to insist that
Indians be excluded because they degraded American labor conditions.
Even the Local Union of Painters, Decorators, and Paperhangers of
America, in Cincinnati, Ohio, petitioned in favor of exclusion.[20]

Caminetti returned to Sacramento for Thanksgiving, announced with
assurance (incorrectly, as it turned out) that the next governor and senator elected in California would be Democrats, and promised to take to

the stump himself the following fall. Whether he expected to campaign for governor or for senator was not clear. He also toured the entire coastline from San Diego to British Columbia, announcing that he would attempt to work out a new system of halting the flood of immigrants that he expected would be smuggled across the border from Canada.

Smuggling in the Puget Sound area was an old problem for the federal government. Countless heavily timbered islands had provided refuge since the 1850s for smugglers intent on avoiding paying tariffs on protected goods. By the 1870s, traffic in opium had developed. When the government excluded Chinese in 1882, smugglers, regarding them as any other excluded commodity, began a lucrative trade of smuggling Chinese immigrants. With considerable public demand for both human and material commodities, smugglers had continued to operate despite expanded attempts of both the bureau of customs and the bureau of immigration. Caminetti conferred with the premier of British Columbia and announced that he would urge appropriations for a fast powerboat on Puget Sound to suppress the smuggling of Chinese, set up a new Canadian office to control immigration, establish a border patrol from the North Cascades to Puget Sound, and settle the Indian problem by taking the matter up with the British foreign office. Back in Washington, D.C., Caminetti told reporters that a secret organization was attempting to smuggle Indians into the country from Manila. In December, he publicly affirmed his commitment to campaign against "Hindu" immigration.[21]

Early in December 1913, Maurice T. Dooling, a federal district judge for northern California, supported Caminetti's decision to exclude Indians from the Philippines. The Indians had argued they had not received a fair trial and that they had a right to enter without further examination at San Francisco. Citing their considerable success as agriculturalists—Indians now held large tracts of land in California—they argued that there was no evidence to support the conclusion that they were likely to become public charges. Caminetti's immigration inspectors maintained that the Indians were obnoxious to many Americans and that this prejudice against them meant that few avenues of employment would be open to them. Dooling upheld Caminetti's new rule requiring a second examination in San Francisco because, he said, there had been some evidence to support the conclusions about prejudice against the Indians and about the lack of demand for their labor. In this sense, he declared, the case was not open for review. Dooling went on to discuss what he called the more basic question, "stripped of all its masks."

Could the department of commerce and labor, in a hearing not open to review, argue that a prejudice existed in the country against aliens of a certain race and that there was no demand for their labor, and then exclude all laborers of that race on the ground that they were thus likely to become public charges?

The United States supreme court had already held that with any testimony at all to support the department, an immigration case could not be reviewed. Dooling was perturbed by the logical implication of this decision, however; if the court conceded to the department of labor the power to exclude Indian laborers for this reason, then it must also concede the power to exclude laborers of any other race. "It is a vast power, and one which, upon the argument of this case, I was very unwilling to believe was lodged in any executive department of the government." With this precedent, the government could exclude persons whom it considered likely to become public charges not because of their physical or mental condition but because of prejudices existing in the country. An alien, whether weak or strong, was helpless if he could not obtain work, according to this reasoning. Even the courts thus accepted the fact that the real basis for the de facto exclusion of Indians was the existence of prejudice against them that would hinder them from obtaining jobs—and yet the basis of the prejudice seemed to be that Indians were actually being employed.[22]

In spite of the fact that Dooling supported his rulings, Caminetti was perturbed. There was no way to keep Indians out of the United States if the courts in a particular area refused to uphold the bureau's interpretation of the law. If California judges questioned the procedures of the bureau of immigration, judges not on the Pacific Coast might be even more critical. Between 1912 and 1914, 60 percent of the Indians admitted to the United States arrived in New York, and Caminetti heard that large numbers in Cuba and Panama were ready to attempt to enter through southern ports. Officially, only 353 Indians entered in 1912 and 1913 and 377 left; an additional 52 had been deported. But by December 1913, Indians in Cuba had already sent a representative to Jacksonville, Florida, to inquire about regulations concerning their entry. Caminetti felt that his position of depending on a policy without full legal authority was "cumbersome, tedious, uncertain, and expensive" to the government. He and the immigration officials wanted definite legislative exclusion.[23]

Raker, meanwhile, had introduced another bill in Congress to exclude all new Asian immigrants and to force registration of those already in the United States. There was not much chance of support for such a measure, but it put California representatives on record as to their sympathies and provided a rearguard action for the exclusionists in Sacramento. With no Democratic senators from California and few other Democratic representatives, Raker found that he had a great deal of federal patronage to dispense. His chances of being appointed to an important committee were enhanced, and he soon found himself on the committee on naturalization and immigration. On 1 May he sent a letter to William Wilson, asking for a report to the speaker of the House on his bill. Wilson replied that Raker's bill to exclude all Asian laborers was in general desirable, and even endorsed registration of all Asians in the United States. Wilson's only objection was that Raker had defined Asia in a vague way that seemed to include Turkey, Persia, and parts of Russia. Wilson wondered whether this was, in fact, the intent of the bill. Raker was not the only congressman to introduce anti-Indian legislation during 1913. Denver S. Church, a Republican from California, suggested a bill based solely on geography rather than on race. It defined Asia carefully and provided that treaty arrangements with Japan on immigration would not be affected.[24]

In the debate on immigration that followed the introduction of these bills, congressmen presented the wide spectrum of views that existed in the country. One representative from Illinois, a Czech immigrant, opposed all immigration restriction and labeled the bill "un-American and unjustifiable." A representative from California defended the bill, saying "Asiatic coolieism is a direct menace. . . . It strikes at the very source of the strength and integrity of American civilization." A congressman from the state of Washington added, "It is only by the practice of eternal vigilance on the part of all people on the Pacific Coast States, regardless of politics, that the Oriental influx has been kept down at all." Hayes, the veteran exclusionist, shouted, "United States for Caucasians."[25]

Despite the racial chauvinism displayed by the House—there had been applause in response to Hayes's shout—1913 passed without congressional action. When Caminetti warned that the old arrangement would no longer hold back the Indians, however, the House immigration and naturalization committee scheduled emergency hearings in December to review the question of Indian immigration.

At the December 1913 hearings, Raker spoke in favor of his own bill to exclude Asians and to force registration. He argued that vital statistics for San Francisco and Sacramento showed that as many Asian children as American children had been born during 1913 and that the agreement of 1911 had not kept the Japanese out. In summing up his argument, Raker introduced an article quoting Herbert Spencer on the dangers of intermarriage of the races. Asians should be excluded to prevent Americans from becoming a "subjective race" or a "bad hybrid."[26]

When the House committee met again a week later, Raker reported that Indians were scattered all over California. "We saw them build the Western Pacific, working for hundreds of miles with their red turbans around their heads when that work should have been done by American citizens." Sacramento was full of Indians, and one could smell their "stench" there. Raker argued that laborers everywhere, and even President Wilson, favored his legislation. To support his argument, he placed in the record an article by the health director at Wilmington, North Carolina, entitled "The Health Menace of Asian Races," which falsely asserted that blacks had brought malaria and hookworm to the South, thus creating the poor physical condition of the southern white, and argued that different races could not live together without great damage to both. "The Chinese, Japanese, and East Indians are racially alien to us," the article continued; "the question of the protection of the white race makes a study of the diseases of these people of more importance to us then even their economic or social characteristics." Apparently the decline of all civilization was caused by alien diseases.[27]

After the hearings, Denver Church was optimistic that some sort of Indian exclusion would be established by the second session of the sixty-third Congress. "I believe my Hindu bill would pass the Committee provided we can get a good, strong report on it from your Department," he wrote to Caminetti. Caminetti went to William Wilson for support.

Wilson sent the necessary support to the speaker of the House. His letter presents the most elaborate argument by an official for the exclusion of Indians. He favored the Raker bill because it would "dispose of the entire matter of Asiatic immigration in one measure," but while Congress was still considering a general immigration bill, he thought that Church's bill could serve as an emergency interim measure. Indian immigration was now an "urgent and imperative" problem, he argued, for Indians were really "coolies" like the Chinese, who had been excluded. Those who were not physically defective had been excluded on the ground that they were likely to become public charges because of "clannishness, caste ideas, superstitions, and habits of life, as well as economic conditions." Because immigration was not systematized and financed, however, the old makeshift holdings were not efficient.

Wilson believed that a concerted movement existed among leaders in India and elsewhere to gain Indians admission to the United States. Steamship companies had helped keep them out, but, Wilson asked, "Can we, and should we, expect these companies to continue to refuse business when offered them if the proposed laws were not enacted or if long delay is permitted?" Referring to the rulings of Canada and of other British colonies, he asked, "Can we, who are not connected by governmental ties or obligations with the Hindus, afford to do less for our people and country than those who are bound by a common citizenship under the Imperial Government?" Unless checked by legislation, Indians would come not only to California and the West but also to the southern states and to other sections of the United States; lack of legislation would be a tacit invitation to potential immigrants.[28]

Wilson liked Church's suggestion that the Asian laborer be defined by geography rather than by race. Wilson thought that the exclusion of natives of any country, district, or island east of an imaginary line drawn across the map of Europe from the Red Sea, through the Mediterranean Sea, Aegean Sea, the Black Sea, the Caucasus Mountains, the Caspian Sea, the Ural River, and into the Ural Mountains—with the exception of Turkey—would be an appropriate policy. Geographers had once considered a roughly similar line as the boundary between Asia and Europe, and Wilson now resurrected it to act as a wall against Asian immigration. Those aliens regulated by existing agreements as to passports—in other words the Japanese—would be excluded from the bill. Since Chinese were already excluded by legislation, Indians were the main group to be affected.

Indians became the focus of exclusionist attention at this time because of the nation's diplomatic situation. British officials raised no objection to anti-Indian agitation as had the Japanese. Woodrow Wilson and William Jennings Bryan therefore cautioned Congress against anti-Japanese legislation but remained silent about the Indian question. President Wilson asked the Senate immigration committee not to release any legislation on Japanese immigration onto the floor of Congress; Bryan made the same request of the House. Congressmen told reporters that there was no necessity for Japanese legislation and that the Indian problem was a great deal more serious. The House committee scheduled hearings on Indian immigration for mid-February.[29]

Caminetti prepared carefully for the hearings. He wired the United States commissioner of immigration in Montreal, John H. Clark, to request information on Canadian exclusion, had tables compiled showing arrivals, exclusions, deportations, and departures of Indians, and had extra immigration bureau circulars on hookworm printed to show committee members. At 10:40 A.M. on Friday, 13 February, he walked confidently into the hearing room. The San Francisco *Examiner* predicted that Indian exclusion would be approved as a salve to California for the committee's having shelved a Japanese exclusion amendment.[30]

Caminetti found many friendly faces in the hearing room. Raker appeared promptly, as did committee member Everis A. Hayes, the Wisconsin-born California representative who had battled long within the Republican ranks for Asian exclusion. Church was there to testify, and so was Albert Johnson, an Ohio-born Republican from Washington who reflected the most extreme exclusionist sentiment of the Northwest. Joseph Moore of Pennsylvania was ready to support the Democrats. Friendliest of all was John L. Burnett, the committee chairman, an old Alabama segregationist.

Several days of testimony followed, much of it by Indians who asserted their desire to work peaceably in the United States. Even the dire warnings by Caminetti and Raker could not bulldoze the committee into recommending the bill, however. One congressman finally suggested that some sort of a gentleman's agreement with India might solve the problem. Caminetti then answered impatiently: "I have come from the Pacific Coast, where we have had two race problems which we have had to fight, and a third one about to be thrown upon us out there, and I have known practically and personally the patience of our people in waiting for diplomatic negotiations upon the Chinese immigration question. . . . The people of California waited very patiently for diplomatic arrangements upon the Japanese immigration problem when that was under consideration, and I do not think they are anxious now for diplomatic arrangements upon the Hindu problem." Caminetti preferred legislation because only legislation could stop what he termed the "menace" descending upon the people of the Pacific Coast. Climatic conditions in California were similar to those in the South, and the Indian problem would soon be a southern problem as well, he warned southern congressmen.[31]

To buttress his argument, Caminetti exaggerated the size of the Indian community to an unbelievable number. Although the bureau of immigration officially estimated that 6,656 Indians had entered from 1907 to 1913 and that 811 had left during the same period, Caminetti used the total immigration number as his base figure. Although the labor department had told Indians who testified at the hearings that it had a record of only 4,794 Indians in the entire country, Caminetti now argued that even the 6,656 figure was too low and that thousands had entered illegally. He claimed that over six thousand were in the San Joaquin Valley alone and estimated that between twenty and thirty thousand were in California, Oregon, and Washington. Through slow and stealthy entrance, he claimed, Indians had become a menace to the whole country. "Shall we allow this experience we have had on the Pacific Coast to be repeated with the Hindu before we take action, or shall we profit by the experience of the past and meet the question now?" he asked.

According to the San Francisco *Examiner*, Caminetti had "ripped into shreds the carefully arranged policy of President Wilson and Secretary of State Bryan" by approving in principle of exclusion of all Asian laborers, even the Japanese. Despite the understanding that Asian exclusion would not be agitated in Congress pending diplomatic negotiations with Japan, Caminetti "shook off the administration muzzle and spoke his mind." Whatever the real reason for Caminetti's action, some Californians were obviously delighted.[32]

Did Caminetti disobey the command of President Wilson and openly support total exclusion? At the time, the *Examiner* speculated that Caminetti was openly defying the administration so that he would be removed from office and thus would be free to run for govenor as a "martyr" to state sentiment on the Japanese question. The author of the article wondered whether Caminetti had had the approval of Bryan in his opposition to state department policy, or whether he was "simply running amuck on his own hook, blissfully oblivious of the State Department and the President." Newspapers quoted President Wilson as saying that he did not know Caminetti was going to testify in this manner before the committee and that the cabinet had discussed his insubordination. Some reporters speculated that the whole episode was prearranged: Bryan was to soothe the Japanese embassy and Caminetti was to soothe the American public. At any rate, the demands for Caminetti's ouster received no support from the president or the secretary of state. Caminetti stayed on.[33]

The committee held one final hearing on "Hindu" immigration. Caminetti made a full report on Canadian exclusion, assuring committee members that the Canadian order-in-council, although framed to exclude all persons not coming to Canada on a continuous voyage from the land of their birth, had in fact been aimed at excluding Indians. He also offered a lengthy review of the cases the bureau had won in Seattle and San Francisco.

Some members still charged that there was politics in the Indian question. Caminetti replied, "So far as I am concerned, I can assure you there is no politics in it, and I have not come up here for the purpose of playing politics." Augustus Gardner, a congressman from Massachusetts and son-in-law of the powerful Henry Cabot Lodge, persisted: "We all know there is an agitation to exclude the Japanese, and as far as I could see in the beginning of the year they tied these things together, but finally separated them, and I wondered why it was. Why did you drop the Japanese end of it if you were anxious to exclude all and begin to agitate only the Hindu's exclusion?" Caminetti replied that he had not dropped the Japanese question but that the Indian situation was an emergency. Gardner snapped back that when fewer than a thousand Indians had entered each year, on average, during the past fifteen years and when only 154 had entered during the first six months of 1913, he did not see the emergency: "You are up here to defend a bill which looks to me like politics. It does not look to me as if there was anything in the Hindu matter except the excuse to show folks out in California that people are hustling around for California, because this 154 Hindu immigration appears to me like a mere drop in the bucket, and as if you said you would exclude every fellow who had zebra-colored eyes." Raker rushed to Caminetti's defense, pleading that it was not politics and warning that "there must be at least 150,000 Hindus in California." The link with reality, even given exaggeration, had now been completely severed. Raker and Caminetti were willing to say almost anything to defend their anti-Indian position. The chairman adjourned the hearings.[34]

Caminetti and Raker did not get a bill out of committee that session. Caminetti continued to be alarmed by reports that Indians in the Philippines were protesting their exclusion despite the fact that no legislation had been passed. Copies of their protests were sent to the state department, to President Wilson, to the new British ambassador, Sir Cecil Spring-Rice, and to colonial officials in London.[35]

The British government did not offer testimony at any of the committee meetings, nor did it make any official representation regarding immigration, as the Japanese continued to do. Indians had appealed to British officials for help, but Spring-Rice had refused his support. He wrote to Duke Arthur Connaught, who had succeeded Grey as governor general, that the United States had a right to exclude anyone it wished and that he did not think "foreign official interference" would be favorably received.[36]

Instead of support for Indians, the British offered unofficial support for exclusionists through their secret agent, W. C. Hopkinson, whose role is discussed in greater detail in the next chapter. Hopkinson arrived in Washington to talk to Spring-Rice in April 1914; from the British embassy he went to see Caminetti to offer to exchange information on Indian nationalists. Caminetti told Hopkinson that, except in special cases, he could not secure information other than that contained in ship's records filled out by immigrants, but he agreed to issue special instructions in the case of Indians "till such time as a serious objection was lodged against this procedure." Hopkinson, in turn, agreed to forward information on naturalization investigations in Canada to Caminetti. Caminetti later wrote that Hopkinson was furnishing him information on Canadian law enforcement in return for information on Indian aliens landing at New York, a reciprocal arrangement that "must not become public." Caminetti asked his subordinates to obtain the following information from Indian immigrants: their father's name, their religion, their address in India, and the address of their nearest relative in India; Caminetti planned to send this information to the British. Before he left Washington, D.C., Hopkinson saw to it that Raker was supplied with a large bundle of documents on the activities of Indians in California to take to the next immigration committee hearings.[37]

While this undercover arrangement benefited the British, it did not immediately help Raker or Caminetti. As for revolutionary activities, Hopkinson reported to London, "I am afraid the whole matter will be considered as of a Political nature and we may look for very little, if not any, assistance from the Government of the United States to eradicate this evil. Our best course seems to be to continue as we have in the past and if the situation becomes serious we can try and meet it by the watchfulness of our secret agents connected with the Consulates in centres of Hindu population in the United States." Congressmen paid little attention to Raker when he raised the political issue at the next hearings on Indian immigration, for they were still not convinced that Indians were a menace to either the economic or the political health of the nation. No legislation had passed in Congress by the time the *Komagata Maru* entered the Vancouver harbor in April 1914.[38]

News of the Sikhs' arrival in Vancouver reached Caminetti almost immediately. Clark wrote to Caminetti from Montreal that a movement was afoot in British Columbia to have all Indians discharged from mills and factories and replaced with white workers. Clark believed that the Indians would then attempt surreptitious entry into the United States.

A similar movement was being planned against the Chinese and Japanese, which meant that they too would be forced to look for work in the United States. On 12 June Caminetti wrote to William Wilson, warning that if Canadian immigration walls broke down, the United States was in for trouble, and even if they did not break down, Indians would still try to get into the United States. They might charter boats, and the government could not expect steamship lines to continue their policy of refusing Asian passengers. "Both in my official capacity and as a citizen of California, I am deeply concerned," wrote Caminetti. President Wilson should be consulted, Burnett should be contacted again, and Congress must pass legislation at the current session, Caminetti insisted. Wilson replied calmly, "I do not think the problem is yet in the shape where it ought to be taken up with the President."[39]

There was no immigration legislation in 1914. President Wilson maintained that the United States was a political asylum and managed to keep Democratic exclusionists in line. In November 1915, however, the supreme court endangered executive exclusion policies by deciding that a band of Russians could not be kept out of the country simply because there was not enough work for them in Portland, their immediate destination. To exclusionists, this ruling seemed to be the prelude to a reversal of the 1913 court decisions that had kept Indians out on the grounds that they were likely to become public charges. "Verdict of United States will admit undesirable aliens into state unhindered," the San Francisco *Chronicle* shrilled.[40]

As American public opinion became more fragmented over the issues surrounding the European war, sentiment for exclusion gradually shifted as well. The exclusionists found the tide running with them. As usual, an election year brought exclusion bills to the floor of Congress but no passage. After the election of 1916, attitudes toward immigrants grew more hostile. The Indians, as the least powerful national group, were the first to be excluded.

When Congress reassembled in December 1916, Caminetti went before the immigration committee again to ask for an amendment to the Chinese laws and the Japanese agreements and to urge passage of the zone law that would keep out all other Asians. According to the now-perfected zone law, inhabitants of most of China, all of India, Burma, Siam, and the Malay states, part of Russia, all of Arabia and Afghanistan, most of the Polynesian Islands, and all of the East Indian Islands would be officially excluded from the United States. Since the Chinese and Japanese were already being excluded under separate laws and agreements, the main Asian country affected was India. Although the bill did not specifically name Indians, as earlier versions had done, it implicitly singled them out as not wanted. Caminetti predicted that a heavy stream of immigration from western Asia would begin after the war and must be headed off.[41]

In the congressional debate that followed, several senators challenged the zone concept presented by the labor department. "There never was anything more farcical attempted in legislation and there never could be anything that would be more offensive to intelligent people in foreign countries than that sort of arbitrary, unreasonable, inconsistent arrangement, to exclude one and to admit the other when there is no difference whatever between them," argued senator Miles Poindexter. "It may be that in the case of members of the same family, born of the same parents, one should be excluded and the other admitted. They would be excluded because they happen to be on the wrong side of a red line that is drawn on the map, a line that includes . . . countries containing white people." Senator James Reed asked: "Why exclude citizens of India, whom you say are of white blood and permit inhabitants of most of Africa to enter?" Senator Thomas Hardwick replied that the words *white person* excluded all Africans but did not exclude a large number of Indians. Reed replied: "The trouble is that instead of drawing this bill by races and excluding men because of character and blood, or even by countries, you exclude them in accordance with parallels of latitude and degrees of longitude. . . . You want to preserve the purity of our race; you want to prevent the influx of great hordes of undesirable people; and starting out with that laudable object—and that laudable object being in the senatorial mind—the Senate absolutely refuses to consider the bad propositions that are loaded into the bill."[42]

On 16 January 1917, Congress finally passed an immigration bill that included both the zone provision excluding Asians and a literacy clause. Thirteen days later, President Wilson returned the bill to Congress with a veto based upon objections to the literacy test, which was, he wrote, a radical change in policy that would allow the secretary of labor to decide who should enter. Such latitude might lead to "very delicate and hazardous diplomatic situations." Gone were Wilson's earlier ringing defenses of the immigrant and the right of asylum; his opposition rested on diplomatic necessities and on the argument that the secretary of labor would have too much control over who should enter. On 1 February, the House repassed the bill over Wilson's veto; three days later, the Senate did the same. The following day the bill became law.

At the same time that Congress passed the bill, Wilson's new secretary of state, Robert Lansing, announced that he had asked the help of western senators in dropping anti-alien land laws then pending in their home states. Whether or not the administration let its Senate supporters allow the bill to pass over Wilson's veto in return for defeat of state measures is not certain. It is certain that state bills would have brought repeated protests from Japan, whereas the federal bill would bring no protest from Britain. Perhaps the administration felt that it was better to sacrifice the Indians and placate Japan, so that the nation could concentrate on European diplomatic issues.

Once the bill was enacted, the labor department enforced it to exclude anyone it wished from emigrating from the barred zone. In April 1919 the acting secretary of labor wrote to Lansing that although in "literal terms" the bill would prohibit persons of pure European or Caucasian stock who happened to have been born within the zone described by the bill, it had been the policy of the department to exempt them from the provisions of the statute. Not only were certain persons judged to be "white" admitted illegally, but Indians were kept out illegally when they wished to come from areas outside the barred zone. A descendant of an Indian in the West Indies who wished to go to the United States was refused a steamship ticket on the basis of exclusion of Indians from the United States. Such an interpretation of the law was wrong, secretary of labor William Wilson admitted to Lansing, for Indians from the West Indies were not excludable. Moreover, the law was also used against Indians already in the United States who wished to go to other countries to visit. One Indian who was lawfully domiciled within the United States asked R. P. Bonham, the inspector at Portland, Oregon, if he would be readmitted after traveling abroad, as were Chinese laborers. There was nothing in the regulations concerning the matter, Bonham wrote, but Caminetti referred him to the new immigration bill, saying, "It would not be competent for the Bureau or Department to undertake to add to this list of special exceptions to a direct provision of law, the presumption obtaining in construing such a statute being that Congress having undertaken to prepare the list has included therein all whom it intended to be included. Hindus living here who leave the United States and who cannot show on returning that they are members of one of these exempt classes will necessarily have to be excluded." Caminetti thus applied the act retroactively to Indian immigrants who had already entered legally.[43]

Nine years after Canada first established its exclusion of Indians by an order-in-council, and almost seven years after executive restriction began in the United States, Congress passed the barred zone act. Congress was, in effect, ratifying the existing executive policy. The action signaled a drastic change in the attitude of Congress and of the public. Indian radical activities alone would probably not have turned the tide. When combined with growing pro-English and anti-German sentiment, however, American response to those activities provided enough support to reverse the traditional concept of political asylum. What was once a California argument had become a national one, receiving support among traditional opponents of exclusion on the East Coast. The Californians had won their fight for exclusion.

8

Students and Spies: Surveillance

The government has sent, my friends,
many Indian traitors
—Ghadar protest song

Political surveillance was still a relatively new government technique for controlling dissent when the first wave of Indian immigrants arrived on the West Coast of North America. Except during wartime, and in the Philippines, the United States had conducted almost no internal surveillance of civilians. Likewise, the Canadian government had no peacetime internal security apparatus. Local governments maintained rudimentary detective forces that normally confined their attention to local lawbreakers. Mexican revolutionaries had been the first persons to lead the United States government into domestic surveillance. The concerns of border officials were always complex. Fear of domestic socialism, intertwined with opposition to Mexican revolutionaries, led officials to establish in 1906 the first clumsy internal security network, composed of police, private detectives, and federal and state officials. Historian W. Dirk Raaf estimates that before 1911, at least seven federal agencies were at work cooperating with the Mexican government in maintaining surveillance over the *revoltosos*.[1]

The first colony in which the British engaged in political surveillance was India. That surveillance followed Indians who immigrated to the West Coast and began to organize. From 1908 through the 1930s, the British, either directly through their own agents, through Canadian agents, or through United States officials, kept a close eye on the Indian community. Eventually, this espionage system provoked a series of assassinations.

The Canadian Indians' refusal of the Honduran proposal of 1908 prompted the Canadian government to establish its first surveillance of the immigrant community. In January 1909, the Laurier government employed W. C. Hopkinson to conduct political surveillance within the Indian community. Hopkinson built his career around the desire of the British to know what Indians were doing to oppose their rule in India. Hopkinson's past is a mystery. According to one account, he was born in Yorkshire in 1876 and taken to India as a child; according to another, in Delhi in 1880 to an Indian mother. It seems most likely that he was the son of a British sergeant and instructor of volunteers and that he grew up in northern India. He was tall (six feet, two inches), lean, and a fluent speaker of Hindi. Sometime in his early twenties, he became an inspector of police in Calcutta, and he left for Vancouver sometime in 1906 or 1907. He married an English stenographer, Constance Frye, and fathered two daughters, born in 1908 and 1912. The Hopkinsons lived in a comfortable house in Vancouver, and Hopkinson soon became an immigration official, donning his blue uniform each morning and going about official business. According to some reports, however, he lived a second life. In a poor immigrant suburb of Vancouver, he also had a shack where he lived part time under the alias of Narain Singh, leading the life of a penniless laborer from Lahore, wearing a turban and a fake beard. Hopkinson attended meetings at the local Sikh temples, paid other Indians to tell him about the activities of immigrants he suspected, and for at least six years acted as an undercover agent in the immigrant community.[2]

Hopkinson was first hired by the Canadian interior department to accompany the Indian delegation to Honduras in the fall of 1908. It is not clear just how he came to be chosen. Perhaps Swayne had known him in India, or perhaps his work for immigration officials led to his recommendation. In January 1909, the Canadian government decided to hire him full time to conduct surveillance of Indians. Because he was technically still on the Indian police force, he had to obtain a leave of absence to work full time as a paid undercover agent for the Canadian government.

During the next six years, Hopkinson established an elaborate surveillance system within the immigrant community. Offering his translating services to the United States immigration authorities in Vancouver and Montreal in return for free entry into the United States for himself and for his Indian informants, he was soon watching Indian activities on both sides of the border. He also provided U.S. immigration authorities with information on suspects in Canada in return for information on Indians entering the United States. Copies of his reports went to the Canadian government as well as to the British colonial office in London.[3]

Hopkinson investigated and reported on many Indians between 1909 and 1914, but perhaps the two best known were Taraknath Das and Har Dayal, both of whom attempted to organize Sikh dissent against British rule in India. While other government officials frequently stressed Sikh opposition to British rule in India, Hopkinson believed that nationalist students were the real cause of unrest among the normally loyal Sikhs and was hence absorbed with the activities of the young intellectuals Das and Dayal.

Hopkinson may have been watching Das long before his official job as a Canadian agent began in 1909. It is possible that Hopkinson may have been sent to Canada by British India officials to watch just such student radicals as Das. Born near Calcutta, Das was one of the young Indians allowed by the British to receive a university education in order to qualify for the Indian civil service. Caught up in the politics of the antipartition movement in Bengal, Das never graduated. He left college in 1905 to become what he later called "an itinerant preacher, explaining the economic, educational, and political conditions to the masses of the people." When the Indian government put out a warrant for his arrest, Das fled to Japan. There, he joined other dissident students who hoped to continue their political activities while obtaining industrial training that would be useful in reviving ancient industries in India or developing new ones in their place. A number of Indian students had congregated at the University of Tokyo, and Das joined them, preaching the cause of Indian freedom. The British ambassador, noting students' criticism of British rule in India and their new freedom with the Japanese students, asked that they be deported. Faced with an inhospitable host, Indian students in Tokyo began to look about for a new place to study. "If you want to see the civilized use of machinery, go to America," one Indian student advised a friend. Japanese students told Das that he could also seek political asylum in the United States.[4]

Das was twenty-two when he arrived in Seattle on 16 July 1906, alone and broke. After working for a while as an unskilled laborer, he drifted down to California, where he worked in the celery fields along with other Indians. Then he worked in a hospital and read books in his spare time, until a professor of medicine helped him get work at the chemistry laboratory at the University of California at Berkeley. Das enrolled as a student and tried to file a declaration of intention to become an American citizen; after being turned down, he took a competitive examination for the position of translator with the United States immigration service. His rating won him a job in Vancouver in July 1907.[5]

By the time of the Vancouver riot, Das was already using his hours after work to organize the Indian community. The first public notice of his political activity came a few days after the riot, when he told a reporter from the Vancouver *Daily Province* that he was secretary of the newly formed Hindustani Association. Indians had come to Canada because of high taxes and bad conditions in India, Das said, and they were now living in conditions worse than cattle because owners would not rent to them. In early 1908, as the Canadian government was moving to exclude Indian workers, Das published the first issue of *Free Hindusthan*, in which he urged Indians both in Canada and in India to resist exclusion. If Canada excluded them, he warned, so would the United States. He also warned that Canadian exclusion would affect British rule in India: "The foundation of the British Empire is undermined on the very day when the legislative body unjustly supports measures, owing to which the natives of Hindusthan cannot go freely to other parts of the British Empire."[6]

Vancouver immigration officials had no difficulty in tracing the newspaper to Das. McInnes, then in Vancouver to investigate the riot, reported to Laurier that Das was using the threat of revolt in India as a bluff to make the Canadian government hesitate in establishing an exclusion policy. The Canadian government promptly protested to Washington about Das's attacks on "British prestige." The American immigration official in Vancouver called Das into his office soon after to inform him that he must either cease editing the *Free Hindusthan* or resign. Das refused to do either. On 18 April 1908, the United States government dismissed him. Das continued to organize.[7]

When Das continued to publish his newspaper, Hopkinson advised the Canadian government to put him under surveillance. Money was being raised by Indians in both Canada and the United States and being sent to India along with instructions in making bombs, Hopkinson warned, and copies of the *Free Hindusthan* and Das's mail should be intercepted. Canadian officials refused to allow the next edition of the *Free Hindusthan* to be mailed, seized one consignment of the paper, and forced Das to cease publication in Vancouver. Das then moved to nearby Millside, where he opened a school, lectured on unrest in India and on unfair treatment of Hindus in Vancouver, circulated newspapers in Gurmukhi (a language of the Punjab) and Bengali, and resumed publication of the *Free Hindusthan*, which he translated into Gurmukhi and sent to the Punjab. Canadian agents followed him to Millside, forwarding information on his activities to the postmaster general, who became convinced that Das's publications were "seditious and disloyal." The justice department maintained that only objectionable issues could be barred from the mails and that the newspaper could not be suppressed legally, but officials were now thoroughly convinced that Canada was being used as a base for agitation against the British government in India. Since legal action could not be taken, Hopkinson arranged for unfavorable publicity in the white community, which forced Das to close his school. Sometime in the spring of 1908, Das fled south to Seattle and started his paper again.[8]

Agents followed Das and found out that Seattle Socialists were printing the *Free Hindusthan* on the presses of their newspaper, the *Western Clarion*. Hopkinson notified the British consul in Seattle, who promised to do something about this "decidedly seditious" paper. Just what the consul did is uncertain, but Das left Seattle soon after. In July 1908, he ceased publishing and moved to Northfield, Vermont, the location of Norwich University, a respected military academy. He entered the university's summer school in engineering and in September enrolled in the regular military program. Hopkinson was convinced that Das was studying military engineering so that he could engineer bombs; soon after Das arrived, the British military attaché, lieutenant colonel B. R. James, mentioned Hopkinson's concern to American brigadier general W. W. Wotherspoon, then in charge of counterintelligence. Wotherspoon ordered an investigation.[9]

The investigation proved that Das was indeed enrolled as a cadet at Norwich. Moreover, as part of his training, he was to participate in the Vermont National Guard. Having received word that the British were concerned about Das, however, the senior army instructor kept him out of the guard, although he interfered in no other way during Das's first year. Das might have been allowed to finish his course of study had he not been such a successful speaker and had he not encouraged ten more Indians to apply for admission in the spring of 1909. Das was very popular; the New England cadets seemed to harbor no racial prejudice against him, and he spoke often in the community on his favorite topic, a free Hindustan. The prospect of more Indian cadets at Norwich so unnerved the British India government that it asked Morley to have Bryce oppose the "gang of Hindu agitators" receiving military training. Meanwhile, the university expelled Das for his speeches denouncing British rule in India. The elated James wrote smugly to the India office that he felt the United States authorities "will always be in sympathy with us in matters of this kind, as they have an idea that the education which they are now giving to the Filipinos may tend to breed the same class of agitator there."[10]

But stopping military training did not alleviate Hopkinson's concern about Das. British officials were already attempting to keep students like Das out of the United States by suggesting that Indians get their education in England. An A.B. from Oxford was preferable to a Ph.D.

from Harvard, officials told young students. Officials also discouraged students from obtaining agricultural or industrial training in the United States. Instead, they encouraged Indians to obtain an English education and join the professions as doctors, lawyers, or lower government officials. Such occupations, officials felt, would direct the interest of young intellectuals from political to professional concerns.

Despite the growing numbers of Indian students in England, surveillance of their activities was sporadic until 1 July 1909, when an Indian student in London assassinated Curzon Wyllie, Morley's political aide-de-camp. Following the assassination, British officials considered even moderate Indian groups dangerous. The government ordered India House closed and assigned Scotland Yard to keep all Indian students under constant surveillance. As a result of the assassination, Hopkinson also increased his surveillance of Indian students in North America. From Seattle, he forwarded lists of students to London.[11]

Hopkinson again turned his attention to Das. Das did not go to Harvard, as some had advised him, but moved to New York, where he contacted Indian students in the Pan-Aryan Association and met George Freeman, editor of the *Gaelic American*. Freeman helped Das to resume publication of the *Free Hindusthan* once more. Before long, the newspaper was circulating in Calcutta. In August 1909 Das returned to Vancouver, where he spoke at the new Sikh temple, urging Indians to bring their wives and children to Canada. Hopkinson sent alarmed reports to Ottawa, for Das had solicited money to help gain Indian independence, talked about the Free Hindustan publicity committee in New York, and circulated postcards picturing famine victims with the caption; "Famine in India as effect of British rule." Hopkinson's alarms were immediately transmitted to the Indian government, and early in October 1909, Indian authorities requested fingerprints and specific information on all societies "cloaking seditious operations" and asked that "seditious" Indians in America be "supervised." The Indian civil service sent a special agent to Canada to inquire about "agitators."[12]

Alerted now to the activities of Das, Indian officials began to look for his literature in India. By May 1910, copies of cards and newspapers printed by the Hindustan publicity committee had surfaced in Calcutta, and C. R. Cleveland, inspector general of the criminal investigation department, hurried to Michael with copies of the publications. The *Free Hindusthan*, Cleveland explained to Michael, was being published in the United States to circumvent Indian sedition laws. It was "revolutionary and anarchical." Cleveland asked whether the police in the United States could do anything about it. Michael obligingly wrote to the state department to see whether the newspaper could be suppressed. Had Indians published the newspaper in India, it would have been banned and its editors and publishers tried or deported summarily, Michael informed the state department. It seemed to Michael that friendly governments such as the United States, which had given refuge to such men, could at least suppress their publications.

Unfortunately for the British, the United States had no federal laws allowing the suppression of newspapers unfriendly to British rule in India. In fact, the First Amendment made such a law unconstitutional. The state department thought that perhaps a New York state law could be used, however, and wrote to the governor of New York asking whether the newspaper might be suppressed under state law. The governor asked the district attorney of New York City for a report. Exactly what action, if any, the district attorney took is not clear, but soon afterward the *Free Hindusthan* ceased publication in New York.[13]

Hopkinson increased his vigilance. On 14 November 1909 an attempt was made to assassinate Minto. The next day Hopkinson wrote that Das and several other Indian leaders in Vancouver were trying to reverse the act of 1907 that barred Indians from voting in British Columbia. Indians should be kept out of politics, he warned, because they were uneducated and susceptible to corruption. They were also encouraging anti-British sentiment and protesting the discrimination of Canadian immigration laws.[14]

Teja Singh, meanwhile, had gone to London to meet with Gandhi to discuss strategy for Canadian Indians. Gandhi advised him to bring all leaders together into a single committee and to call on all educated Indians to take up the cause of immigration in Canada. Teja Singh returned to Vancouver in March 1910, and in April, Vancouver Indians issued a protest over the discrimination of Canadian immigration laws. The government responded that no discrimination existed. The two-hundred-dollar entrance fee applied to all Asians except to Chinese, who were covered by special statutory regulations, and to Japanese, who had a special agreement. The continuous voyage ruling applied to all immigrants and did not exclude Indians, for a resident of British India could purchase a direct ticket for Canada and travel by continuous voyage on that ticket. If Indians complied with the law in regard to monetary qualifications and passed the usual medical examination at the point of landing, officials insisted that there would be no difficulty about entering Canada.[15]

This growing concern of the British with Indian activists combined with domestic political necessities to drive the Canadian government deeper into political surveillance of Das and other students in the United States after 1910. That year the Indian government began to require students to obtain government certificates of identity before traveling abroad. These certificates allowed the government to keep track of wandering scholars. Certificates were issued freely since their purpose was to maintain surveillance of students, not to restrict their departure. By 1911, there were approximately a hundred students from India in the United States—mostly men, because practically all Indian women who studied abroad went to England. The men were scattered across the country: the son of the maharaja of Baroda was at Harvard, the son of the poet Tagore was at the University of Illinois at Urbana, and other Indians were at Columbia and at midwestern universities in Nebraska and Iowa. Most Indian students were on the Pacific Coast, however, at agricultural colleges in Oregon, at the University of Washington at Seattle, and at the University of California at Berkeley. It was these western students who organized first and who then became the objects of intense concern by British agents.[16]

Hopkinson soon discovered that Das was encouraging students to organize. Das joined the students at the University of Washington at Seattle in January 1910, where, with the help of a history professor, he organized the Association for the Promotion of Education for the People of India. He also organized a Hindustan club for Indians. From Seattle, Das went on to organize students at the University of California at Berkeley. The routine for Indian students traveling to Berkeley was already well established by the time Das arrived in 1910. The *Modern Review* of Calcutta gave explicit advice for students who wished to study in the United States. They must arrive with a good knowledge of English, a hundred dollars in pocket, and the government certificate of identity. Students had already organized to help others make the trip. One Berkeley student wrote an article for the *Modern Review* outlining how to study on the Pacific Coast. He advised a year of high school in the United States, which could be obtained without fee at Berkeley High School, only an eight-minute walk from the university. Prospective students could get a letter of recommendation from the American consul general to the immigration inspector at Seattle and identification papers from the organization sponsoring the student. When the immigration inspector asked whether the student believed in polygamy, he should answer no. At Seattle, a friendly American would meet the newcomer and take him to New India House. From Seattle, the student was to write to Berkeley, and another student would arrange to meet him. It was best to leave India at the end of February, arrive in Berkeley at the end of April, and then work during the summer or take a summer course. At Berkeley, students could live on twelve dollars a month. A student could get by on $250 a year; for $350 he could live in luxury. He could make twenty-five or thirty cents an hour working, or he could sell shawls or other Indian products.[17]

Das found more than thirty Indian students enrolled at Berkeley in 1910. Students chose Berkeley primarily because tuition was only fifteen dollars per semester. Classes were large at Berkeley, some over five hundred, and often students were assigned seats alphabetically. There were thus few personal contacts between professor and students—a difficult adjustment for students who had experienced small classes in India, close rapport with their Indian professors, and emphasis on wide reading rather than on textbook cramming for exams. Those who asked for special attention from American professors with heavy teaching loads sometimes received an unsympathetic response from faculty members annoyed with students who did not willingly conform to convention. Nor were most Berkeley professors at that time sympathetic to Indian students' criticisms of the university or of British imperialism. "They are generally revolutionaries, or if not such when they come, are soon taken in hand by their fellows and converted to revolutionary ideas," complained one Pacific Coast professor.[18]

Students at Berkeley had already encountered West Coast discrimination before Das arrived. In the Northeast, a turban could be a passport to high society. When traveling in the Southeast, Indians had to wear their turbans lest they be taken for black Americans and encounter even more discrimination. Because of the opposition to Indian laborers in West Coast cities, however, most students learned not to wear turbans. Hotels and boarding houses, including the YMCA, usually turned students away regardless of their head covering because of their color. One student remembered spending a cold winter night in a Southern Pacific depot in northern California after being turned away from a dozen hotels. When students found rooms, they were often refused use of the kitchen to prepare their own food. Most public restaurants, including those at the University of California, which were run by students, refused to serve Indians. Typical fare for the Indian college student was graham bread, fruit, milk, eggs, and nuts. In an era when college clubs determined all social activities on campus, Indians were refused membership in the clubs. A few Berkeley Indians formed a fraternity, but they were refused admission to the interfraternity council.[19]

Such discrimination made students feel, sometimes for the first time, that political organizing might be necessary. Many had been sponsored by societies that looked forward to a nationalism that would eliminate caste in India, and students writing for the *Modern Review* had warned Indians to leave their caste prejudices behind if they wanted to come to America to study. Although many of the students had not worked in India, they often accepted the tradition of working their way through college at Berkeley. One student worked cleaning house in return for room and board. Another became a linen keeper in a San Francisco hospital. Many students joined Sikh laborers doing summer farm work in the fields. In answer to the question of caste, one Berkeley student wrote, "We do not pay any more respect to a Brahman than we do to Pariah, Hindu or Muhamadan, Christian, Brahman or Khsatriya, Namasudra or Chandal, all are equally welcome in this Temple of Lord Jagannath. In fact, we never know or care to know to what caste anyone belongs." To find the earmarks of caste in a country that provided an example of political democracy seemed wrong, then, and being treated as outcasts deepened the students' nationalism. Discrimination led to a growing consciousness of their common political oppression. They now felt like Indians and were ready to act collectively as Indians.[20]

Students had already found their way to the Vedanta temple in San Francisco, an elaborate three-story edifice that combined Gothic, Hindu, Shiva, and Muslim designs in an aggregation of towers, minarets, and colonnades topped by a precariously perched American eagle. Because it housed the Vedanta Society, the building also became a home for new students. Euro-American women who attended services at the temple often helped students to find jobs and lodging, and Unitarian ministers often invited them to speak to congregations about India. At these church lectures, Indian students from Berkeley felt free to speak out against British rule. At one YWCA meeting, where missionaries denounced the Hindu religion and praised British rule, sixteen Indian students stationed themselves in the front row and arose one after another to defend their culture until the speaker abruptly closed the meeting. Life for these student exiles in California, wrote a Swiss student at Stanford who later married one of the men, was "rather pathetic, an uncertain hovering between two worlds, permeated by a sense of irremediable hopelessness and futility."[21]

Nationalism was a powerful antidote to the feeling of helplessness.

When Das arrived in the Bay Area, he told students about restrictions on immigration, collected funds to fight cases in court, and urged students to remain vocal in their opposition to British rule. When the Friends of Hindustan was formed in September 1910 to help poor students, Das urged that the group become political. By March 1911, the student community was split between loyalists who wished to support the British in India and nationalists such as Das who continued to speak out against British rule. The Friends of Hindustan dissolved that month. Some students joined California radicals, but most nationalist students concentrated on getting more students to join them. The nationalists formed the Hindustan Association of the United States. Das returned to the University of Washington, where he obtained his master's degree in 1911. He then applied for citizenship again.

Hopkinson's informants told him about Das's citizenship attempt late in June. He immediately advised the Canadian minister of the interior, W. W. Cory, asking him to interrupt the proceedings by giving information to the American government that Das was an anarchist agitating against British rule in India. Das, he claimed, wanted to return to India at the time George V was to be crowned emperor of India, claim the protection of the American flag, and raise international complications. Cory informed Bryce of these predictions, and Bryce in turn informed the state department informally that this was why Das was seeking naturalization. In a letter to secretary of state Philander Knox, Bryce warned that Das was suspected of being an anarchist and a revolutionist. The state department replied to Bryce that it had no evidence that Das was trying to obtain citizenship papers or that he was an anarchist. Das was allowed to file his application for citizenship. He then applied to the University of California at Berkeley to work on a doctorate in political science and moved to Berkeley.[22]

Informants within the Indian student community, now regularly reporting to Hopkinson, noted Das's departure for Berkeley. Late in September 1911, Hopkinson arrived in San Francisco, where he went to Angel Island to find out what officials knew about Das and other nationalist Indian students. These officials said they were surprised that the British government had not been aware of the situation created in California by the Indian students. Hopkinson then saw the secretary of the AEL, who provided him with clippings of lectures made by Das. Back in Seattle, Hopkinson obtained the promise of immigration inspectors to testify against Das if he proceeded with his application for citizenship. There, Hopkinson also discovered that on 16 October, Indians had called a mass meeting to commemorate the anniversary of the partition of Bengal. The Indian national flag was hoisted, and the meeting ended with the singing of "Bande Mataram." Hopkinson dutifully reported all this information and warned that Indian students had been influencing white women to help them in the name of humanity. When he made a report in early October 1911, he also suggested that the British consulate in San Francisco should take more note of the Berkeley students. An agent should be assigned specifically to watch Das, who was gaining prominence by assisting immigrants to secure their "alleged rights" when they received no protection from consular officers. The situation in the Bay Area was a good opportunity for agitators, Hopkinson concluded. There was no doubt in his mind that Berkeley was now the main center of agitation.[23]

In Washington, Bryce was still attempting to prevent Das from becoming a citizen, but the state department insisted that there was not sufficient evidence to deny Das citizenship. Bryce then wrote to Connaught asking for information on Das that could be used officially in court to oppose naturalization on the grounds of "anarchist tendencies." In December 1911, Das left Berkeley and moved to Bandon, Oregon. There he purchased sixty acres of land and opened the Bandon Clay Products Company. Then, on 10 January 1912, he appeared in the circuit court of Coos County at Coquille, Oregon, and filed a petition of intention to become a citizen. Connaught sent a secret telegram to Bryce, saying that all the evidence was in the hands of Hopkinson, who was to use it at his discretion, in cooperation with Hunter in Seattle, in opposing Das's naturalization. Hopkinson was still not sure whether the bureau of naturalization would reject Das's application, but the Seattle office forwarded the information to Washington, D.C., and the department of commerce and labor notified the justice department that its files suggested that Das would not make a desirable citizen. The department asked the United States attorney at Portland to oppose Das's naturalization. There is no evidence that Das engaged in any political activity for the next two-and-a-half years.[24]

The movement still went on. Hopkinson had been investigating Indians for almost two years, and there seemed no end to their activities. The Canadian government decided to give Hopkinson a raise and to keep him watching students. As soon as Das left the Bay Area, another leader arose to worry Hopkinson. His name was Har Dayal.[25]

Dayal spent less than three years in the United States, but he was responsible for leading Hopkinson more deeply into surveillance of the student movement. Whereas Das would resume his espousal of Indian independence after he received his American citizenship in 1914 and would remain an activist in defense of Indian rights, Dayal would eventually recant his views and embrace British control. He was one of the most controversial Indian radicals. Mercurial, brilliant, and an appealing leader, Dayal studied in Lahore and London, then returned to the Punjab in 1907 to organize boycott activities. He left the Punjab in 1909, after police had successfully curtailed his political work there, and returned to London. From London he went to Paris to help Indian nationalists edit the *Bande Mataram*, a journal for Indian independence. Disagreement with the socialist principles of Indian leaders in Paris and the expense of living there soon prompted him to leave for Martinique. After a few weeks of isolation there, he went on to Puerto Rico, and then, on 9 February 1911, at age twenty-six, he arrived in steerage on the East Coast of the United States.[26]

Although the British already considered Dayal a dangerous revolutionary, he apparently entered the United States unknown to them. According to Dayal, he went first to Harvard to study Buddhism in the library there. Before long, however, he was in touch with Teja Singh, who asked him to come to California to lead the agricultural workers. By late April 1911, Dayal was in Berkeley. Shortly after arriving in the Bay Area, he wrote an article for the *Modern Review* saying that there were four types of Indians in the United States—Sikhs, swamis, students, and spies. Spies, he said, had nothing to do because Indians were frank and outspoken. The United States, he told his readers, was the perfect environment for political and social freedom. Dayal then went to Hawaii for two or three months, where he later said he studied the works of Karl Marx.

By late 1911, Dayal was back on the West Coast, still undetected by Hopkinson. In Palo Alto he found a part-time job lecturing at Stanford on Indian philosophy—a job for which he received no pay, but one that left him time to engage in political activities. By January 1912, he had devised a plan for the Guru Govind Singh Sahib education scholarships at the University of California, to be financed by Jawala Singh, a wealthy Stockton rancher. Students were to pay their own passage to Berkeley, but all expenses and return passage were to be paid by the scholarship. Arthur Upham Pope, a new assistant professor of philosophy at Berkeley, agreed to be on the committee to select recipients; two thousand Indian newspapers announced the fellowships. By May the first six recipients had been selected.

Until the summer of 1912, everyone seemed happy to have Dayal
around. He lived like a true guru in a small room near the railroad, with
a single chair for the occasional guest, sleeping on the floor and living
on milk and unbuttered bread. He lectured in an old brown tweed suit.
The Stanford administration liked the lectures he delivered to the afflu-
ent white students and agreed to allow him to lecture a second semester,
though still without compensation. The young Indian made friends
among Bay Area radicals. Palo Alto was the center of a flourishing
intellectual radical movement when Dayal arrived. He was soon in contact with the Socialist Radical Club, which usually met at the home of
Alice Park in Palo Alto or at Campe's, an Italian restaurant in the basement of the old Call Building on Market Street in San Francisco. Manuel
Larkin, an economics instructor at Stanford, was president of the club,
and Clarence Darrow, John D. Barry, Mrs. Fremont Older, and Rose
Markham (then called Emma Goldman, Jr.) were among the radicals
who went to the meetings to discuss socialism, feminism, and social
change. Dayal became secretary of the club.

Dayal received considerable publicity in the San Francisco *Bulletin*
in a series of articles published by John Barry, a member of the Anti-
Imperialist League and a well-known journalist. In the form of conversations with Dayal, the articles presented arguments for Indian
independence in very sympathetic terms. The articles were reprinted by
Dayal with exhortations to Indians in India: "Our voice is stifled at home,
but it is heard in other lands. The sympathy of all who love freedom is
with you. You are not alone in your struggle." Such views were, of
course, exactly those that were putting Indian nationalists in jail in India.
During 1912, in a ceremony of great pomp and splendor, George V
became emperor of India. He began his reign by quietly canceling the
unpopular partition of Bengal, but the Liberal secretary of state for India,
Robert Crewe, was nevertheless explicit about the possibility of self-
government: "I see no future for India on these lines." The India government refused soon after to issue certificates of identity to students
traveling to the United States, but the number of students making inquiries at the American consulate in Calcutta increased. The state department continued to allow the students to enter.[27]

Dayal still went about his activities unhindered by the British. In the
summer of 1912, he lectured before the IWW in Oakland on the future
of the labor movement. He sketched his plan for world solidarity among
workers—a labor movement that cooperated with the woman's movement, uniting two enslaved classes that had to fight their battles to-

gether. Leadership was to rest with a vanguard of ascetics based at a central labor college who renounced riches and respectability to prepare workers for moral and intellectual as well as economic emancipation.

According to author Van Wyck Brooks, who was teaching English at Stanford that year, Dayal began at this time to elaborate plans for a "fraternity of the red flag" modeled on Jesuit discipline. Novices were to submit to the guidance of one member for a year, accept eight principles of radicalism, take vows of poverty, homelessness, humility, purity, service, and propaganda. Brothers must renounce wealth, must not earn money or become parents, and must repudiate all social ties. The goal of the fraternity was to establish a universal brotherhood without private property, patriotism, religion, or marriage. Through organizing and a general strike, private property would be abolished and communism established. Dayal used the terms *brotherhood* and *fraternity* loosely, for the group was to include women, and the goals included the establishment of the complete economic, moral, intellectual, and sexual freedom of women as well as the abolition of prostitution, marriage, and other institutions based on the enslavement of women. A woman "comrade" promised to donate six acres of land and a house near Oakland for an institute to train anarchist propagandists. This was to be the first monastery of anarchism of the Order of the Red Flag, and was to be called the Bakunin Institute, named for Russian nihilist Mikhail Bakunin.[28]

By late September, rumors began floating around Stanford about Dayal's extreme ideas. It was said that he advocated free love, that he was attempting to establish a free-love colony near Palo Alto, and that he had issued a manifesto calling for the abolition of government, religion, marriage, prostitution, and all racial discrimination. Stanford had just weathered an attack by outraged moralists against Thorstein Veblen, a professor who had been inviting women students out into the woods for weekends at his cabin. The annoyed administration dismissed Veblen and was in the process of notifying Dayal of his dismissal when he heard about the complaint and resigned.[29]

As long as Dayal stayed away from the Berkeley students, however, Hopkinson remained ignorant of his plans. Dayal's difficulties began when students invited him to help them celebrate "Nation Day" at Styles Hall at the University of California on 12 October 1912. Students also invited professors from the departments of philosophy, political science, political economy, and languages. Political science professor R. H. Reed said that he favored Indian self-government and assured Indians of the sympathy of the Berkeley faculty and of the American people. The wife of philosophy professor Arthur Pope read an article by anti-imperialist Jabez Sunderland on the new nationalist movement in India, and Pope then spoke on American ideals and the new spirit in India. Pope criticized British rule but urged the people of India not to be hasty in bringing about change. Das spoke on the scope and aim of Indian nationalism. Young India, he promised, would demand a revolution in social ideals so that humanity and liberty would be valued above property, special privilege would not overshadow equal opportunity, and women would not be kept under subjection. Dayal gave a welcoming address, but he identified himself as an internationalist who did not believe in the narrow views of nationalism and thanked the Americans for their cordial treatment of students. On the whole, it was a mild gathering. Still, convinced that Berkeley was the base of operations on the Pacific Coast for all Indian political agitators, Hopkinson was alarmed when he heard about the "Nation Day" celebrations, and had informants report on each speaker. Hopkinson routinely reported that Dayal had been there, but in response, the Canadian government sent a hurried order to collect more information on Dayal.[30]

Early in January 1913, Hopkinson returned to San Francisco to take a closer look at Dayal's activities. The British consul, A. Carnegie Ross, warned him that student informants had reported sedition against the British government. Students, Ross said, had received with great joy the news of the wounding of Viceroy Hardinge by a Bengali bomb thrower and had prepared a pamphlet titled "The Significance of a Bomb," which they intended to print and send to all parts of the world, including India. Loyalist students had asked Ross for permission to form their own organization and wanted to elect him president and to counter the activities of Dayal and the nationalists. Ross, unimpressed with the leader of the loyalists, had opposed the plan and suggested that the students just keep aloof, but he sent Bryce copies of articles written by Dayal and a list of his followers. Ross also warned Hopkinson to be careful in Berkeley, as he was a marked man. From the consulate, Hopkinson went to the Vedanta temple. There, the swami confirmed that the situation was worse than when Hopkinson had visited in 1911, because Dayal had assumed leadership of the nationalist students.[31]

Hopkinson then visited American officials to see if any law existed under which the student activities might be stopped. A 1903 law, passed after an anarchist had assassinated President McKinley, excluded anarchists who believed in the overthrow by force and violence of the

United States government and "all governments or all forms of law." But Hopkinson had to convince the immigration authorities that the students not only were advocating overthrow of the British government in India but were opposed to "all" governments. Some American officials were eager to deport students if incriminating evidence could be found. Clayton Herrington, special agent of the bureau of investigation in San Francisco, asked for a list of the students and promised that he would have the postmaster at Berkeley look over all incoming mail. Later, Hopkinson introduced a loyalist student to Herrington, so that the student could repeat his stories about student activists. Herrington asked the student to collect information for him.[32]

When Hopkinson made his report after his trip to Berkeley in 1913, he recommended intensification of surveillance. He suggested that someone be stationed at San Francisco for six months, or even permanently. The reply came quickly. Early in March, Connaught received a secret telegram from London: "Secretary of State for India attaches great importance to Hopkinson's investigation and I hope your Ministers may be able to keep him on the work." The Berkeley investigations would continue.[33]

Most alarming to Hopkinson was the fact that Dayal was not only meeting with students but also attempting to make contact with Sikh workers along the Pacific Coast. The organizational networks that West Coast Indians developed from 1912 to 1914 are difficult to sort out, but at least two groups—the Pacific Coast Khalsa Diwan and the Hindustan Association—were important aids to political organizing. Each group provided support for Indians seeking to redress injustices encountered in the United States and a place where Indians could express bitterness about British disregard of their equities at home and abroad.

The most important of the three Indian organizations was the network linking all the Sikhs on the Pacific Coast, the Khalsa Diwan. Sikhs in Canada had already established half a dozen temples when the California Khalsa Diwan was formed at a meeting near Holt on 1 April 1912. Teja Singh played an important role as impartial arbitrator between regional groups of Sikhs in northern California, convinced them that they had a common interest in providing a hostel and aid for newly arrived immigrants and Indian students, and was elected the first president of the California Khalsa Diwan. Previously, there had been discussion of establishing a temple in Oakland. Now the men favored Holt, but since no land was available there, they settled for a lot next to the railroad tracks on the southwestern side of Stockton. The house on the lot was to serve as a gurdwara until a real temple could be built. According to the minutes of the first meeting of the Khalsa Diwan, the group's purpose was to provide for the welfare of students and of the laboring class. To achieve this goal, the Khalsa Diwan planned to incorporate in the state and to hold property in common. By 27 May 1912, the group had incorporated and was at work establishing the gurdwara.[34]

The Khalsa Diwan was the social organization that ran the temples and served as the Sikhs' cultural structure in the United States. In India the gurdwaras had been more than a place of worship; they had been village meeting centers, hostels, schools, places where free meals were served, and the focus for political discussion of community issues. The Khalsa Diwan, to which every Sikh automatically belonged, provided political representation for the community, and the gurdwara provided a home base for that community. Sikhs envisioned the Khalsa Diwan and the gurdwara in Stockton functioning in the same manner they had in India. In addition, and less formally, the Khalsa Diwan was to serve more specific political functions. Before the first meeting, the question of raising bail bonds for political prisoners in India and providing funds for education in India was discussed. Although no information has survived on how much money, if any, was sent to India to assist political prisoners, one source said that $200,000 had been sent to various schools by 1920. We also know that Doaba and Majha Sikhs, traditionally the most politically radical in India, dominated the Khalsa Diwan and held most offices. The gurdwara soon became a place where political discussions occurred, political newspapers were read, and contributions were solicited for independence plans. No sooner had the gurdwara been established in Stockton than an Indian nationalist spoke there, asking for funds to pursue a scheme to establish headquarters in Japan for a freedom movement. Sikhs gave him a generous donation.[35]

The second Indian group was the Hindustan Association, organized in Oregon and Washington in May 1913, a year after the formation of the Khalsa Diwan. Its centers were Portland and Astoria, but it soon spread south to California. Pandit Kashiram, a founder, was one of several hundred Indians in Oregon who had prospered and was rumored to have made a fortune in lumbermill contracts. Another founder, Pandurang Sadashiva Khamkhoje, who had arrived from India in 1908, had been a protégé of the nationalist Bal Tilak and the founder of a short-lived Indian independence league in California before leaving for Portland in 1909. Kashiram supplied the funds and Khamkhoje the plans for a local political network that would encourage Sikhs to return to India to fight against British rule.[36]

Dayal soon visited both the Khalsa Diwan and the Hindustan Association to discuss plans for a propaganda center in San Francisco. All previous Indian publishing ventures had been short-lived. Das had been harassed by the British and was unable to keep his paper going, and other publications in British Columbia and the Bay Area had proved equally fugitive. Newspapers were usually poorly printed, sometimes as no more than ditto sheets, and seldom lasted for more than a few issues. By June 1913, Dayal was in Oregon, talking to workers in lumber camps about plans to establish a publishing center in San Francisco that would print news of both the struggle against Britain for independence and the struggle for equal rights in North America. Dayal met with 120 Indians, a third of whom were representatives sent by towns and factories in Oregon and Washington, and visited groups at Saint Johns, Oregon, and other lumber towns. At a meeting in Astoria, Dayal told Indians that there was no hope for reform of the British government, that it must be abolished. The workers pledged several thousand dollars to support a newspaper.[37]

As he rallied workers, Dayal also recruited students who could work with him on the newspaper and spoke out publicly against British rule. He wrote to students in India during this time, urging them to study French, German, Italian, and Spanish, to abandon the "stale stew of philistinism and hypocrisy" at Harvard and Oxford, to travel, and to study sociology instead of theology and metaphysics. "There is no short cut to liberty and knowledge passing through the tropical jungles of religious bigotry and obscurantism," he counseled. "India cannot evolve new laws of social growth. She must obey the universal form of social movement."[38]

San Francisco immigration officials were now watching Dayal constantly, hoping to find evidence that he was a deportable anarchist. Early in July 1913, when the IWW announced that Dayal, along with Emma Goldman, would speak at one of its meetings, Ainsworth rushed to the meeting, only to find that although Dayal was there, he did not plan to speak as scheduled. Ainsworth, who was now making reports regularly to Hopkinson, grumbled that there was simply not enough information to prove Dayal an anarchist. Then, on 3 May 1913, a federal court in Washington state quietly admitted the first West Coast Indian to citizenship. Now Hopkinson was truly upset. "The matter of granting citizenship papers to Hindu residents in the United States is a serious one for Canada as regards immigration," he wrote to Ottawa officials. Herrington, now also sending reports to Hopkinson, had told him in a "strictly confidential" memorandum why Dayal had resigned from Stanford. On 18 June Hopkinson reported with satisfaction that, because of his confidential information, immigration officials in Washington had ordered Seattle and Portland officials to attend Dayal's lectures and take notes.[39]

London officials carefully digested Hopkinson's January reports on San Francisco and found them "especially helpful." They decided that Hopkinson should visit San Francisco regularly and send reports directly to the agent of the government of India in London. Hopkinson would be given sixty pounds a year in addition to his regular salary from Canada, and another sixty pounds to pay Indian informants. The Canadian minister approved this arrangement early in August, and the India office began to send Hopkinson requests for investigations of individual Indians. Beginning in the fall of 1913, the British Indian government thus had its own surveillance structure in the United States.[40]

The additional funds allowed Hopkinson to expand his force considerably. He hired his own investigator, A. Tilton Steele, and paid Indian informants to work under cover for him. Steele threw himself into the investigations with gusto. He went to the IWW headquarters in San Francisco and reported back in colorful language about the gathering of the "big Guns and Gunnesses of Anarchism." Emma Goldman, "the most rabid and dangerous revolutionary leader" in the United States, held her gatherings there, Steele reported, but Dayal was seldom there, nor were other Indians. Steele did claim that he had met Dayal at one of the meetings and that Dayal had boasted of being president of the Bakunin Club, an organization of young people who were studying the teachings of Mikhail Bakunin. Dayal said the group met each Sunday at 10 A.M. in San Francisco but would not allow Steele to attend any of the meetings.

Steele was sure that Dayal was poisoning the minds of students with the "virus of revolutionary thought" at the Bakunin Club. "Dayal thinks he is safe," Steele wrote to Hopkinson on 22 November, "that this is a 'free country' where 'free speech' prevails and political agitators, and criminals, can find a safe retreat—and rendezvous, for their various schemes. He should be taught a lesson that there are limitations to 'free speech,' that only 'law abiding' persons are wanted here in the United States and that people with 'lawless aims and objects' can, under the

law, be sent out of the country." By this time, Steele was using code
names for his informers and for Indians being investigated. Steele was
"Spender," Indian informer H. E. Pandian was "Peters," Teja Singh
was "Sutton," Das was "Delta," and Dayal was "Dawson." Dayal appeared to be by far the most dangerous to Steele, who said that Das
had refused to allow Dayal to make any more speeches because of his
violent denunciations of the British government. Steele's reports were
all sent to Ottawa, with the suggestion that Dayal's activities be brought
to the attention of the United States justice department. Hopkinson
himself joined Steele in San Francisco soon after for a third visit.[41]

Hopkinson found that students now looked to Dayal as a leading
patriot in the movement to liberate India and that Indian laborers found
him a champion of their cause in the exclusion controversy in North
America. With two thousand dollars raised by Indian workers, Dayal
purchased a building in San Francisco to house and board a newspaper
staff and named the group the Yugantar Ashram. He called the paper
Ghadar, which means "revolt" in Urdu, the main language of northern
India; he printed twenty-five thousand copies a week in Urdu and circulated them free everywhere. He maintained that *Ghadar* would serve
as a means of communication for Indians in North America and encourage work for the independence of India. On 1 November 1913, the
first issue of the newspaper appeared. It carried the advertisement:

> Wanted—Brave soldiers to stir up Ghadar in India;
> Pay—Death;
> Prize—Martyrdom;
> Pension—Liberty;
> Field of battle—India.[42]

That fall Dayal was still corresponding with Van Wyck Brooks, who
was now in England and was forwarding letters and packages of literature for him. Late in December, Dayal wrote to warn Brooks: *"Never
tell anyone anything about me.* . . . The British government sends spies
all the time, which affords a revolutionist much amusement and relax-
ation in an otherwise intense and strenuous life." Dayal, Brooks wrote,
had said he would gladly have been burned alive in front of the post
office at Palo Alto if it would have brought forth ardent apostles.

Dayal's actions were considerably less dramatic than his writings, but
his rhetoric was increasingly alarming to Hopkinson. On 31 December
1913, the Hindu Association called a large meeting in Sacramento,
where, according to informants, Dayal delivered a lecture on the decline

of British power in India. Using lantern slides, he showed statistics and pictures all pointing to the conclusion that the British Empire was crumbling. He urged Indians to return to India to help in the coming revolt. A war between Britain and Germany would be the signal for revolution, he prophesied. On 7 January, Hopkinson sent a report to London that Berkeley students were arming. Twenty revolvers and sixteen Winchester rifles had been purchased at the Berkeley Gun Store.[43]

San Francisco immigration inspector Samuel Backus had, meanwhile, also decided to investigate Dayal. On 6 October 1913, he reported to the inspector of immigration that Pacific Coast Indian students were presenting the cause of the immigrant laborers so well to the press that they had enlisted the sympathies of "well meaning" people in California and had even led a few to speak out in favor of the immigrants. There were, he had good reason to believe, "extremist revolutionaries" among the students.[44]

The commissioner of immigration sent his own investigator, Henry Weiss, to California to check the Backus report. Weiss reported that the political movement in India was confined mainly to Bengalis and that no Bengali colonies existed in the United States. He found only twenty-five on the Pacific Coast, most of them students, scattered in Washington, Oregon, and California.[45]

Backus sent on his own report, however. Most Bengali students on the coast were said to belong to a Hindustani student association pledged to foment rebellion. Not twenty-five but sixty-eight Bengalis were in the United States, twenty of them in California. Some of these Backus labeled as "notorious agitators" who used their studies as a cover for their main interest, rebellion. Berkeley students, he had heard, were actively engaged in rifle and revolver practice in the hills behind the University of California campus. Dayal, secretary of the Yugantar Ashram, was not only editing a newspaper with revolutionary content but also conducting speaking tours of the Pacific Coast sponsored by "anarchists." Dayal had been so successful, Backus concluded, that even white residents, some of whom were citizens, were listening to his talks. Worse, some Indian radicals were filing applications for citizenship. On 19 January 1914, Das had appeared in a San Francisco court dressed in a spruce dark American suit and requested an application for citizenship. For these reasons, Backus wanted a warrant for Dayal's arrest and deportation as an anarchist.[46]

The years of surveillance had finally paid off for Hopkinson. Caminetti informed the state department soon after he received Backus's report that he intended to arrest and deport Dayal and that he was strongly opposed to the naturalization of Das, whose case the attorney general himself was planning to take charge of. The state department promptly informed Cecil Spring-Rice, who asked that he be informed before Dayal was deported to any British possession.[47]

Was there an alternative to Hopkinson's spreading surveillance system among students? The translator at the immigration office in San Francisco, D. S. Dady Burjor, recommended that Hopkinson adopt a different response to the activities of the students. He suggested that attention to the grievances of students and other Indian immigrants would undercut their growing militance. The students, Burjor admitted, were being affected by revolutionary ideas and were appealing to the laborers to join them, but he argued that the British should attempt to prove that they had not neglected the Indians and that the British India government was as solicitous of Indians as was the Japanese government of Japanese. Chinese and Japanese governments had associations to care for immigrants, but the British consuls at San Francisco and Seattle did not take any interest in their nationals. And while consuls could not intervene directly, they could help to organize and support a British India association. Such an association could help immigrants by explaining the laws and defending them from the hostility of the Americans.[48]

Such protection of civil rights should, of course, have been extended by the British years earlier. But years of inaction had paralyzed British officials to the just claims of the immigrants, and the growing violence of Indian rhetoric only evoked fear and increased dependence on informants, undercover agents, and repression of protest. Hopkinson continued to collaborate with American immigration officials in deportation investigations. When Don S. Rathbun, the new bureau of investigation agent, arrived in San Francisco, Hopkinson promptly briefed him on the dangerous activities of Indian students. Hopkinson reported student activities to Canada and to London, secretly photographed Indian students who volunteered information about other students, and made his own further investigations of other students. These types of surveillance helped to drive students and Sikhs to greater opposition of British rule in India.[49]

By this time hundreds of copies of *Ghadar* were circulating weekly through the Indian colonies in Oregon and California, and bundles of the paper were on their way to Canada and India. The Ghadar Press began publication of an Indian version of the rebellion of 1857, books of patriotic songs, and volumes of poetry. The hand press had been exchanged for an electric printing press, and a Gurmukhi press was brought from England to publish *Ghadar* in Punjabi.

According to Harish Puri, an Indian historian who has made a careful study of the Ghadar publications and of Dayal's political career in California, the ideology that emerged was immensely attractive to Indian migrants. Although Dayal was impulsive and erratic, he was able to draw on a broad range of ideas of nationalist, revolutionary, and anarchist movements to formulate his opposition to British rule. He concentrated on the necessity of independence, seldom discussing the form that the post revolutionary government of India should take. At times he stressed setting up a republic. Ghadar literature, however, simply supported a revolution. *Ghadar* seldom cited the discrimination and oppression that immigrants had experienced as a reason to support a revolution. Sikh poets, on the other hand, revealed bitter awareness of their humiliation, of the fact that they were called "coolies" and were subject not only to compulsion at home but also to oppression in foreign lands. These oppressive experiences in America were the result of British control of India. British consuls in the United States did nothing to protect Indians from American hooligans. Only armed struggle in India by the Sikhs could right the wrongs committed in America as well as in India. Patriotism was to become the religion of all immigrants—Muslim, Hindu, and Sikh—who would unite against foreign rulers. The Ghadar poems thus provided a powerful unifying ideology that was, Puri concludes, far different from that in the Punjab, where culture and politics had never been reconciled. In America, politics came first.[50]

Dayal's strength and the strength of the group that gradually emerged as the Ghadar Party rested on rhetoric, not on organization. Dayal could evoke a sense of commitment and unity but was unable to build a strong organization. Ghadar leaders considered political education as their main role, a role that did not include molding Bengali students and Punjabi farmers into a "rationally organized secret militant organization." While some Bengali students saw the movement as a terrorist conspiracy, others considered it a mass movement based on political education. The Punjabi peasants viewed it as a call to violent and spontaneous combat. Because Dayal did not try to reconcile or integrate the different views, he had increasing difficulty in controlling the Ghadar Party. He conceived of Ghadar as a sort of spontaneous popular movement dependent less on the analysis of existing conditions in India than on direct action to arm civilians and mutinous soldiers, to legitimate violence, and to rouse a passion for independence among the masses and soldiers. Apparently neither Dayal nor others expected the opportunity for such action to occur before 1920. Political education was to be the first stage. What was to come after remained comfortably vague.[51]

British informants chose to emphasize the rhetoric of the most militant of the Ghadarites and to focus on Dayal as the center of conspiracy. According to Pandian, Hopkinson's Indian informant, Dayal was contemplating organizing political *dacoits* (robberies and assassinations) on a guerrilla basis along the borders of the Punjab in the northern mountains of India. The government must prevent such talk or there would be far-reaching consequences and unnecessary trouble, reported Pandian. Hopkinson insisted that this evidence proved that Dayal was an anarchist and thus eligible for deportation, and he urged Backus to act. On 24 February, the San Francisco immigration office received a warrant for Dayal's arrest, and Backus ordered that Dayal be taken into custody as soon as he arrived back in the city. On 25 March, Dayal was arrested at a Socialist meeting at Bohemian Hall in San Francisco on suspicion of being "an anarchist or advocating the overthrow of the United States government by force." Rumors quickly spread that other Indians who had advocated independence would also be arrested.[52]

Ainsworth interrogated Dayal following his arrest. No lawyer was allowed to be present at the interrogation, but a transcript was kept, one of the first full records of a political interrogation conducted by federal officials. The questions concerned Dayal's approval of violence, terrorist activity, student activities, whether he was using San Francisco as a base from which to spread propaganda among Hindus advocating the overthrow of the British government, and whether he believed in or advocated the overthrow of the United States government or all governments. Dayal answered each question carefully. Yes, he approved of violence in some circumstances but opposed it in India because it was not expedient. No, he did not support most terrorist activities because little was gained by individual acts. Yes, he admitted, he was in the United States to educate, and if he could not do it, he would go to another country. No, he did not believe in overthrowing governments or condone assassination of public officials as a general principle, but he believed tyrannical governments should be overthrown by the masses.[53]

The friends Dayal had made in the San Francisco radical movement rallied to his defense. By 27 March, Dayal was free on bail and talking to friendly reporters. "The Democratic administration is licking the boots of England," he told them, for he had never advocated or committed an act of violence in the United States. Furthermore, he went on, the arrest had been illegal, for he had arrived in New York on 9 February 1911, and the warrant had not been issued for his arrest until more than three years later, but the law against anarchists was operative for only three years after they entered the country. John D. Barry wrote a friendly account in his San Francisco *Bulletin* column, arguing that Dayal could not be considered an anarchist because he favored an uprising by force of arms, not by massacre or assassination. The San Francisco *Chronicle* also published an editorial defending Dayal and insisting that he had violated no law. Although the San Francisco *Examiner* denied that the British had requested the deportation of Dayal, the New York *Times* insisted that the British indeed wanted Dayal deported to India, where they could keep an eye on him. Caminetti issued a formal statement saying that Great Britain had not inspired the arrest and had "had no part in the matter nor has it either directly or indirectly requested either the arrest or deportation of the alien."[54]

After Dayal's arrest, Spring-Rice received a request from the British foreign secretary to raise formally the matter of the Berkeley student agitation with the Wilson administration. The British in India had built a case against Dayal during the last two years. In 1912, the British had considered New York a place to be watched. Now, two years later, the criminal intelligence office in India believed that the Bay Area was the headquarters of a "gang of highly dangerous conspirators headed by Har Dayal." The situation was grave, and it was necessary to put an end to the pernicious activities of Dayal, the intelligence officers in India agreed. During a subsequent conspiracy trial in Delhi, the prosecuting attorney claimed that Dayal was writing seditious literature against the British India government, advocating murder of officials in *Ghadar* and training revolutionaries in California. He accused Dayal and others of conspiring as early as October 1910 to commit a murder that occurred on 17 May 1913 at Lahore, India.[55]

Spring-Rice responded to the request with a long letter to the foreign office, outlining what should be done to deal with the Berkeley student agitation. He judged that the time was not right for an official protest to the United States about the students. Fear of competition from Indians, opposition of admission of groups that the native population could not assimilate, fear of the spread of anarchistic propaganda, and violent proceedings of the IWW—all might cause the administration to act against Indian students, limiting their free admission to the universities. On the other hand, the United States government did not like to interfere with the right of political asylum and took pride in the fact or supposition that the government of China was overthrown and the monarchy in Japan was being threatened by students educated in the United States. As far as Spring-Rice could judge, the latter attitudes were still predominant in the Wilson administration. Organized labor had a great influence on the president, the ambassador warned, and there was undue tolerance of anarchists, which made it particularly difficult for a foreign government to complain about the activities of its own subjects in the United States. Spring-Rice also believed that anti-British sentiment among the Irish would be sparked by British complaints and that Bryan might not have changed his critical opinion of British rule in India. Spring-Rice wanted to wait for a change in the balance of American political forces operating for and against the Indian revolutionary cause. In the meantime, he suggested that the best course would be caution in allowing subjects to leave India and that each applicant be investigated and his activities noted on his passport so that American officials could reject him as an anarchist if necessary. The home office should employ American private detective agencies, as it had already done, to keep watch on Irish nationalists conspiring in the United States and its territories.[56]

The silence of the United States government continued through April. Early in May, Caminetti admitted to officials in San Francisco that Dayal had been in the country for more than three years and that they therefore had no legal jurisdiction. Dayal had landed three years and a day before the warrant was issued on 10 February, and although there was some evidence that Dayal had left the country at one point, officials could not prove it. On 12 May immigration officials publicly admitted their mistake. The semiofficial publication for the government of India, *Pioneer* sniped: "Apparently in the land of the free an anarchist is under no penalty unless he be an immigrant of less than three years' domicile. Har Dayal, having been more than this period in the States, is a citizen who may preach anarchy as freely as he pleases. That his activities have in no way been curtailed is apparent from the flood of literature from California that still reaches Bombay." Despite a subsequent complaint from Henry D. Baker, the American consul at Bombay, that the literature coming from California was a source of continual anxiety to the government of India, the American government was not ready to interfere with Indian nationalists in California. Dayal, meanwhile, had quietly left the United States for Switzerland.[57]

The British continued to depend on surveillance. "I look upon the rabid discontent among the Sikhs and other Punjabis on the Pacific Coast as one of the worst features in the present political situation in India," the director of the criminal intelligence division wrote to Lewis V. Harcourt, the secretary of state for the colonies, that spring. Connaught also sent a worried letter to Harcourt suggesting that another man be assigned to the surveillance of Indians in the United States. If anything were to happen to Hopkinson, the careful network of intelligence in the United States and Canada would collapse. He suggested that Hopkinson be transferred entirely to the service of the government of India. Canadian officials also warned London to take special care of Hopkinson's correspondence on Indians in America: files were to be kept in special steel cases.[58]

Steel cases could not contain the Ghadar movement after the outbreak of war between Germany and Great Britain in August 1914. For many Punjabi workers in America, the war was a signal for revolution in India. "Hindus go home to fight in revolution," announced the Portland *Telegram* on 7 August 1914, reporting that large numbers of Indians had already left Astoria and that one lumber company where many had worked was deserted. On 22 August, a number of Indians left Vancouver on the *Empress of India*; three days later more left from Victoria on the *Shidzukoa Maru*, and on 29 August, sixty-two men, including Jawala Singh, the rancher who had helped Dayal to establish student scholarships, boarded the *Korea* in San Francisco. Informers reported that Ram Chandra, the new editor of *Ghadar*, had given a farewell address urging the Indians to start a revolution in India.[59]

During August, three leaders of the Ghadar Party, Ram Chandra, Bhagwan Singh, and Maulvi Mohamed Barakatullah, toured the Pacific Coast from Seattle to the Mexican border, urging men to return to India. The leaders, a Hindu, a Sikh, and a Muslim, provided a display of unity that encouraged Indians in America to put aside their regional and religious differences and to work together for the overthrow of the British. At Sacramento, over five thousand Indians gathered at a mass meeting to hear them urge unity and protection of Indian rights. Barakatullah, who had earlier helped to organize an association of Indo-American nationals and to publish the *Free Hindusthan* in New York, had just returned after five years in Japan and threw himself immediately into the West Coast movement. He explained what the Ghadar Party planned to do in a letter to Dayal, who was now settled in Geneva. Most men had paid for their own expenses back to India, Barakatullah wrote; the Ghadar Party had helped only a few. The plan was to start a revolt in

India, which would spread to the outer provinces of Indochina near Siam and finally to Shanghai and Hong Kong.[60]

Indians continued to leave in small groups for northern India during September. They organized in bands of four or five at mills and ranches, collected money, and booked passage. Each group, called a *jatha*, was autonomous. The main call, according to Harish Puri was "Come, let's become martyrs." On 21 October, the *Tenyo Maru* left San Francisco with over a hundred men who had been refused admittance at Vancouver and fifty Sikhs from California headed for Calcutta. Another group left three days later on the *Manchuria*. The San Francisco *Chronicle* claimed that this was the advance guard of Sikhs who planned to lead a revolution against British rule. According to reporters, almost two thousand men left the Pacific Coast in the first three months of the war. The men did not, however, organize a military expedition in the literal sense. Germany did not offer them any funds, nor did they leave as an organized expedition. The men simply left in small groups with the intent of working for a spontaneous revolt when they arrived in India. Nevertheless, Hopkinson was alarmed. Steele, still under cover in California, wired Hopkinson: "Hindus in California arranging return to India by Japanese steamer for great revolt." Hopkinson added his own information on Canada in his report to Connaught, who wired Harcourt in London.[61]

As the British increased surveillance, the call "come, let's become martyrs" affected the men left behind as well. Late in August, Canadian Indians began to eliminate the British surveillance structure by using a response they had found effective and popular against police spies in India—assassination. Two of Hopkinson's informers were found dead, their heads severed by a razor. In a shoot-out at the Sikh temple, two more Sikhs were killed and several others were wounded. In October, when Hopkinson appeared to testify against an Indian accused in the temple murders, a Sikh named Mewa Singh shot and killed him. Mewa Singh said he had done it "to lay bare the oppression exercised upon my innocent people." Although the Canadians promptly tried and hanged Mewa Singh, immigration officials ordered an end to Canadian surveillance of the activities of Indian nationalists. When Connaught asked Harcourt if he wanted to set up a new system of watching the movements of seditious Indians on the Pacific Coast, Harcourt replied no. For the next two years, the British handled surveillance directly, sending their own professional agents and continuing to infiltrate the Ghadar Party. Gradually, British agent Harish Chandra was able to discredit Ram Chandra, to support friends as leaders, and thereby to disorganize the party. The British were also able to convince United States officials to intervene against the party.[62]

In India, meanwhile, the British relied primarily upon their new wartime internal security system for protection against the returning Sikhs. In the Punjab, the government obtained special authority to arrest persons carrying arms under suspicious circumstances or people suspected of revolutionary activities, as well as anyone trying to protect such suspects. The Punjab government was also granted the power to bring suspects before special tribunals with no right of appeal. The government planted undercover agents among released Indians, opened all mail coming into India, and confiscated papers of the Ghadar Party. Sikhs returning from America thus found the internal defenses of India well secured.

The experiences of Jawala Singh and Tuly Singh Johl were typical of those Sikhs who left California to return to India. By the time Jawala Singh reached Hong Kong in October 1914 on the *Korea*, he had assembled a group of almost three hundred men. The British allowed the men to transfer to the *Tosa Maru* and to continue on to Calcutta, but when the *Tosa Maru* arrived there on 29 October, all the men were loaded on special trains and interned under wartime subversive laws. Officials jailed a hundred men, including Jawala Singh, and released seventy-three on security.[63]

Tuly Singh Johl, the young Sikh who had left his home in Jundialla for America in 1907, returned on the *Manchuria*. Early in October, he had gone into Fresno, the town that he had been working near for the last six years, withdrew all of his savings from the bank, and joined fellow countrymen in San Francisco. Their motivation to return to India, he recalled, was the Ghadar Party, whose leaders had told them that the outbreak of war between Germany and Great Britain was the signal for revolution in India. The words of the Ghadar leaders, but even more the protest songs that the immigrants sang, moved Sikh immigrants like Tuly to act. One Ghadar song counseled Sikh workers:

> The time for prayer is gone;
> It is the time to take up the sword.
> Empty talk does not serve any purpose.
> It is time to engage in a fierce battle.
> Only the names of those who long for martyrdom
>   will shine.[64]

The Sikhs who boarded the *Manchuria* needed little encouragement, however. Their resentment of Great Britain had deepened during the last five years. They knew about the lack of help from Britain in their attempts to obtain equal rights in North America and about the spies who had reported on their activities. The men carried no arms or ammunition on board the *Manchuria*, according to Tuly, and they were not organized as an army. Their plans were informal: some would try to get Sikh troops to mutiny, others would damage property, blow up railroad tracks, or encourage people not to pay taxes. The *Manchuria* was first delayed at Hong Kong for a month until Indian soldiers there struck in protest. When the ship reached Calcutta, the government put the returned emigrants on a train for the Punjab. When the men got off the train at Ludihana, troops surrounded them and locked them up in the police station. The police brought the men food but asked them to pay for it, and the men refused to pay, Tuly recalled. Warrants were then issued for the arrest of many of the men, charging that they had guns, ammunition, and bombs with which they planned to overthrow the government. Some men were imprisoned for life, one was exiled to the Andaman Islands, and a few like Tuly were imprisoned in their home villages.[65]

In Jundialla, a town long suspected of fostering disloyalty, the British held villagers responsible. Because three men from Jundialla had sailed with Gurdit Singh on the *Komagata Maru* and had been imprisoned for life, the village had to pay a fine of twenty-five thousand rupees. The village paroled Tuly by posting bail of forty thousand rupees, but the police set up a special unit of six men to watch him. Every three hours they checked to see if he was home, and he was required to report to them each morning and evening. "The Brahman policeman asked me to salute him," remembered Tuly, "but I told him, 'If you want me to salute, you can do it to me first.' " The police kept Tuly confined to his village of Jundialla for almost eight years.[66]

Repression simply fired the fervor of the Punjabi nationalists and insured that the revolutionary tradition was to live on in the Doaba, a region in the central Punjab. The harsh treatment of Ghadar Party members created resentment among Sikhs who had been hastily mustered into the European war and had fought in France, Egypt, and Mesopotamia. Elsewhere, however, Indians rallied to the British, raised money, and recruited troops. The failure of India to rise in revolt forced nationalist students to search for new allies among Britain's enemies. For revolutionaries seeking aid, Germany now seemed India's hope.

Parsi merchants arrive at Ellis Island, 1907. Source: "Some of Our Immigrants," *National Geographic* (May 1907): 328.

Sikhs aboard the *Komagata Maru* at Vancouver, May–July 1914. Source: Vancouver Public Library, Vancouver, Canada (VPL 6232).

Taraknath Das in cadet
uniform at Norwich
University, 1909. Source:
William Arba Ellis,
*Norwich University 1819–
1911: Her History, Her
Graduates, Her Roll
of Honor*, 3 vols.
(Montpelier, Vt., Capital
City, 1911), 3:490.

Indian railroad workers take time out to have their picture taken in Plumas County, Ca.
1910. Source: Plumas County Museum, Quincy, Calif.

Indians in Canadian sawmill, ca. 1910. Source: University of British Columbia, Vancouver, Canada (BC 489/4).

Indians in Canadian lumberyard, ca. 1910. Source: University of British Columbia, Vancouver, Canada (BC 489/7).

After three years in the gold mines, Indian adventurer awaits passage to India, 1857–1859. Source: R. R. Olmsted, ed., *Hutchings' Illustrated California Magazine* (Berkeley: Howell-North, 1962).

Sikhs pose for formal studio photograph in Sacramento, 1910. Source: California State Library, Sacramento, Calif.

9
Germany: India's Hope

Peacefulness has made you impotent.
There is no strength left in your youths.
—Ghadar protest song

In 1914, a forty-one page pamphlet titled *Deutsch-land—Indiens Hoffnung* (*Germany—India's Hope*) was published in Göttingen. The pamphlet was probably meant for captured Indian soldiers, but it signaled publicly the opening of a new battlefront. Henceforth, Germany would look to India and support anti-imperialism as a way to weaken the British war effort in Europe. While the German attempt to weaken Britain by attacking its colonial empire ultimately failed, it was a great concern to the British and a major opportunity for Indians abroad to gain experience from foreign allies for their independence movement.[1]

In the more than sixty years since the Germans opened their third front, historians have not been able to answer the questions raised at the time. There is no consensus as to when the Germans began to assist Indians in Germany and in the United States. It has not been settled how much assistance was given or for what purposes. Nor has there been any analysis of the effect of German activities in terms of the experience gained by the Indians and the potential for foreign assistance to the liberation forces in India. The third front was far more important than the British acknowledged publicly and was an important transition in the experience of some Indian nationalists, who moved to the left after the war to work with the Russian Bolsheviks and to found the Communist Party in India.[2]

The question of when Germans began working with Indians was the most important issue involving India during World War I because it was linked to the question of war guilt. If the British could prove that the Germans were stirring up revolt in India before the war in Europe began, it would help them to establish their national innocence and make the upsurge in the Indian liberation movement coincide with German assistance rather than with the outbreak of the European war. There were three areas in which the British suggested that German assistance had preceded the war: the attempt by Sikhs aboard the *Komagata Maru* to challenge Canadian exclusion laws and the subsequent riot in Budge Budge; the formation of the Ghadar Party and the return of Sikhs to

India to foment rebellion; and the formation of an Indian independence committee in Berlin (thereafter referred to as the BIC). German foreign ministry records and other available documents give answers to most of these questions.

The *Komagata Maru* episode is not mentioned at all in German documents. An analysis of Canadian and British sources indicates that there was little basis to the claim that this voyage was engineered by the Germans to embarrass the British. In early December 1914, the London *Daily Chronicle* announced that the Canadian government had definite evidence that the *Komagata Maru* enterprise was arranged by the German government. A Canadian immigration agent said that the German consulate in Canada was involved, and a member of parliament from British Columbia announced that a German brokerage firm in Hong Kong had chartered the vessel and worked with Gurdit Singh.

There is no doubt that the Germans were aware of the disruptive influence of Indian nationalism. But German interest focused first on the possibilities in the Middle East and the potential of Pan-Islamism in India. After military leaders discussed the potential for such a movement in India and Germany, German newspapers began to report revolutionary nationalist activity in 1913. The German consul general first recommended an active anti-British policy in India in 1913. The *Berliner Tagblatt* published an article on 6 March 1914 titled "England's Indian Trouble," which said that secret societies of revolutionaries were being assisted from outside. A young English scholar visiting Bonn in July 1914 found professors and students full of talk about the coming war, in which it was predicted that the British colonies would rebel. The benefit of such activity, and the itch to become involved in it should conflict develop with Great Britain, increased as international tensions arose. On the eve of war, Wilhelm II wrote: "Our Consuls in Turkey and India, agents, etc. must get a conflagration going throughout the whole Mohammedan world against this hated, unscrupulous, dishonest nation of shopkeepers—since if we are going to bleed to death, England must at least lose India." General Helmuth von Moltke wrote to the German foreign office on 2 August 1914, the day that the German-Turkish treaty was signed: "If Britain becomes our opponent, attempts will have to be made to instigate a rebellion in India." According to Nirode Kumar Barooah, an Indian historian who studied the official relations between India and Germany during this period, however, no prewar preparations were made for such a Pan-Islamic movement. The Göttingen pamphlet appeared in fall after the war began.[3]

Nor is there evidence from undercover agents in Canada or India that Indians were working with the Germans before war was declared. Hopkinson had reported that Gurdit Singh was said to have had a stack of seditious literature in a safe in his cabin and that guns were thought to have been supplied by local Indians, but he made no mention of German involvement. During the stay of the *Komagata Maru* in Vancouver, Canadian officials and newspapers often said that financing had been handled by the German government. After war was declared, the old rumors were revived and given more credence, but the Canadian government admitted that it had "no definite evidence that the enterprise was arranged by the German government."[4] Finally, an inquiry by the Indian government confirmed that there was no evidence of German participation in the *Komagata Maru* incident beyond the fact that the ship was chartered from a German agent at Hong Kong. There was no record of financial assistance, and some reports indicated that the German agent had even tried to dissuade the men from chartering the ship. The inquiry suggested that Indian revolutionary societies in America were in touch with societies in Germany, but it also pointed out that most of the emigrants had fully expected that they would be allowed to land. Leaders had misled them, and court decisions had encouraged their delusion. Revolutionary organizations promoted dissatisfaction while the ship was in Canadian waters, and the Indians were in a dangerous frame of mind when they left. They should have been searched for weapons before being allowed to land in India, the report concluded. None of the later claims of German involvement offered any more evidence than the inquiry. The *Komagata Maru* voyage seems to have been entirely an Indian idea; the participants neither sought nor received the assistance of the German government.[5]

The second question, concerning the involvement of Germans in the prewar formation of the Ghadar Party, is more complex. The major source for claims of German involvement is the transcript of a conspiracy trial held in Lahore in September 1915. According to testimony in this trial, the German consul in San Francisco, Franz Bopp, was a special guest at the 31 December 1913 meeting of the Ghadar Party, where plans were made to send a military force and arms to India. These claims were repeated in the subsequent conspiracy trial for violation of neutrality laws in the United States, a trial that is discussed in chapter 10. These claims originated with an Indian who was testifying for the government in India, however. Detailed reports made at the time by Hopkinson do not mention Bopp's presence at the meeting. Nor did Har Dayal mention any German involvement while he was still in the United States. While Dayal might have concealed the presence of the consul, it is unlikely that Hopkinson would have done so. There is nothing in the German foreign office records to indicate any meeting. The papers of Bopp or of the British foreign office might provide conclusive evidence, but the British claims of Bopp's prewar involvement with the Ghadar Party remain highly suspect.[6]

The third question, concerning when the Germans formed the BIC, is easier to answer. If Dayal was working with the German consul, then his flight from San Francisco to Europe in April 1914 was simply a transference of activities. While it is true that Dayal may have made some contact with the German consulate in San Francisco, he did not go directly to Germany but went instead to Switzerland. Some letters sent by Dayal to Ghadar Party members during this period, which might have shed light on his first months in Europe, were destroyed by Frieda Hauswirth, who was married to an Indian and transmitted letters for Ghadar Party members. Letters from Dayal to Van Wyck Brooks, however, indicate only that Dayal was writing for the Ghadar papers. The British criminal intelligence division reported that Dayal was working actively in Geneva for the Indians after war was declared, and German records confirm that Dayal made contact with the German consul in Geneva soon thereafter. Dayal later traveled to Constantinople, but he paid his own way; though he proposed a plan to gain help from Germans, the first mention in the German records of a contact with Dayal is dated 1 September 1914.[7]

While Dayal was developing contacts in Geneva, the German foreign office was already contacting Indians in Europe. The initiative to do so came from Baron Max von Oppenheim, a man who appears to have been somewhat like a German counterpart of Britain's Lawrence of Arabia. Oppenheim, a scholar and writer of travel books, had long been interested in the colonial possessions of France and England. He had traveled to Morocco, Egypt, and other colonies in northern Africa to lend support to revolutionary movements there. Oppenheim brought his Middle Eastern interests to the German foreign office. He wrote on 18 August 1914, two weeks after the war began, that unrest in India could force Britain "to conclude an early peace favorable to us." It was Oppenheim who apparently first suggested that Indians in Germany be contacted. By 31 August the German foreign office had a list of the names of specific Indians and the name of the Hindustan Association as a possible group from which to recruit.[8]

The documents generated during this first organizing attempt indicate that the Germans realized the importance of the Indian front as soon as the war began. They do not, however, indicate any prior organization or contact. One piece of evidence indicates that the German foreign office felt that peacetime support for revolution was not an acceptable policy. At the end of the war, the BIC asked Otto Gunther Von Wesendonk, the German official with whom it had worked, to arrange a continuing relationship; Wesendonk penned his response in the margin: "In peace as before?" The Germans made no plans to continue their official support for Indians in peacetime. This reluctance resulted in part from the lack of any ideology that saw Great Britain as a permanent enemy and in part, no doubt, from the lack of an anti-imperialist ideology such as that which led the Bolsheviks to seek Indian allies after the war. Collaboration with Indians appears to have been strictly a wartime measure.[9]

The war, however, provided a rich and complex range of possibilities for collaboration between the Germans and Indian nationalists. For simplicity, only four aspects of this collaboration are dealt with here: relations between the German government and the BIC; Germans' relations with agents sent by the committee to the United States; Indians' relations with German officials in the United States who helped nationalists to send arms to India; and Germans' relations with the Ghadar Party.

Most important, for both Germans and Indians, was the BIC, and most important for the BIC was its leadership. German documents establish beyond a doubt that Viren Chattopadhyaya was the leader of the BIC from its beginning, and that his concept of the nationalists' relationship with the German government dominated it. The BIC began when the German foreign office contacted Oppenheim to ask him which Indians in Germany and in neutral countries might be willing to work with the committee. During the first week of September 1914, Oppenheim met with Indians in Berlin and asked some of the hundred Indians scattered around the rest of Germany to come to Berlin for talks. He requested that money be deposited in a Swiss bank to pay for Indian students to go to Bombay, Lahore, and Calcutta and planned to send an Indian to the United States to organize. Both Dayal and Chattopadhyaya would be good men for an expedition to Afghanistan, Oppenheim told the foreign office, which was at that time interested primarily in the northwestern provinces of India. There, Germans hoped to contact the border tribes and convince them of the necessity of Indian-Afghan friendship. Oppenheim could find no Indians as capable as Dayal and

Chattopadhyaya among the group of Indian patriots in Switzerland who had already formed themselves into a committee called the *Deutscher Verein der Freunde Indien* (German Society of Friends of India).[10]

Dayal, the brilliant young Oxford student who had renounced his scholarship and then gone to the United States in 1911, is the better known of the two men. His prominence resulted in part from the fact that the British wished to emphasize the contact between Ghadarites in the United States and the German government, and in part from his flamboyant history. It is clear that Dayal had arrived in Constantinople from Geneva by 14 September for the German embassy there asked the German foreign office to transmit a telegram from him to Indians in America, asking them to come to Constantinople. The telegram, sent to New York, requested that Indians be sent from New York and California, that they have British passports for travel to India, and that they bring six months' expense money. By early October, the first two Indians had left Berlin for America. They were to work with an Indian in New York in locating other men for the Afghanistan expedition. The German foreign office asked Dayal to send suggestions for participants in the expedition.[11]

The embassy informed the foreign office that Viren Chattopadhyaya was also a good man to work with. Chatto, as he came to be called, was an ardent nationalist who spoke German, French, and English fluently. The eldest son of an Indian educator who had studied chemistry in Germany and founded a school in Hyderabad, Chatto had gone to England in 1901 to study but had failed the Indian civil service examination. Turning to law and politics, he joined a group of Indian nationalists who talked of independence, became an editor of the *Indian Sociologist*, and met students involved in the assassination of Curzon Wyllie. These political activities led to his expulsion in 1909 from the Middle Temple, where he was studying law, and his continued involvement with Indian nationalists to a warrant for his arrest in June 1910. The cause for the warrant was apparently a letter intercepted by the English police in which Chatto discussed his willingness to send rifles from Europe to India.

Fleeing to France, Chatto worked with Indian nationalists there and joined the French Socialist Party. In 1913, after the French suppressed nationalist activity, he went to Switzerland, and from there to Germany in 1914. He began working with the Soviets late in 1917, eventually moved to Russia, and died mysteriously in 1925 in Moscow, where he had gone to continue his revolutionary activities after the end of the war. Unlike Dayal, however, Chatto never recanted the nationalist goal of an independent India. According to recent biographers of Agnes Smedley, who went to Germany to work with Chatto from 1919 to 1925, he was the most widely respected Indian nationalist in Europe. As one observer noted, he had "a tongue like a razor and a brain like hell on fire."[12]

At the urging of the German foreign office, Chatto went to Berlin along with a man named Champarkaraman Pillai to help organize the BIC. Pillai, who headed the Indian group in Switzerland, had been taken to England by missionaries as a young child. From England, he went to Italy and then to Switzerland, where he started the International Pro-Indian Committee, composed of about twenty Indian students, mostly nationalists. Like Chatto, Pillai immediately shifted his interest to Germany when the French curtailed nationalist activities. He began organizing a volunteer corps of Indians, to be composed of men already in Europe as well as Indian prisoners of war captured by the Germans. Pillai probably arranged for publication of the 1914 pamphlet, *Deutschland—Indiens Hoffnung.*[13]

It was Chatto who finally convinced Dayal to join the others already in Berlin—something Chatto later regretted. At the time, however, Dayal seemed to be an important link in the Indian network. After contacting the German embassy in Constantinople, Dayal had disappeared without a word and turned up in Geneva, where he grumbled to the German consul general that his proposals were not accepted in Constantinople and it was useless to remain there. Dayal refused to go to Berlin until the foreign office wired the consul at Bern to give Dayal travel money and a ticket. Chatto had wired: "Must speak you immediately request you start at once Berlin for a few days intend leaving shortly don't let any consideration prevent your coming." Dayal put off going to Berlin, telling the German consul that he wanted to remain in Zurich and work as an independent writer for India, that his assistance in Berlin was not necessary, and that he had heard that German help would be only for the duration for the war. He turned down all offers of money to go until Chatto went to Zurich to talk to him. By the time the two men had finished their discussion, Dayal was ready to accept a "loan" to continue his work in Zurich and had promised to go to Berlin to help later.[14]

The German general staff had just approved the sending of weapons to India when Dayal arrived in Berlin in November 1914. The German consul in Bern thought that Dayal was growing ambitious and that he was no longer satisfied to work in Switzerland. At any rate, both Dayal and Basant Singh, a young representative from the Ghadar Party in San Francisco, were in Berlin by the end of November. During the next six months, Dayal made another trip to Constantinople to set up a propaganda center aimed at reaching Indian troops sent by the British to guard the Suez Canal. Again he disappeared mysteriously from Constantinople. Chatto left Berlin to meet Dayal in Constantinople at the end of July 1915 after going to Italy to arrange for propaganda work there.[15]

The two men agreed to attempt action in Bucharest, Sofia, and Athens. Chatto then contacted members of the Young Turk Party and met with the Rumanian anarchist P. Musoiu, whom he encouraged to increase literary work against the war and to preach among the peasants to stir up revolt. Chatto asked Berlin to send copies of William Jennings Bryan's article attacking British colonialism in India and of an article by the Italian anarchist Malatesta. Dayal, meanwhile, abandoned the whole scheme and went back to Berlin, where he wrote in mid-August that the secret police were after Chatto and that he should leave Sofia. Dayal insisted that he was not aware of or responsible in any way for Chatto's plans of work in the Balkans, and he held up the promised funds in Berlin.[16]

From Dayal's correspondence in the German foreign office, it is clear that he wanted California and the Ghadar Party to be the focus of the work of the BIC, whereas European-based nationalists like Chatto were more interested in the Near East. Ram Chandra, editor of *Ghadar*, complained to Dayal in the spring of 1915 that he was receiving little help from the Germans, and Dayal urged the BIC to send money to Chandra if it wanted help from California. Again in June, Dayal urged the committee to be more active in working among students in the United States, to secure new workers, and to keep contact with Chandra. In August, Dayal demanded to know whether the German consul general at San Francisco had been authorized to give financial support to Chandra. Dayal had already asked several Americans to join him in Berlin to work on plans and had written a number of letters to friends in the United States, including some to anarchist Alexander Berkman, copies of which were obtained by the British and turned over to the United States government.[17]

Indians in Berlin were not sure how Dayal's letters had been obtained by the British. Some thought that other Ghadar Party members in San Francisco had shown the letters carelessly or perhaps that an American anarchist friend of Dayal, John Sloan, was working under cover for the British. After Dayal's letters became public in the fall of 1915, the BIC gave him no further assignments. In October 1915, after the collapse of the Near East venture, Dayal wrote to the German foreign office that he was going to Amsterdam to cable money to American friends and to secure the services of "socialist and anarchist comrades" for important work in England and India. The committee knew nothing of his departure. By early January 1916, conflict between Chatto and Dayal finally reached a climax. Dayal had asked a couple named Gustav and Alta Stiller, along with two California women, to come to Berlin. The BIC believed that the Stillers should not come to Germany and asked that they return to the United States from Amsterdam, where they had just landed. The committee also asked Pillai to send a telegram to the two Californians, Ethel Dolson of San Francisco and Amy Dudley of San Diego, saying "Do not risk voyage to Europe."[18]

Dayal, who had returned to Berlin, was now disaffected from his fellow revolutionaries. He complained to the German foreign office that he thought the committee was annoyed with him because he had talked frankly to the Germans about the defects and mistakes of the work of the Indians, that he did not care about the committee, and that he would rather conduct business with only the two experienced members of the committee—Pillai and Chatto—and the foreign office. Dayal announced to his friends at the BIC that if they would not work with him, he would work alone or return to Switzerland. He agreed to "the principle of constitutional procedure and the authority of the committee," insisting he had proven his acceptance of the BIC's authority by engaging in no active work for two months. At the same time, however, Pillai sent word from Amsterdam that Dayal had been visiting the German consul there. Chatto concluded that the foreign office had refused to abide by the decision of the committee and was working directly with Dayal. He wrote angrily: "We have decided to withdraw from all cooperation with the Foreign Office until we get . . . a final statement as to the exact position taken by the Foreign Office towards us and towards Mr. Har Dayal."[19]

Dayal discounted the uproar over the authority of the committee. Although the BIC had asked the foreign office to send the Stillers back to New York, Dayal still wanted them to work in British East Africa or China. "Well, let the Committee try to write a book, or deliver lectures, or start revolutionary work in Northern India, or get men for work, or establish the Ghadar party. . . . Let them all combined try to do this," wrote Dayal petulently. The foreign office supported the BIC, however, and early in February 1916, Dayal announced that he was going to

Wiesbaden for a rest and cure. The committee promised to publish and circulate his book, and Dayal said he would work on it there. He later complained that he was under virtual arrest. There is no indication that he was, but he offered it as a reason for recanting his nationalism in 1919.[20]

As complex as was the leadership in Germany, the relationship between German diplomats and the BIC was even more complicated. There is no doubt that the Germans had their own goals for the Indians. As early as 20 August 1914, the German foreign ministry had talked about an expedition from Constantinople to Afghanistan. At that time, several Germans and an Italian were to go to Calcutta, under the guise of a commercial trip, to contact Indian princes, apparently to explore the possibility of supporting an uprising against British rule. The Germans were also concerned about Indian troops being sent to Egypt and planned to distribute anti-British pamphlets there. The policy was stated by German chancellor Theobald von Bethmann-Hollweg in a message to the Constantinople embassy on 4 September: "England seems determined to carry through a war to the knife. France seems to support this plan with its military operations. One of our chief tasks, therefore, is to gradually make England weary through disturbances in India and Egypt, which will only be possible from Constantinople."

By the middle of October, four Indians were in Berlin ready to start an Afghanistan expedition. Pamphlets were being prepared to drop from balloons and airplanes on the Indian border, and the foreign office was anxious to set up a propaganda office in Constantinople. Alfred Zimmermann, under secretary to the foreign minister, believed that passive resistance against the English would start a revolution in India if Turkey joined the war and that terrorism in Afghanistan would make it the Achilles' heel of Russia and England. On 20 October 1914, Turkey joined the Central Powers, and the British rushed Indian troops to safeguard the Suez Canal and the Persian oil fields. Roger Casement, leader of the Irish revolutionaries, who arrived in Berlin early in November and found Zimmermann "warm hearted and warm handed," wrote with enthusiasm from Berlin on 28 November 1914: "India and Egypt will both be in arms."[21]

German officials all over the world began to help with the expected uprisings. Arms were an important element. German ambassador Johann von Bernstorff wrote to the foreign office in Berlin in October 1914 that he had located a firm willing to ship arms to India on a neutral ship if the value was not over sixty thousand dollars and if security for half the purchase cost were given. A few days later military attaché Franz von Papen forwarded a report from New York that Krupp, the weapons dealers, had helped him find some twenty thousand United States army rifles discarded after the Spanish-American War, complete with cartridges, and two or three hundred automatic pistols, all available for $140,000. The weapons could be shipped from South America to Kabul, Afghanistan, and from there smuggled into India. Bernstorff telegraphed early in December that arrangements had been made to purchase for the Indians eleven thousand rifles, four million rounds of ammunition, 250 Mauser pistols, and 500 revolvers with ammunition. The military attaché telegraphed that the troops in Turkey could be bribed, so that weapons would be unnecessary there.[22]

Early in December, the BIC formulated serious plans for a great uprising in India. It expected that as soon as the emir of Afghanistan declared war on England, the British would mobilize Indian troops along the border. Then the revolutionary organization would make an effort to disrupt telegraph and railway communications and to take arsenals. During December, nationwide conferences would take place in India, and revolutionaries would contact local leaders to urge them to support the rebellion. The Germans could capitalize on the great dissatisfaction of Indians in Europe, Africa, and America, especially because of the treatment of Indians in South Africa and Canada and the *Komagata Maru* affair, and build on the revolt already under way against England. Three or four thousand immigrants and workers would return to India and work with the masses, the Germans believed, and the hundreds of students in America who had a national organization of intellectuals and middle-class men would encourage anti-British feeling.

Men sent to America would explore the possibility of setting up a central revolutionary committee in Shanghai. From there, weapons and proclamations could be smuggled into India. The weapons question was of extraordinary significance for the revolution in India. Weapons would be smuggled to Batavia, where more than a thousand Indian workers and merchants lived. The BIC had already picked men to go to Shanghai and Batavia. There was a possibility of purchasing about sixty thousand weapons in Tokyo through the influence of the son of Sun Yat-sen, in addition to the twenty thousand weapons from the United States. The Germans would help the revolutionaries to buy another forty thousand weapons.[23]

A second proposal contained specific plans for work in America. The British, said the committee, were spreading false news of the war, and before the revolution could be successful, accurate news had to be circulated. In September 1914, the BIC had sent two men to the United States with no financial help and no knowledge of conditions in America; these men accomplished little except sending five students to Berlin. Nevertheless, the BIC believed that there were many excellent revolutionaries in America who would be a valuable addition to the cause if sent back to India. The BIC plan was to send students from America to India with information only. A second group of young men was to be sent with instructions in revolutionary work and entrusted with detailed plans of the organization. A third group would be sent with small sums of money, about a hundred pounds each, to do initial organizing work. A fourth group of Punjabis, mainly Sikhs, who were willing to fight for the cause but who were still in America because of lack of funds, would be sent to India later. Three men would also be sent to Indonesia and Shanghai to establish news centers and to carry out the smuggling of arms.

A man with good judgment, business capacity, and full information about the whole movement, as well as a perfect knowledge of the American situation, would be sent from Berlin. In America he was to select men and arrange passage, supervise instruction in explosives, advise the Ghadar Party, and supply them with the funds necessary for sending people from their party back to India. German authorities would make all payments and would receive reports from the Indians. The BIC asked for a hundred thousand marks, fifty thousand for New York and fifty thousand for San Francisco. The overall plan was to capture and hold a piece of land in India, establish a temporary military government in the occupied territory, and then obtain diplomatic recognition for the provisional government established in Berlin.

On 17 December 1915, the BIC wrote to the secretary of state for foreign affairs in the German foreign office to ask for a formal written assurance that if the Indian princes and national leaders waged war against England to establish an independent Indian government, the German government would supply arms, ammunition, officers, money, and eventually diplomatic recognition. Chatto asked that the German government pledge that it had no interests other than commercial and cultural in furthering the cause of Indian national independence. Another uprising was planned for spring of 1916, and Indians wanted additional assurances of the Germans' intentions. A few days later, the German government replied formally that it was ready to give "all the material and moral assistance which it is possible to render under present circumstances." Should the princes and the people of India succeed in establishing a provisional government, the German government was ready to recognize it. Germany, the foreign office affirmed, had only commercial and cultural interests in furthering the cause of national independence in India and was the "true friend of all oppressed nations."[24]

The BIC began to take on the semblance of a provisional government during 1915. The German foreign office established the committee in a comfortable three-story modern house with a German cook. A number of young Indians arrived from the United States. Amin Chand Chaudhry, who had attended high school in Oregon and had studied two years at the Polytechnic College in Oakland, joined them. Shivadeo Singh Ahluwalia came to Berlin from the University of California. Reshi Kesh Latta, who had studied for six months at a private agricultural college in Nevada, also came from California. All told, more than a dozen students made the journey to Berlin to work with the committee, most of them from the United States. They received three hundred marks a month for their work and planned to return to India if their movement was successful.[25]

During 1915 and 1916, the BIC made its main effort to work in America with the official support of the German government. Two Indian officials left Berlin for the United States, Heramba Lal Gupta early in January 1915 and Chandra Chakraberty early in 1916. These two men and the Ghadar Party were to be the main American components in what British and American officials later called the German-Hindu conspiracy.

Heramba Lal Gupta was the first man sent from Berlin to organize Indian collaboration in the United States. Little is known about Gupta's background. He is not mentioned in any of Hopkinson's reports previous to the war, and he first appears in the German records in early February 1915, after he had arrived in New York to talk to von Papen. The BIC then asked that he send men from the United States. The British later intercepted a telegram to Bernstorff, dated 27 December 1914, announcing that Gupta was leaving for America and requested that Bernstorff pay him for his services. According to later German telegrams, Gupta arrived in New York on 20 January, went on to Boston, Chicago, and finally San Francisco where he met the German consul and arranged for collaboration. He apparently made at least one trip to Los Angeles before returning to New York. Gupta helped to coordinate plans for the shipment of weapons and the expected uprising in Afghanistan.[26]

No further mention of Gupta appears in the documents until a December 1915 BIC communication, which reports that the German consul in New York gave Gupta four thousand dollars and that Gupta was able to settle the quarrel between the San Francisco consul and the Ghadar Party. In January 1916, the BIC confirmed that Gupta had left for Japan. He returned to the United States late in 1916, found that a new agent from Berlin was organizing, and refused to cooperate with him. This is the last information about Gupta in the BIC papers until a letter of 11 December 1916, advising the German consul in New York that Gupta should not be paid a hundred dollars monthly because he was not cooperating.[27]

The second Berlin agent, Chandra Chakraberty, left Berlin in early 1916. A schoolteacher and writer, Chakraberty had engaged in anti-British political activity in Calcutta, fled after warrants for his arrest were issued, arrived in the United States sometime in 1910, and settled in New York. He was an avid reader who spent much of his time reading in the Bronx Park and the Bronx Public Library. He later claimed that he had met Leon Trotsky in the library. When Hopkinson investigated him in August 1913, he found nothing suspicious. Chakraberty lived with a German doctor named Ernest Sekunna and had friends among Indian nationalists in New York. He spoke publicly in support of independence but apparently had no connection with the West Coast Indians except through Har Dayal.[28]

Chakraberty is first mentioned in the German records in September 1914, when Har Dayal asked that he come to Germany with Indians from California, bringing British passports and six months' expenses. In March 1915, the BIC asked the German consul in San Francisco to pay Chakraberty eighteen hundred dollars for a trip to India via Italy to take messages to the people of India. Conflicts with the consul caused delays, however, and Chakraberty was not able to leave the United States until late 1915. By that time Gupta had left for Japan, and the BIC decided to send Chakraberty back to the United States to organize work and form a committee. The BIC wanted him to send more Indians to India and to publish literature for India secretly. The BIC asked the German foreign office to provide Chakraberty with passage and a fund of ten thousand dollars; the foreign office approved the request and notified von Papen's office in New York of the arrangement. Von Papen had already left New York at the end of 1915, but his private secretary, Wolf von Igel, had remained as a contact person.[29]

Chakraberty arrived in New York early in February 1916, collected the ten thousand dollars from von Igel, and went to Washington, D.C., to talk to Bernstorff. Before he could start organizing, however, he was involved in a serious auto accident which resulted in a skull fracture and spent almost a month recovering. By May 1916, he was printing leaflets and circulars, but he complained to the foreign office that he needed more money. He planned to go to the Pacific Coast. The Germans gave him another twenty thousand dollars in May.[30]

Four months and thirty thousand dollars had now passed, and Chakraberty seemed to have little to show for it. The BIC wired him on 13 July reminding him that the primary object of the work was "to produce a revolution at home *during* this war." By September he was requesting another thirty thousand dollars to start a new Pan-Asian journal. He was making arrangements to buy arms through the Chinese, he reported to the BIC in September. The Chinese were to buy guns in large quantities in the United States and send them to India in return for financial aid. In January 1917, Chakraberty asked for another twenty thousand dollars. Although warned by the committee that he should leave if it appeared dangerous, he remained in New York.[31]

Although Chakraberty had accomplished little, the British decided to intervene. An agent tipped off the New York bomb squad, and shortly after midnight on 6 March 1917, eight men arrived at Chakraberty's house. One pretended to be a messenger delivering a package, and when the door opened, all eight forced their way in and began a search. They rifled rooms, scooped up bundles of literature printed in Urdu, confiscated a supply of suspicious-looking little aluminum boxes, and hustled Chakraberty and his red-goateed roommate Sekunna down to police headquarters. The inspector made no formal arrests. This was to be only a friendly interrogation. He began with questions about the little boxes. Sekunna explained that they were pillboxes for a patent medicine he had promoted. The investigator went on to the literature, which he could not read but which he thought looked seditious. The bomb squad inspector began to ask questions about the relations of Indians in the United States with Germany. For three hours, Chakraberty refused to answer the questions. Finally, he admitted that he had gone to Berlin to confer with officials in the German foreign office and made a full confession on the condition that it not be used against him in court. After two more hours of questions, Chakraberty was taken to the justice department to be arrested. There, a complaint was drawn up for violation of neutrality laws. Police gave reporters this front-page news while Sekunna and Chakraberty were incarcerated in the Tombs. On 9 March, a grand jury returned indictments against Chakraberty and Sekunna. Two bonding companies refused bonds for the prisoners. One company said it that would not furnish bonds to persons arrested for "un-American activities." Said Chakraberty, "A couple of days in jail will do me no harm. It will rest my nerves." The next day he complained of being ill and was taken to a hospital.[32]

It is not possible to tell from the correspondence just what role Chakraberty was playing. He accomplished very little during the year the BIC stationed him in the United States. He seems not to have taken his arrest and imprisonment very seriously. He later pleaded guilty, testified against other Indians, and served only thirty days in prison. After the war, he worked for the India office. Whatever his relations with the British, his work with the Germans was at least ineffectual and careless.[33]

While Chakraberty may simply have been ineffectual, Gupta eventually worked directly with the British. Gupta was heard from again. He was mentioned in Canadian wires as one of the Indian students at Columbia willing to cooperate with the British. He was arrested in the spring of 1917, confessed to his activities, and was one of four men tried in Chicago for setting a military expedition afoot. Later he testified against other California-based Indians. Since he spent only a few months in the United States, he could describe little of their activities, but he did testify to the relationship between *Ghadar* editor Ram Chandra and the German consul.[34]

Although neither Gupta nor Chakraberty had close ties to the Ghadar Party, the BIC spent considerable time attempting to link up with this group. Barakatullah developed the closest ties with the BIC. He had returned from Japan in the summer of 1914 and helped to coordinate the first group of Sikhs to return to India. Members of this group, returning in August and September, either paid their own expenses or had assistance from the Ghadar Party, but there is no evidence of German involvement until September 1914, when Indians contacted the San Francisco consulate to ask for weapons and officers for the revolt they expected to bring about in India. The consulate agreed to send two men, apparently Taraknath Das and Barakatullah. Barakatullah planned to leave in October, but in late November he was still in New York, waiting to go to Berlin. Das had already gone, but the German ambassador did not know where. By January 1915, Barakatullah was in Berlin, urging the German foreign office to support the plans for revolution. He soon left on a mission to Kabul to gain Muslim support for the Indian revolution. With another Indian, he established a provisional government of India in independent territory between British India and Afghanistan and became prime minister. The British, by increasing financial pressure on the emir, were able to keep Afghanistan neutral throughout the war, but in early 1919, Afghan nationalists assassinated the emir for his pro-British leanings, and his successor proclaimed independence from the British. In any event, Barakatullah did not return to the United States to continue organizing. Das went to China and Japan to conduct propaganda work and was also out of the country for most of the war.[35] Two other California Sikh leaders, Bhagwan Singh and Santokh Singh, had also left the country to participate in direct activity for the revolution. Ram Chandra was the principal West Coast Ghadar organizer and link to the Germans.

Chandra had taken over much of the control of the Ghadar Party by the end of 1914. He was a relative latecomer to the West Coast Indian community. The son of a labor merchant and teacher, he had edited a newspaper called *Akash* in Delhi before going to Japan and on to the United States in 1913. He and his wife Padma both attended high school in Washington, then left for Berkeley, where Padma intended to enroll as a student, in January 1914. Hopkinson reported on their plans in the summer of 1914. Chandra soon joined the Ghadar Party and became editor of *Ghadar*. After Dayal left, he became the leading Hindu member of the party, and after the Sikhs and Barakatullah left, he controlled the finances and most of the party machinery, as well as the editorial policy.[36]

The BIC did not attempt to make direct contact with the Ghadar Party, but it did try to get Indians in California to come to Berlin, and a number did join Dayal and Chatto there. By December, after Barakatullah's arrival, the BIC knew much more about the Ghadar Party. Barakatullah apparently told the committee that there were thousands of Sikhs in California and British Columbia who wanted to return to the Punjab to work for the revolution but who lacked funds. By March 1915, Chandra was giving information to the German consul in San Francisco about conditions in India, but the committee was having difficulty establishing communications with Chandra. A series of BIC telegrams that month specifically instructed him to send men to Berlin to help with propaganda and to confer with the San Francisco consul. Chandra seems not to have been involved in the shipment of arms, although he apparently knew of it and sent several men and Ghadar literature along.

In May 1915, however, he complained that he had still received no financial help. Dayal proposed sending Chandra money and in August 1915 asked him if he had received the money that had been authorized. The problem, evidently, was that the German consul did not trust Chandra because letters from Dayal had become public. Gupta finally straightened the matter out and obtained money from the New York consul to help finance some of the returning Punjabis. By the fall of 1915, some sort of working relationship and financial support had finally been obtained for returning Indians. The total amount of aid was only four thousand dollars, however, and the distrust continued. The BIC avoided working with Chandra and the Ghadar Party and in July 1916 explicitly warned Chakraberty to avoid them as well. "Ghadar men cannot be sent home. They will ruin our work everywhere. They do not understand how to work secretly." By December the BIC was writing; "We do not think the Ghadar organization is doing work justifying the expenditure of so large a sum of money upon them."[37]

It is clear that Chandra did receive financial help from the Germans between March and December of 1916. Just how much he received is uncertain, however. By December, the Ghadar Party had also decided that Chandra was not trustworthy. In January 1917, he was expelled from the party. Soon after, arrests of Indians began in New York and on the Pacific Coast, and the United States joined Britian in its war against Germany. With that alliance, hopes for a German victory—and with it hopes for an independent India—began to decline.[38]

As the prospect of German victory faded, the BIC began to make peace plans. The German and Austro-Hungarian empires were already disintegrating. Before the armistice was signed, left-wing revolts had broken out at Kiel, a socialist republic was formed in Bavaria, and revolutionaries controlled important rail centers and supply depots in Germany. On 9 November the kaiser abdicated and a German republic was proclaimed. Indians were to keep the BIC headquarters building for another year, but the BIC prepared to conclude its work that year. "Four years we have worked together and our mutual interests all this time have been absolutely identified," read the final report of the committee. "The kind help and sympathy that we got from the German Government has now become historical. Whatever interpretation our mutual enemies give to this help it has been inspiring to us, and has opened a new vista before the eyes of the Indian public." The committee asked that sixteen Indians who had come from the United States to Berlin be given German citizenship. The United States government had destroyed the Indian movement there, and forty or fifty Indians were in prison in the States; some of the students could not go back because they were still under indictment. New immigration laws kept out the rest. The students' only option was therefore to remain in Germany. The German government agreed to finance their postwar education in Germany so that they could support themselves.

Some BIC leaders hoped that work with the German government would continue. An unarmed India could not revolt, wrote one committee member, Bhupendra Datta. Indians needed men and money for organizing, as well as a supply of arms, but rich Indians would not help the revolutionaries unless they could see a sure chance of success. Support was needed from outside and a network from inside to import and store arms, distribute propaganda among the masses and soldiers, and maintain communication with foreign countries. Foreign governments could also work to bring the question of Indian independence before international political organizations, make proposals for independence, circulate literature on India, form pro-India parties, teach Indians to manufacture firearms, give them military training, and import arms to India. India needed the help of other nations to become free, Datta concluded. It was his query that brought the response "In peace as before?"[39]

The Germans had embarked on their India venture purely as a war measure. There was no indication of interest in continued support for the struggling revolutionaries. Even if the German government had had any flicker of interest, it would have been difficult to fan it into open support. Germany faced a civil war, and with the tide of revolution still rising at home, the government had no interest in assisting revolution elsewhere. In late 1921, a delegation of fourteen Indians left Germany to discuss future support from the Bolsheviks. When they returned, the German government, at the instigation of the British, attempted to deport them. The group went underground. Chatto and a small number of other Indians migrated to Russia, and the Soviets began to support the Indian Communist Party and revolution in India.

The entry of the United States into war with Germany as an ally of Great Britain meant that the situation of Indian revolutionaries in the United States would be far different from that of the BIC in Germany. The British government now had an opportunity to portray nationalist organizing in the United States as disloyal to the American government. Prosecution of Indian nationalists followed the growing support of British war aims by the United States government.

10

"Hindu Conspiracy": Neutrality Laws

When the people are not even free to write and speak,
How can any invention take place there?
—Ghadar protest song

During World War I, United States diplomatic officials
took little interest in India. American policy toward India was slow to
develop and did so primarily in response to British concern over the
activities of Indian nationalists in the United States. Central to U.S. policy
was the prosecution of Indian nationalists for conspiracy to violate the
neutrality laws of the United States. In April 1918, a San Francisco federal
jury found twenty-nine defendants guilty of conspiring to violate the
law prohibiting military expeditions against countries with which the
United States was at peace. These men were convicted for activities that
formed the basis of what British and United States officials called the
"Hindu conspiracy." United States officials halted the activities of the
most militant nationalists by using the conspiracy statute to expand the
number of activities that could be prosecuted under the neutrality laws.

At the trial, the United States attorney presented the first historical
interpretation of the "Hindu conspiracy." The activities of the militant
Indian nationalists, he said, were a reprehensible but relatively ineffectual response to British rule. Indians had participated in an insidious
conspiracy that "permeated and encircled the whole globe" and was
directed by the Germans against the United States as well as against the
British Empire. Documentation in the massive court record, together
with numerous newspaper articles about the trial, Indian publications,
and a number of popular spy accounts, formed the basis for the histo-
riography of the "Hindu conspiracy" for almost half a century.[1]

As new archival sources in India became available in the late 1950s
and early 1960s, a second interpretation of the "Hindu conspiracy" began to undermine the older version.[2] While still accepting the idea that
the activities of Indians were a conspiracy, scholars began to question
whether those activities were reprehensible, ineffectual, or inherently
anti-American. These scholars looked at nationalist activities in the
United States in a positive light and considered them preliminary steps
in India's struggle for freedom. Arun Coomer Bose, for example, saw

the early actions of Indians in the United States as a prelude to national self-determination.[3]

This new evaluation of the significance of American-based efforts to achieve Indian independence led eventually to a third interpretation, which focused on government activities and on those of the Indians and examined the way British and American officials responded to the Indian movement. In a 1971 article based on British documents, Don Dignan attempted to answer this question from the British side. Using diplomatic correspondence between Spring-Rice and the British foreign office, Dignan demonstrated the great concern of British officials about the Indian revolutionary movement in the United States. More recently, Rhodri Jeffreys-Jones has used American state department records to argue that the purpose of the San Francisco trial was to discredit the revolutionaries and was "the occasion of an attempt to justify retrospectively the administration's harassment of a nationalist group at a time when the United States was going to war to further the cause of self-determination."[4]

Canadian and American justice department documents show that British officials translated their concern into pressure on the American government to arrest political activists. Justice department officials responded by using the conceptual framework of conspiracy as an ideological and legal weapon against the Indians. The term *Hindu conspiracy* became part of the government attempt to discredit Indian revolutionaries. *Hindu* was a common term of opprobrium in early-twentieth-century America and was used to identify all Indians, regardless of religion. *Conspiracy*, likewise, was a negative term that confused ideological and legal issues. By designating Indian revolutionary activities as a conspiracy and then by applying the conspiracy statute to them, government officials were able to arrest the men legally and justify the interruption of their political activities as an enforcement of the neutrality laws.

The conspiracy statute, then section 37 of the penal code, prohibited conspiracy to violate a federal law. Only two neutrality laws applied to the activities of persons within the United States. One law, section 10, prohibited the enlistment of men to fight in a foreign army at war against a nation with which the United States was at peace. The second, section 13, prohibited the organization of a military expedition against such a nation. For simplicity, I refer to these statutes as the recruiting law and the military expedition law.

The justice department used only the military expedition law against the Indian activists. This tactic may appear strange at first since one of the important points made in the trial was that German money was given to the Indian Ghadar Party to help Indians return to India. Evidence showing that large numbers of men did return was offered as documentation of conspiracy. There were apparently two reasons why the recruiting law could not be used effectively by the justice department. First, Indian leaders did not actually recruit and organize in a strict military sense. They simply urged men to return to India and lent money to those who needed it. Second, the justice department probably did not use this statute because the British had earlier insisted on a very narrow definition of recruiting.

By 1917 the United States had a long history of prosecutions under the 1794 military expedition law. During the nineteenth century the government had prosecuted Irish Fenian revolutionaries and Cuban *insurrectos*. Such trials were generally not popular in the United States, and the government had great difficulty in obtaining convictions, particularly against the Cuban insurrectos, who had gained much public support for Cuban independence.

During the Mexican revolution, the attorney general originally interpreted the military expedition law strictly, and United States attorneys along the Mexican border occasionally clashed with military officers who wanted to use the military expedition law to put down the revolution. Beginning in 1906, the United States arrested and tried a number of Mexican rebels, or revoltosos, under the military expedition law. There was such popular support for these men, however, that only a few were successfully prosecuted. To surmount the reluctance of juries to convict these men, the justice department began charging the men with conspiracy to violate the neutrality laws. The department successfully prosecuted several individuals under the conspiracy law in 1908.

Under President Taft and Secretary of State Knox, the government returned to a strict interpretation of the neutrality laws. Despite the attempts of the attorney general to continue prosecuting Mexican revolutionaries from 1908 to 1912, few actual prosecutions took place. The public was sympathetic to the revoltosos, the border was long, and the support from the president was minimal. Groups met freely to discuss and plan their activities. Only when revolutionaries engaged in overt action did the government attempt to prosecute, and courts usually refused to define a small group of men as a military force. While the justice department continued to argue that the conspiracy statute could be applied in neutrality cases, its lack of success was evident. In 1912 the department filed indictments against two groups of Mexican revolutionists for conspiring to violate the military expedition statute, but neither case was brought to trial. In mid-1915, the department charged two prominent revolutionaries, generals Victoriano Huerta and Pascual Orozco, with conspiracy to violate the statute. Orozco escaped and Huerta died before the trial could begin.[5]

At the time Indians engaged in most of the activities later labeled the "Hindu conspiracy," then, the courts had been reluctant to accept conspiracy as a connecting link between the activities of individual revolutionaries, and usually defined overt action very narrowly in military expedition cases. The Germans did attempt to ship arms to India, and five Indians planned to sail with the arms. In addition, Indians participated in several attempts to further the cause of the Indian revolution. None of these activities, however, constituted a clear-cut violation of neutrality laws unless the conspiracy statute was applied. Conspiracy required only that two people "conspire" to commit some illegal act and then that one person make an overt act toward executing the plan. An action of a single person thus might not violate neutrality statutes, but the same action, if discussed with another person, would constitute a violation. Although the conspiracy statute was of great assistance in obtaining convictions, it confused the legal issues involved. As one legal researcher said of the statute after reviewing the government's widespread use of it in the 1960s: "It distracts the courts from the policy questions or balancing of interest that ought to govern the decision of specific legal issues and leads them instead to decide those issues by reference to the conceptual framework of conspiracy. . . . It gives the courts a means of deciding difficult questions without thinking about them."[6]

Conspiracy was not a new legal concept. It had a history in England dating back to the thirteenth century. American workers had fought a long and ultimately successful battle during the nineteenth century against the application of conspiracy laws to their organized attempts to raise wages and improve working conditions. In 1921, the supreme court ruled that the conspiracy statute could not be applied to labor unions. By then the federal government had given the statute new life by applying it to internal security cases involving political activists. Later convictions for conspiracy to violate the Selective Service and Espionage acts of 1917, the Smith Act of 1940, and the Selective Service Act of 1967 are better known than the Indian neutrality convictions, but all were part of the tradition that expanded the conspiracy statute to hinder the activities of political groups. In the Indian trial, the justice department achieved its first important successful application of the statute to the military expedition law. Success in the trial depended upon creating the concept of "Hindu conspiracy."[7]

There were three stages in the creation of this concept. The first stage began in December 1908, when Roland Brittain investigated the "alleged Hindu conspiracy" in British Columbia, and it ended with the assassination of W. C. Hopkinson in 1914. During this period, the British began surveillance of Indian nationalists in Canada and the United States.[8]

During the second stage, from 1914 to mid-1916, the British exerted diplomatic pressure on the United States to suppress the movement for independence in India, continued covert surveillance activities in the United States, and engaged in anti-Indian propaganda.

The cause of the heightened concern of the British government in 1914 was the large number of Indians who, after war broke out between Britain and Germany, returned to India from North America to work toward revolution. Of an estimated ten thousand Indians in North America in 1914, as many as two thousand may have left for India during the first three months of war. There were no laws against Indians leaving the United States, whatever their intent, as long as they did not organize a military expedition and had not been recruited for a foreign army. The British Empire in India had well-fortified defenses against these men: a widespread network of surveillance and informers, and the Ingress into India Ordinance, passed by the British India government at the beginning of the war, which allowed subversives to be arrested summarily and held without trial. Even after large numbers of men had been arrested, however, revolutionaries continued to smuggle in copies of *Ghadar* which openly advocated the overthrow of the British government in India.[9]

During 1915 Spring-Rice asked that a shipment of arms the Germans had purchased in New York for shipment to Mexico on the *Annie Larsen* be investigated. British undercover agents knew that the Germans planned to transfer the arms to the *Maverick* in Mexico and to ship them to Batavia for distribution to Indian revolutionaries. There was no discussion by Spring-Rice or by U.S. justice department officials of conspiracy regarding this arms shipment. The only question was about a violation of neutrality laws. There was no evidence of such a violation at the time of shipment or after the fact.[10]

At this time, the British made no attempt to link the arms shipment to the activities of Indian revolutionaries in the United States. Early in

1915, the British government began to forward informal complaints about the Ghadar Party to the U.S. state department, but Spring-Rice refused to lodge an official complaint about the Indian nationalists for another year. At first, he told the British foreign office that he feared unfavorable newspaper publicity. Later, he said Americans would resent British interference. Finally, in February 1916, Spring-Rice agreed to register an official protest, in part because of the anxiety exhibited by the Wilson administration about the activities of German officials in the United States, who had been exposed and publicized primarily by the British, and in part because of the extreme concern in London about unrest in India.[11]

With his protest of February 1916, Spring-Rice sent a transcript of the judgments in the 1915 Lahore conspiracy trial and a military intelligence memorandum showing that German officials had been cooperating with Indians. During the Lahore trial, the British India government had argued that California had been the location for planning a revolution in India. According to the prosecution, five or six thousand Indians had met in Sacramento in August 1914 to launch the conspiracy, and their success had encouraged similar action in India. "The conspiracy had the object of waging war on his Majesty the King Emperor and overthrowing by force the government established by law in India, expelling Europeans and establishing a Swadeshi, or self government," said the governor advocate in summing up his case. As a result of the trial, twenty-four Indians were executed for conspiracy and another twenty-seven were sentenced to long imprisonment.[12]

Later in February, Spring-Rice forwarded to secretary of state Robert Lansing a protest from Charles Hardinge, the viceroy of India, about the Ghadar propaganda and an article by a British newsman purporting to prove that Indian revolutionaries were attempting to overthrow British rule. The reporter claimed that the Ghadar Party was advocating wholesale massacre of all Europeans in India and that Indians were being urged to come to California to learn the manufacture of bombs. He quoted Edwin S. Montagu, the secretary of state at India House in London, who stated that infinite harm was done to British rule in India by the shelter given the revolutionary Ghadar Party and its newspaper in California. Spring-Rice promised to send the state department a memorandum from the British government on revolutionary activities in the United States.[13]

Frank Polk, in charge of neutrality matters in the state department, forwarded the journalist's article to the justice department and urged "radical action" if the article was correct, because the agitation was "causing a great deal of irritation in England." Assistant attorney general Charles Warren, Polk's counterpart in the justice department, replied that his staff had already given considerable attention to the activities of the Ghadar movement but that he had no evidence of a violation of the law.[14]

At the end of February 1916, the British colonial office dispatched Robert Nathan, one of its top intelligence agents in the Indian police, to Canada. Nathan was to coordinate and supplement investigations already under way by detectives hired through the British consul in San Francisco and by Indian informants working under cover among the Indians. About the same time, British military intelligence officials sent a second agent to New York, Colonel Norman Thwaites, who was to work on Indian investigations with William Wiseman, an agent of the British foreign office. Reports were funneled from Nathan and Thwaites to London, and selected information was then forwarded to the embassy in Washington. Bundles of papers on the revolutionary activities of the Indians began to arrive regularly in the state department, accompanied by ever more excited memorandums from Spring-Rice, linking the activities in Berlin and San Francisco to *Annie Larsen* guns shipment, which he called an international conspiracy. The justice department soon had two of its own investigators working on the British complaints, but it still found no evidence of illegal activities.[15]

Among the papers forwarded by the state department to the justice department was a batch of photographs of British atrocities published by the Ghadar Press. These "horrible pictures," as Warren called them, provoked him to instruct legal researchers to "devise some method of prosecuting criminally the Editor of this paper, which has been producing a great deal of trouble on the Pacific Coast." Warren asked John W. Preston, the United States attorney in San Francisco, to conduct a special investigation into the activities of Ram Chandra, editor of *Ghadar*, on the grounds that the newspaper appeared to be inciting murder, arson, and assassination. After dutifully sifting the pictures and articles, Warren's assistant reported back that while the pictures were brutal and offensive to aesthetic taste, they did not violate the law prohibiting the use of the mails for matter tending to incite murder, arson, or assassination. Everything in the material mailed by the *Ghadar* editor was legitimate criticism of governmental activities of the British Empire in India.[16]

Warren's attempt to interfere with the publication program of *Ghadar* in mid–1916 marked the beginning of the third stage of the creation of the concept of "Hindu conspiracy," during which American officials began to share the British opinion. Attorney general Thomas Watt Gregory was under increasing pressure from other members of the administration to halt German activities in the United States even though Congress had refused to expand the internal security laws. In two minor cases involving Germans, the justice department tried to link the *Annie Larsen* shipments to the Ghadar Party in order to show, as the British had argued, the existence of a German-Indian revolutionary plot. Warren's assistant made up long lists of persons connected with what he called the "Hindu insurrection." Any men involved with the shipment of arms, with the San Francisco Ghadar Party, or with the BIC were on the list. Late in June 1916, the justice department considered prosecuting the men involved in the *Annie Larsen* arms shipment. Indictments were to be sought for conspiracy to defraud the United States by filing false manifests and for organizing a military expedition against a friendly nation. The difficulty with this plan, as assistant attorney general S. J. Graham admitted to the state department, was that the justice department had no direct evidence stating the purpose of the expedition and thus could not connect it with the plots to foment revolution in British India. It seemed "reasonably clear" to him that the true destination of the arms was India, but he still needed proof.[17]

During the fall of 1916, a British court at Lahore sentenced seventeen more men for conspiracy and announced that it believed the United States to be the chief center of the movement to overthrow the British Empire. Spring-Rice subsequently complained to the state department that the British government considered the "continuance of German intrigues against British possessions in the East a grave menace and negligence of the United States incompatible with the duties of a neutral power." His accusation that the United States was tolerating "Indian and German intrigues" brought an angry retort from Gregory that the British had not furnished any evidence that would warrant indictment. Any witnesses who might provide evidence, Gregory wrote Lansing, were either "in the hands of British authorities as prisoners, or else have been executed," and "neither a British prisoner nor a corpse is available as a witness in the courts of this country." There were no United States laws against "intrigues," said Gregory, unless they violated a neutrality law or constituted a conspiracy to violate federal law.[18]

In January 1917, Spring-Rice made one more effort to link American intrigues to the Indian conspiracy. He reviewed for Lansing the activities of the Indians in the United States and the statements of the Lahore conspirators. There could be no doubt about the aims of the men who left the United States, he argued. Their purpose was "deadly war against the King, and the overthrow of the government by law established in India." He cited as evidence the papers and pamphlets published by the Ghadar Party, as well as statements that 83 of the 686 men who had returned to India from the United States in 1915 had passed through sedition centers in the United States and that 10 of the 26 convicted in supplementary trials had been influenced by seditious preachings in the United States. He also reviewed the *Annie Larsen* case and included confessions of arrested Indians and a statement by J. B. Starr-Hunt, a purser on the *Maverick*, that five revolutionaries had sailed with him. He titled the whole batch of documents "German-Indian Conspiracy in America." Late in January, Spring-Rice sent more documents to the state department, including additional testimony linking Chandra to the Indians who had sailed on the *Maverick*.[19]

As soon as the state department forwarded these documents to the justice department, Warren rushed them to the U.S. attorney in San Francisco, telling him that the activities of the Ghadar Indians were giving the British "grave concern" and that they were "anxious that the revolutionary movement in this country looking to the liberation of India should cease." He instructed Preston: "I desire that as many as possible be brought to book." January 1917 also brought a big breakthrough for the justice department: it obtained its first conviction for conspiracy to violate the neutrality law in a case involving Franz Bopp, the German consul general at San Francisco. With the conviction of Bopp, the way seemed clear for Warren to push for indictments of the Indians.[20]

While Warren was anxious to push for prosecution, Gregory was still concerned about the accusations of Spring-Rice. He wrote to Lansing in February, explaining that there was nothing illegal about the *Annie Larsen* shipment unless it was part of a military expedition. Starr-Hunt's testimony concerning Indian passengers on the *Maverick* was hearsay and of no value in proving violation of law; moreover, the British had not offered to send him to the United States to testify. The justice department, insisted Gregory, had been "particularly scrupulous" in maintaining its obligation to enforce the neutrality laws. With Gregory's arguments in hand, Lansing composed a memorandum defending the United States from the ambassador's "intemperate" language and insisting that neither the *Annie Larsen* nor the *Maverick* had violated the neutrality laws of the United States. On 28 February 1917, President Wilson approved the Lansing memorandum.[21]

Britain and the United States obviously did not yet share the same goals or strategy in the Indian neutrality case. During the first week of April, however, British undercover agents in New York engineered the arrest of Chakraberty, who immediately confessed that he had received money from the German military attaché to purchase arms and ammunition. Warren, who knew nothing of the role of the British agents in the arrest, was infuriated because he felt that the San Francisco prosecution would be endangered. The British agents, on the other hand, felt popular opinion would now keep the case alive, and they offered to exchange information directly with Warren on Indian suspects. By the time the United States joined Britain as an ally against Germany, the two governments were already collaborating on the case below the diplomatic level.[22]

On the morning of 6 April, before President Wilson had signed the House resolution declaring war, Warren ordered Preston to arrest Ram Chandra and other Indians involved in the "German-Hindu conspiracy." Preston immediately arrested Chandra and sixteen other Indians in San Francisco. The first suspects arrested by the federal government after the United States went to war with Germany were thus Indians. Not until that afternoon did Warren order the arrest of seventy Germans whom he considered the most prominent and dangerous agents in the United States.[23]

Even after these arrests, Preston was not optimistic about obtaining indictments. The *Annie Larsen* case looked good, he wrote to Warren, but not the case against the Ghadarites. He must not continue to think of the Ghadar Party case and the *Annie Larsen* case as two separate cases, Warren replied to Preston. The only difficulty, he admitted, was in proving the connections between Chandra and the German agents in the United States and between Chandra and the five men on the *Maverick*. "There has for some time been no doubt in my mind on these two points," Warren concluded. "The only difficulty has been in the proof." The British rushed Preston more documents and brought Starr-Hunt down from Canada, where he had been secreted, to testify before the San Francisco grand jury. On 1 May 1917, the grand jury brought indictments against Chandra and seven other Indians.[24]

In May, the British agent Nathan met with Preston in San Francisco, and they decided that, because of a lack of evidence, the cases started in Chicago and New York should be combined with the one in San Francisco. Preston supported this consolidation later that month at a strategy conference in Washington with Warren and the United States attorneys from New York and Chicago. The New York case was undeniably weak: two individuals had been sent out separately—hardly a military expedition. Matters in Chicago seemed only slightly better. The prosecution could show only that four or more men had gone out "more or less in a body to commit hostilities against India."[25]

The officials decided to drop the charges against the Indians in New York but to indict Chandra and the other San Francisco men in a Chicago court in order "to give fuller color to the conspiracy in the introduction of evidence." Once indictments had been obtained in Chicago, the San Francisco men would not be tried there. Chicago would be a test case for applying the conspiracy theory to the Indians. If the case was successful, the justice department would make San Francisco the showcase of a "Hindu conspiracy" trial in which convictions would be sought for all the Germans and Indians mentioned in the British documents. On 7 July 1917, the San Francisco grand jury returned secret indictments for conspiracy against 105 men and on 12 July indicted 19 more. The conspiracy, according to the indictments, had begun on 1 August 1914 at a meeting of Indian and German conspirators to prepare a military expedition.

In Chicago, one Indian and three Germans were convicted of violating the neutrality law against military expeditions and of conspiracy to violate this law. Warren commented later that the courts had made a "broad ruling" and that the words *military expedition or enterprise* were given their "broadest definition" in this "Hindu plot" case.[26]

Preston was optimistic by the time the trial began on 12 November 1917. "The evidence is in very good shape," he wrote to Gregory. "The British agents have worked very hard in putting the evidence in accessible form, and I have every reason . . . to believe that the case will result favorably as to all important defendants." The trial, which dragged on for more than five months, revolved around the British version of a worldwide "Hindu conspiracy" dictated by the Germans, who allegedly sought to stir up a revolution in India as part of a master war plan against England.[27]

The advantages that a government has in a conspiracy trial were exploited fully in San Francisco. The charge of conspiracy branded the Indians with the image of secrecy and evil plotting, which heightened apprehensions already present in San Francisco during that first winter of the war. Hearsay evidence rules were relaxed to allow the words of alleged conspirators to be used against each other. The defendants were confronted with the recitation of a hodgepodge of alleged acts and with the statements of other defendants, which the government hoped might persuade the jury of the existence of a conspiracy. All the government had to prove was that two defendants conspired to bring about some illegal act and that one person then made an overt act to further that conspiracy. The government did not have to prove actual criminal acts. Assistant U.S. attorney Annette Adams summed up the government's case against the "Hindu conspirators" by labeling them tools of German agents and appealing to the jury to "hold the line for democracy." The jury found all the defendants, with the exception of an American ship-builder and millionaire from Long Beach, California, guilty of conspiring to launch a military expedition in violation of the criminal code.[28]

The political cost of the trial was high for the Indians. Undercover agents, informers, and government witnesses demoralized and divided the revolutionaries and made it difficult for them to know whom to trust. The trial so heightened tensions within the Indian community that one of the accused went mad in his cell. A second man shot and killed Ram Chandra during the trial itself and was, in turn, shot by a marshal. Publicity emphasizing Indian nationalist collaboration with German officials made the Indian revolutionary movement appear to be a conflict essentially different from that waged by the American colonies against Great Britain 160 years earlier.[29]

Convictions meant more to Britain than to the United States, as Preston admitted to Gregory. Success in the case, he explained, resulted from the "able and exhaustive" investigations by the British, which supplemented his own. The British had assigned their best agents to the case. They furnished complete and accurate reports, provided at least three key witnesses and several confessions, and coached Preston and Adams in presenting the case. Preston told newsmen that he thought the verdict showed "that this country is now realizing that we must teach the non-assimilable, parasitic organizations in our midst that while this is a land of liberty, it is not a country of mere license."[30]

The trial had in fact made the United States less a land of liberty. It openly established the United States government as opposing the movement for political liberation in India and put a seal of disapproval on participation by Americans in that movement. Government disapproval did not stop Americans from continued participation in the Indian liberation movement, but it did signify that the government would deal with the issue of Indian independence from a position essentially the same as that of Great Britain.[31] That position included translating what the British termed the "Hindu conspiracy" from historical to legal terms. This is not to say that there was a British "conspiracy" or that the British manufactured their evidence—only that historians need to look more carefully at the activities of officials who responded to the Indians' movement. In the words of German chancellor Theobald von Bethmann-Hollweg, this was to be a "war to the knife." In such a war, it was difficult to separate anticolonialism from conspiracy. Certainly, the Indians were conspiring against the British. Political refugees had long used the United States as a base for revolutionary activities. Some men had violated the neutrality laws as well. But to equate political conspiracy with violation of the law through the conspiracy statute was to move the United States one step away from the political refuge it had been. That step also made it more likely that the government would move to a yet more extreme position—the deportation of Indian political prisoners to India.

11

Friends of the Freedom of India: Deportation

Why do we feel low and humiliated?
—Ghadar protest song

Arrest and imprisonment for violations of neutrality laws ended one battle for the Indians and began another. As convicted aliens, the imprisoned men might be deported upon their release from prison. Deportation to India for men convicted of revolutionary activities was far more serious than imprisonment in the United States, for it could mean a much harsher sentence or even execution. The Indians knew that only through organizing further and garnering the support of American citizens could they avoid deportation of the revolutionaries.

The American government had a long tradition not only of harboring political revolutionaries but also of refusing to deport political offenders. Such deportation clearly put the United States in the position of supporting the government against which the revolutionaries had acted. Handing over a political offender often meant certain death, and American officials were reluctant to take that responsibility. During the Mexican revolution, for example, the state department had consistently opposed the deportation of political offenders. Extradition agreements with foreign governments normally carried an article that excluded persons charged with crimes of a "purely political character." Most Mexican revoltosos were able to escape deportation because of these articles and because of the legal assistance they were able to obtain. The state department, in reviewing the issue in 1906, determined that only anarchists could be deported. Despite arrests and detentions of a large number of revoltosos, few were actually deported. Now, however, the success of the neutrality convictions of the Indians reopened the question of deportation of political prisoners.[1]

Fear of deportation was not new in 1918. The labor department had already used the process against Indian workers on the West Coast and had threatened its use against Har Dayal in 1914. Deportation of Sikh laborers had been fairly easy for the labor department to accomplish during the years when West Coast politicians were pressing for exclusion. Deporting radicals had not proven so simple. As long as the country was not willing to exclude Indians from using the United States as a political asylum, there was little basis for deporting Indians for their political activity. After the arrest of Dayal in 1914 and the outburst of support from liberals and radicals, Caminetti had been more careful. The British occasionally asked him to investigate immigrants who were allegedly aiding rebels in India, but Britain made no official protest about the activities of the men.[2]

Caminetti did cooperate informally with British officials, however. The United States deportation laws required that a deportable alien be returned "to the country from whence he came." This apparently straightforward wording became complex when it had to be interpreted. Indians came from Shanghai, from Hong Kong, and from Canada. The labor department had to decide whether the men should be deported to Canada, to China, or to India. It did not take long for immigration officials to decide that the clause really meant "to remove as far as possible." Each Indian to be deported was booked through to India.[3]

The policy still presented difficulties, for every ship going from San Francisco to India had to stop to coal at Yokohama. As soon as a ship docked, the Indians would walk down the steerage gangplank and simply disappear. These disappearances bothered the British, and authorities in Hong Kong volunteered to arrange for transshipment of the deportees to India if the United States would deliver them to Hong Kong. One consul suggested that the Indians be deported only in American ships so they could be watched better, but immigration officials in Washington, D.C., worked out a system that was to be used increasingly as the European war continued. In May 1916, the immigration bureau asked West Coast immigration officers to send immigration officials in Vancouver weekly abstracts showing available data on Indians sailing from ports in their districts to Asia. This information allowed the British not only to arrest anyone they considered suspicious, but also to keep track of men more carefully when they were deported.[4]

When Indians were deported, however, most were deported directly to India. In the spring of 1917, the government ordered the deportation of Dhanna Singh, a Sikh who had entered California in 1908, gone to British Columbia in 1915, and then reentered the United States surreptitiously. Singh admitted his illegal reentry but argued that since he had entered illegally from Canada, he should be returned there. If Dhanna Singh had acquired a domicile in Canada, the judge said, he could be returned there. But, the judge concluded, eleven months in Canada— including eight months working for a lumber mill and purchasing a lot with several other Indians—was not proof that he had been domiciled there. In a second case, decided the same day as that of Singh, the same judge held that two Indians could be deported to India if they denied they had been to Canada, even though the charge brought against them by immigration officials was that they had entered illegally from Canada.[5]

When the first Indians were arrested in March 1917 on charges of conspiring to violate neutrality laws, civil libertarians raised the issue of possible deportation of these men. Charles James, secretary of the Single Tax League in Los Angeles, wrote a letter of concern to fellow single taxer Louis Post, then assistant secretary of labor, about possible deportation. James feared that the Indian revolutionists would be executed by the British if deported to India. Post replied that no proceedings had been instituted by the bureau of immigration against Indian revolutionaries. Indians would not be turned over to the British without their "day in court," Post assured James, for such a procedure would violate constitutional rights and was not the general practice in cases of this nature.[6]

At the time of the San Francisco "Hindu conspiracy" trial in 1918, attorneys for the Indians requested certificates from the judge that would prevent deportation to India. Preston opposed granting the certificates, however, arguing that while some men seemed harmless, others were "anarchists of a dangerous variety." He suggested that perhaps the British could be requested not to execute the deported men. Gregory asked Lansing and Post what to do. Lansing replied unequivocally that the Indians should be considered "undesirable aliens" and deported to India and that Preston should oppose issuance of the certificates. Post also agreed that the justice department should take no part in helping to obtain the certificates. If the attorney general were concerned about executions, said Post, he should make representations to the British. The British decided to oppose deportations during the war, and the men were imprisoned to serve their terms.[7]

By the end of the war, the government had several possible statutes under which the men might be deported. The first was a 1917 statute that allowed aliens convicted of certain crimes to be deported. This law, however, specifically excluded deportation of "persons convicted, or who admit the commission or who teach or advocate the commission of an offense purely political." Moral turpitude was a deportable crime, but it had been defined previously as "an act of baseness, vileness, or depravity in the private and social duties which a man owes to his fellow man or to society." This seemed clearly not to apply to the convicted men. The second statute, passed in 1918, provided for deportation of anarchists, "those who believe in the forcible overthrow of the Government, or who are opposed to organized government, those who believe in or teach the unlawful assaulting or killing of public officials or the unlawful destruction of property, and those who become members of organizations advocating such destruction after entering the United States." A third statute was pending in Congress in February 1919. This new legislation would allow deportation of all aliens convicted during the war who had been in the country too long to come under the old deportation laws. Washington state representative Albert Johnson, an exclusionist, had tacked on a provision for direct deportation to India of Indians convicted during the war, and on 5 February Gregory and Post wrote a joint letter to the Senate committee on immigration and naturalization urging that the law be passed.[8]

The labor department was not confident that it could use any of these statutes to deport Indian revolutionaries. Nevertheless, in December 1918, immigration authorities appeared at Fort Leavenworth to interview Indians convicted during the war, with the intention of deporting them all to India. By mid-February 1919, the first load of aliens arrested during the war had arrived at Ellis Island for deportation. When critics of the Wilson administration condemned the rush to deport aliens who had questioned the politics of the government, Caminetti insisted that reports of wholesale deportations were unjustified. When Gopal Singh emerged from prison on 23 February 1919, however, the labor department announced its intention to carry out deportation plans by arresting him at the gate.[9]

Indians, meanwhile, had been attempting to create coalitions of American reformers to continue support for Indian independence. The success of the British in suppressing the radical Ghadar Party during the war had not stopped the organizing of the moderate Home Rule League founded in 1917 in New York. Leaders of the home rule movement continued to function during the war, with Lajpat Rai as their president. In September 1917 Rai published an open letter to British prime minister David Lloyd George, deprecating revolt in India but seeming to advocate ultimate revolt unless the reasons for revolt were removed. "The talk about ending the war for all times to come is pure and simple nonsense," Rai wrote. "No one believes it to be possible." The war, he argued, would only result in greater complications in European politics and sow the seed for future war. A discontented India would be a source of constant danger, and British statesmen must decide whether they preferred a self-governing India as a part of the Empire or no India at all.

The Home Rule League also circulated Rai's book, *Young India*. A similar league in London did the same, putting a copy of *Young India* in the box of each member of the House of Commons.

Suppression of the Home Rule League in England soon followed. The remaining copies and unbound sheets of *Young India* were seized by the police under the direction of the home office, and postal censors intercepted a packet of Rai's open letter. The British embassy in Washington asked the state department to "take steps to prevent the dissemination and exportation" of the pamphlet, and Spring-Rice sent a memorandum promising a confidential report on "the mischievous activities of Lajpat Rai." After receiving the memorandum, which mentioned *Young India*, the justice department asked Preston whether Rai could be prosecuted and the magazine suppressed. On the advice of British undercover agents, Preston replied that *Young India* did not at the moment seem particularly harmful, although eventually it might prove a menace. The censorship board decided that Rai's open letter should be suppressed at once, however, and promised to take similar action against such publications in the future. The board refused to give any reason for the suppression. After Rai gave a speech defending home rule at a dinner given by the People's Council in mid-February of 1918, army intelligence officials put him on their list of "dangerous" radicals. After a Home Rule League meeting in May 1918, where Rai and nine other Indians discussed the growing revolutionary spirit in Asia, intelligence agents had New York police tap league members' phones, intercept Rai's mail, and place visitors to his apartment under surveillance. Finally, the league sent a letter to Gregory insisting that it had no sympathy with the Germans. It survived the war with no prosecutions.

The goal of the Home Rule League was to get official United States support for home rule in India. Publicly, President Wilson had stated that the Germans must recognize Czechoslovakia and Yugoslavia as independent nations, but he was silent about recognition of India by the British Empire. Privately, Wilson had told his subordinates that he would not apply the fifth point of his Fourteen Points for the Treaty of Versailles—the one endorsing self-determination—to the colonial empires of France and Britain. In October 1918, he approved a memorandum by Frank I. Cobb and Walter Lippmann affirming that the fifth point applied only to German colonies. Wilson's retreat from application of the Fourteen Points to the British Empire was not made public, however, and in the absence of any stated United States policy toward

India, the Home Rule League continued to promote its verson of self-determination.

The Home Rule League celebrated its first anniversary on 20 November 1918 with a huge dinner. Oswald Garrison Villard, editor of the *Nation*, presided over the program at the Grand Hotel in New York and three hundred guests joined the celebration. Nine days later the league sent a telegram to President Wilson, reviewing India's services in the war and asking for support of progressive measures of home rule such as the Wilson administration had inaugurated in the Philippines. Leaguers circulated a petition to be sent to the peace conference to remind Wilson of his pronouncements regarding self-determination. "India has fought for world democracy. Is she to remain a mere dependency? We, the undersigned, urge you to use your influence in considering India's case at the International Peace Conference." In the first flush of peace, there was growing support for Indian independence from critics silenced during the war but determined to work for reform in the postwar world. Jeannette Rankin, a pacifist congresswoman, spoke at a second league meeting, while in Washington the league lobbied senators with copies of *Young India*. Liberal Republican senators Frank Norris and A. J. Gronna, both of Nebraska, responded sympathetically. Other leaguers spoke to groups of Theosophists, Socialists, and Unitarians, asking them to appeal to Congress for home rule in India.[10]

As the home rule movement grew, the British were determined to repress it. When a member of parliament denounced Lajpat Rai for stirring up anti-British sentiment in America, secretary of state for India Edwin S. Montagu replied, "steps have been taken to counteract them." Whatever the British did to counteract the activities of Rai, they were effective. In a manuscript dated June 1919, Rai denounced Indian revolutionists in the United States. Chandra, wrote Rai, was an "absolutely unscrupulous man without moral and ethical principles, a frank anarchist who believed in no principles and was not a nationalist," and all Bengalis in San Francisco were "revolutionists more mercenary than patriotic." Har Dayal denounced the revolutionaries about the same time and announced that he too had had a change of heart. In an article reprinted in the New York *Times*, Dayal wrote that he now believed that the consolidation of the British Empire in the East was in the best interests of the people of India, Burma, Egypt, and Mesopotamia. The British allowed Dayal to return to England and Rai to return to India.[11]

Even before the end of the war, support for an independent India and opposition to deportation of Indian political prisoners had taken root among a coalition of radicals who opposed the imposition of a peace that did not provide for self-determination of all nations. This group had its origins not in the moderate Home Rule League but in a revived Ghadar Party with more radical demands for self-determination.

The campaign built on wartime attempts to influence American foreign policy regarding India. Ram Chandra had begun this campaign to influence Wilson on behalf of Indian independence in late June 1917, in a letter to Wilson saying that the president's recent declaration of war aims raised "the hope that the time may be near at hand when the cry of India for freedom and self-government will receive sympathetic response by the Great Nations of the world." Chandra's letter was forwarded to the state department, sent to the division of Far Eastern affairs, and filed. That December, Das took up the campaign to attempt to influence Wilson in favor of independence for India.[12]

Das began to gather American support for a new policy on India. After voluntarily offering himself for arrest upon learning that he had been included in the indictments, Das was released on bail in late 1917. During this period, he introduced Salindra N. Ghose, a slender young Indian of twenty-three, to the Wotherspoons, American friends who had put up bail for him. W. A. Wotherspoon, a retired Iowa attorney, had been active in the Democratic party in the 1880s and then became interested in cooperatives, which he attempted to establish in Sinaloa, Mexico, in southern California, and in Kansas. A Socialist for a time, Wotherspoon later became a staunch supporter of Wilson and now found his political friends among left-wing Democrats. Marion Foster Washburne Wotherspoon, author and one-time school editor of the Chicago *Evening Post*, had been active in reform politics and in the women's suffrage movement. She had met Vivekananda at the World's Parliament of Religions in Chicago in 1893, studied theosophy, and later opened her salons to Indians who lectured on various topics. After moving to San Francisco in 1915, the Wotherspoons continued to entertain Indians in their home, as well as friends from the People's Council, a pacifist group that opposed the war and that the government suppressed in 1917.[13]

The Wotherspoons entertained Ghose, wrote letters of introduction for him to personal friends in the East, such as Post, and allowed him to use their address for his mail. They also sympathized with the desire of Ghose and Das for Indian independence and apparently promised to try to gain support for the Indian National Committee, a group formed by the two men to achieve this purpose.

The involvement of the Wotherspoons was symptomatic of growing support among left-wing liberals for Indian independence. Just as symptomatic of British concern about that involvement was the response of the British agents. British intelligence officers attached to army headquarters in San Francisco had become friendly with United States military intelligence agents during the conspiracy trial. British agents visited army headquarters, furnished agents there with information on Indian activities, including copies of translated letters from revolutionaries, and convinced the Americans of the danger of Indian revolutionaries. Sometime in February 1918, British agents discovered that Indians were meeting at the home of the Wotherspoons. Agents then contacted the San Francisco post office, where they found that the inspector "displayed a great willingness to cooperate with the military intelligence in intercepting mail," and British agents promised to turn over additional information in return for photostats of the intercepted letters.[14]

One of the letters that soon turned up was a letter to Ghose from Agnes Smedley, a young radical who was working with Indians in New York. The agents contacted British agent George Denham, who suggested that they search Das's house because he was a known friend of Ghose. The army agent and Denham raided Das's home while he was away and found a copy of a letter to the Workingmen's and Soldiers' Council of Russia, dated 12 December 1917, Tagore Castle, Calcutta, and addressed to Leon Trotsky, Petrograd, Russia. The letter, from the Indian Nationalist Party, supported the revolutionary government in Russia, identified the position of India as parallel to that of Russia in 1905, and explained that the British were influencing the actions of the United States government against Indian revolutionists. It asked Russia to support the revolutionists on trial in San Francisco. This information was quickly transmitted to New York, where military agents arranged for Agnes Smedley and Salindra Ghose to be arrested immediately.[15]

Ghose could not be found, but according to Smedley, who left an account in her semi-autobiographical book, *Daughter of Earth*, British and army intelligence agents collaborated with city detectives in her arrest. Smedley was a twenty-five-year-old reformer who had become interested in the cause of Indian independence while living in California. After being fired from her college job for being a member of the Socialist Party, she had moved to New York to work with Indians there and had become a communication center for them, keeping their correspondence, codes, and foreign addresses.[16]

The British wanted Smedley's information. It was not difficult to convince army intelligence officers that they should become involved in the case, and they arranged for the illegal search of Smedley's apartment after she was arrested. Agents assumed that Smedley was somehow involved in the "conspiracy" and thus that the technicalities of due process were not necessary. No search warrant was asked for or obtained. Agents also placed a twenty-four-hour watch at Smedley's door, and two days later Ghose appeared and was arrested. On 19 March the New York *Times* announced that this was one of the most important cases that had developed in months in connection with the worldwide German-directed conspiracy. Ghose was accused of being the "directing genius," a man who was collaborating with Das on propaganda. Smedley, the newspaper claimed, had refused to aid her country by exposing the conspiracy. Smedley's bail was set at ten thousand dollars, that of Ghose at twenty-five thousand dollars.[17]

These arrests were significant because they extended the battles of the neutrality period into the war. American government officials now felt a greater distrust of Indians and of the Americans who supported the effort to obtain independence for India. Das emerged as the central figure in this supposed conspiracy and was considered the link between American radicals and Indians who feared deportation. Das himself was soon the focus of officials' deportation attempts. Upon hearing of Ghose's arrest, Das wired President Wilson that he and Ghose were members of a three-man commission representing the Indian Nationalist Party in the United States. Wotherspoon also wrote a letter to Wilson, enclosing an open letter from Das asking that Ghose be allowed to present his credentials, arguing that the federal courts were being used to discourage and prevent the aspirations of Indians toward freedom, and accusing British secret service agents of directing the entire prosecution.

Military intelligence agents notified Preston about Das's role in the new movement. Preston then demanded that the judge give a warrant for Das's arrest because he was "one of the leaders of a deep-laid plot to enlist the aid of the Bolshevik party in Russia through Leon Trotsky to precipitate the overthrow of British rule in India." According to Preston, Das was a paid German agent, his actions "near treason," and contemptible. Declaring that these "anti-American" plots must be halted, the judge sent Das to jail for the duration of the trial. Preston also decided that the Wotherspoons should be arrested for harboring persons passing as representatives of a foreign government, and ordered that they be charged with violation of the Espionage Act. In New York, Agnes Smedley and five Indians were also indicted under the Espionage Act for attempting to stir up rebellion against British rule and for representing themselves as diplomats. Wotherspoon's defense of Das was promptly turned over to the justice department, where Charles Warren decided that it should be reason to disbar Wotherspoon.[18]

In Washington, meanwhile, military intelligence officers had already begun compiling lists of Indian suspects and a summary of Ghadar activities, claiming that the conspiracy trials had not silenced the revolutionaries. The head of military intelligence sent the labor department insinuating reports about the sexual lives of Indian men and American women. Publicity of these "facts" among Indians might interfere with their anti-British propaganda, suggested the chief. In San Francisco, more indictments were returned against Indians and their American supporters on charges of conspiring to deceive Wilson and his cabinet and to defraud philanthropic Americans of a million dollars in violation of the Espionage Act.

Wotherspoon wrote a second letter to Wilson, protesting that citizens should be allowed to address the president safely and freely on the welfare or supposed welfare of the country. "We recognize that, in wartime, Free Speech has its dangers," he wrote, "but suppression of speech is at all times dangerous." Wotherspoon also wrote to Wilson's secretary, Joseph Tumulty, that the president was endangering his peace proposals by allowing suppression of radicals and pacifists. The very people supporting the president's peace terms were being indicted because the administration was concentrating on winning the war and not preparing for peace, he wrote. These letters, together with an appeal from Marion Wotherspoon to Post, finally brought an inquiry from Gregory. Adams explained that the American supporters of the Indians were all part of a "Hindu-Bolshevik clique." Thus the "German-Hindu conspiracy" gave way to the "Hindu-Bolshevik" danger, laying the groundwork for the deportation movement and its opposition.[19]

Throughout 1918, Preston stubbornly insisted that the case must continue. He accused Wotherspoon of being "a man whom you would immediately brand as a crook if you saw him . . . a Socialist, a Bolshevik, a lover of Lenin and Trotsky, a Pacifist, anti-war, and generally crooked from all viewpoints"; he called Wotherspoon's letter to Wilson a "contempt of court." Marion Wotherspoon had displayed a "disgusting friendship and familiarity" with Das, had dwelt on "this Hindu Indian philosophy and Pacifism" until she was absolutely un-American and disloyal. Das, according to Preston, had published a pamphlet which was "nothing short of popular treason." There was no doubt in Preston's mind that this was one of the most complete conspiracy cases he had seen. After several reviews in Washington, the attorney general finally asked Preston to drop the indictments in San Francisco. But the indictments remained, as did those in New York, although they were drawn up so poorly that officials there assumed the case would be thrown out of court. Ghose and Smedley were finally released on bail and allowed to stay in New York pending their appeal to the supreme court for a writ of habeas corpus.[20]

Reformers raised the issue of deportation directly with the labor department early in 1919. Historian Charles Beard was the first reformer to write to Post, in February 1919, asking for discriminating attention to every case that might involve violation of personal liberty and common justice. Secretary of labor William Wilson replied to Beard that there were no cases pending before the department charging Indians with advocating independence. Furthermore, he continued, the department would have no authority under law to deport an alien simply because he advocated political reforms or changes in his native country. The one case before him, Wilson told Beard, involved the conviction of an Indian within five years of entry for a crime involving moral turpitude. Similar cases would arise out of the "Hindu conspiracy" trial, Wilson admitted, but each case would receive careful consideration as to deportation and place of deportation.[21]

Late in 1918, Smedley and Ghose helped to organize the Friends for the Freedom of India (FFI), dedicated to full independence for India and to defending Indians from deportation threats. The FFI drew together a group of left-wing reformers who had previously been active in a variety of civil liberties causes. The idea for the organization came originally from Das, who met Rose Strunsky and other Socialists in New York. Norman Thomas, Roger Baldwin, and Margaret Sanger joined an executive board, and Robert Morss Lovett, professor of English at the University of Chicago and editor of the *Dial*, became president. Dudley Field Malone and Frank P. Walsh, civil libertarian lawyers who had continued to defend critics of the war, became vice-presidents. According to the first letterhead of the FFI, the group proposed to maintain the right of asylum, to see that Indian political prisoners and refugees received justice, and to assist in an open discussion of conditions in India.[22]

The most immediate problem was the threat of deportation of Indians arrested during the war. Arrests continued throughout the spring and summer. In each case, the bureau of immigration charged the men with moral turpitude for making false statements upon entering the country and argued that they were likely to become public charges. The latter charge had been upheld by the courts before, and the bureau of naturalization hoped to fall back on this old standby should the new charge of moral turpitude not hold. In June, three men—Bhagwan Singh, Santokh Singh, and Gopal Singh—were notified that the department of labor intended to deport them. Attorney Gilbert E. Roe, who had volunteered his services to Smedley, Das, and Ghose free of charge, agreed to defend any Indians in deportation proceedings. Supporters established a New York office, made contacts with the men attempting to revive the Ghadar Party on the West Coast, and installed Smedley as secretary of the FFI. With these actions, the group began to mobilize, working primarily through the American Federation of Labor at both the national and local levels. At the June 1919 meeting of the AFL in Atlantic City, James A. Duncan of the Seattle Central Labor Council introduced a resolution opposing deportation as equivalent to a death sentence. The FFI sent two Indians and one FFI member to the council to present a brief for the Indians, along with thousands of pamphlets analyzing the deportation cases.[23]

Given its tradition of opposition to Asian immigration, the AFL might seem to have been a poor choice. Smedley did not at first think that the AFL would pass a resolution. To her surprise, not only did the AFL pass Duncan's resolution, but Samuel Gompers promised to submit the brief to the department of labor. The brief was then printed as a pamphlet and put in the hands of each senator and representative in Washington.[24]

The Home Rule League, meanwhile, opposed continued talk of Indian revolution. "This is not the time for any revolutionary activities on the part of the Hindus in this country," wrote Jabez Sunderland, the new head of the league. Sunderland felt that the movement to fight deportation cases should be free from suspicion of any kind. This attitude served only to alienate the FFI, which had no intention of pursuing such a course. At least one Indian who was on the deportation list agreed that a cautious policy was proper, but Smedley argued that the extent to which actions might be interpreted as "pro-German" was not a consideration, that possible distortion of pro-Indian and anti-British feeling to mean pro-Germanism was no cause to retreat from deeply held views. The FFI proceeded to ally itself with the more militant wing of the Indian movement and to continue its work. On both the East and the West coasts, the Ghadar Party and the FFI worked to have union locals introduce resolutions similar to that passed by the national body and to send copies to the departments of labor and immigration. The Home Rule League decided not to become involved in the deportation battle or to associate in any way with the FFI.[25]

The FFI thus took the lead in protesting deportations and soliciting defense funds. Smedley contacted liberal, socialist, and labor newspapers, which all printed their opposition to deportation. Said the *Commonwealth*, "The accusation against [Gopal Singh] was none other than that he tried to do for the Hindus precisely that which Washington did for the Americans." Said the socialist Oakland *World*, "Should these men be sent to India to be shot or to lie in prison for life for propaganda? LIBERTY PROPAGANDA?" The *World Tomorrow* noted impatiently, "Our Immigration Bureau would have deported Garibaldi." Political refugees of all nations had preached their cause in England and America undisturbed previously.[26]

Lovett opened up the *Dial* to discussion of the case against deportation. The Indian cases, he wrote, illustrated "how far we have wandered from our former proud estate of political asylum. . . . As long as a Government, however corrupt or tyrannical, or vicious, is formally recognized, refugees have not the right in the United States to advocate the overthrow by force of that government. . . . Even 10 years ago it never would have occurred to us to deny a Hindu refugee the right to say exactly that, if he thought it was true." Lovett called on Illinois senator Medill McCormick to try to get the amendment for direct deportation eliminated from the still-pending deportation bill. McCormick promised that the amendment would not pass. The FFI organized a mass meeting to be held at the Central Opera House in New York on 10 April 1919, passed a resolution protesting deportation, and delegated Lovett to send a letter to President Wilson to urge him to drop the charges against Indians who had already been punished for their offenses. Lovett's open defense of the Indians joined him in combat with Richard Gottheil, a professor at Columbia University. In a letter to the New York *Times*, Gottheil argued that Indians would not ordinarily be condemned to death and that the "guiding hand of Great Britain" was necessary for their own protection. Lovett retorted in another letter, never published, that the British had already executed Indians returning from France and Canada.[27]

Some historians have dismissed India as an insignificant issue for the peace conference agenda. That situation was true only because the British successfully kept their colonial questions out of the conference. The application of the principles of self-determination to victor and vanquished alike could have been a bargaining point for Wilson to exploit in favor of home rule for India, had he been so inclined. On 25 June 1919, Tumulty wired Wilson, urging him to take an interest in the British possessions: "There are no boundary lines between free peoples anymore." Wilson replied that he would take up the question of Ireland. Three days later, the peace treaty was signed at Versailles amid rising fear of worldwide revolution by the capitalist countries. It was a harsh peace, and although it included the League of Nations—Wilson's hope for righting all the wrongs left at the end of the war—Germany was not to be included in the League, nor was Russia, nor was India except as British India. In July 1919 Wilson presented the peace treaty to the Senate.[28]

The movement for self-determination for the colonies of France and England had, meanwhile, died on the tables of the peace conference. Secretary of state Robert Lansing had noted in his diary in December 1918 that self-determination was "simply loaded with dynamite." The British Labor Party platform of November 1918 had asked for self-determination for Ireland and India, and the British delegation to the Socialist Conference held at Bern also advocated home rule for India, but at Paris there was no such talk. Prime Minister George maintained that enemy propaganda had poisoned neutral opinion and that Britain was being criticized for selfish and imperialistic aims as a result. He argued publicly that the loyalty of India and Ireland had caused the widening of war aims. At the peace conference, the British insisted that questions regarding their colonies were strictly internal affairs.[29]

Although Wilson had already indicated that he would not apply the principles of the Fourteen Points to British colonies, a recommendation from his advisors for Indian home rule might still have kept the issue open. The Inquiry had been set up by Wilson late in 1917 under the supervision of E. M. House to conduct research for the coming peace conference. One of the men originally suggested for the group was Arthur Pope, then considered an outstanding authority on Persia. When Pope's name was sent to the justice department for approval, however, the department sent it to the United States attorney in San Francisco, who asked the British agents for a report on Pope. The reply was extremely disparaging, and Gregory reported back that Pope had been "closely associated with the most dangerous of the German Hindu agents, both those now in Germany, in Mexico, and those on trial." He opposed using Pope for any sort of government work.[30]

Although British agents managed to keep Pope off the Inquiry, their success did not prevent criticism of British rule. Dorothy Kenyon, the lawyer who drew up the reports on India, submitted such a damning criticism of British rule that James T. Shotwell, the Canadian-American history professor who headed the Inquiry, said that they were based on propaganda against British rule and read "like an indictment of an enemy country." He refused to use the reports in making recommendations to the peace delegation. The peace treaty that Wilson presented to Congress was immediately attacked by Wisconsin senator Robert La Follette, who asked why India had been omitted from the peace treaty and why no peace settlement had been made in Asia.[31]

The deportation cases, meanwhile, finally came before Post for his approval late in August 1919. Petitions against deportation were now piled high on his desk. A glass bottle blowers' local in Pennsylvania, a ladies' kimono and housedress makers' local in New York, and a carpenters' and joiners' local in Oakland protested against the deportation of Indians. The California State Federation of Labor, the American Labor Party, the League for Democratic Control, the National Civil Liberties Bureau, and senators Frank Norris, William S. Kenyon, and George Huddleston—all sent their objections. Medill McCormick also wrote to Lansing to ask what was being done with the Indians under arrest and enclosing a protest from the Chicago Federation of Labor. There was, of course, no guidance from President Wilson, who had left on a speaking tour of the United States to warn Americans of the danger of revolution at home and abroad and to urge support for his peace treaty. His tour ended in collapse, stroke, and paralysis.[32]

The FFI redoubled its efforts, sending copies of resolutions denouncing deportation to unions and speaking at union meetings. While Smedley wrote and Ghose spoke, Dudley Field Malone prepared a brief on the case for senators, and Frank P. Walsh and Arthur Pope, who had joined the FFI, also wrote letters. By the end of September, the FFI had nine senators and six representatives who agreed to meet with Roe, the Indians' attorney, to hear him explain the case. The FFI feared that the deportation hearings might be held quietly and quickly, without enough time to present the Indians' case adequately. When the bill to allow deportation of any alien convicted of a crime was introduced into the Senate, Robert La Follette, Thomas Gore, and David Walsh kept it off the floor despite the fact that the new attorney general, A. Mitchell Palmer, defended the bill as a way to keep the United States from becoming a "place of temporary sojourn for the purpose of fomenting plots against friendly countries."[33]

Momentum against deportation seemed to be growing. Late in October, Roe, a senator, and a labor leader talked to William Wilson for three hours and obtained his assurance that the Indians would be given the opportunity for a full and adequate defense. The FFI had by this time begun a weekly news bulletin to furnish information to labor magazines and newspapers. David Walsh and Joseph France had both made speeches in the Senate. Concern focused on the alien bill that the senators had so far managed to keep off the floor but that now seemed to have a chance of passage. La Follette promised to propose an amendment that would protect the Indians from deportation under the bill.[34]

Roe was also attempting to get Palmer to drop the case still pending against Ghose, Smedley, and Das in San Francisco. Palmer's assistant, R. Steward, told him the charge seemed of a "manifestly political character and so subversive of the political ideals of this Government, and the spirit of its laws, that the United States should not be a party to further pressing this case." The indictments against the Wotherspoons had already been dropped, and Steward recommended that those against Smedley and the Indians should also be dropped. Palmer's solicitor general supported Steward's recommendation on the basis that the case had probably resulted from "the close relations between this Government and the English Government, and the supposed connection of these defendants with some effort to raise disturbances in India under German instigation." This time Palmer penciled his approval, and the San Francisco indictments were dropped. When Das emerged from prison in December, he thus had no need for bail. The FFI gave a huge banquet to celebrate his release.[35]

The Indians also began to work openly with the Irish in 1920. Irish-Americans had given support informally to Indians in New York before. The proclamation of the Irish Republic in 1918 and its suppression by the British brought new Irish militance, which, in turn, fueled American collaboration with the Indian independence movement. Senators Frank Norris and William E. Borah and Illinois representative William E. Mason spoke in favor of Indian rights in Congress, and the Irish and Indians joined hands to work for independence. Late in February, at a dinner sponsored by the FFI, Eamon DeValera, leader of the Irish Republicans, offered his support to the movement for Indian independence: "The Indians are 'mere' Asiatics, we are told. We were the 'mere' Irish. Irishmen, anyhow, should not be deceived by the British cant about the Indian. We have never been able to achieve anything except when we compelled England to rule us with the naked sword." Over five hundred people attended the banquet, and hundreds more crowded in to hear and applaud DeValera's words. The alliance was symbolized by a Saint Patrick's Day parade in New York where Indians marched side by side with Irish, demanding complete and unconditional independence for Ireland and India. Ghose rode on horseback as a special aide to the grand marshal of the parade in a green turban and sashes of red, gold, and green. Other Indians carried the banner of the FFI, accompanied by Smedley and other American women who blacked their hair and wore saris. Their banners demanded independence. The work of the FFI seemed to be paying off. Post began to cancel the deportation orders. In May, deportation proceedings against Bhagwan Singh, Gopal Singh, and Santokh Singh were dismissed.[36]

The celebration soon ended. Early in June the FFI discovered that the alien bill had slipped through Congress unamended. La Follette had been ill, and two other senators who had promised to watch the bill were away when, without any publicity, the committee passed the bill and brought it onto the floor of the Senate with only a half dozen senators present. It passed both the Senate and the House and became law on 10 May 1920. The bill provided that the labor department could deport any alien convicted of violating or conspiring to violate the neutrality law that prohibited the organization of a military expedition against a nation with which the United States was at peace. "Your deportation dismissal amounts to nothing, practically," Smedley wrote bitterly to the Ghadar leaders in San Francisco, "since under this law, if the Department of Labor wishes, you can be arrested for deportation." It was, she concluded, "a treacherous piece of work." Although the labor department had assured Das that no new proceedings were contemplated, in August the government began a wholesale roundup of Indians for deportation. Thirty-nine were held for deportation at Ellis Island, and the FFI believed that all Indian workingmen might be deported, for the arrested men were not radicals but men who had been employed by Bethlehem Steel. Some were escaped seamen and ten had been in the United States only a few months, but others had come before 1917. The

FFI planned to make a test case with the ten and also to bring suit against Caminetti and other immigration officials for conspiracy to violate civil rights.[37]

Linking deportation threats to British control in India, the FFI renewed its campaign for Indian independence. Friends organized large parades and public gatherings, staged public coming out parties for the men as they were released from prison, and encouraged the men to speak out for independence. They also urged support for the noncooperation movement that Gandhi had launched in India.[38]

Events in the Punjab during 1919 had led to a resurgence of militant opposition to the British raj. Most important was the Amritsar massacre, which took place in a park called Jalianwala Bagh. There, British troops fired upon Punjabi protesters, killing hundreds and wounding thousands more. Following the massacre, large numbers of Sikhs had supported Gandhi's nonviolent resistance movement. In the districts of Jullundur and Hoshiarpur, many Sikhs who had returned from abroad took up noncooperation with such vigor that the government used the Seditious Meetings Act to halt meetings. Sikhs boycotted the November elections, and at Delhi polling stations volunteers picketed on horse and on foot. Returning Sikh veterans of the Akali sect banded together late in 1920, and on 20 February 1921 a group of Akalis were massacred after trying to seize a Sikh temple that was under the control of government managers. Following the massacre, a movement called Babbar Akali spread, and the British arrested two hundred men and executed a number of soldiers before the movement was suppressed.[39]

As repression spread in India, Sikhs in the United States grew more militant. Late in 1919, West Coast Sikhs revived the Ghadar Party, and by November 1920 the first issue of the *Independent Hindustan*, the new party paper, had appeared. Its purpose was to contact Sikhs and other Indian workers in California and to marshal support for a free India. Armed rebellion, leaders predicted, would follow Gandhi's nonviolent movement. Leaders promised to raise money for the families of imprisoned Sikhs.[40]

The FFI's work thus coincided with resurgent organizing along the Pacific Coast, as well as with Gandhi's movement in India. On 5 December 1920, the FFI held a convention in support of the Indian National Congress. At other meetings Ghose demanded suffrage in eastern Africa and solicited contributions from the Irish to equip Indian fighters. The British, meanwhile, continued to watch the Indians and to pass on information to the United States government. Wartime statutes were still in force in the United States because the war had not been declared ended. Postwar was less than peace.[41]

We know from military intelligence agents, who continued to report on Indian activities, that the FFI held several more meetings in 1921. On 13 February 1921, according to one agent, the group expressed fear that violence and bloodshed could not be avoided in India and that large numbers of Indians should be brought to the United States, trained in "radical and liberal revolutionary ideas," and then sent back to India to preach these doctrines. According to another intelligence report, the FFI called a "British peril" meeting for 20 March, where six hundred people heard Das speak again on the need for action in India, and collected money for India.[42]

After that, the momentum of the FFI began to falter. Smedley had resigned from the group in December 1920 and left for Germany. With Smedley gone, the old East and West conflicts among the Indians appeared, and Das was soon quarreling with the West Coast leadership. By May 1921, all ties were severed between the West Coast Ghadarites and the East Coast support group. The FFI ceased its activities soon after. With the demise of the FFI, the main national source of information on Indian independence and Indian rights also disappeared. The Ghadar Party continued to publish its newspaper in English, but now it had no organized American support group to help it present the Indian cause to the American public.

In December 1921, a small group of liberals in the United States who had fought for self-determination for India for more than two years issued a Christmas message to the people of India. The signatories included senators, progressive mayors, ministers, and judges, who sent their support to the people of India in their struggle. Ghose told reporters that posters being displayed in India pledged American support of nationalist campaigns to overthrow the British.[43]

At the June 1922 annual convention of the AFL, workers adopted a resolution sympathizing with the just aspirations of the people of India for self-government. Some of the delegates wanted to offer positive support for Gandhi, who had recently been arrested in India, and for his noncooperation movement, but the majority of delegates were not willing to offend delegates from the British Trade Union Congress and thus settled for a vague resolution of sympathy. The Home Rule League ceased publication of *Young India* about the same time, and it too died at the end of 1922. Lajpat Rai, who had returned to India, promised to send someone from India to revive the league, but by the end of 1922 he too was in jail for political activities in India.[44]

How many Indians were deported is difficult to say. Twenty-nine of the Philadelphia men agreed to deportation, and the FFI estimated that a total of between seventy and a hundred were finally deported. None of the political prisoners were deported, however, and in this sense the movement was successful.[45] The threat of deportations kindled support for independence in India during the first few postwar years, but with that issue ended, Friends for the Freedom for India could not hold the interest of Americans on the Indian cause. After 1921, American liberals and radicals found themselves fighting for their own rights more frequently. What little time, effort, or money there was to spare for fighting Indian battles went to support the new battles over naturalization.

12

Brown Is Not White: Naturalization and the Constitution

She has no love for you,
She only has to rob you in every way.
—Ghadar protest song

Naturalization is the official act by which people become nationals of countries other than their own. Through naturalization, foreign-born residents are legally and symbolically transformed
from aliens into citizens. And yet this crucial process is one of the least
studied by historians. Part of the neglect stems from the very ritualistic
quality of naturalization—it seems inaccessible to analysis—and part is
the result of the diffusion of authority for the process. In the United
States, Congress has the authority to establish rules for naturalization,
but the courts review those laws and also have charge of administering
them. In the twentieth century, the executive, through the bureau of
naturalization, has also played a large part in determining who may
become a citizen. It is thus no surprise that the process remains so little
analyzed.

The process of becoming a citizen was one from which Asians were
excluded through an increasingly complex maze of laws and regulations.
The first Congress decided in 1790 that to become a naturalized citizen,
a person must be "white." White women could be naturalized or could
marry an United States citizen to obtain citizenship. Children under
twenty-one were included in their parents' citizenship. For many years
no one knew exactly what the word *white* meant. Most controversies
arose over whether to extend the waiting period for certain white
males—particularly Irish and French.[1]

Congress always considered American Indians a separate group. During the early nineteenth century, most were excluded on the basis that
they belonged to separate nations. Congress denied citizenship to native
Americans in Alaska when it acquired that territory in 1867, and courts
subsequently held that the Fourteenth Amendment did not apply to
native Americans unless Congress specifically included them. Despite
special treaties and laws that admitted individual American Indians to
citizenship, most remained outside the political community until well
into the twentieth century.[2]

Although Americans agreed about excluding American Indians, they did not agree about whether to exclude blacks from citizenship. On this issue northern and southern courts disagreed, and the Dred Scott case of 1856 fueled rather than settled the debate. After the Civil War, Congress amended the naturalization statute to allow persons of African nativity or descent to become citizens but rewrote *white* into the naturalization law for all other immigrants.

The issue of Asian citizenship was not seriously discussed by Congress until the 1880s. Legal scholar James Kent had speculated in his *Commentaries on the American Law* in the 1820s that "the tawny races of Asia" could probably not be admitted to the privileges of citizenship under the term *white*. Such commentary was academic until the Chinese began to arrive in California in large numbers in the 1860s. Congress added a clause to the treaty signed with China in 1868 that the agreement was not to be construed as giving the Chinese the right of naturalization. With the prodding of Californians, Congress explicitly voted to deprive Chinese of the right of naturalization in 1882. After Chinese exclusion, Congress made no further laws regarding naturalization for several decades, leaving the local and federal courts, which had the power to naturalize, and the executive to interpret the law. In 1893 one court excluded a Japanese from citizenship on the theory that he was "mongolian," but the supreme court made no decision on non-Chinese Asians. Nor did it make any decision on a whole range of people who did not neatly fit into the then commonly accepted racial categories of Caucasian, Mongolian, and Negro. Courts in Florida, Indiana, New York, and Washington continued to naturalize "tawny races" from Asia. Even in California, courts naturalized Japanese and admitted one to the bar.[3]

Naturalization of Asians was only part of the confusion that pointed to the need for reform. Scandals and frauds existed in all parts of the country. There was a brisk business in the sale of first papers. Even when the naturalization process was clear of fraud, the two-tiered state and federal court system and the lack of clear regulations often resulted in chaos. In 1904 attorney general Charles J. Bonaparte recommended that only federal courts be given the power to naturalize, but Congress was not yet ready to face the complex and politically volatile question of naturalization reform.[4]

In the absence of action by Congress, the executive branch began to assume the responsibility for deciding the increasingly complex question of eligibility for citizenship. During the first decade of the twentieth century, the bureau of naturalization began to warn clerks of court that they should inform persons who appeared to be "nonwhite" that their applications for naturalization might be turned down by the courts. In July 1906, Bonaparte specifically held Japanese to be ineligible, and the clerks generally did not allow Japanese to become citizens. President Roosevelt, at that time interested in allowing naturalization in exchange for Japanese restriction of their own immigrants, urged Congress to pass an act permitting their naturalization. Generally, however, the clerks did not allow Japanese to become citizens.[5]

When the first Asian Indians began to apply for citizenship, the question of who was "white" and therefore eligible for citizenship was still being decided by clerks of the courts. The clerks refused applicants who seemed to belong to excluded groups and discouraged with a warning those who might be turned down. Some clerks arbitrarily turned down Indians as ineligible without further question. Taraknath Das, the Bengali translator who had been employed by Canadian immigration officials at Vancouver before moving to the United States, was simply refused when he applied in San Francisco. Other clerks were not so sure. The question of how a clerk should respond to a "tawny" Indian was first raised officially late in 1906 when two Sikhs, Iasar Singh and Sohan Singh, appeared before the clerk of the superior court of Santa Clara County in California to request applications for declarations to become citizens of the United States.

Sikhs were, of course, British subjects and therefore had to renounce allegiance to the king to become American citizens. Under an 1870 convention between the United States and England, citizens of either country could become citizens of the other country through naturalization, but subjects of a British colony were not clearly eligible. These men were also brown, and the clerk was not sure whether they came under the statute limiting naturalization to "white" men. When the clerk asked the bureau of naturalization what to do, the secretary of commerce and labor passed the query on to the justice department. Early in 1907, the justice department replied that it could "not venture to express an opinion." There the matter rested for seven months, until Robert T. Devlin, United States attorney at San Francisco, repeated the query. "There is considerable uncertainty as to just what nationalities come within the term white person," he wrote. On 14 August 1907, Bonaparte replied to Devlin, "It seems to me clear that under no construction of the law can natives of British India be regarded as white persons."[6]

Bonaparte's decision was publicized first in an American Press dispatch from San Francisco, then by the Toronto *Globe*, and finally in an editorial in the New York *Outlook* with the headline "British Indians and citizenship in white men's countries." The British government could not object to exclusion, wrote the editor, but it would add to the difficulties of the British in confronting the problem of the 112,000 Indians in Natal and the Transvaal, for the colonial government at Pretoria was taking the same stand as Bonaparte in saying that the Indians were not white.

The article brought inquiries. Das, the Bengali who had been refused an application in San Francisco, immediately wrote to Bonaparte to ask on what law the attorney general had based his action. "May I ask you," wrote Das, "if the Hindus who belong to the Caucasian stock of the Human Race have no legal right to become citizens of the United States, under what special law the Japanese who belong to a different stock according to the statements of various scholars of all parts of the world, are allowed to declare their intention to become citizens of the United States." Bonaparte replied curtly: "It is contrary to the practice of the Department of Justice for the Attorney General to give advice as to questions of law, except in cases prescribed by the statutes." When Cornell University professor W. F. Willcox wrote asking for a copy of the ruling, he received a reply that the department rendered no opinion on this subject. Willcox sent a copy of a newspaper article announcing the decision, and only then did Bonaparte send a copy of his letter to Willcox.[7]

While Bonaparte could not keep his decision secret, he also could not determine what the courts would do about naturalizing Indians. California courts, in the heightened atmosphere of anti-Asian sentiment, might accept his opinion, but others need not, and indeed did not, honor it. Das found a Seattle court willing to accept his application in February 1908. The following month, in New Orleans, the court admitted the first two Indians to citizenship.

The bureau of naturalization did not give up. When it became clear in the summer of 1908 that the British government would make no objection to the exclusion of Indians from American citizenship, the bureau moved from a policy leaving the decision in the hands of the clerks of court and the courts to one actively opposing Indian citizenship. On 3 November 1908, the chief of the bureau of naturalization asked all United States attorneys to oppose actively the granting of naturalization to "Hindoes or East Indians" and to instruct clerks of courts in their districts to refuse to accept declarations of intention or to file petitions for naturalization. He also asked attorneys to file motions for orders to cancel declarations of intention already filed by Indians. The United States attorney in Seattle prepared to serve notice on Das.[8]

Although attorneys followed orders and opposed naturalization of Indians in 1909, they were unsuccessful in convincing the courts. Take, for example, the case of a merchant, Abdullah Dolla, who applied for admission as a citizen in 1909. Dolla had arrived in New York in 1894 and had lived in Savannah, Georgia, for twelve years, where he made a living as an importer of silks, linens, and other Indian goods. Dolla's parents were Afghans, but he was born in Calcutta. The United States attorney opposed admission on the basis that Dolla was a native of India and therefore not white and not eligible for citizenship. Dolla argued that he had been accepted as a white in Savannah. The deputy collector of the Port of Savannah and a United States attaché were willing to testify to his reputation in Savannah, a white doctor was ready to swear that he was of "pure Caucasian blood," and Dolla testified that he owned a cemetery plot in Savannah's white cemetery.

The judge looked Dolla over. His complexion and eyes were dark, his features regular and rather delicate, his black hair very fine and soft. The judge asked him to pull up the sleeves of his coat and shirt to look at the skin protected from the sun. It was much lighter than his face and hands and was sufficiently transparent for the blue veins to show clearly. The judge scrutinized his appearance closely, gave him a rigid and detailed examination, then declared him white and granted his petition. The government appealed the naturalization.[9]

Or take the case of a Parsee named Balsara, who applied for citizenship in a federal court in New York in May 1909. This time the attorneys for the government argued that *white* pertained only to those races who had settled in the country before the American Revolution and who had helped to established the new country. Presumably this theory would exclude all Asians and, once accepted, could be extended to exclude other groups as well. The court decided that it would be unscientific to accept the argument that Congress had intended to include only persons of races building up the community that declared itself a new nation, and admitted Balsara to citizenship. The judge added that it would be good to have an authoritative interpretation of the statute. The government appealed this case as well.[10]

A third case occurred in Massachusetts in December 1909. An Armenian named Halladjian, who requested citizenship, was opposed by United States on the basis of the bureau notice of 1908 opposing naturalization of Indians. The U.S. attorney presented a new theory, that there was an "Asiatic race" to which Halladjian belonged and that, although the "average man" could not define this "Asiatic race," he himself understood distinctly who belonged to it. The judge rejected this argument summarily, saying that the idea of an "Asiatic race" was not supported by history or ethnology. He commented acidly that the clerk had no right to refuse any petitions, even if the United States attorney general thought so. The clerk's official duty was to accept all petitions. The court would decide whom to exclude from citizenship. Another Indian Muslim was admitted to citizenship in Galveston, Texas, in 1909.[11]

Early in January 1910, a judge once again explored the question of who was white in a case involving a Syrian. The statute needed clarification, the judge concluded, for the old Caucasian/Mongolian/Negro classifications were no longer thought to be valid by most ethnologists, and for court decisions to rest on these classifications would mean that the results depended on an abandoned scientific theory. Yet no modern theory had gained general acceptance. Hardly anyone classified a human race as "white," and the distinctions would surely not be the same as the original meaning in the statute. Classification by ethnological race would be almost impossible. To use the meaning first intended by the statute, on the other hand, would make naturalization depend upon "the varying and conflicting classification of persons in the usage of successive generations and of different parts of a large country."[12]

The bureau persisted. In July 1910, it used the Balsara argument again in an Oregon case involving a Syrian. The United States attorney admitted that Syrians were Caucasians, as were Indians, but he argued that the statute applied only to those members of the white race whose ancestors had lived in Europe at the time of the formation of the American government and who were inured to European governmental institutions or who lived upon the American continent. The statute included only those of the "white" races who from "tradition, teaching, and environment" would be predisposed toward the United States' form of government and who would thus be readily assimilated by the people of the United States.

The judge agreed that there was some authority for the government's view, but he decided that legislation and debates in Congress indicated that the word *white* was employed at that time to distinguish between the Caucasian, Negro, and Mongolian races. Therefore, he concluded, the elementary rule of construction should be applied to this case, and that words and phrases should be assumed to have been used in the popular sense if they had not acquired a technical meaning. Applying this rule, he concluded that since the simple term *white* had been used, it must have been intended in the popular sense to denote members of the Caucasian race. If there was any doubt or ambiguity, said the judge, it was better to resolve the doubt in favor of a Caucasian "possessed of the highest qualities which go to make an excellent citizen, as the applicant appears to be." If this definition of *white* in the popular sense was too broad, then Congress should legislate on the matter. He ordered that the applicant be admitted to citizenship.[13]

While government attorneys were now actively opposing the naturalization of Indians, courts still had to make the final decision, and courts were still not sure just who was "white." In March 1910 the Dolla appeal was thrown out of court because the judge declared that the court had no jurisdiction to review the decision on a writ of error. Then in the Balsara appeal, the court agreed with the defense's contention that what Congress really meant when it used the word *white* was the Caucasian race. Balsara's ancestors had emigrated from Persia to India twelve hundred years before. Balsara was therefore a Caucasian.[14]

The census of 1910 was very clear on who the department of commerce thought should be classified as white. For that census the population of the United States was divided into six groups: white, Negro, American Indian, Chinese, Japanese, and other. Census takers classified the 2,545 Asian Indians as "other," along with Koreans and Filipinos. In a footnote, the compilers explained why these "Hindus" were being classified as an "other" race. Although "pure-blood Hindus" were ethnically white, and in several cases had been declared so by naturalization proceedings, the footnote said, "the popular conception of the term 'white' is doubtless largely determined by the fact that the whites in this country are almost exclusively Caucasians of European origin." Indians had been classified with nonwhite Asians because they represented "a civilization distinctly different from that of Europe." Race was thus already being defined in two significant ways—by "popular conception" and by culture.[15]

Courts continued to ignore the arguments of United States attorneys and naturalized according to their own interpretation of the statute. Indians were naturalized along with a whole range of other persons who were "brown." By 1913, even West Coast courts were adopting the decisions of other parts of the country. On 3 May 1913, a court in Washington state quietly admitted Akhay Kumar Mozumdar, the first West

Coast Indian granted citizenship. A year later, a Los Angeles court naturalized the first Indian in California. On 9 June 1914, Das appeared in a federal court in San Francisco with two professors from the University of California to testify to his good character, and he was also admitted to citizenship.[16]

Between 1913 and 1924, courts continued to struggle with the concept of race in naturalization and to arrive at differing conclusions. One South Carolina court moved to a position in 1913 that supported the government's contentions about citizenship, giving the bureau of naturalization new hope. Faras Shahid, a fifty-nine-year-old Christian Syrian, applied to federal district court judge Henry A. Smith in South Carolina for citizenship. Shahid wrote Arabic but not English and understood English very imperfectly. He was, the record showed, "the color of walnut, somewhat darker than a mulatto." The judge had to decide whether this man "the color of walnut" was white.   Smith studied the case carefully and then announced that *white* did not mean Caucasian because the term had not been used generally until after 1830. Nor did it mean Aryan. Neither word had been in currency in 1790, when the statute using the word *white* had been enacted. Nor did it refer to persons belonging to the Indo-European race that included Hindu and Dravidian inhabitants of India and Ceylon, or to the mixed races of Persia. In 1790, said Smith, *white* described persons who were known as "white Europeans" and their descendants. The governing or controlling element or strain in all these people was that of "a fair-complexioned people of European descent." A modern Bengali, Parsee, or Persian might be partly of Indo-European descent, since the conquerors of India and Persia probably were fair-complexioned, but Smith went on, "In India the conqueror seems to have been soon swallowed up in an enormously preponderant brown or black people of different race." In Persia the same result followed, and in most Asian countries, Smith claimed, the governing or controlling element or strain was apparently that of a "dark-colored people" not of European descent.

Smith then elaborated his own racial theory. "To say that a very dark brown, almost black, inhabitant of India is entitled to rank as a white person, because of a possible or hypothetical infusion of white blood 30 or 40 centuries old, and to exclude a Chinese or Japanese, whose parent on one side was white, and who thus possesses manifestly at least one-half European blood, would seem highly inconsistent." If that were the case, he concluded, then Japanese and "certain Chinese" would be entitled to stand with many of the so-called white nations and with the

Parsee, Brahman, and Persian, far above the Negro race. Therefore, Smith concluded, the term *white* could only be interpreted as applying to persons of European habitancy or descent. All the inhabitants of Asia, Australia, the South Seas, the Malaysian peninsula and archipelago, and South America who were not of European descent, or of mixed European and African descent, could not be admitted. Nor could inhabitants of Syria, like the present applicant Shahid, be admitted. Geography rather than color must be the criterion. After establishing support for the government's position, Smith went on to decide the case on personal qualifications. He decided that Shahid could not become a citizen.[17]

Smith was still on the bench in February 1914 when George Dow, another Syrian, applied for citizenship. In contrast to Shahid, Dow was an acceptable candidate in every way to the judge, except that he was a bit darker than the usual person of European descent. Courts, Smith said, had rejected ocular inspection, color, and race as ways to determine who was a white person. The term *white person* clearly referred to geography. With a geographical definition, he argued, the meaning of *white person* became "plain, understandable by the multitude as well as by the learned, and not difficult of enforcement." The American people might be as capricious and unreasonable as they saw fit about the question of admission to citizenship, Smith concluded, for it was their privilege to reject whom they wished. He, in turn, rejected the Syrian.[18]

Two months later Dow was back in Smith's courtroom for a rehearing. He had rallied other Syrians to his cause, but Smith remained unmoved. Syrians should not feel humiliated just because they were not admitted to citizenship, Smith told Dow. Many other Asians and the American Indians had also been excluded from voting and being on juries, and, after all, Syrians had at least been admitted to the United States. After discussing again the findings of ethnologists and philologists, Smith concluded once more that the term *white person* simply could not conform to any racial classification. If the statute seemed arbitrary, illogical, unjust, or even absurd, then the Syrians should not come to him but should go to Congress or to the supreme court to settle "this most vexed and difficult question."[19]

During 1917, Oliver B. Dickinson, a Pennsylvania federal judge, applied Smith's logic to Indians in a decision on the eligibility of Sadar Bhagwan Singh for citizenship. The naturalization bureau had refused Singh's petition, contending that the geographical interpretation should be applied and that citizenship could not be conferred on someone of a different social and political condition. Singh appealed, arguing from an ethnological standpoint that he was white. The court immediately rejected the ethnological argument of race, and Dickinson went on to reject the geographical argument as well. "Congress had a vision of what the United States has since become," he said, "the melting pot of almost all the nations of the world"—a vision that forbade adopting the narrow geographical definition argued by the bureau. Although the original 1790 statute probably was not intended to include the Latin races, Dickinson continued, later immigration expanded the term to cover Latin Europeans. Later, southeastern Europeans had brought a broader meaning to the term. Still, Dickinson reasoned, he had no power to enlarge the accepted class; he could only determine whether an individual belonged to that class. The term *Caucasian* did not mean the same thing as the term *white*, and since the Indian had not yet been accepted by Congress, the court could not extend the word *white* to him without usurping the lawmaking powers of Congress. Singh could not become an American citizen through Dickinson's court.[20]

Indians continued to apply to and be accepted in other states, however. In eighteen states, courts interpreted the word *white* broadly and assumed that, in the absence of congressional legislation, Indians should be naturalized. Between 1908 and 1922, at least sixty-nine Indians were admitted to citizenship, the peak coming in 1917–1918, when thirteen gained citizenship. In California alone, federal and state courts had already admitted at least seventeen men to citizenship by the time Mohan Singh applied for citizenship early in 1919 in Los Angeles.

Naturalization examiners appeared in court to object that Indians were not covered by the term *white* and therefore that Mohan Singh could not become a citizen. Singh's Indian attorney, S. G. Pandit, based his case on three "arguments": legal opinion, anthropological authority, and the fact that other Indians had become citizens. Pandit argued that in legal cases a "preponderance of respectable opinion" included Hindus in the Caucasian race. Anthropologists likewise classified Hindus as Caucasian. He offered proof that Indians had been admitted to citizenship in Georgia, New York, and Washington, as well as in California. As final proof, he offered himself. Pandit had arrived in California in 1909, had become a citizen in 1914, and was admitted to the bar of California as a practicing attorney on 20 December 1917. Convinced by the force of these arguments, the federal judge decided on 24 March 1919 that Mohan Singh was entitled to citizenship. The naturalization examiners did not appeal the case.

In California, the courts had no doubt that Indians were white. Despite antimiscegenation laws that allowed marriage only among whites, early in 1920 Pandit married a white American woman who had been born in Michigan. Sant Ram Mandal, a senior at the University of California at Berkeley, gained his citizenship papers in 1920 without a fight from naturalization officials. Mandal had been born in India and argued that he was Aryan by proving his former caste status. The courts thus forced Indians back into a reliance on caste that they might otherwise have left behind in India. Still, the question seemed to have been settled in California.[21]

In Oregon, however, the bureau refused the naturalization of Bhagat Singh Thind, a veteran of the United States army, when he applied in 1920. Indians, like other aliens, had been drafted during World War I. Some Indians volunteered, and one Indian died on active duty in Pearl Harbor. The number of Indians in the United States army was not large, and there are few traces of their experiences. They undoubtedly suffered the same discrimination in uniform as out of uniform; one was refused restaurant service in Lansing, Michigan. Some Indians wore their turbans in the military, and they probably were not segregated into colored regiments. Thind wore his turban during the six months he spent in the army and received an honorable discharge. Had he been in the army three years, he might have tested the law that three-year veterans were eligible for citizenship. Several Chinese and 184 Japanese were granted certificates in Hawaii under this clause, and almost thirty-four thousand other aliens were granted citizenship in May and June of 1918.[22]

Thind brought his case under the 1906 naturalization law. He was a high-caste Hindu born in the Punjab, had graduated from Punjab University, and had entered the United States in 1913, probably as a student. He began his studies at the University of California at Berkeley and was on friendly terms with Ram Chandra and others connected with the Ghadar Press, but he denied any connection with Ghadar propaganda or approval of the activities of his friends. He was, he admitted, an advocate of the principle of India for the Indians and would like to see India rid of British rule, but he did not favor armed rebellion.

Federal district court judge Charles E. Wolverton thought that the question of Indian citizenship revolved around whether Indians should be allowed to remain in the United States without becoming citizens or should be deported because they were ineligible for citizenship. The zone bill of 1917 had barred Indians from the United States and had been applied retroactively for deportation, but it did not say that Indians should be barred from citizenship. Wolverton felt that the law should not be applied retroactively with regard to citizenship and that Thind should be admitted. He ordered the petition granted. The bureau of naturalization appealed the case to the supreme court.[23]

It took over two years for the Thind case to make its way onto the crowded docket of the highest court of the land. Naturalization of Indians continued during the interim. On 17 January 1922, the western division of Pennsylvania, ignoring the previous decision of the court of eastern division of the state, admitted an Indian to citizenship. In 1922, the supreme court also decided the Ozawa case. In order to understand the Thind case, one must understand the Ozawa case. Takao Ozawa was born in Japan and resided in the United States for twenty years. He spent three years as a student at the University of California, educated his children in American schools, attended an American church with his family, and spoke English at home. Ozawa was well qualified by character and education for citizenship. Since 1911, however, the bureau of immigration and naturalization had opposed the acceptance of papers from Japanese, just as it had opposed Indian naturalization. Over four hundred Japanese had already become citizens at that time, and almost as many had made declarations of intention to become citizens. Nonetheless, the bureau opposed Ozawa's application on the basis that he was not white.

The Ozawa case was argued before the supreme court in October 1922, and the next month justice George Sutherland delivered the opinion of the court. Sutherland, an English immigrant who had been educated in the United States and elected a senator from Utah, had been appointed to the supreme court in 1922 by Warren Harding. The question, said Sutherland, was not one of color, for the courts had decided that color was not a test. Color varied among the same race even among Anglo-Saxons, so there was no practical line of separation. The courts had applied the words *white* to persons of the Caucasian race, including Indians—a conclusion with which Sutherland saw no reason to differ. The assumption of the synonymous meaning of the words *white person* and *Caucasian* simplified but did not dispose of the problem, Sutherland went on, because borderline cases were still debatable and would have to be decided individually. Ozawa was clearly not Caucasian—a conclusion sustained by numerous scientific authorities. The supreme court had no other function than to ascertain and declare the will of Congress, Sutherland went on, and the court had decided that the will of Congress had been that Ozawa was ineligible for citizenship.[24]

Since Sutherland had referred specifically to Indians being admitted to citizenship within the definition of *white* as Caucasian, the attorneys for Thind assumed that they would have little trouble proving his eligibility. Thind based his case on the now-traditional combination of anthropological evidence and judicial precedent. Indians were Aryans and therefore Caucasians according to anthropologists, and the courts had accepted the term *Caucasian* as an equivalent of *white*.

The government had a different theory. It simply refused to accept the arguments of social scientists that Indians were Aryans, and hence Caucasians. The government argued that *white* should be interpreted according to the usage of the common man, and in that usage Indians were not white. Sutherland delivered the opinion for a unanimous court on 19 February 1923. Yes, the justices agreed, *free white persons* were words of common speech, words to be interpreted in accordance not with science but rather with the understanding of the "common man." And according to the "common man" *white* was not synonymous with *Caucasian* but had a considerably narrower definition. Indians could not be included in this popular definition. Furthermore, the 1917 exclusion of Indians by Congress must be taken as evidence that Congress did not want Asian immigration, and this conclusion was "persuasive of a similar attitude toward Asiatic naturalization as well."[25]

The supreme court had rejected science, history, legal precedent, and logic to put the Constitution at the disposal of a legal fiction called "the common man." Now ignorance would be bliss, one lawyer commented, for "the most ignorant man would believe that he could infallibly say who belonged to the white race."[26]

California exclusionists were delighted with the Thind decision. "This is surely an instance in which a court has decided on facts and not on inferences," noted the Fresno *Morning Republican* with satisfaction. The decision, said the San Francisco *Chronicle*, was "as important as the recent ruling holding Japanese ineligible to vote." Indians did not deserve naturalization, according to the *Chronicle*, for the "low-caste Hindus are degraded, and the high castes made this country a center of agitation for their domestic feuds."

In the celebration following the Sutherland decision, Californians did not forget the land held by the Indians. The Asiatic Exclusion League reminded Californians that Indians owned over two thousand acres of land and leased eighty-six thousand acres of "the most fertile land in the state." Actually, much of the land had been desert and marginal land reclaimed by the Indians after being considered worthless by Californians, but now they wanted it back. The San Francisco *Chronicle* demanded that the attorney general of California make a statement on what would be done to end the "menacing spread of Hindus holding our lands."

California attorney general U. S. Webb lost no time in replying. Within a few weeks district attorneys in Sacramento, Sutter, Colusa, and Glenn counties had instituted proceedings to revoke Indian purchases of land. Webb assured a *Chronicle* reporter that Indians would be forbidden from farming lands on leaseholds or contracts.[27]

After the Thind decision, clerks in California courts also began to refuse to issue marriage licenses to Indians applying for them with white women. One Indian man was refused a license even though neither the woman's parents nor the communities of the two young people opposed the marriage. Indians even heard rumors that Californians were attempting to have Indian children born in the United States declared ineligible for citizenship. The government had already prepared petitions asking for the cancellation of naturalization papers of Indians. The editor of *Nation* wrote, "it seems unthinkable that the law can be used retroactively."[28]

That was exactly what the justice department intended to do. Armed with the Thind decision, it filed a petition to denaturalize Das on 1 May 1923. During the spring of 1923, the bureau of naturalization also prepared petitions asking for the cancellation of naturalization of all Indians. Bureau officials argued that the provision in the Naturalization Act of 1906 authorized denaturalization if certificates had been procured illegally or by fraud. Since Indians had at no time been eligible for citizenship, the argument went, their certificates had been obtained through fraud and were illegal.

The clause included in the 1906 act was the first to allow denaturalization in cases of fraud. It was up to the courts to decide what the clause meant, however, and until 1915 courts interpreted it to mean bribery by the applicant—that is, a jurisdictional defense, not an error of law. In that year, a man was stripped of his citizenship after nineteen years because he had acted as a pimp for prostitutes in Montana. This man was not of good moral character when admitted, the judge decided, and therefore his certificate had been obtained by fraud and could be cancelled. During the war, the clause was further broadened by being used against German-Americans accused of disloyalty during World War I. In one 1918 case the judge assumed that comments considered disloyal in 1917 must presuppose greater disloyalty in 1888, when the defendant had been naturalized. On 22 May 1918, the justice department ordered

United States attorneys to bring denaturalization proceedings against any naturalized citizen evidencing disloyalty, whether or not he was German.[29]

Despite the success of the government in court, the United States did little denaturalizing. The British denaturalized 101 persons between 1918 and 1921, the French 368 between 1914 and 1918, but the United States only 6—all Germans—between 1918 and 1921.

The issue of denaturalization had been raised during the San Francisco conspiracy trial. At that time, Preston had told reporters that denaturalization proceedings might be brought against Das, but since Das was in jail, nothing was done. When immigration authorities began interviews of convicted Indians in preparation for their deportation, however, they ordered that Das could not be deported because he held citizenship papers. The United States attorney in San Francisco immediately brought proceedings to revoke his citizenship.[30]

Although still in the federal prison at Leavenworth, Kansas, Das began his own defense, aided by the Friends for the Freedom of India. The FFI argued that the situation of Indians was far more difficult than that of any denaturalized German alien. Because they had renounced their British citizenship to become Americans, they would have had to be naturalized again under British law to have a country, and the British would not permit naturalization of Indians who had been in the United States because they claimed the Indians had worked against the interests of Britain during the war. Das also wrote to attorney general A. Mitchell Palmer in May 1919, pointing out that he had not been involved in the shipment of arms to India and that he had returned voluntarily to stand trial when he learned that he had been indicted in San Francisco. Senator Joseph Ransdell interceded on behalf of Das.

Palmer asked Louis Post and the United States attorney in San Francisco, Annette Abbott Adams, for their opinions. Post replied with a strong endorsement of denaturalization because he felt that Das had procured his citizenship through fraud and had not been a person of good moral character when naturalized. Adams was even more vehemently opposed to allowing Das to remain a citizen. Denaturalization was entirely justified, she told Palmer, because Das had Russian anarchist bomb manuals in his possession at the time he became a citizen, his publications were anti-American, and he had exhibited a belligerent attitude at the trial. Preston, Adams's predecessor, agreed that Das was a "dangerous character" and not a credit to the United States as a citizen. Adams refused to drop the proceedings.

The continuing movement to denaturalize Germans made the position of Das even more precarious. In December 1919, a court decided that any act of disloyalty subsequent to naturalization could be considered to show continued disloyalty and thus "fraud." A judge in Washington state held in 1920 that "the fact that not until afterwards, in time of stress, is it made manifest that the desires, suffered to lie dormant, are stronger for their native than their adopted country, although this fact may not be fully realized at the time of their naturalization, renders it none the less a legal fraud for the applicant to fail to disclose his true, though latent feelings in such a matter." Adams soon argued a case carrying the interpretation of fraud in denaturalization even further. She maintained that there was no need to impute fraud at the time of naturalization. Even though good faith might have been in evidence at that time, "the criterion of original fraud must be the later conduct." Soon after, Adams was replaced by a new United States attorney in San Francisco, who wrote that the case seemed doubtful and suggested that it be dismissed. The case was left standing, however, and when Palmer left the office of attorney general and Post left his position in the labor department in the spring of 1921, denaturalization proceedings were still pending against Das. Not until September 1922 did the courts finally dismiss the proceedings against him.[31]

In 1923, courts also refused to continue denaturalization of German-Americans for their activities during the war. Activities in 1914 were no evidence of fraud and were not indicative of attitudes ten years earlier, when the man was naturalized, said an Oregon judge, William B. Gilbert, in reviewing a case brought there. "Citizenship, once bestowed upon proceedings in the federal courts, should not be lightly taken away," said Gilbert. Despite his ruling, the justice department filed new papers in May 1923 to denaturalize Das.

The justice department also brought cases to denaturalize all Indians, regardless of their political activities. At the end of November 1923, the first Indian case came up. Akhay Kumar Mozumdar had become a citizen on 30 June 1913 in the state of Washington, but proceedings for denaturalization were brought in California, where he was then living. Pandit defended Mozumdar and criticized the Thind decision. The judge rebuked Pandit for his criticism, told him that "an alien when he lands on the shores of this country, comes with no right at all of any natural kind to have extended to him the privilege of citizenship," and upheld the cancellation. Pandit appealed the case, but the circuit court of appeals upheld the Mozumdar decision. The justice department then filed a petition to denaturalize Pandit.[32]

Pandit argued his own case before a court of equity in February 1924.

The fact that he had been engaged by the Labor Defense League during the war to defend IWW members arrested in southern California was among the activities mentioned as reason for his denaturalization. Pandit argued, however, that he had conducted himself as a responsible member of society, had practiced law for over ten years in the courts of California, owned a fifteen-thousand-dollar home in Los Angeles, and that cancellation of his citizenship would deprive him of his livelihood and his property, call into question the legality of his marriage, and, under current laws, cause his wife to lose her citizenship. In September 1922, before either the Ozawa or Thind cases had been decided, Congress had passed a law providing that American women marrying aliens ineligible for citizenship would lose their citizenship. The intent of the act was apparently to keep American women from marrying Asian men. Denaturalization of Indians who had already married American women would now deprive native-born women of their citizenship rights ex post facto, and they would have to apply for naturalization. Seeing the merits of Pandit's arguments, the judge ordered that the case was not open for review because the government had waited too long.[33]

Indians expected the case to stop there. The United States attorney in Los Angeles, Joseph C. Burke, was reluctant to pursue the case any further, but the justice department replied that Pandit's objections were "wholly without merit" and ordered Burke to appeal the case. At the end of 1925, therefore, the Pandit case was still in the courts. Samuel McNabb, new attorney at Los Angeles, again questioned whether the case should continue. The commissioner of naturalization urged the justice department to proceed because the case had a "vitally important bearing upon the uniform administration of the naturalization law," particularly because similar cancellation suits were still pending. The government appealed the Pandit case once more.[34]

In the justice department there were lengthening lists of Indians who were to be denaturalized. The chief of the naturalization division denied that there was a drive against Indians and argued that he was just bringing cases as they came to his attention. Still, he went after Das, and when he could not locate Das to serve cancellation papers, he had them published in the newspapers. Das had somehow eluded the government long enough to receive his doctorate from Georgetown University in June 1924 and to marry an American woman. Das again took up the cause of the Indian-Americans in June 1926, after his wife, Mary K. Das, had been refused a passport on the grounds that her husband was ineligible for citizenship. Das, who gained an interview with supreme court justice Howard Taft to argue the injustice of Indians being deprived of citizenship, was able to get Taft to write a letter to the secretary of labor, calling the condition a "real injustice" and recommending special legislation.[35]

Pandit, meanwhile, was attempting to attack the whole concept of the understanding of the common man. If it meant the common man in the 1870s, when the term *white* had been reenacted into law by Congress, Pandit argued, then it must include Indians, for school geography books from that time identified five races, and the white or Caucasian race included Indians and Arabs. Children who were to become the common men of the 1870s recited this definition of the races and therefore could not possibly think Indians were not white. The prejudice against Indians dated from a later period, Pandit argued, when there had been an influx of laborers and prejudice had arisen against Chinese and Japanese. The act of 1917 did not deal with citizenship at all, and the rule of the common man was "inequitable and illogical." The decision, he said, had been a political one based on public policy and should not be retroactive. Early in November 1926, when the court upheld the decision that Pandit could not be denaturalized, the naturalization officials immediately announced that the decision did not change the Thind decision and that the case would be appealed again. McNabb again pleaded with the justice department to drop the case. Cancellation of Pandit's certificate was "an unequitable and unconscionable thing" from a moral standpoint, and McNabb was reluctant to proceed with the legal fight. The secretary of labor asked that the case proceed because there were a dozen denaturalization cases still pending.[36]

Das continued to lead the opposition to the denaturalization drive. He convinced Republican senator David Reed of Pennsylvania, who had had Indians in his regiment during the war, to introduce a resolution to confirm the citizenship of the men and to affirm that no American women would lose their citizenship through marriage to any of them. The bill went to the Senate committee on immigration and naturalization, and hearings were held in December. Members of the committee told Das that the bill did not make it out of committee because the administration was opposed to it. Das then took a copy of Taft's letter to the heads of the departments of state, labor, and justice. All of the men assured Das that they would not oppose the bill to validate citizenship but that they would oppose any bill classing all Indians as eligible for citizenship. The justice department continued to denaturalize. By December, forty-three men had been deprived of citizenship, and twelve more cases were pending.[37]

Das appealed to Reed again. "Everyone realizes that it is a simple justice to the persons concerned," Reed replied. "The whole trouble comes through the fear on the part of many Senators that it will set an uncomfortable precedent which would embarrass us if a similar bill were introduced for the benefit of Japanese." New York senator Royal S. Copeland had, meanwhile, introduced another bill declaring all Asian Indians white, a bill that the AFL supported. The committee did not support this bill either, and no hearings were held. Early in February 1927, Copeland wrote to Das, "I am sorry to say there is some opposition from the Administration to the Hindu Bill. I am doing what I can to straighten it out, but it is a difficult undertaking." At the beginning of the first session in 1927, the bill died.[38]

The following year, the justice department decided to appeal the Pandit case to the supreme court. There, on 14 March 1927, the government finally lost its case when the court refused a writ of certiorari. Only then did the commissioner of naturalization recommend that the pending denaturalization cases be cancelled. The labor department grudgingly concurred, and by April 1927, all of the cases had been dismissed. In reviewing the denaturalization cases, one commentator in the *Harvard Law Review* wrote that certainly the cases extended the language of the original act beyond its natural meaning or that intended by the legislature. To argue that the certificate was "illegally procured" when it was granted in accordance with the prevailing judicial opinion of the time seemed to him "an even greater perversion."[39]

The uniformity that the justice department had sought was still not possible, for although the forty-five pending cases had been cancelled, sixty-five Indians had already been denaturalized. Indians appealed through both Copeland and their attorneys to have the other men re-naturalized but without success. Two Indians who attempted to regain citizenship through the courts had their cases dismissed after long and expensive litigation.[40]

The test of "common understanding," as it came to be known, remained the law of the land and became part of the Constitution. Since the rule of "common understanding" had no legal definition, however, it was based on how well a person passed in his or her community for social purposes, and this test of social relationships was now applied to legal rights. Even in the slave states before the Civil War, laws had been governed by statutory or judge-made rule of degrees of blood rather than by social standards. Yet now, over half a century after the end of the Civil War, the courts accepted a national standard of discrimination based on color. Immigration and naturalization were now linked, with the 1917 immigration law imputing to Congress a narrow prejudice far beyond even the necessities of an exclusion policy based on race. The Thind decision was to spin out its implications in a 1934 case decided by justice Benjamin Cardozo, a case against the state of California. In this case, the court held that persons qualified as white "if the strain of colored blood in them is a half or a quarter, or, not improbably, even less, the governing test always . . . being that of common understanding."[41]

Into such a racist quagmire would the Thind decision drag the Constitution. As legal scholar Dudley McGovney said in opposing the rule of "common understanding," there might be an almost nationwide standard of discrimination against persons of African descent in matters relating to social intercourse, but there was little evidence of a national standard with respect to the Chinese, the Japanese, or the Indians. Even if there were such a standard, he said, how could Americans assume "that Congress intended to apply it to naturalization, which does not affect the relations in which this standard is supposed to operate?"[42]

The Thind case had even broader consequences for Asians in California. In November 1923, the supreme court held that the California alien land law did not violate the Fourteenth Amendment. With the Thind and Ozawa decisions, the attempt to take land away from Asians began. On 9 January 1924 Webb, longtime leader of anti-Asian sentiment in California, advised private attorneys that contracts to sell land to Indians were void and that Indians were not eligible to buy land under the 1920 alien land law. Three days later, in a conference in San Francisco with district attorneys from forty-nine counties in California, Webb decided that no landowner could make any contract with Japanese or Indians that would give the Asians a right or interest in the produce of California's soil. Even cropping contracts with Japanese and Indians were to be considered a violation of the law. All Indians still owning land in Yuba and Sutter counties were ordered to negotiate immediately for disposal of property and to make plans to terminate all leases at the close of the season. "The laudable verdict of the conference," wrote one Indian in California, "is that the Japanese and East Indians either must take to day labor or get out of the country."[43]

There was more to the case than just discrimination against Indians in America, as the India office well knew. While the British refused to protect Indian rights in the United States, Indians were expected to grant special privileges to white Americans in India. "It must appear as a sort of international irony," wrote the editor of the *Modern Review* in Calcutta, "that whilst the Racial Distinctions Bill in India places the Americans in a privileged position, in America the natives of India are discriminated against and placed in a humiliating condition. The thing cannot rest where it is." In the Indian National Congress, a representative from Allahabad made a motion to double the taxes of British and American residents and to refuse them the right to own land. There was no hope for the motion to pass, but it expressed an indignation as strong as that over the insulting treatment Indians were receiving in British colonies.[44]

American missionaries feared that discrimination in the United States might endanger their special status in India. The *Nation* published a memorandum signed by American missionaries in India that the Thind decision had "caused a deep resentment in the mind of India" which would widen the gulf between East and West and "give added impetus to the rising tide of resentment and bitterness against the white exclusiveness." The missionaries regretted that their country had augmented the Indians' bitterness and asked that the alien land law not be applied to Indians because Americans held large quantities of land in India. Landholding should be equal in the two countries.[45]

California Indians appealed to the British ambassador in Washington to protest the land law. Under a United States treaty with Britain, British subjects were allowed to own property in the United States and Americans to hold property in British possessions. In May 1924, the British embassy did notify the state department that the land law was causing undue hardship to the Indians, but instead of protesting the law, the ambassador simply complained that Indians were being given too short a time to dispose of property and suggested an extension of time. The question of discrimination in the United States was raised briefly in the House of Commons and then dropped. In India, the British blocked attempts of Indians to withhold concessions to Americans in retaliation for the actions of the Californians.[46]

Asians, often with the help of their white neighbors, bankers, and lawyers, developed many ways to evade these laws. Sometimes Asians sold property to trusted friends, other times friends held leases, and frequently there were simply verbal leasing agreements or land was registered in the name of American-born children. In the Imperial Valley, bankers and lawyers held land for Punjabi farmers or formed corporations for them. The law certainly did not end access to land by Asian aliens, as politicians had expected. Still, the law did cause hardship to Asians, who never could be quite sure that some event might not expose and end their illegal access to land.[47]

The Pahkar Singh case was one example of how the law could lead to violent conflict. Pahkar Singh had leased his ranch in the Imperial Valley with only a verbal agreement. With an investment of $14,000 in 320 acres of lettuce, his harvest in 1925 was worth an estimated $50,000. Just as he was harvesting the lettuce, however, his Anglo partners claimed the entire product of his labor. In a rage, Singh murdered the two men. He spent fifteen years in jail. Ironically, however, the case also proved that there was considerable community support for agreements to evade the law. Many small Anglo farmers saw the partners' action as an example of the ruthlessness of big growers and shippers. They sympathized with Singh's response and continued to shelter Indians from the law. Some Sikhs believed that Singh's violent defense of his rights in the verbal agreement would make Anglos afraid to cheat them. Mainly, however, the Pahkar Singh case revealed the continuing search for ways to surmount a law based on racial discrimination.[48]

Discrimination against Indians also widened as Congress applied the same standard of exclusion against other immigrants. Once the supreme court had decided that Congress had meant that Asians could be excluded from naturalization, Congress no longer felt restrained in its adoption of a national law excluding aliens ineligible for citizenship. Washington state representative Albert Johnson introduced the bill, the administration offered no opposition, and the bill became law in May 1924. The San Francisco *Examiner* wrote exultantly, "This is not race prejudice. It is race preservation."[49]

The immigration law of 1924 openly and officially committed the government of the United States to the ideology developed by the labor department years before. Immigration policy would now foster culturally homogeneous communities, composed as far as possible of people of the same race with a uniform ethnic and political outlook. To maintain a stable national character, immigrants had to be thoroughly assimilable. "To all appearances the question of colour is one that will increase rather than lessen in importance, and it appears to be hopeless even to suggest a basis of agreement that would meet conditions so fundamentally different," wrote one commentator in 1924. There was no possibility of worldwide law, he concluded.[50]

The reactions of Asians to the great white wall erected by Americans was one of outrage. Madame Sun Yat-sen told reporters that she was the wife of a "coolie" and that she would not return to the United States to visit her husband unless America repealed the exclusion law. Japan promised again to bring up the issue before the League of Nations. The *Modern Review*, once the eager exponent of a meeting of East and West, ran a scalding editorial on "anti-Asiatic fever," demanding that some criteria other than race be used as a standard to select immigrants. Exclusion of all Asians would only lead to further wars—a foolish policy after all the American boasts of plans and points to attain universal peace. Immigration, wrote an Indian commentator in the *Modern Review*, should not be "a question of national sovereignty, but a question of national decency." Mary Das voiced the feelings of Indians in another article: "In America today, as well as in other countries, there exist double standards of international morality—one for the superior White-man and the other for the Asiatics. The people of India are enslaved Asiatics, and they cannot, under the existing circumstances, expect to have equal rights with the *superior Whites*." Gandhi said America had nothing to give to India and India, for the present, had nothing to give to America.[51]

The reaction of the internationally acclaimed Nobel laureate Rabindranath Tagore to the Indian policies of the United States was perhaps the most important. Tagore had visited the United States, had many American friends, and had formerly praised America for its international leadership. Now he denounced Asian exclusion and refused to return to the United States. The poet said he did not intend to revisit America. Praise from American authors and publication of his *Reminiscences* by Macmillan could do little to restore the faith Tagore had had in the United States when he had sent his son to college there in 1906. To the editor of the *Atlantic* who wrote to ask Tagore why he would not visit the United States, Tagore decried the "utter lack of freedom with which the atmosphere is charged."[52]

In fact, the immigration law did not eliminate Asians entirely from the body politic. The law allowed for the reunification of families by allowing wives and unmarried children under eighteen to enter. Moreover, children born in the United States were American citizens with all the rights of non-Asian citizens. The law did signify more than that racial discrimination lay behind the exclusion of "aliens ineligible for citizenship." It also signaled the end of the period of Asian participation in the international migration that had so clearly marked the late nineteenth and early twentieth centuries. The law seemed to Asians to end that period of migration on a particularly ominous note, for they were apparently being excluded not for economic reasons but for racial reasons. A period that might have led to greater international understanding thus ended with misunderstanding. The industrialized nations had developed a labor policy to use the workers of Asian nations to meet their own economic needs and had then discarded them as unworthy to become permanent members of the host nations. The United States was no different from European nations, but the government's policy did signify that the United States was not ready to move beyond racialism to cultural pluralism. The economic need was over, as the restriction on immigration of Europeans as well as Asians showed. But the restriction first of Asians and then of Southern Europeans indicated that economics was still inextricably combined with ethnicity in America.

Pacific Coast exclusionists could look back with satisfaction on the results of their twenty-year battle against the "Hindu invasion." Excluded from immigration, prosecuted for their political activities, threatened with deportation, excluded from citizenship, denaturalized, excluded from land ownership, and regulated even in the choice of a mate in the states where most of them lived, Indians now formed a small band of people set apart from Americans by what truly must have seemed a great white wall.

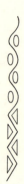

Epilogue: The Pioneers

We are all inhabitants of India,
Offspring of one—Mother.
—Ghadar protest song

After 1925, immigrants settled down to make the best of their restricted life in America. The majority continued to farm or perform manual labor, and a small minority, most former students, entered professions or became merchants. Large numbers of Indians continued to organize for the independence of India and for the rights of Indians in North America, and to recruit American allies for their cause. Some men married; others chose to remain in all-male living groups. Most attempted to maintain their old networks with other Indian immigrants. Together they faced the difficult task of living on the margins of United States and Canadian society.

Regardless of restrictive immigration laws, Indians would almost certainly have settled in the United States and Canada. Immigrants, no matter how much they initially intend to return home, tend to develop support communities that give them roots within the once-alien population. Restrictions probably encouraged some Indians who would have left to remain and join permanent Indian enclaves. By returning to India, new immigrants might suffer British retaliation for their political activities and might not be allowed to return to North America later, should they wish to do so. Restrictions meant that few of the male immigrants could bring their wives and families, so many formed attachments with American-born women or other immigrant women, thus loosening their cultural ties to India.[1]

The older immigrant workers who remained in California typically married Mexican women and formed families at the edge of the Mexican migrant community. Of some four hundred Indian families formed in California before 1946, almost 80 percent involved Mexican women and Indian men. These unions were often uneasy. The wives were mostly young Mexicans, from female-centered families, who insisted on raising the children in their own culture, teaching them Spanish or English, bringing them up as Catholics, and rooting them in the Hispanic community. Indian husbands, most of whom were Punjabis, were typically tolerant of their wives' religions but often attempted to reassert their patriarchal traditions of family control. Although the men usually retained control of the family income, they could not discipline or control their younger wives. According to one study, at least 20 percent of Imperial Valley marriages ended in divorce—an even higher average than for other divorce-prone Californians. Both men and women found these marriages unsatisfactory. In divorce proceedings, the women demanded—and usually received—from the courts a division of community property and custody of the children. Even where divorce did not occur, children seldom married Indians or even children from other "Mexican-Hindu" families. Most chose to marry Anglos or Hispanics, moving away from these transitional families back into the cultural mainstream.[2]

Although their homelife was sometimes troubled, the men achieved a surprising degree of economic success in California. Indeed, some familial conflict probably resulted from the overriding determination of Punjabis to invest family income in land even when their wives wanted to use it to raise the material standards of the families. Many Mexican women were from migrant communities whose members commonly chose factory work rather than landowning and disposable income rather than land. Punjabi farmers valued working their own land above other types of work and also above material comfort. Income for them meant a chance to lease or buy more land.

This desire to possess land prevailed even against the alien land laws of California. Karen Leonard, who has studied the Punjabis in the Imperial Valley, has found that the Indians, like the Japanese, evaded the alien land laws. Punjabis used both the American legal system and carefully developed networks among American businessmen to obtain control of farmland. Not until 1933, when a grand jury in the Imperial Valley indicted sixty-five Indians for conspiracy to evade the alien land laws, did these farmers encounter much difficulty. The conviction of these men in 1934, however, was followed by a supreme court ruling that made it virtually impossible for the state of California to use the conspiracy statute in land cases. Thereafter, Indians had little difficulty in controlling land.[3]

Despite their economic success in the Imperial Valley, immigrant communities did not live out the interwar years removed from either American or Indian politics. Immigration restrictions and the continuation of revolutionary activities provided points of contention. The center for these conflicts was primarily in northern California. While Punjabis in the Imperial Valley concentrated on devising ways of developing landholding families, those in the northern part of the state, who married less frequently, seemed to have combined their concerns for farming with more active resentment against British control in India.

Officially, of course, the United States government continued to maintain a hands-off policy toward British India. Although Gandhi received support from some Americans committed to nonviolence, there was generally little interest in his crusade. Arthur Brisbane, a New York columnist who was considered by many to be the voice of popular American values during the interwar years, explained the negative attitude toward Gandhian methods: "In these days you only get justice when you fight for it. Even then it is slow." Taraknath Das sent a copy of Brisbane's article to the *Modern Review*, in Calcutta, with the advice that Indians must be more assertive to impress the West.[4]

Sikhs also saw assertiveness as the only way to achieve Indian independence. In India, Sikhs fought for control of their temples through the gurdwara reform movement and for workers' control of the land through the Kirti Kisan, a workers' and farmers' party. Although the gurdwara reform movement was elitist, it provided a focus for unification of rural and urban elements, gave the Sikh community political representation, and provided a method of organizing and making community resources available for political activities. The British arrested, imprisoned, and executed some leaders of the Sikh Akali movement in the early 1920s. Following the arrest of the Akalis, Sikhs in California and British Columbia began to raise money for the men's families. When the Akalis condemned the use of Sikh troops in defense of Shanghai, the British were concerned that West Coast Sikhs might support a revolution in Shanghai.[5]

The struggle for equality in North America remained linked to the larger issue of political independence for India. Indians continued to believe that political independence was essential for equality, and they did not forget their martyrs. For many years the Sikhs commemorated the death of Mewa Singh, the man who assassinated Hopkinson, in their temples in North America. By 1922, Sikhs also dominated a revitalized Ghadar Party which continued its interest in freedom for India throughout the interwar period. The party relied, as it had done earlier, on the bitterness of the Sikhs and on their willingness to use a religious base for their political organizing. While becoming predominantly a Sikh organization, the Ghadar Party retained its nationalism; Ghadarites envisioned an independent and united India as their goal.

The Ghadar Party continued to collect money and to search for international allies. Although the Berlin Indian group had no official recognition from the German government after the end of World War I, Agnes Smedley and a handful of Indian revolutionaries continued to work for independence there. After 1923, however, the British government pressured the Germans into expelling Indian nationalists, and thereafter the German government began to restrict the political activities of Indians. Chatto, Smedley, and others went underground to continue their activities.[6]

Russia, which had indicated an interest in promoting revolution in colonized nations in Asia as early as 1918, seemed to be the only nation willing to support the Indians after 1923. Mao Tse-tung and Ho Chi Minh, as well as Indian communist H. M. Roy, had received early support from the Soviets, and Chatto moved to Moscow to continue his revolutionary work in the 1920s. The California Ghadarites, expecting no help from either America or western European countries, also looked to the Soviets for encouragement. They sent two representatives to the fourth congress of the Comintern in November 1922. There is no clear indication of what relation the Ghadar Party developed with the Soviets, but Ghadarites probably received little more than encouragement.[7]

Whatever interest Russia had in Indian revolution declined after 1924. During that year, British officials arrested all Indian Communist leaders, tried them for conspiracy, and silenced the revolutionary movement. Britain also pressured Russia into reducing its support for revolution in India, and Russia thereafter turned its interest from India to the growing revolutionary movement in China. Russia offered support to nationalists Sun Yat-sen and Chiang Kai-shek, as well as to Communist revolutionaries. Soon, however, the Chinese revolution began to threaten British interests in Shanghai. As Chiang Kai-shek's forces swept northward from Canton in 1926 to threaten Shanghai, British India rushed a detachment of Sikh troops to defend the international settlement there. The Sikh Akali Dal group condemned the dispatch of troops to China as a "national humiliation" and offered support to the Chinese struggle for freedom. By 1927, the British believed that Sikh revolutionaries were leaving the West Coast to work for revolution in China.[8]

The British continued to monitor the situation in North America during the 1920s. By paying propagandists such as Rustom Rustamji, an Indian Parsee, to denounce nationalist activities and agents such as Canadian special immigration officer M. J. Reid to conduct surveillance, the British were able to contain Indian activities on the West Coast. The British knew that the Indians were raising their own funds and that after 1924 Indians had little support from Russia for armed revolution in India. But the Chinese threat to Shanghai and the Sikh opposition to British defense plans there caused the British great concern about the West Coast Ghadarites.[9]

The viceroy of India himself wrote to the secretary of state for India in January 1927, asking that police officers watch California Sikh communities and censor their correspondence. "The main object is to enable us to keep a close watch on developments of Bolshevik or Sikh propaganda in Shanghai as affecting Indians." In February, the viceroy wrote again, urging the secretary of state to watch the activities of agitators and the literature of the Ghadar Party, as well as to censor all mail to Indians in China. The Ottawa government subsequently reported that it was systematically watching the Sikhs in British Columbia and the publishers of *Ghadar*.[10]

Such surveillance was less important than British action in Shanghai. Accepting British support for Chinese nationalists in return for suppression of the Communists, Chiang Kai-shek turned on his former allies and saved Shanghai for the British. The Ghadar Party lived on in California during the 1930s, and the British frequently complained to the U.S. state department regarding the party's activities. The United States government never again prosecuted the Ghadarites. The California Bureau of Criminal Investigation, a state agency that investigated violations of the law, did infiltrate the party with informants and conducted a public campaign against Ghadarites calling them Communists. The restrictive immigration laws and the violation of those laws by some Indians made the immigrant communities vulnerable to government attacks in the 1930s.[11]

Some Indians did violate immigration laws. Indians crossed borders illegally in part because they felt that the laws were an unjust restriction on their right to free movement, in part because they felt immigration officials were collaborating with the British, and in part because it was easy to cross the unguarded frontier along with other immigrants. It is not known how many Indians entered the United States illegally during the interwar period. Probably most were Sikhs. The Ghadar Party undoubtedly helped some, particularly political refugees whom it feared immigration authorities might hand over to the British. At least some Ghadarites were crossing the Mexican border and traveling to the Panama Canal Zone to mail literature from there in an effort to elude British censors. The Ghadar Party may also have aided Sikhs who simply wished to cross the border from Canada or Mexico to work in the United

States. Since so many immigrants left the United States during the Great Depression because of the lack of jobs, however, it seems more likely that British suppression of political activities was the major reason for these illegal entries by 1930. In 1931, the British asked informally for an investigation of California Sikhs.[12]

Whatever the cause of immigrant involvement in illegal immigration, the result was tragic. By early 1931, California's criminal investigation bureau had thoroughly infiltrated the Ghadar Party. The bureau's chief, Clarence S. Morrill, had recruited informants who were apparently suspected within the Indian community to be agents for the British government. One informant, who had served as an interpreter for the Berkeley police department, was the son of a Punjabi police official and was known as a British undercover agent as well. Between 1927 and 1931, more than twenty-five murders occurred in the Indian immigrant communities of California, and most were committed by other Indians.[13]

All these murders could not have been connected with the Ghadar Party or with investigations by California officials. Some apparently occurred before immigration officials had infiltrated the party, and others had little to do with politics. California officials, however, attributed most of the murders to the Ghadarites, who, they claimed, had organized a smuggling ring to bring men in from Mexico to spread Communist doctrine. What began as a "discreet inquiry" by San Francisco immigration authorities in 1931 ended as a public crusade against the Ghadarites by Morrill, who announced unequivocally that the Ghadar Party was being financed by funds from the Communist Party and that it was responsible for at least fifteen murders in the previous five years.[14]

Ghadar Party officials maintained their commitment to United States democracy as a model and attributed the murders to private feuds. Most murders probably were purely private matters, but a few were retaliations against undercover agents who were furnishing information to American officials. Most Ghadarites did see the United States as their model for the Indian nation; only a few supported Communism as the way to obtain independence. Once again, British concern, together with the quickness of Californians to distrust and condemn Asian communities, resulted in conflict over the activities of the Indians. Despite the controversy, however, the Ghadar Party continued to support Indian independence. When it disbanded in August 1947, it turned all its assets over to the new Indian government.[15]

Indian immigrant communities maintained a strong commitment to nationalism. The same nationalist spirit that had nurtured the growth of the Ghadar Party also helped immigrants to find an outlet for their frustration at finding their rights restricted in North America.

During the interwar period the British made their last stand in India. They adjusted foreign policy to reduce the influence of the Communist Party, which had strong support in Bengal, and of the Akali Party, which had strong support in the Punjab. They kept nonviolent noncooperation at bay by arresting Gandhi and other Indian National Congress leaders, and they embarked on a policy of supporting religious differences as a way of maintaining control. Nothing worked completely, but each policy helped to prevent an Indian revolution and maintained constitutionalism as the only viable policy for Indian nationalists.

The British continued to allow Canada to regulate immigration from other commonwealth nations, and Canadians chose to continue restriction of Indian immigration. A few Indians held trading licences in Vancouver and Victoria, but most remained at work in the British Columbia lumber industry. During the 1920s, a few Indian wives and children were admitted—five wives and four children in 1923, for example. The total pioneer population, probably only about a thousand in 1921, had dwindled to 720 by 1932. British Columbia steadfastly denied Indians the franchise, and repeated attempts by Indians to regain voting rights failed until 1938, when Indians, Japanese, and Chinese were granted the right to vote there. Canadian officials watched Indians closely. Indians had few opportunities to engage in political activities beyond supporting the California-based Ghadar Party.[16]

The British also successfully maintained United States government support of British colonialism in India. During the 1920s, however, American religious periodicals, once hostile to Indian independence, gradually moved toward support of the nationalist movement because of Gandhi's nonviolent crusade. This shift was followed by a similar movement in secular journals in the 1930s. During the 1920s, middle-class Indians continued to build organizations with which American supporters could work. In 1928, after the death of Lajpat Rai, the man who had headed the Home Rule League in the United States during World War I, a memorial meeting was held in New York. It was sponsored by the Hindusthan Association of America, the Indian Freedom Foundation, the India Society of America, the Maha-Bodhi Society of America, the Sat Sanga, and the Vedanta Society. But these organizations had only narrow support among religious leaders, Socialists, and a number of liberals, many university-based. Not until the late 1930s, when a greater number of Americans began to oppose racial injustice at home and abroad, was there renewed interest in Indian independence.[17]

The movement was led by a group of Indians who were successful businessmen or professionals. The most well-known Indian to foster American interest in India and to work toward regaining Indian citizenship rights in the United States was Sirdar Jagjit Singh, who became president of the newly formed India League of America in 1938. J. J., as he was known, arrived in the United States in 1926, a six-foot Sikh in his twenties who had already been a member of the Indian National Congress. As an importer of Indian goods in New York, J. J. flourished during the 1930s, developing a wealthy clientele among social and theatrical circles. Once established as a successful merchant, he began in the late 1930s to act as an unofficial lobbyist for India and Indians. Donating money to the league and then gaining control of it, he advanced the group's cause effectively by drawing on his connections with columnists and radio commentators. He arranged a trip to India for Claire Booth Luce, managed to get *Time* magazine to support Indian nationalists, and began to corner congressmen and diplomats. He was able to combine westernization with ethnic individualism—he wore a black homburg rather than a turban and shaved daily rather than maintaining the traditional Sikh beard, but continued to wear a *kara*, the thin iron bracelet that was one of the five distinguishing marks of a Sikh and seemed to symbolize the westernized Indian.[18]

Sirdar Jagjit Singh was not the only middle-class Indian to forge new links with Americans. Mubarak Ali Khan, founder of the Indian Welfare League in 1937, worked to help the unemployed and lobbied for civil rights for Indians in America. Khan had come to the United States in 1913 and had become a successful farmer. He farmed in the fertile Salt River Valley in Arizona and gained considerable community support for Indians, despite the prejudice that lingered there. Khan wrote to U.S. attorney general Francis Biddle in 1944, arguing that granting citizenship to Indians would provide an important link to Asia and would be proof of the permanence of the United Nations doctrines, then being espoused by Franklin Roosevelt and by many liberal Americans. Members of the National Committee for India's Freedom, the All-India Muslim League, and several other Indian groups joined in the movement to promote the cause of Indians and to help build important support groups within crucial American constituencies.[19]

A number of Indians had battled for restoration of citizenship throughout the 1920s and 1930s. Each time, however, Congress had balked. Still committed to Asian exclusion, Congress saw no reason to reverse its exclusionary position. The work of active Indian organizations, together with the outbreak of World War II, finally reversed the wall of discrimination established years before. Many Britons, most notably Winston Churchill, clung tenaciously to the failing colonial empire. During the war, when the United States needed Asian allies, an independent India seemed very attractive. In 1942, President Roosevelt suggested dominion status for India as a war measure but backed off when he realized the depth of Churchill's opposition to an independent India. Roosevelt hoped to use India as a back door to Japan, but diplomacy with both Indians and British proved difficult. Caught between a stubbornly entrenched colonial power and nationals who wanted Britain to "quit India," Americans accepted their difficult role in India and waited. On 1 February 1944, Roosevelt assured Indians that American troops were there only to defeat Japan, but the Indians were not so sure.[20]

In 1942, only 40 percent of Americans could locate India on a map. Yet by Christmas of 1943, thousands of American troops were in India—the first sizable number of Americans to reach there. American soldiers celebrated Christmas by doing a snake dance through the streets of New Delhi and eating turkey at camps. From Ramgarh, in Bihar Province, where there was a training center for Chinese troops, Americans sent home greeting cards that reflected their attempts to adopt something of the Indian environment. A turbaned Santa Claus, with a wreath of holly on one side of his turban and a China-Burma-India insignia on the other, grinned over the message, "Salaams from India." Americans kept out of Indian politics, but Indians worried about foreign designs as Americans established air bases, supply depots, repair centers, defense works, and frontier outposts. Individual encounters with Indians—whether good or bad—had little to do with the growing anti-American sentiment in India. As Americans yielded to British colonial policy needs, Indian disillusionment grew. By late 1945, after the war had ended, Indians were rioting against American troops still stationed in India.[21]

The attempt to show Indians some goodwill by restoring citizenship and establishing a token quota of immigrants seemed one small way for the United States to counter growing antagonism toward American troops. Previously, several bills to naturalize Indians already in the United States had been introduced into Congress, but none made it out of committee. After October 1943, when Congress lifted both immigration and naturalization barriers for the Chinese, the India League broadened its support and its demands to obtain similar rights for Indians. Sirdar Jagjit Singh convinced Republican Clare Booth Luce and Democrat Emmanuel Celler to introduce identical bills in Congress that would grant the same rights to Indians that the Chinese had obtained. Despite arguments by Luce that the bill was a pragmatic one to keep India as an ally, and Celler's argument that it would remedy the racial arrogance of American immigration policy, the committee was stubbornly opposed to these bills or any of the several others introduced in the House. At hearings held by the House committee on immigration and naturalization, Indians spoke eloquently in favor of the bills, but still nothing happened. Finally, in March 1945, Roosevelt sent William Phillips, who had gone to India as his personal representative, to testify secretly in favor of the bill. Statutory discrimination against Indians, Roosevelt wrote to the chairman of the committee, "now serve no useful purposes, and [is] incongruous and inconsistent with the dignity of both our peoples."

Roosevelt's action moved the bill out of the House committee and onto the floor of the House, where it was finally passed in October 1945. In the Senate, however, southern Democrats and midwestern Republicans joined to oppose it. Despite spreading anti-American riots in India, the Senate was unconvinced that the gesture was harmless, let alone useful. Not until July 1946 did Congress pass a bill granting naturalization and allowing an immigration quota for both Indians and Filipinos.[22]

As Indian immigrants had always predicted, nothing ensured the respect of Indians in foreign countries better than independence for India. Achieved only after agonizingly slow negotiations with Britain and a bloody civil war that shattered the Punjab, independence in 1947 nevertheless brought great satisfaction to Indians in the United States who had long worked for it. For Sikhs in America, who had always envisioned a unified India, the partition of India was deeply disappointing. Rather than Indians, they were now to be Indians and Pakistanis, in addition to the traditional division of Sikhs, Hindus, and Muslims. These divisions were difficult for men who had come from a united if unfree India, who had suffered successes and failures together for decades in America, and who had begun to feel united. Still, the pride of nationhood moved the old-timers, especially when prime minister Jawaharlal Nehru visited the United States and Canada in October 1949.

After addressing Congress and the Canadian parliament, Nehru spoke before a huge crowd in the Greek Theater at the University of California at Berkeley. It was a fitting culmination for the years of exile and hope.[23]

Although United States immigration laws did not yet admit Indians in the same numbers as the peoples of other countries until 1965, Nehru's visit signaled the end of the first phase of the Indian immigrant experience in America. Indians moved rapidly into the political mainstream in the United States. Best known for his political success was Dalip Saund, who farmed, worked for citizenship in the United States, and, after Indians regained their citizenship in 1946, became a congressman. Saund had immigrated to the United States from a middle-class though uneducated family in the Punjab in 1920. He earned three degrees from the University of California at Berkeley, including a Ph.D. in mathematics, before settling down to farming in the older Indian immigrant community in the Imperial Valley. Saund worked first as a foreman on a cotton farm for Indian friends, then as a farm owner. By 1928, he had married an American woman, and together they became involved in civic activities. Saund helped to organize the Indian National Congress Association of America and, after helping to fight for citizenship, became a judge. In 1956, he successfully ran for Congress. He was elected twice, but his political career was cut short in 1962 by a disabling stroke.[24]

The immigration law of 1952 maintained a small quota for Indians. A similar law passed in Canada established a quota of 250 immigrants a year from India and Pakistan. Gradually, the process of reuniting families began. Wives and children joined aging pioneers. At last, Indian communities began to resemble other immigrant communities. Indians continued their work in Canada and in the United States to gain freer entry for other Indians.

After 1965 in the United States and after 1967 in Canada, immigration laws were revised to admit Indians in numbers equal to those for people of other countries. The United States law, fully implemented by 1968, allowed large numbers of Indians and other Asians to immigrate. The law gave preference to highly trained and educated professionals, however, and the second wave of Indian immigration was thus much different from the first, when workers had crowded the ships. These Indians brought their families, fleeing competition for professional jobs in India that were the only alternative to landed indebtedness. Almost a hundred thousand engineers, physicians, scientists, professors, teachers, business people, and their dependents had entered the United States by 1975. Urban, educated, and English-speaking, these families experienced a relatively smooth transition from life in India to life in America. The professionals, who were mostly male college graduates between twenty and forty years of age, found well-paid employment in hospitals, corporations, and academic institutions. Some women were also professionals, but many were technical and clerical workers, who also found jobs easily. Birth rates were low among these immigrants; most families were small, usually with three to five members, and with both parents present. With careful financial management, these families were able to invest in land, houses, and shops. They took pride in the fact than an independent India stood ready to guarantee that they received the same civil liberties granted to other immigrants. The postwar interest of Americans in Indian religion, philosophy, literature, and music ensured a better welcome for these Indians than that received by earlier immigrants, who had competed economically with American laborers.[25]

These new immigrants had to sacrifice much to succeed, however. They worked long hours, at highly competitive jobs, and encountered discrimination when they attempted to move into administrative positions. American life-styles contrasted with those in India in ways that seemed to threaten traditional family roles. The economic independence of some women concerned their husbands. Working wives were not always able to provide traditional care and services even if they remained committed to traditional roles, for they lacked the support of relatives who would have helped in India. Parents also worried about the erosion of family authority. Daughters, whose occupation and marriage could be closely controlled by the family in India, asserted their right to choose work and husband or to remain single. Sons did not feel the responsibility toward the family that was expected of them. Children found it difficult to maintain both an Indian and an American identity. Still, most Indians adapted to American life and at the same time recreated important aspects of Indian culture in the United States. More than eight thousand became citizens between 1966 and 1975. During these first years many women retained their Indian citizenship, thus keeping open the possibility of returning to India. Still, Indians sought citizenship more quickly than most other Asian groups during the years from 1969 to 1978, and Asians as a whole sought citizenship more quickly than non-Asian groups.[26]

Despite their desire to integrate through acquiring United States citizenship, these Indians were in many ways more traditional than the early pioneers. The earlier immigrants shared a "political memory" not only of a time when India was a united mother country and of their

struggles to obtain justice in an inhospitable land, but also of their experiences as rural, isolated individuals who formed separate communities. Those differences were particularly evident in California, where
pioneer agrarian communities still existed. There was an uneasy truce
between the old and the new immigrants. And some of the older Sikhs
felt great distress when Sikh-Hindu conflicts broke out in the Punjab.
Their militance had been directed at a unified India. The new Sikh
separatism confused and saddened them.[27]

Beyond the concerns of the new and old immigrant communities,
there was the undeniable fact that the Asian population as a whole was
growing and changing in the United States. By 1985, Indians formed a
community of more than five hundred thousand—10 percent of the more
than five million Asians and their descendants in the United States.
Though fewer in number than Chinese, Filipinos, Japanese, Vietnamese,
and Koreans, Indians formed an important part of the new Asian immigrant population, which by the mid–1980s accounted for almost half
of all immigrants to the United States. In California and Hawaii, where
almost half of the Asian immigrants live, tensions have begun to increase
again. This time it is the middle classes of the United States and India
that confront the tensions.

Today, however, the Pacific Rim is also an area influenced by the ties
and tensions of trade. The tensions caused by the interaction of countries
along the Pacific Rim have extended over several centuries, but the
period when Asian countries allowed their workers to emigrate overseas
to solve economic problems is largely over. Instead, workers stay home,
and the countries export the products of their industry. Trade, like immigration, produces tensions.

For Asian immigrants, San Francisco and Vancouver had been the
storm centers of many of the earlier tensions. No Statue of Liberty welcomed Asian immigrants to the West Coast. And unlike Ellis Island,
Angel Island did not come to symbolize an easy transition into the land
of liberty. It produced, as one Asian immigrant remembered, "a bowl
full of tears." Americans and Canadians had erected a great white wall
against Chinese, Japanese, Korean, Filipino, and Indian workers.[28]

The United States and Canada had been the destination of only a few
Indians. By the time Indians arrived on the West Coast of America, anti-
Asian attitudes and activities of workers of European heritage were
already forcing governments to restrict the future immigration of Asians
and the civil liberties of those who had already entered. Despite the
small number of Indians who entered the United States and Canada

during the first two decades of the century—probably not more than ten thousand—their history in North America was one of the most complex of any immigrant group. Because Indian migration coincided with the first great upsurge of twentieth-century militance by American workers and of nationalism by Asian workers, Indian immigrants' struggle to enter North America became more than just a local or even a national issue.

From the time the first several thousand Sikhs arrived on the West Coast between 1900 and 1910, the stage was set for a drama of international proportions. Organized workers responded to the new immigrants from India as they might have to an invading army. Alexander Saxton has called the Chinese an "indispensable enemy," in the formation of late-nineteenth-century West Coast unionism.[29] So too were the Indians. One after another, old policies supporting open immigration succumbed to pressure by workers to halt the immigration from India. The barriers erected against Indian workers, like those established against Chinese, Japanese, Korean, and Filipino workers, assured that each Asian nation would eventually have to deal with its economic problems without the safety valve offered by immigration to North America.

For the United States, Asian exclusion led to admission of Mexican immigrants to solve employers' labor needs. United States immigration policies soon encouraged Mexican workers to flow north in times of seasonal demand and south again in times of surplus. This flexible border policy, combined with an increased dependence upon agricultural technology and upon the labor of women, allowed agriculture to expand along the West Coast even with the restriction of Asian immigration. Exclusion policies thus led directly to the expansion of the Hispanic population in the United States and to another cycle of confrontation that has not yet ended. For the time, Mexican immigrants were considered "white," their labor welcome, their naturalization as citizens secure because of earlier treaties, and their culture tolerated.

During the early twentieth century the United States government, like the Canadian government, responded to the continued political opposition that Indian immigration engendered by discriminating against Indians. None of the major political parties championed the cause of the Indians. Yet the erection of the great white wall came slowly, with many people opposing its construction. The injustice done to Indians roused many Americans to action on their behalf. The collision of Euro-American workers and Asian workers made the Indian pioneer experience in America a significant one. Asian and American workers continued to struggle to control their economic destinies by using political means. They had, after all, far more in common with each other than they had ever suspected.

Abbreviations

BIC	Berlin India Committee
CH	*Canadian History*
CHR	*Canadian Historical Review*
CSL	California State Library, Sacramento
FFI	Friends for the Freedom of India correspondence, University of California at Berkeley
GFMA	German Foreign Ministry Archives
GFO	German Foreign Office
GGC	Governor General's Correspondence
GPO	Government Printing Office
HL	Hoover Library, Stanford University, Palo Alto, California
HMSO	His (Her) Majesty's Stationery Office
JAH	*Journal of American History*
LC	Library of Congress
MR	*Modern Review*
NA	National Archives, Washington, D.C.
PAC	Public Archives of Canada, Ottawa, Ontario
PHR	*Pacific Historical Review*
RG	Record Group
UCB	University of California at Berkeley
UO	University of Oregon at Portland
YU	Yale University, New Haven, Connecticut

Notes

The opening epigraph and the epigraphs intro-
ducing each chapter are from Ved Prakash and Sylvia Vatuk, "Protest
Songs of East Indians on the West Coast, U.S.A.," *Folklore* 7 (October 1966):
370–82.

Prologue

1. Emory Upton, *The Armies of Asia and Europe: Embracing Official Reports on the Armies of Japan, China, India, Persia, Italy, Russia, Austria, Germany, France and England* (New York: Appleton, 1878), p. 83.
2. Gene D. Overstreet and Marshall Windmiller, *Communism in India* (Berkeley and Los Angeles: University of California Press, 1959), pp. 7, 20; Ramparkash Dua, *The Impact of the Russo-Japanese War on Indian Politics* (Delhi: Chand, 1966), p. 46; Howard Beale, *Theodore Roosevelt and the Rise of America to World Power* (Baltimore: Johns Hopkins, University Press, 1956), pp. 211–20; and Roosevelt to T. C. Friedlander, 23 November 1905, in Elting Morison, ed., *The Letters of Theodore Roosevelt*, 8 vols. (Cambridge: Harvard University Press, 1958), 5:90.
3. For this interpretation, see Louis L. Cornell, *Kipling in India* (New York: St. Martin's, 1966), pp. 140–65.
4. W. S. Churchill, *A Roving Commission: My Early Life* (New York: Scribner's, 1930), pp. 104, 133; and Randolph S. Churchill, *Winston S. Churchill*, 2 vols. (Boston: Houghton Mifflin, 1966), 1:284–307.
5. Stanley A. Wolpert, *Tilak and Gokhale: Revolution and Reform in the Making of Modern India* (Berkeley and Los Angeles: University of California Press, 1962), pp. 83–89. This version differs greatly from accounts by British historians such as Ronald Hyam, *Elgin and Churchill at the Colonial Office, 1905–1908: The Watershed of the Empire-Commonwealth* (London: Macmillan, 1968), p. 31; Hyam called Viceroy Victor Alexander Bruce Elgin's handling of the famine "deft" and of the plague "resourceful."
6. R. C. Majumdar, *History of the Freedom Movement in India*, 3 vols. (Calcutta: Mukhopadhyay, 1963), 2:18–21, 62–64, 469–83; Naeem Gul Rathore, "The Indian Nationalist Agitation in the United States: A Study of Lala Lajpat Rai and the Indian Home Rule League of America, 1914–1920" (Ph.D. diss., Columbia University, 1965), pp. 15–16; and Syed Razi Wasti, *Lord Minto and the Indian Nationalist Movement, 1905 to 1910* (Oxford: Clarendon, 1964), p. 90.
7. Stanley Wolpert, *Morley and India, 1906–1910* (Berkeley and Los Angeles: University of California Press, 1967), p. 100.

8. Norman Barrier, *The Punjab Alienation of Land Bill of 1900* (Durham, N.C.: Duke University Press, 1966), p. 24; interview with Tuly Singh Johl, 28 May 1975; and Kushwant Singh, *A History of the Sikhs*, 2 vols. (Princeton: Princeton University Press, 1963–1966), 2:119–20.

9. Denzil Charles Jett Ibbetson, *Punjab Castes* (Patiala, Punjab, GPO, 1916), p. 102. The best discussion of late-nineteenth-century conditions is in Tom G. Kissinger, *Vilyatput, 1848–1968: Social and Economic Change in a North Indian Village* (Berkeley and Los Angeles: University of California Press, 1974), pp. 76–103.

10. Barrier, *The Punjab Alienation of Land Bill*, pp. 33–50, 89; Deva Singh, *Colonization in the Rechna Doab* (Lahore: Punjab Government Record Office, 1929), pp. 4, 28, 35.

11. Singh, *A History of the Sikhs*, 2:119; Baldev Raj Nayar, *Minority Politics in the Punjab* (Princeton: Princeton University Press, 1966), p. 64; and Stephen P. Cohen, *Indian Army: Its Contribution to the Development of a Nation* (Berkeley and Los Angeles: University of California Press, 1971), p. 49.

12. Emily Datta, in "The Gurdwara Reform Movement: Religion and Politics in Twentieth Century Punjab," (a paper written in 1969 at the University of California at Berkeley), pointed out the significance of the increase in the Sikh population.

13. Paul Bass, *Language, Religion and Politics in North India* (Cambridge: Cambridge University Press, 1974), pp. 310–11; and Richard G. Fox, *Lions of the Punjab: Culture in the Making* (Berkeley and Los Angeles: University of California Press, 1985), p. 7.

14. Hugh Tinker, *A New System of Slavery: The Export of Indian Labour Overseas, 1830–1920* (London: Oxford, 1974), pp. 5, 40, 49, 236, 273.

15. Charles A. Price, *The Great White Walls Are Built: Restrictive Immigration to North America and Australasia, 1836–1888* (Canberra: Australian National University Press, 1974), pp. 226–75; B. R. Nanda, *Mahatma Gandhi: A Biography* (Boston: Beacon, 1958), pp. 90–94.

16. For the background of the Cape Colony Act, originally passed in 1902 but approved only with the proviso that the clause regarding European illiterates be amended, see Robert A. Huttenback, *Gandhi in South Africa: British Imperialism and the Indian Question, 1860–1914* (Ithaca: Cornell University Press, 1971), pp. 209–18; Robert A. Huttenback, *Racism and Empire: White Settlers and Colored Immigrants in the British Self-Governing Colonies, 1830–1910* (Ithaca: Cornell University Press, 1976), pp. 139–44; and M. Vane, "Indians in Natal," *Contemporary Review* 174 (July 1948): 44.

17. Peter Richardson, *Chinese Mine Labour in the Transvaal* (London: Macmillan, 1982), pp. 166–87; Churchill, *Winston S. Churchill*, 1:186; and Mohandas Gandhi, *Autobiography: The Story of My Experiments with Truth* (Washington, D.C.: Public Affairs Press, 1954), pp. 134–64.

18. L. W. Hollingsworth, *The Asians of East Africa* (London: Macmillan, 1960), pp. 53, 76–77; Hyam, *Elgin and Churchill*, p. 418.

19. William Bentley, *The Diary of William Bentley*, 5 vols. (Salem: Essex Institute, 1905), 1:228. James Duncan Phillips, *Salem and the Indies: The Story of the Great Commercial Era of the City* (Boston: Houghton Mifflin, 1947), p. 364; James

Duncan Phillips, "Captain Stephen Phillips, 1764–1838, " *Essex Institute Historical Collections* 76 (April 1940): 130; and Walter Muir Whitehill, *The East India Marine Society and Peabody Museum of Salem* (Salem: Peabody Museum, 1949), pp. 34, 39.

20. Reel 22, Series 4, Manumissions, Indentures, and Other Legal Papers, 1758–1865, Indentures of Asiatic Persons, 1788–1811, Pennsylvania Abolitionist Society Collections at the Historical Society of Pennsylvania, Philadelphia.

21. Friedrich Gerstacker, *Scenes of Life in California*, trans. George Cosgrave (San Francisco: John Howell, 1942), p. 178; "Whiskey Hill's Cook," Oakland *Tribune*, 14 July 1957, c2; and R. R. Olmstead, ed., *Hutchings' Illustrated California Magazine* (Berkeley, Calif.: Howell-North, 1962), pp. 388–89.

22. E. R. Schmidt, "American Relations with South Asia, 1900–1940" (Ph.D. diss., University of Pennsylvania, 1955), pp. 15–16.

23. Charles Carrington, *Rudyard Kipling: His Life and Work* (London: Macmillan, 1955), p. 129; Pramath Nath Roy, the port doctor, is mentioned in *The Hindustanee Student* 2 (September-October 1926): 9. On Japanese businessmen see T. Scott Miyakawa, "Early New York Issei: Founders of Japanese-American Trade," in Francis Hilary Conroy and T. Scott Miyakawa, eds., *East Across the Pacific: Historical and Sociological Studies of Japanese Immigration and Assimilation* (Santa Barbara; Calif.: ABC-Clio, 1972), p. 178; and Haru Matsukata Reischauer, *Samurai and Silk: A Japanese and American Heritage* (Cambridge: Harvard University Press, 1986), pp. 191–242.

24. Carl T. Jackson, *The Oriental Religions and American Thought: Nineteenth Century Explorations* (Westport, Conn.: Greenwood, 1981), pp. 243–49. See also John Lovell, Jr., "Appreciating Whitman: 'Passage to India,' " *Modern Language Quarterly* 21 (June 1960): 131–41; Malcolm Cowley, "Guru, the Beatnick and the Good Gray Poet," *New Republic* 141 (26 October 1959), 17–19; "Phillips Brooks's Letters from India," *Century* 44 (1893): 754–63; and Roger Lipsen, *Coomaraswamy: His Life and Work* (Princeton: Princeton University Press, 1977), pp. 5–9. Coomaraswamy's father was a Tamil, his mother English.

25. Rajani Kanta Das, *Hindustani Workers on the Pacific Coast* (Berlin: de Gruyter, 1923), p. 16.

26. L. Edwin Dudley to Elihu Root, 5 November 1906, numerical file, 1906–1910, vol. 612, NA, RG 59.

27. Baldwin quoted in Holden Furber, "Beginnings of American Trade with India, 1784–1812," *New England Quarterly* 12 (June 1938): 239; Sushil Madhava Pathak, "American Protestant Missionaries in India: A Study of Their Activities and Influence, 1813–1910," (Ph.D. diss., University of Hawaii, 1964), pp. 9–17, 55–65.

28. Karl Marx, "India Under British Rule," *Living Age* 328 (23 January 1926): 177–83; Diwakar Prasad Singh, *American Attitude Towards the Indian National Movement* (New Delhi: Munshiram Manoharlal, 1974), pp. 18–19; Robert L. Beisner, *Twelve Against Empire: The Anti-Imperialists, 1898–1900* (New York: McGraw-Hill, 1968), p. 168; Bernard Stern, "American Views of India and Indians, 1857–1900," (Ph.D. diss., University of Pennsylvania, 1956), pp. 27, 30, 48, 51.

29. Marie Louise Burke, *Swami Vivekananda in America: New Discoveries* (Calcutta:

Advaita Ashrama, 1958), p. 75; Julian Hawthorne, "England in India," *Cosmopolitan* 23 (1897): 653–58.

30. Diwakar Prasad Singh, "American Official Attitudes: Towards the Indian Nationalist Movement, 1905–1929" (Ph.D. diss., University of Hawaii, 1964), p. 171.

31. Roosevelt to Cecil Spring-Rice, 11 August 1899 and 2 December 1899, in Morison, *Roosevelt*, 2:1052; *The Works of Theodore Roosevelt*, 16 vols. (New York: Colliers, 1889–1896), 3:128–30.

32. Fred Harrington, "The Anti-Imperialist Movement in the United States," *Mississippi Valley Historical Review* 22 (September 1935): 211; William J. Pomeroy, *American Neo-Colonialism: Its Emergence in the Philippines and Asia* (New York: International Publishers, 1970), p. 114.

33. Theodore Roosevelt, *California Addresses* (San Francisco: California Promotion Committee, 1903), pp. 95, 109; Singh, *American Attitude*, p. 22.

34. William B. Hixson, *Moorfield Storey and the Abolitionist Tradition* (New York: Oxford, 1972), pp. 46, 196.

35. Rathore, "Indian Nationalist," p. 69; Wasti, *Lord Minto*, p. 90.

36. Singh, *American Attitude*, pp. 44–46; Wolpert, *Morley and India*, p. 108; Wolpert, *Tilak and Gokhale*, p. 203.

37. Wolpert, *Morley and India*, pp. 106–07; William Michael to Elihu Root, 10 May 1907, file 6971, NA, RG 59.

38. "Students and Politics," file 6971, NA, RG 59.

39. Taraknath Das, "India and America," *MR* 49 (July 1931): 91; Michael to Alvey A. Adee, 18 October 1906, numerical file, 1906–1910, vol. 612, and Michael to Root, 29 May 1907, file 6971, NA, RG 59; Singh, *American Attitude*, p. 49.

40. Wolpert, *Morley and India*, p. 48.

41. Rathore, "Indian Nationalist," p. 8.

Chapter 1

1. "Indians in Canada," *MR* 35 (April 1925): 448.

2. My understanding of the family arrangements and trip preparation was helped by conversations with Nahn Kahr Singh, Bruce La Brack, and Tuly Singh Johl, as well as by two books on British Sikh immigrants: G. S. Aurora, *The New Frontiersmen: A Sociological Study of Indian Immigrants in the United Kingdom* (Bombay: Popular Prakashan, 1967); and Alan J. James, *Sikh Children in Britain* (London: Oxford University Press, 1974). See also Prakash Tandon, *Punjabi Century, 1857–1947* (Berkeley and Los Angeles: University of California Press, 1968), p. 97.

3. Girindra Mukerji, "Hindu in America," *Overland* 51 (April 1908): 305; Saint Nihal Singh, "The Picturesque Immigrant from India's Coral Strand," *Out West* 30 (January 1909): 47–49; "British Indians and Citizenship in White Men's Countries," *Outlook* 87 (7 September 1907): 7–8; and Adrian Mayer, *A Report on the East Indian Community in Vancouver* (Working paper, Institute of Social and Economic Research, University of British Columbia, 1959), p. 11.

4. S. A. Waiz, ed., *Indians Abroad*, 2d ed. (Bombay: Imperial Indian Citizenship Association, 1927), p. 648.

5. Prices given in Frank Oliver to Grey, 18 November 1907, vol. 199, GGC, PAC. Fare from San Francisco to Calcutta via Japan was about seventy-five dollars.

6. Aurora, *New Frontiersmen*, p. 27; James, *Sikh Children in Britain*, p. 10; interviews with Nahn Kahr Singh, 27 May 1975, and with Tuly Singh Johl, 28 May 1975; "The Position of Hindus in Canada," *British Columbia Magazine* 8 (1912): 667.

7. For views attributed to employers, see *Winnipeg Telegram*, 22 October 1907, quoted in J. Castell Hopkins, *The Canadian Annual Review of Public Affairs* (Toronto: Annual Review, 1908), p. 388. Similar views were frequently cited in the press.

8. Aurora (*New Frontiersmen*, pp. 67–73) discusses prostitution, drink, and talk in a way that seems to agree with the scattered references on the subject in the literature on the Sikhs in Canada. See also Marian W. Smith and Hilda W. Boulter, "Sikh Settlers in Canada," *Asia and the Americas* 44 (August 1944): 359, 362–63; Waiz, *Indians Abroad*, p. 651; Tien-Fang Cheng, *Oriental Immigration in Canada* (Shanghai: Commercial Press, 1931), pp. 138–39.

9. Interviews with Tuly Singh Johl, 28 May 1975 and 24 August 1975.

10. Bellingham *Reveille*, 5 September 1907, 1:6–7, and 7 September 1907, 1:3; Bellingham *Herald*, 5 September 1907, 1:5; Frederick Lockley, "The Hindu Invasion: A New Immigration Problem," *Pacific Monthly* 17 (May 1907): 587; interview with Tuly Singh Johl, 28 May 1975; and R. L. Olson, interview at N & M Lumber Company, Rochester, Washington, 22 July 1924, series A, file 210, Smith Collection, UO.

11. Interview with Tuly Singh Johl, 28 May 1975; Ann Louise Wood, "East Indians in California: A Study of Their Organizations, 1900–1947," (M.A. thesis, University of Wisconsin, 1966), p. 25.

12. The best description of the railroad construction is in Frederic Bennett Whitman, *"Western Pacific"—Its First Forty Years: A Brief History (1910–1950)* (New York: Newcomen Society of North America, 1950). Railroad files at the Plumas County Museum in Quincy, California, and various issues of the *Plumas National Bulletin* were also helpful in piecing together the history of construction problems. On economic questions, see John William Kendrick, *A Report Upon the Western Pacific Railroad* (Chicago: n.p., 1917). The Ghadar Collection at the UCB, box 21, has materials from research of I. S. Gurem in 1937 that mention Indians working on the railroad near Palermo.

13. Senate Commission on Immigration, *Immigrants in Industries: Japanese and Other Immigrant Races in Pacific Coast and Rocky Mountain States*, 3 vols., 61st Cong., 2d sess., 1909–1910, S. Doc. 633, 1:332–33.

14. Interview with Tuly Singh Johl, 24 August 1975. Bruce La Brack, "Occupational Specialization Among California Sikhs: The Interplay of Culture and Economics," *Amerasia* 9 (1982): 29–56, presents a convincing argument for Indians' preference for agriculture. Conversations with La Brack greatly deepened my understanding of Punjabi agricultural life in California and forced me to expand my evaluation. See Bruce Wilfred La Brack, "The Sikhs

of Northern California: A Sociohistorical Study" (Ph.D. diss., Syracuse University, 1980), pp. 76–81.

15. One of the best descriptions of farming in the early nineteenth century is in *History of Yuba County, California* (Oakland: Thompson and West, 1879), pp. 130–37; Kenneth Thompson, "Irrigation as a Menace to Health in California," *Geographical Review* 59 (1969): 195–214, describes early fears about irrigation; Peter S. Murchie, *The Life and Letters of Emory Upton* (New York: Appleton, 1885), p. 304, quotes a letter of 27 July 1875 in which Upton commented with wonder at the mechanized farming and the wheat harvests of the San Joaquin Valley. California harvesting equipment of the period was immense. Examples are in the Museum of American History in Washington, D.C.

16. Senate Immigration Commission, *Immigrants in Industry*, 3:333; Dhan Gopal Mukerji, *Caste and Outcast* (New York: Dutton, 1923), pp. 269–77.

17. Willard A. Schurr, "Hindus in Los Angeles," file A273, Smith Collection, UO; "Interview with J. M. Hamer," 8 July 1924, William C. Smith, "Interview with Inder Singh," 31 May 1924, and Schurr, "Hindus in Los Angeles," file A273; "Hindus and Intermarriage," file 46–B, Smith Collection, UO.

18. Report on Fresno, California, part IV, Smith Collection, UO.

19. Of 258 Singhs who died between 1905 and 1929, 60 (23 percent) died in the five counties of the Sacramento Valley, 94 (36 percent) in the five counties of the San Joaquin Valley, and 40 (16 percent) in the Imperial Valley, CSL.

20. For information on the Imperial Valley see La Brack, "Occupational Specialization," pp. 29–56. See also "Commonwealth Tenancy Studies, April-June 1923, file A–277; "Interview with L. C. Lee of El Centro, California," June 1924; William C. Smith, "Interview with Dr. E. E. Chandler," 23 August 1924, and E. E. Chandler to George Gleason, 2 May 1924, file A–84; William L. Smith, "Interview with Inder Singh," 31 May 1924, file A–237; William C. Smith, "Life History of R. Chand," 1 June 1924, file 232; and William C. Smith, "Hindus and Intermarriage," file B46, Smith Collection, UO. Indians also thought whites were lazy, according to Robindra C. Chakravorti, "The Sikhs of El Centro: A Study in Social Integration" (Ph.D. diss., University of Minnesota, 1968), p. 128.

21. "General Summary of the Oriental Situation in California Agriculture," file A2; Commonwealth Club Tenancy Studies, April-June 1923, file A–277, Smith Collection, UO; and Ann Foley Scheuring, *Tillers: An Oral History of Family Farms in California* (New York: Praeger, 1983), p. 113.

22. Leona A. Gagai, *The East Indians and the Pakistanis in America* (Minneapolis: Lerner, 1972), pp. 42–43; and Salim Khan, "A Brief History of Pakistanis in the Western United States" (M.A. thesis, California State University, Sacramento, 1981), p. 40.

23. Smith, "Interview with Dr. E. E. Chandler," 23 August 1924, and E. E. Chandler to George Gleason, 2 May 1924, file A–24, Smith Collection, UO.

24. Khan, "Brief History," p. 43.

25. Chakravorti, "The Sikhs of El Centro," p. 80. In 1940, a sociologist found that twenty-two of twenty-five Indians in California who had married were married to Mexican women; see Yusaf Dadabhay, "Circuitous Assimilation

among Rural Hindustanis in California," *Social Forces* 33 (December 1954): 140. The pattern continued after 1924, according to Karen Leonard, "Marriage and Family Life among Early Asian Indian Immigrants," *Population Review* 125 (1981): 67–75.

26. The years 1910 and 1911 were an important dividing line in terms of Indians' desire to stay. H. A. Millis, "East Indian Immigration," pp. 379–86, reported that thirty-six of seventy-nine Indians interviewed in Washington in 1909 intended to return to India, thirty-seven were in doubt, and six intended to remain. More California Indians may already have made up their minds to stay, but the lack of organization among early immigrants seems to indicate that attitudes began to change after 1911.

Chapter 2

1. Otto Dalke, "Riots: A Study of the Typology of Violence," *Social Forces* 30 (1952): 425. See also Bellingham *Reveille*, 7 September 1907, 1:1; Bellingham *Herald*, 30 September 1907, 1:7. The only historical study of the riot, Gerald L. Hallberg, "Bellingham, Washington's Anti-Hindu Riot," *Journal of the West* 12 (January 1973): 163–71, unfortunately accepts many of the biased terms and opinions of the day and erroneously calls Indian immigrants "virtual indentured workers" (p. 163).

2. Black quoted in *The Coast* 14 (September 1907): 133. Edmond S. Meany, Jr., "The History of the Lumber Industry in the Pacific Northwest to 1917" (Ph.D. diss., Harvard University, 1935), p. 348.

3. The best discussion of racism as a historical theme in the western United States is Lawrence B. deGraff, "Recognition, Racism, and Reflections on the Writing of Western Black History," *PHR* 44 (February 1975): 22–51. See also Roger Daniels and Harry H. L. Kitano, *American Racism: Exploration of the Nature of Prejudice* (Englewood Cliffs, N.J.: Prentice-Hall, 1970); Lerone Bennett, Jr., "The Road Not Taken," *Ebony* 25 (August 1970): 70–77; Stuart Creighton Miller, *The Unwelcome Immigrant: The American Image of the Chinese, 1785–1882* (Berkeley and Los Angeles: University of California Press, 1969), pp. vii, 1–7; Doris Marion Wright, "The Making of Cosmopolitan California: An Analysis of Immigration, 1847–1870," *California Historical Society Quarterly* 19 (December 1940): 329; Rodman W. Paul, "The Origins of the Chinese Issue in California," *Mississippi Valley Historical Review* 25 (1938): 181–96; People v. Hall, 4 California Reports 399 (October term 1854); Gerald Stanley, "Racism and the Early Republican Party: The 1856 Presidential Election in California," *PHR* 43 (1974): 173–86; and Joel Stephen Franks, "Boot and Shoemakers in Nineteenth Century San Francisco, 1860–1892: A Study in Class, Culture, Ethnicity, and Popular Protest in an Industrializing Community" (Ph.D. diss., University of California at Irvine, 1983), pp. 7–21, 65–73, 203–16.

4. Ronald Olson, "The Orientals in the Lumber Industry in the State of Washington," series A, file 198, Smith Collection, UO.

5. R. L. Olson, interview at N & M Lumber Company, Rochester, Washington,

22 July 1924, series A, file 198, Smith Collection, UO. At that time thirteen of the forty-five Asians employed at this mill were Indians.

6. Robert Edward Wynne, "Reaction to the Chinese in the Pacific Northwest and British Columbia, 1850 to 1910" (Ph.D. diss., University of Washington, 1964), p. 409; New York *Times*, 10 September 1907, 1:7, 11 September 1907, 4:3.

7. Bellingham *Herald*, 2 September 1907, 1:7; Bellingham *Reveille*, 5 September 1907, 1:6–7.

8. Details of the riot are from the Bellingham *Reveille*, 5 September 1907, 1:6–7, the Bellingham *Herald*, 5 September 1907, 1:5, and Lockley, "Hindu Invasion," p. 587; San Francisco *Chronicle*, 6 September 1907, 1:3; San Francisco *Call*, 7 September 1907, 6:1.

9. Bellingham *Herald*, 6 September 1907, 2:3, 7 September 1907, 1:1, 3:5, and 17 September 1907, 3:5.

10. Vancouver *Daily Province*, 11 September 1907, 2:3, 14 September 1907, 3:4; Bellingham *Reveille*, 17 September 1907, 5:4; New York *Times*, 15 September 1907, 3:1–2; Seattle newspapers quoted in "Pacific Coast Press on the Anti-Oriental Riots," *Literary Digest* 35 (5 October 1907): 465–67.

11. New York *Times*, 10 September 1907, 1:7, 12 September 1907, 1:3, 15 September 1907, 3:1–2, 16 September 1907, 2:4; Bellingham *Reveille*, 12 September 1907, 3:3; "Race Riots on the Pacific Coast," *Outlook* 87 (21 September 1907): 89; William Hemmingway, "A Japanese Hornet's Nest for John Bull," *Harper's Weekly* 51 (5 October 1907): 1448; and Oscar Straus, *Under Four Administrations, from Cleveland to Taft* (Boston: Houghton Mifflin, 1922), pp. 220–27. Denver *Post* quoted in Bellingham *Reveille*, 12 September 1907, 3:3.

12. Werter D. Dodd, "The Hindu in the Northwest," *World Today* 13 (November 1907): 1160.

13. Bellingham *Herald*, 10 September 1907, 3:3, 12 September 1907, 2:3, 14 September 1907, 4:1–2, 16 September 1907, 1:6; New York *Times*, 19 December 1915, VI:1:1; F. B. Moorhead, "Foreign Invasion of the Northwest," *World's Work* 15 (March 1908): 9992; and Harold Hyman, *Soldiers and Spruce: Origins of the Loyal Legion of Loggers and Lumbermen* (Los Angeles: Institute of Industrial Relations, University of California, 1963), pp. 66–80.

14. Bellingham *Reveille*, 12 September 1907, 4:1–2; "Pacific Coast Press," p. 465.

15. Bellingham *Herald*, 16 September 1907, 1:2; Bellingham *Reveille*, 17 September 1907, 5:4. Fowler, the self-proclaimed champion of the white Northwest, moved from Seattle to Bellingham shortly after the riot to solicit money for continuing the league's fight. Later, he was found ripping up sheets in his hotel room and was removed to the state mental hospital at Steilacoom. South Carolina senator Ben Tillman, who had recently defended the lynching of blacks, also arrived in Bellingham soon after the riot to campaign for the repeal of the Fifteenth Amendment. He called the race question at Bellingham so insignificant that it bordered on the ridiculous: "You people get excited over a few Hindus, where we have to contend with 9,000,000. Why the very hypocrisy, the absurdity of the affair." A few days later *Organized Labor*, the weekly of the California State and Local Building Trades Council, quoted Washington governor Albert Mead with approval as hav-

ing said, "The Bellingham outbreak is only an instance in the battle between American labor and the cheap labor from the Orient. . . . The Bellingham people adopted the best methods of settling it." Bellingham *Herald*, 18 September 1907, 1:7, 19 September 1907, 5:2, 23 September 1907, 1:7, and 25 September 1907, 1:7; Wynne, "Reaction," p. 338.

16. Bellingham *Herald*, 2 October 1907, 1:3, and 4 October 1907, 1:2.

17. W. R. McInnes to Frank Oliver, 14 March 1908, GGC, vol. 211, PAC.

18. R. L. Olson, interview at Bay City Mill, Aberdeen, Washington, 28 July 1924; R. L. Olson, interview at N & M Lumber Company, Rochester, Washington, 22 July 1924; Ronald Olson, "The Orientals in the Lumber Industry in the State of Washington," p. 5. (All interviews are from series A, file 198, Smith Collection, UO.) Twelve of the two hundred workers at Bay City Mill were Indians. Japanese workers decreased by almost 50 percent, from 2685 to 1458, between 1907 and 1924; series A, file 198, Smith Collection, UO. Senate Commission on Immigration, *Immigrants in Industries*, 1:331–32, discusses Indian work in lumber mills briefly and attributes their general disappearance from the industry primarily to the hostile attitude of white workingmen but also to cultural and racial prejudice. The commission located fifty-three Indian men in the six mills it visited.

19. Letter of K. Kahn, Chico, California, 5 November 1906, in NA, RG 59, file 2376.

20. The Live Oak riot is described in the Sutter County *Farmer*, 10 January 1908, 31 January 1908, 7 February 1908, and 14 February 1908; the Sutter *Independent*, 30 January 1908; and the Sacramento *Bee*, 27 January 1908, 7:1.

21. San Francisco *Call*, 15 November 1907, 9:7, 8 March 1908, 12:4, 21 November 1908, 8:3; San Francisco *Examiner*, 6 December 1911, 1:4.

Chapter 3

1. Beale, *Theodore Roosevelt*, p. 186; Svend Petersen, *A Statistical History of the American Presidential Elections* (New York: Ungar, 1963), pp. 62–65, lists the 1896 election results as follows: McKinley received 49.13 percent of the vote, and Bryan received 48.44 percent. For James see Robert L. Beisner, *Twelve Against Empire: The Anti-Imperialists, 1898–1900* (New York: McGraw-Hill, 1968), p. 43.

2. J. Oliver Curwood, "The Effect of the American Invasion," *World's Work* 10 (September 1905): 6607. According to Gerald Clark, *Canada: The Uneasy Neighbor* (New York: McKay, 1965), p. 257, a survey in 1964 showed that 29 percent of British Columbians still favored joining the United States.

3. Phillip Jessup, *Elihu Root*, 2 vols. (New York: Dodd, Mead, 1938), 2:391–92.

4. Charles J. Woodsworth, *Canada and the Orient: A Study in International Relations* (Toronto: Macmillan, 1941), pp. 215–31. The advertising was confirmed by Indian immigrants in Vancouver. See T. R. E. McInnes to Frank Oliver, 2 October 1907, GGC, vol. 199, PAC; confidential memorandum by Mackenzie King, 2 May 1908, GGC, vol. 200, PAC; and Das, *Hindustani Workers*, p. 6.

5. Nand Singh Sihra, "Indians in Canada," *MR* 14 (August 1913): 140–49; and "Canada's Newest Immigrant," *Review of Reviews* 35 (March 1907): 367–68.

6. R. Macgregor Dawson, *William Lyon Mackenzie King: A Political Biography* (Toronto: University of Toronto Press, 1958), pp. 174–75.

7. F. A. McGregor, *The Fall and Rise of Mackenzie King, 1911–1919* (Toronto: Macmillan, 1962), p. 25; Dawson, *King*, p. 215; Oscar Douglas Skelton, *Life and Letters of Sir Wilfred Laurier*, 2 vols. (Toronto: Century, 1921), preface to vol. 1; Joseph Schull, *Laurier, the First Canadian* (New York: St. Martin's, 1965), p. 464; and Samuel F. Wells, Jr., "British Strategic Withdrawal from the Western Hemisphere, 1904–1906," *CHR* 49 (December 1968): 348.

8. An 1894 treaty between Great Britain and Japan provided for self-governing colonies to adhere to the treaty without granting the right of free movement, but Canada did not apply this restriction; see Harold Hiroshi Sugimoto, "Japanese Immigration, the Vancouver Riots and Canadian Diplomacy," (M.A. thesis, University of Washington, 1967), pp. 36, 41.

9. Mukerji, "Hindu in America," p. 306; Munro quoted in "Canada's New Immigrant," p. 367; T. R. E. McInnes to Frank Oliver, 14 March 1908, GGC, vol. 211, PAC; J. Barclay Williams and Saint Nihal Singh, "Canada's New Immigrant," *Canada Magazine* 28 (February 1907): 385–86, 388; Cheng, *Oriental Immigration*, p. 141; and Singh, "The Picturesque Indian," pp. 47–49.

10. According to a memorandum on Indian immigration to Canada, prepared by the India office on 26 August 1915, there were twenty-eight thousand Chinese in British Columbia by 1911; see Canadian Department of External Affairs, *Documents on Canadian External Relations, 1909–1918* (Ottawa: GPO, 1967), vol. 1. Hopkins, *Canadian Annual Review* p. 397, quotes the Japanese commissioner's figures on Japanese immigrants as eight thousand. That white laborers were not wanted is described in Hopkins, *Canadian Annual Review*, pp. 382–98; "White Canada Forever" is quoted in Khushwant Singh and Satindra Singh, *Ghadar 1915: India's First Armed Revolution* (New Delhi: R and K, 1966), p. 2.

11. Grey to Elgin, 4 October 1906, Grey Papers, vol. 13, and Grey to Laurier, 8 October 1906, Grey Papers, vol. 2, PAC; Wynne, "Reaction," p. 401; memorandum by Grey, 25 August 1907, Grey Papers, vol. 2, PAC. Hopkins, *Canadian Annual Review*, p. 215, lists 774 Chinese, 86 Japanese, and 55 Indians and Hindus employed on Vancouver Island, where Lieutenant Governor Dunsmuir ran a mine.

12. Lockley, "The Hindu Invasion," pp. 588–90.

13. Williams and Singh, "Canada's New Immigrant," p. 390; undated newspaper clipping in GGC, vol. 199, PAC.

14. Laurier to Grey, 10 November 1906, Grey Papers, vol. 2, PAC; L. Edwin Dudley to Alvey A. Adee, 22 November 1906, file 2376, NA, RG 59. A total of 2,124 Indians arrived in Canada in 1906.

15. Henry Borden, ed., *Robert Laird Borden: His Memoirs*, 2 vols. (Toronto: Macmillan, 1938) 1:213; Howard Sugimoto, "The Vancouver Riots of 1907: A Canadian Episode," in Francis Hilary Conroy and T. Scott Miyakawa, eds., *East Across the Pacific: Historical and Sociological Studies of Japanese Immigration and Assimilation* (Santa Barbara, Calif.: ABC-Clio, 1972), p. 111.

16. Canadian Department of External Affairs, *Documents on Canadian External Relations, 1909–1918*, pp. 660–66.
17. Sugimoto, "Japanese Immigration," pp. 32, 52.
18. Ibid., 113.
19. San Francisco *Call*, 7 September 1907, 6:1, and editorial, "Harrying the Man With the Turban," 6 September 1907, 5:1; San Francisco *Chronicle*, 6 September 1907, 1:3; Vancouver *World*, 5 September 1907, 1:6.
20. Vancouver *Daily Province*, 7 September 1907, 1:1.
21. Ibid., 9 September 1907, 9:2–3; Vancouver *World*, 9 September 1907.
22. Dodd, "Hindus in the Northwest," p. 1158; Cheng, *Oriental Immigration in Canada*, p. 76; San Francisco *Chronicle*, 9 September 1907, 1:1; Wynne, "Reaction," pp. 415–25; Vancouver *Daily Province*, 9 September 1907, 1:1–2; New York *Times*, 10 September 1907, 1:7, 2:1–2. The most detailed recent account is W. Peter Ward, *White Canada Forever: Popular Attitudes and Public Policy Toward Orientals in British Columbia* (Montreal: McGill-Queen's University Press, 1974), pp. 53–76.
23. Bellingham *Herald*, 12 September 1907; Vancouver *World*, 11 September 1907, 1:6–7, 12 September 1907, 1:4.
24. Cheng, *Oriental Immigration in Canada*, p. 76; Grey to Laurier, 13 September 1907, Grey Papers, vol. 2, PAC; New York *Times*, 13 September 1907, 5:3, 14 September 1907, 6:1–2.
25. Vancouver *World*, 11 September 1907, 1:6–7; Vancouver *Daily Province*, 12 September 1907, 1:7, 14 September 1907, 1:6.
26. Vancouver *World* quoted in "Pacific Coast Press," p. 466.
27. Wynne, "Reaction," pp. 435, 441. Clippings from Victoria *Daily Colonist*, 17 September 1958, 9, and Ottawa *Free Press*, 18 September 1907, are in GGC, vol. 199, PAC.
28. "Race riots in Vancouver," 394; "Pacific Coast Press," p. 465.
29. Newspaper accounts cited in Wynne, "Reaction," 419; James Bryce to Edward Grey, 20 September 1907, GGC, vol. 199, PAC.
30. T. R. E. McInnes to Frank Oliver, 2 October 1907, GGC, vol. 199, PAC.
31. Memorandum accompanying McInnes to Oliver, unsigned, 2 October 1907, GGC, vol. 199, PAC.
32. Laurier to Grey, 10 September 1907, Grey Papers, vol. 2, PAC.
33. McGregor, *The Fall and Rise*, pp. 1–33; Dawson, *William Lyon MacKenzie King*, pp. 36, 144. King later worked for and became a close friend of John D. Rockefeller, Jr. He also became an avid spiritualist. See Bruce Hutchinson, *The Incredible Canadian* (New York: Longmans, Green, 1953), p. 86.
34. Grey to Elgin, 27 December 1907, Grey Papers, vol. 14, PAC; McInnes, *Oriental Invasion*, p. 18. The translator of the documents was later found shot. He apparently committed suicide. See also Sugimoto, "Japanese Immigration, the Vancouver Riots and Canadian Diplomacy," pp. 199, 227.
35. Grey to Laurier, 10 December 1907 and 27 December 1907, Grey Papers, vol. 14, PAC.
36. Grey to Elgin, 27 December 1907, Grey Papers, vol. 14, PAC.
37. Elgin to Grey, 30 December 1907, Grey Papers, vol. 14, PAC; Nanda, *Gandhi*,

pp. 99–100; Morley to Bryce, 6 January 1908, in H. A. L. Fisher, *James Bryce*, 2 vols. (London: Macmillan, 1927), 2:94.

38. Laurier to Grey, 19 September 1907, and Grey to Laurier, 20 September 1907, Grey Papers, vol. 2, PAC.

39. Grey to Bryce, 12 September 1907, and Grey to Laurier, 9 September 1907, Grey Papers, vol. 2, Grey to Elgin, 9 September 1907, Grey Papers, vol. 14, PAC; undated clipping, GGC, vol. 199, PAC; "Pacific Coast Press," p. 466.

40. Grey to Laurier, 13 September 1907, Laurier to Grey, 16 September 1907, Grey to Laurier, 17 September 1907, Grey to Elgin, 18 September 1907, Laurier to Grey, 19 September 1907, and Grey to Laurier, 20 September 1907, Grey Papers, vol. 2; Grey to Elgin, 11 November 1907, Grey Papers, vol. 14; Grey to Elgin, 15 November 1907, Grey to Laurier, 16 November 1907, Grey to Laurier, 20 November 1907, Grey Papers, vol. 2, PAC.

41. Grey to Elgin, 1 October 1907, Grey Papers, vol. 14, PAC.

42. Grey to Elgin, 17 February 1908, GGC, vol. 200, PAC; "The Canadian General Election," *Outlook* 90 (7 November 1908): 512; and Woodsworth, *Canada and the Orient*, p. 94.

43. Elgin to Grey, 2 February 1908, and copy of a telegram from the government of India, 22 January 1908, GGC, vol. 200, PAC.

44. Grey to Bryce, 28 February 1908, Grey Papers, vol. 8, Grey to Elgin, 3 March 1908, Grey Papers, vol. 14, PAC. John O. Foster to Robert Bacon, 5 March 1908 and 7 March 1908, file 8880, NA, RG 59.

45. Canadian Department of the Interior, *Report on East Indian Immigration* (Ottawa: GPO, 1908) contains King's official report, which was reprinted in House Committee on Immigration and Naturalization, *Hindu Immigration Hearings*, 63d Cong., 2d sess., 1914, p. 55. King's confidential memorandum of 2 May 1908 (GGC, vol. 200, PAC) is much more explicit. Wynne, "Reaction," p. 452.

46. McInnes to Oliver, 14 March 1908, McInnes to Laurier, 15 March 1908, GGC, vol. 211, PAC.

47. Foster to Bacon, 13 March 1908 and 7 March 1908, file 8880, NA, RG 59. L. W. Crippen to London *Times*, 21 March 1908, GGC, vol. 200, PAC; London *Times*, 19 March 1908; Grey to Bryce, 23 March 1908, Grey Papers, vol. 8, PAC; Grey to Elgin, 23 March 1908, Grey Papers, vol. 14, PAC.

48. Foster to Bacon, 24 March 1908, file 8880, NA, RG 59; *The Free Hindusthan*, vol. 1, no. 1 (April 1908); and Ameer Ali, "Anomalies of Civilization: A Peril to India," *Nineteenth Century* 63 (April 1908): 570–74.

49. Unidentified clipping, GGC, vol. 199, PAC; Toronto *Globe*, quoted in [A Hindu-Canadian], *India's Appeal to Canada or An Account of Hindu Immigration to the Dominion* (n.p.: Indian Association, 1915), p. 16.

50. Confidential memorandum by Mackenzie King, 2 May 1908, GGC, vol. 200, PAC.

51. Wynne, "Reaction," 457, 453.

52. Dawson, *King*, pp. 194–95.

53. Minto to Laurier, 1 March 1909, and Laurier to Minto, 13 April 1909, quoted in Skelton, *Laurier*, 2:353–54.

54. Grey to Laurier, 12 May 1908, and Laurier to Grey, 26 May 1909, Grey Papers, vol. 3, PAC.

55. Das, *Hindustani*, pp. 6, 8; Cheng, *Oriental Immigration in Canada*, p. 141; Andracki, "Immigration," p. 102.

Chapter 4

1. For the relation of immigration to foreign policy, see especially Demetrios G. Papademetriou and Mark J. Miller, *The Unavoidable Issue: U.S. Immigration Policy in the 1980s* (Philadelphia: Institute for the Study of Human Issues, 1983), pp. 1–39.

2. See Roger Daniels, *The Politics of Prejudice* (Berkeley and Los Angeles: University of California Press, 1962), pp. 31–45.

3. William R. Braisted, "The United States Navy's Dilemma in the Pacific," *PHR* 26 (1957): 242; and Seward W. Livermore, "American Naval-Base Policy in the Far East," *PHR* 13 (June 1944) 113–45.

4. Ralph E. Minger, "Taft's Missions to Japan: A Study in Personal Diplomacy," *PHR* 30 (1961): 279–94; Singh, "American Official Attitudes," p. 171.

5. New York *Times*, 7 September 1907, 2:3, 11 September 1907, 4:3.

6. Edith Roosevelt to Cecil Spring-Rice, 25 June 1907, in Beale, *Theodore Roosevelt*, p. 134; "Irregular Diplomacy," *Nation* 83 (27 December 1906): 550; Edmund Ions, *James Bryce and American Democracy, 1870–1922* (New York: Humanities, 1970), p. 211; Charles Neu, "Theodore Roosevelt and American Involvement in the Far East, 1901–1909," *PHR* 35 (November 1966): 440; James Bryce, "Difficulties Encountered in Colonial Government," *Annals of the American Academy of Political and Social Science* 30 (July 1907): 19; Bryce to Adee, 12 September 1907, numerical file, 1906–1910, NA, RG 59.

7. New York *Times*, 11 September 1907, 4:3.

8. Roosevelt to St. Loe Strachey, 8 September 1907, in Morison, *Roosevelt*, 5:786–88.

9. Lodge to Roosevelt, 10 September 1907, in Thomas A. Bailey, *Theodore Roosevelt and the Japanese-American Crises* (1934; reprint, Gloucester, Mass.: Peter Smith, 1964), p. 253; Roosevelt to Lodge, 11 September 1907, in Morison, *Roosevelt*, 5:790; New York *Times*, 10 September 1907, 1:7.

10. Taft to Hayes, 11 September 1907, quoted in Ralph Eldin Minger, *William Howard Taft and United States Foreign Policy: The Apprenticeship Years, 1900–1908* (Urbana: University of Illinois Press, 1975), p. 151. Wheeler to Loeb, 19 September 1907, Roosevelt Papers, series 1, LC.

11. Bryce to Adee, 12 September 1907, Adee to Mead, 16 September 1907, Mead to Adee, 19 September 1907, and Black's letter quoted in Root to Bryce, 24 September 1907, 6:1, numerical file, 1906–1910, vol. 612, NA, RG 59; Bellingham *Sunday American Reveille*, 22 September 1907, 6:1.

12. Root to Roosevelt, 25 September 1907, quoted in Bailey, *Theodore Roosevelt*, p. 255; Bryce to Adee, 27 September 1907, numerical file, 1906–1910, vol. 612, NA, RG 59. This activity was typical of diplomatic maneuvering. With prodding by foreign governments, however, Congress usually indemnified

injured aliens. See Jules Alexander Karlin, "The Indemnification of Aliens Injured by Mob Violence," *Southwestern Social Science Quarterly* 25 (1945): 235–46.

13. New York *Times*, 19 December 1915, VI:1:1, clipping in GGC, vol. 199, PAC.
14. Roosevelt to Root, 19 November 1907, and Roosevelt to Charlemagne Tower, 19 November 1907, in Morison, *Roosevelt*, 5:851, 853.
15. Henry Fowles Pringle, *The Life and Times of William Howard Taft* (New York: Farrar and Reinhart, 1939), p. 304.
16. Bryce to Grey, 11 January 1908, Grey Papers, vol. 8, PAC; King's account is in GGC, vol. 210, PAC; Grey to Elgin, 5 February 1908, GGC, vol. 209, PAC.
17. Grey to Elgin, 5 February 1908, GGC, vol. 209, PAC.
18. Laurier to Grey, 30 January 1908, and Grey to Laurier, 30 January 1908, Grey Papers, vol. 3, PAC.
19. Dawson, *King*, p. 153; King's account is in GGC, vol. 210, PAC; Roosevelt to Laurier, 1 February 1908, Roosevelt Papers, series 2, LC; Roosevelt to Lee, 2 February 1908, in Morison, *Roosevelt*, 6:918; Bryce to Grey, 2 February 1908, GGC, vol. 209, PAC.
20. Grey to Elgin, 5 February 1908, GGC, vol. 209, PAC; Laurier to Grey, 6 February 1908, and Grey to Laurier, 5 February 1908, Grey Papers, vol. 3, PAC; Bryce to Grey, 4 February 1908, Grey Papers, vol. 8, PAC; Grey to Bryce, 5 February 1908, GGC, vol. 209, PAC; Roosevelt to Laurier, 1 February 1908, Roosevelt Papers, series 2, LC; "Yankee trick" quoted in Dawson, *King*, p. 155.
21. Memorandum of interview with Roosevelt in Washington, D.C., 10 February 1908, GGC, vol. 209, PAC. Present were Ralph Smith, Dr. McIntyre, Dr. Thompson, and B. C. Nicholas. Capital letters are in the original.
22. Bryce to Grey, 14 February 1908, GGC, vol. 209, PAC.
23. Grey to Elgin, 17 February 1908, and Elgin to Grey, 19 February 1908, Grey Papers, vol. 14, PAC; King's diary for 17 February 1908, is quoted in Dawson, *King*, pp. 158–59.
24. Laurier to Roosevelt, 20 February 1908, Roosevelt Papers, series 1, LC. Grey to Elgin, 3 March 1908, Grey Papers, vol. 14, PAC; Donald C. Gordon, in "Roosevelt's 'Smart Yankee Trick,' " *PHR* 30 (1961): 357, concludes that the consequence was the assumption of wider powers by Canada and Australia. It seems, however, that the incident was part of a larger trend. See Braisted, "The United States Navy's Dilemma," p. 242.
25. The accusation that Bryce suggested exclusion of Indians from the United States is in Elizabeth S. Kite, "An American Criticism of 'The Other Side of the Medal,' " *MR* 41 (February 1927): 169. For the British actions see Singh, "American Official Attitudes," pp. 172–73, 182.
26. Singh, *American Attitude*, pp. 134–35; Michael to Adee, 30 April 1908, numerical file, 1906–1910, vol. 612, NA, RG 59.
27. William Roy Smith, *Nationalism and Reform in India* (New Haven: Yale University Press, 1938), pp. 66–72; report of committee of privy council, 21 July 1908, GGC, vol. 200, PAC; confidential memorandum from King on sedition,

quoted in Lemieux to Grey, 15 July 1908, GGC, vol. 209, PAC; M. K. Gandhi, *Satyagraha in South Africa* (Stanford: Academic Reprints, 1954), p. 202.

28. Bryan, "British Rule in India," reprint by the British committee of the Indian National Congress, copy in HL; Alan Raucher, "American Anti-Imperialists and the Pro-India Movement, 1900–1932," *PHR* 43 (1974): 83–110.

29. Michael quoted in Singh, *American Attitude*, pp. 101–02; Morley to Minto, 23 April 1908, quoted in Wolpert, *Morley and India*, p. 112.

30. Roosevelt to Reid, 3 September 1908, in Beale, *Theodore Roosevelt*, p. 163; Roosevelt to Brooks, 20 November 1908, in Morison, *Roosevelt*, 6:1370.

31. Sidney Brooks, "The Real 'Pacific Question,'" *Harper's Weekly* 51 (12 October 1907): 1484; Brooks to Roosevelt, 11 November 1908, and Roosevelt to Brooks, 20 November 1908, in Morison, *Roosevelt*, 6:1368–70; Sidney Brooks, "British and Dutch in South Africa," *Harper's Magazine* 100 (January 1900): 304–10.

32. Roosevelt to Reid, 26 November 1908, and Roosevelt to Morley, 1 December 1908, Roosevelt Papers, series 2, LC; Roosevelt to Brooks, 28 December 1908, in Morison, *Roosevelt*, 6:1443–46; Beale, *Theodore Roosevelt*, p. 164.

33. New York *Times*, 19 January 1909, 2:4.

34. Beale, *Theodore Roosevelt*, p. 164; Singh, *American Attitude*, pp. 89–93; Roosevelt to Lee, 7 February 1908, Roosevelt Papers, series 1, LC; copies of press clippings are in Roosevelt Papers, series 1, LC; Sidney Brooks, "American Opinion and British Rule in India," *North American Review* 190 (December 1909): 774.

35. Singh, "American Press Opinion," pp. 127, 131.

Chapter 5

1. Asiatic Exclusion League, *Proceedings* (February 1908): 8; San Francisco *Call*, 8 January 1908, 40:3, 6 January 1908, 7:2, 19 January 1908, 5:1.

2. McInnes to Grey, 7 February 1908, McInnes to Oliver, 13 February 1908, McInnes to Laurier, 22 February 1908, McInnes to Oliver, 16 February 1908, GGC, vol. 211, PAC; Seattle *Daily Times*, 5 February 1908, Grey to Elgin, 17 February 1908, GGC, vol. 200, PAC.

3. Policies discussed in William R. Wheeler to Charles P. Neill, 11 August 1910, file 52903/110, NA, RG 85.

4. San Francisco *Call*, 7 October 1908, 4:3, 19 October 1908, 7:5; San Francisco *Examiner*, 19 October 1908, 3:2.

5. San Francisco *Examiner*, 28 January 1898, 2:1; Hart H. North, "Chinese and Japanese Immigration to the Pacific Coast," *California Historical Society Quarterly* 28 (1949): 343–50; and Daniels, *Politics of Prejudice*, p. 46.

6. San Francisco *Chronicle*, 4 September 1904, 41:2, 7 October 1904, 16:1; San Francisco *Call*, 7 February 1905, 9:5, 8 February 1905, 11:5, 10 February 1905, 11:7, 26 April 1905, 16:3, 4 June 1909, 5:1.

7. Figures for Indian immigration in 1909 do not agree. Exclusionists maintained that 600 entered at San Francisco during the last six months of 1909, but immigration officials said that 337 entered and 331 were excluded. The

league probably used the total number landing rather than the number
admitted; see Asiatic Exclusion League, *Proceedings* (January 1910): 5. See
also memorandum on Indian immigration, file 52903/110C, NA, RG 85;
H. A. Millis, "East Indian Immigration to the Pacific Coast," *Survey* 28 (1
June 1912): 381; A. E. Yoell to Charles Nagel, 28 December 1909, quoted in
Asiatic Exclusion League, *Proceedings* (January 1910): 6; Daniel J. Keefe to
A. E. Yoell, 8 January 1910, quoted in Asiatic Exclusion League, *Proceedings*
(January 1910): 6.

8. Asiatic Exclusion League, *Proceedings* (January 1910): 6–11.

9. Salvio J. Okesti, "Plague, Press and Politics," *Stanford Medical Bulletin* 13
(February 1953): 9; San Francisco *Call*, 19 April 1907, 9:3, 17 July 1907, 5:4,
11 December 1907, 10:2.

10. Mary Naka, "Angel Island Immigration Station," 1922, Smith Collection,
UO.

11. San Francisco *Call*, 31 January 1910, 1:7, 1 February 1910, 5:7.

12. San Francisco *Chronicle*, 2 October 1921, 11:5; Kahn to Keefe, January 1910,
file 52903/110, NA, RG 85.

13. "Hindu Invasion," *Collier's Weekly* 45 (26 March 1910): 15. Ruth St. Denis
had the misfortune to arrive in California at this time to perform her Indian
dances. From 1906 to 1909, she had toured the East Coast and Europe with
a cycle of solo dances—"Radha," "Incense," "The Cobras," "Nautch," and
"Yogi" —in which she attempted to interpret Asian dance for Westerners.
Audiences had applauded her in the East. In California her exotic dances
drew so little interest that her show closed a financial failure; see Christena
L. Schlundt, *The Professional Appearances of Ruth St. Denis and Ted Shawn: A
Chronology and Index of Dances, 1906–1932* (New York: New York Public Li-
brary, 1962), p. 17.

14. San Francisco *Call*, 21 April 1910, 1:4, 22 April 1910, 16:1, 23 April 1910,
11:4, 24 April 1910, 23:1.

15. Keefe to North, 27 April 1910, file 52903/110, NA, RG 85; Millis, "East Indian
Immigration," p. 381.

16. San Francisco *Call*, 1 May 1910, 42:1. Oakland *Enquirer* quoted in San Francisco *Call*, 13 May 1910, 18:6.

17. San Francisco *Call*, 15 May 1910, 29:2, 21 May 1910, 18:1.

18. Ibid., 11 June 1910, 1:3.

19. Ibid., 13 June 1910, 4:3.

20. Ibid., 18 June 1910, 18:3; Michael is quoted in Schmidt, "American Relations," p. 220.

21. San Francisco *Call*, 26 June 1910, 43:4, 29 June 1910, 7:1, 19 September 1910,
3:1.

22. Ibid., 3 July 1910, 31:4, 13 July 1910, 5:1; W. Stanley Hollis to Alvey Adee,
11 September 1908, numerical file, 1906–1910, vol. 612, NA, RG 59; U.S.
Immigration Commission, *Annual Report* (Washington: GPO, 1910), pp. 148–
49.

23. San Francisco *Call*, 16 July 1910, 5:3, 20 July 1910, 2:2, 6 August 1910, 3:2.

24. Protest from citizens of the Glen Park and Mission districts of San Francisco,
5 August 1910, file 52903/110, NA, RG 85.

25. Pattison to Taft, 12 August 1910, and Wheeler to Neill, 11 August 1910, file 52903/110, NA, RG 85; San Francisco *Call*, 14 August 1910, 46:2, 17 August 1910, 4:1, 15 August 1910, 7:5.

26. Michael's attempts to halt the exodus earlier are discussed in Schmidt, "American Relations," pp. 218–20; Michael to Philander Knox, 10 August 1910, 11 August 1910, file 150.456, NA, RG 59. Clippings from San Francisco *Bulletin*, 10 August 1910; San Francisco *Call*, 11 August 1910, 5:6; and *Calcutta*, 11 August 1910, are in file 52903/110, NA, RG 85. Michael's cable was not sent to Nagel until 12 August 1910, and North was notified only then.

27. Clippings from the *Englishman*, 28 August 1910, file 52903/110, NA, RG 85; San Francisco *Call*, 5 September 1910, 3:7.

28. Michael to assistant secretary of state, 1 September 1910, file 150.456, NA, RG 59.

29. Letters to Keefe and his letters of response are in file 52903/110, NA, RG 85. Nagel's trip is discussed in San Francisco *Call*, 28 September 1910, 4:5.

30. Walter R. Bacon to W. G. Stanton, 23 July 1910, and Otis to Taft, 8 August 1910, Taft Papers, presidential series 2, file 844, LC. George E. Mowry, *The California Progressives* (Berkeley and Los Angeles: University of California Press, 1951), pp. 129–34, does not consider the anti-Asian aspects of the campaign of 1910. Roger Daniels, *Politics of Prejudice*, p. 50, emphasizes the dominant role of the Democrats, but the anti-Indian campaign of 1910 indicates that Republicans were also concerned about exclusionists.

31. San Francisco *Call*, 16 September 1910, 1:4.

32. Ibid., 19 September 1910, 3:1.

33. San Francisco *Chronicle*, 29 September 1910, 1:4; Nagel to Keefe, 20 October 1910, file 53100, NA, RG 85; Knox to Michael, 25 October 1910, file 150.456, NA, RG 59.

34. C. B. Walters, "The Treatment of Hindus in America," *MR* 8 (October 1910): 439.

35. North to Keefe, 14 September 1910, and Yoell to Keefe, 28 September 1910, file 52903/110, NA, RG 85.

36. Richard Taylor and Samuel Bond to Daniel J. Keefe, 17 October 1910, file 52961, Nagel to Keefe, 20 October 1910, and Keefe to Nagel, 1 November 1910, file 53100, NA, RG 85; San Francisco *Call*, 23 October 1910, 29:2, 30:6.

37. San Francisco *Call*, 28 October 1910, 1:7, 29 October 1910, 1:3.

38. Schmitz to Nagel, undated, and Yoell to Taft, 17 December 1910, file 52903/110A, NA, RG 85.

39. San Francisco *Call*, 19 December 1910, 41:6; Millis, "East Indian Immigration," p. 381.

40. Schmidt, "American Relations," p. 279; "Hindu, the Newest Immigration Problem," *Survey* 25 (1 October 1910): 2, gives estimates of five thousand; Das, *Hindustani*, p. 10, gives official figures.

41. Asiatic Exclusion League, *Proceedings* (April 1911): 107.

42. The four-volume investigation is in file 53108/24, NA, RG 85; Nagel Hilles, 19 May 1911, Taft Papers, presidential series 2, file 1492, LC.

43. San Francisco *Chronicle*, 12 April 1930, 7:5; Ella Sterling Cummings, *The Story of the Files: A Review of California Writers and Literature* (San Francisco, 1893),

p. 187; Rockwell D. Hunt, ed., *California and Californians*, 3 vols. (San Francisco: Lewis, 1932), 3:51; San Francisco *Call*, 29 June 1911, 1:4, 30 June 1911, 4:3, 11 July 1911, 3:1.

44. Quotation from diaries of John B. Sawyer, Bancroft Library, UCB, vol. 3, 13 March 1918. For graft see vol. 2, 22 October 1917 and 17 November 1917.

Chapter 6

1. San Francisco *Call*, 8 December 1907, 40:3.
2. Asiatic Exclusion League, *Proceedings* (February 1908): 9.
3. E. J. E. Swayne, "Confidential Memorandum on Matters Affecting the East Indian Community in British Columbia," GGC, vol. 200, PAC; Grey to Crewe, 7 January 1908, GGC, vol. 200, PAC; San Francisco *Call*, 16 October 1908, 5:5.
4. Swayne, "Confidential Memorandum."
5. Waiz, *Indians Abroad*, p. 650; Saint Nihal Singh, "The Triumph of the Indians in Canada," *MR* 4 (August 1908): 103.
6. Singh, "The Triumph," pp. 106–08. Swayne said that Teja Singh first went to Vancouver on 2 October 1908 and was called back to Vancouver on 11 November to dissuade Indians from going to Honduras; GGC, vol. 200, PAC.
7. Vancouver *Daily Province*, 23 November 1908, Toronto *World*, 24 November 1908, and Swayne, "Confidential Memorandum," all in GGC, vol. 200, PAC.
8. Rowland Brittain to assistant director of intelligence, 12 December 1908, GGC, vol. 200, PAC; T. R. Buchanan, India office, to under secretary of state, colonial office, 22 December 1908, GGC, vol. 200, PAC; W. C. Hopkinson to W. W. Cory, deputy minister of the Interior, 24 November 1908, GGC, vol. 200, PAC; and Singh Sihra, "Indians in Canada," *MR* 14 (August 1913): 144.
9. Grey to Laurier, 3 December 1908, Grey Papers, vol. 3, PAC; W. D. Hunter to John Hanbury-Williams, 2 December 1908, Rowland Brittain to assistant director of intelligence, 12 December 1908, deputy minister to Hanbury-Williams, 18 December 1908, Grey to Bryce, 29 December 1908, and Grey to Crewe, 29 December 1908, GGC, vol. 200, PAC.
10. Hunter reports of 23 and 24 November 1908, Brittain to assistant director of intelligence, 5 December 1908, and Hunter to Hanbury-Williams, 2 December 1908, GGC, vol. 200, PAC; Laurier to Grey, 8 December 1908, Grey Papers, vol. 3, PAC; and Brittain to assistant director of intelligence, 12 December 1908, GGC, vol. 200, PAC.
11. Vancouver *World*, 11 December 1908, quoted in Nand Singh Sihra, "Indians in Canada," pp. 144–46.
12. Crewe to Grey, 18 December 1908, GGC, vol. 200, PAC. T. R. Buchanan to under secretary of state, colonial office, 22 December 1908, with regard to viceroy's letter of 17 December 1908, GGC, vol. 200, PAC.
13. Sehra, "Indians in Canada," p. 147.
14. Ibid., p. 148; Hopkinson to Cory, 26 September 1911, GGC, vol. 201, PAC.

15. Cheng, *Oriental Immigration in Canada*, pp. 146–48; "East Indians' Grievances in Canada," *Literary Digest* 47 (23 August 1913): 276–77.

16. "East Indians' Grievances," p. 277. The court cases are described in Hugh Johnston, *The Voyage of the Komagata Maru: The Sikh Challenge to Canada's Colour Bar* (Delhi: Oxford University Press, 1979), p. 12.

17. "The Position of Hindus in Canada," *British Columbia Magazine* 8 (1912): 665; Sehra, "Indians in Canada," p. 149; Hopkinson to Cory, 27 December 1912, GGC, vol. 203, PAC.

18. "East Indians' Grievances in Canada," pp. 276–77.

19. Cheng, *Oriental Immigration in Canada*, pp. 148–51; see also In re Norian Singh, 18 *British Columbia Reports*, 506 (1913). Seattle newspaper quoted in House Committee on Immigration and Naturalization, *Hindu Immigration*, p. 3; various clippings, 2–5 December 1913, file 52903/110, NA, RG 85.

20. Clippings in file 52903/110B, NA, RG 85.

21. Gandhi, *Satyagraha*, p. 339.

22. Holderness to under secretary of state, colonial office, 9 December 1913, GGC, vol. 103, PAC. For order-in-council see Cheng, *Oriental Immigration*, p. 151. In a letter to Caminetti (17 December 1913, file 52903, NA, RG 85), Malcolm Reid explained that the order-in-council, though it appeared to include all nationalities, was directed at Indians.

23. Cheng, *Oriental Immigration in Canada*, p. 152; Montreal *Star*, 22 May 1914, in file 52903/110D, NA, RG 85. Some accounts say that Gurdit Singh made part of his wealth in Canadian timber, but according to Fanja Singh, *Eminent Freedom Fighters of Punjab* (Patiala: Punjabi University, Department of Punjab Historical Studies, 1972), p. 101, he was never a Canadian immigrant. The most detailed account of the affair is Sohan Singh Josh, *The Tragedy of Komagata Maru* (New Delhi: People's Publishing House, 1975).

24. Johnston, *Voyage of the Komagata Maru*, pp. 31, 61.

25. Montreal *Star*, 20 May 1914, *Victoria News-Advertiser*, 22 May 1914, in file 52903/110D, NA, RG 85.

26. Fresno *Republican*, 23 May 1914, Montreal *Gazette*, 23 May 1914, in file 52903/110D, NA, RG 85.

27. Robie L. Reid, "The Inside Story of the 'Komagata Maru,' " *British Columbia Historical Quarterly* 5 (January 1941): 9–10; San Francisco *Examiner*, 4 June 1914, 21:8.

28. Hopkinson to Cory, 6 June 1914, GGC, vol. 211, PAC.

29. "Sikhs Besieging Canada," *Literary Digest* 49 (18 July 1914): 96.

30. Clipping from Vancouver *Sun*, 22 June 1914, and Hopkinson to Cory, 22 June 1914, GGC, vol. 211, PAC; San Francisco *Chronicle*, 22 June 1914; Eric W. Morse, "Some Aspects of the Komagata Maru Affair, 1914," *Canadian Historical Association Annual Report* (1936): 104; minutes of the meeting are in GGC, vol. 211, PAC; the resolution is described in "Sikhs Besieging Canada," p. 96; John H. Clark to Anthony Caminetti, 30 June 1914, file 52903, NA, RG 85.

31. Hopkinson to Cory, 6 June 1914 and 22 June 1914, GGC, vol. 211, PAC.

32. Hopkinson to Cory, 10 July 1914, GGC, vol. 211, PAC; San Francisco *Examiner*, 8 July 1914, file 5290311/0D, NA, RG 85.

33. Reid, "The Inside Story," p. 4; Hopkinson to Cory, 10 July 1914, GGC, vol. 211, PAC. The *Sea Lion* is described in an undated, unnamed clipping in file 52903, NA, RG 85.
34. R. L. Borden to Martin Burrell, undated, GGC, vol. 211, PAC.
35. Reid, "The Inside Story," p. 17; San Francisco *Examiner*, 21 July 1914, 2:8.
36. Vancouver *Saturday Sunset*, 25 July 1914, in GGC, vol. 212, PAC.
37. San Francisco *Examiner*, 21 July 1914, 2:8; Hopkinson to Cory, 20 July 1914, Borden to Connaught, 21 July 1914, and Burrell to Borden, 22 July 1914, GGC, vol. 211, PAC; Hopkinson to Cory, 27 July 1914, Harcourt to Connaught, 29 July 1914, Borden to Connaught, 1 August 1914, and Hopkinson to Cory, 8 August 1914, GGC, vol. 212, PAC; "Notes and Comments," *British Columbia Historical Quarterly* 6 (1942): 297–99; Percival Spear, *India: A Modern History* (Ann Arbor: University of Michigan Press, 1961), p. 171.
38. I have relied upon the accounts of L. P. Mathur, *Indian Revolutionary Movement in the United States* (Delhi: S. Chand, 1970), p. 69; Josh, *Tragedy of Komagata Maru*; pp. 73–78; Johnston *Voyage of the Komagata Maru*, pp. 96–111; and Ted Ferguson, *A White Man's Country: An Exercise in Canadian Prejudice* (Toronto: Doubleday Canada, 1975), pp. 99–134. The New York *Times*, 3 October 1914, 5:3, carried the British press release from London about the Budge Budge incident.
39. Majumdar, *History of the Freedom Movement in India*, 2:467; Jawaharlal Nehru, *Glimpses of World History* (New York: John Day, 1942), p. 669.

Chapter 7

1. For Cleveland's veto see *Congressional Record*, 54th Cong., 2d sess., 1897, 29, pt. 3:2667–68. The response to immigration is surveyed in John Higham, *Strangers in the Land: Patterns of American Nativism, 1820–1925* (New Brunswick, N.J.: Rutgers University Press, 1955).
2. Flint quoted in Bellingham *Herald*, 30 September 1907, 1:1.
3. Senate Commission on Immigration, *Immigrants in Industries*, pp. 348–49; H. A. Millis, "East Indian Immigration to British Columbia and the Pacific Coast States," *American Economic Review* 1 (March 1911): 72, 76.
4. Nagel to Taft, 8 November 1910, Taft Papers, presidential series 2, file 77, LC; Eleanor Tupper and George E. McReynolds, *Japan in American Public Opinion* (New York: Macmillan, 1937), p. 71; Eleanor Tupper, "American Sentiment Toward Japan" (Ph.D. diss., Clark University, 1929), pp. 278–81.
5. Office of solicitor, department of commerce and labor, Memorandum for Charles Nagel, 12 April 1912, file 1512–20, NA, RG 85.
6. For Taft's veto see *Congressional Record*, 62d Cong., 3d sess., 1912, 49, pt. 4:3156. Ray Stannard Baker, ed., *Woodrow Wilson: Life and Letters*, 8 vols. (New York: Doubleday, 1927–1937), 6:106. Arthur S. Link, ed., *The Papers of Woodrow Wilson*, 78 vols. (Princeton: Princeton University Press, 1966–1985), 41:52–53; 39 *U.S. Statutes at Large* 874 (1917). For Wilson's veto see

House Immigration Committee, *Message from the President of the United States*, H.R. 10384, 64th Cong., 2d sess., 1918, H. Doc. 114.

7. Perhaps Raker's most famous legislation was the Raker Act of December 1913, which signaled the end of John Muir's battle to save the Hetch Hetchy Valley; see John Muir, *The Yosemite* (New York: Doubleday, 1962), p. 202n. See also Joan M. Jensen, "Annette Abbott Adams: Politician," *PHR* 35 (1966): 187–90; Raker to Taft, 20 June 1911, Taft Papers, presidential series 2, file 77, LC; and San Francisco *Call*, 13 August 1911, 17:1, 7 September 1911, 2:6.

8. Robert Hennings, "James D. Phelan and the Woodrow Wilson Anti-Oriental Statement of May 3, 1912," *California Historical Society Quarterly* 42 (December 1963): 291–92.

9. Lodge to Taft, 7 December 1911, Taft Papers, presidential series 2, file 77, LC; Hilles to Knox, 8 December 1911, and memorandum to Wilson, 14 December 1911, file 150.456, NA, RG 59.

10. Cable to Knox, 20 September 1912, file 52903/110, NA, RG 85.

11. Taft to C. C. Moore, 6 June 1912, quoted in Pringle, *Taft*, 2:787.

12. Phelan to William F. McCombs, 11 November 1912, quoted in Robert Hennings, "James D. Phelan and the Wilson Progressives of California," (Ph.D. diss., University of California at Berkeley, 1961), p. 134; Hennings, "James D. Phelan," p. 296; see Svend Petersen, *A Statistical History of the American Presidential Elections* (New York: Unger, 1963), pp. 78–79, for the 1912 election results. See also Alexander Saxton, "San Francisco Labor and the Populist and Progressive Insurgencies," *PHR* 34 (1965): 432.

13. Daniels, *Politics of Prejudice*, pp. 58–62; see Kathleen Long Wogelmuth, "Woodrow Wilson's Appointment Policy and the Negro," *Journal of Southern History* 24 (May 1958): 457–80, for a discussion of Wilson's domestic racism.

14. Albert H. Elliot, "Present Status of Alien Land Law in California," survey of race relations, reports, Smith Collection, UO.

15. Joseph Giovinco, "The California Career of Anthony Caminetti, Italian-American Politician" (Ph.D. diss., University of California at Berkeley, 1973), pp. 364–91; Herbert P. Le Pore, "Prelude to Prejudice: Hiram Johnson, Woodrow Wilson, and the California Alien Land Law Controversy of 1913," *Southern California Quarterly* 61 (1979): 99–110; San Francisco *Call*, 20 August 1912, 5:1, 20 October 1912, 4:5, 21 May 1913, 1:3, 1 February 1913, 1:4; San Francisco *Examiner*, 18 February 1914, 4:1.

16. House Committee on Immigration and Naturalization, *Hindu Immigration*, pp. 49–50, 80.

17. Various clippings and letters regarding Hindu Immigration, "Immigration," file 52903/110C, NA, RG 85; see also correspondence in file 150.456, NA, RG 59.

18. "East Indians' Grievances in Canada," pp. 276–77; Shund Singh to Woodrow Wilson, 3 July 1913, and R. S. Miller to J. B. Moore, undated, included with Miller to Parker, 10 July 1913, all in file 150.456, NA, RG 59.

19. Ex parte Moola Singh, et al., 207 Fed. 780 (1913).

20. For petitions of September, October, and November 1913, see immigration file 52903/110B, NA, RG 85.

21. San Francisco *Examiner*, 29 November 1913, 9:1; House Committee on Immigration and Naturalization, *Hindu Immigration*, pp. 47, 212; Giovinco, "The California Career," p. 426; and Roland L. DeLorme, "The United States Bureau of Customs and Smuggling on Puget Sound, 1851 to 1913," *Prologue* 5 (Summer 1973): 7788.

22. In re Rhagat Singh, 209 Fed. 700 (1913); San Francisco *Examiner*, 7 December 1913, 68:8.

23. Bureau of Immigration memorandum regarding Hindu immigration, acting immigration commissioner to Caminetti, 10 December 1913, and immigration inspector to Caminetti, 5 December 1913; all in file 52903/110B, NA, RG 85; House Committee on Immigration and Naturalization, *Hindu Immigration*, p. 68.

24. 63d Cong., 1st sess., 1913, H. Doc. 56, reprinted in House Committee on Immigration and Naturalization, *Hindu Immigration*, pp. 138–40; San Francisco *Call*, 29 December 1912, 17:4.

25. *Congressional Record*, 63d Cong., 2d sess., 50, pt. 3:2781, 2783, 2823.

26. House Committee on Immigration and Naturalization, *Hindu Immigration*, pp. 3–18.

27. Ibid., pp. 334–36; and Nesbitt, "The Health Menace of Asian Races," in ibid., pp. 75–76.

28. Church to Caminetti, 12 January 1914, file 53903, NA, RG 85; Wilson to James B. Clark, 20 January 1914, file 53640, NA, RG 85.

29. San Francisco *Examiner*, 24 January 1914, 1:1, 2:4, 20 January 1914, 4:2.

30. Ibid., 10 February 1914, 4:1.

31. House Committee on Immigration and Naturalization, *Hindu Immigration*, pp. 4–20, 37–53; Sudhindra Bose testified for the Indians. "A Hindu Professor of an American University," *MR* 9 (1910): 438–40; Frank P. Miller, "Dr. Sudhindra Bose: Pioneer Indian Educator in America," *MR* 67 (March 1940): 345; and Sudhindra Bose, "Asian Immigration in the United States," *MR* 25 (May 1919): 524.

32. San Francisco *Examiner*, 14 February 1914, 1:5.

33. San Francisco *Examiner*, 18 February 1914, 4:1.

34. House Committee on Immigration and Naturalization, *Hindu Immigration*, pp. 130–48.

35. Protest addressed to consul general, Philippine Islands; undated, received 14 March 1914, file 150.456, NA, RG 59.

36. Spring-Rice to Connaught, 16 February 1914, GGC, vol. 204, PAC.

37. In a letter to the acting commissioner of immigration at Ellis Island (8 May 1914, file 52903, NA, RG 85), Caminetti discussed Hopkinson's visit. Raker described receiving a bundle of papers about Indian revolutionaries in House Committee on Immigration and Naturalization, *Hindu Immigration*, p. 164.

38. Hopkinson to Wallinger, 30 April 1914, GGC, vol. 205, PAC.

39. John H. Clark to Caminetti, 27 May 1914, and Caminetti memorandum to William Wilson, 12 June 1914, file 52903, NA, RG 85. Wilson did, however, write to Burnett on 3 July 1914, reviewing the need for legislation.

40. San Francisco *Chronicle*, 8 November 1915, 1:5.

41. San Francisco *Examiner*, 8 December 1916, 6:5.

42. *Congressional Record*, 64th Cong., 2d sess., 1916, 54, pt. 3:2619–22.
43. Acting secretary of labor to Lansing, 30 April 1919, and assistant secretary of labor to Lansing, 28 June 1923, file 53854, NA, RG 85; Bonham to Caminetti, 8 May 1918, Caminetti to Bonham, 22 May 1918, W. F. Watkins to Caminetti, 15 August 1918, and Watkins to Caminetti, 2 October 1918, file 53640, NA, RG 85. On ethnic control see Ian R. H. Rocket, "American Immigration Policy and Ethnic Selection: An Historical Overview," *Journal of Ethnic Studies* 10 (Winter 1983): 1–26.

Chapter 8

1. See Joan M. Jensen, *War Plans White: The Army and Internal Security* (in press); W. Dirk Raat, *Revoltosos: Mexico's Rebels in the United States, 1903–1923* (College Station: Texas A & M Press, 1981), pp. 166–99.
2. At the time of Hopkinson's death, the Vancouver *World* of 21 October 1914 said that he was born in Yorkshire in 1876 and that he had gone to India as a child. Clipping and biographical information in GGC, vol. 206, PAC. However, Johnson, *Voyage of the Komagata Maru*, pp. 1, 142, says that Hopkinson was born in Delhi in 1880 and that his mother may have been Indian.
3. Cory to Hanbury-Williams, 19 January 1909, GGC, vol. 200, PAC; Hopkinson to John L. Zurbrick, 29 June 1914, Zurbrick to commissioner of immigration, 1 July 1914, and Caminetti to acting commissioner of immigration, Ellis Island, 8 May 1914, file 52903, NA, RG 85.
4. Das gave some biographical details in a Norwich University history, William Arba Ellis, *Norwich University 1819–1911: Her History, Her Graduates, Her Roll of Honor*, 3 vols. (Montpelier, Vt.: Capital City, 1911), 3:490–91.
5. The best description of the early activities of Das is in Gobind Behari Lal, "Dr. Taraknath Das in Free India," *MR* 91–92 (July 1952): 36–38.
6. Vancouver *Daily Province*, 12 September 1907, 1:7, 14 September 1907, 1:6; *The Free Hindusthan*, 1, no. 1 (April 1908), copy in GGC, vol. 199, PAC.
7. McInnes to Oliver, 3 April 1908, and E. J. E. Swayne, "Confidential Memorandum on Matters Affecting the East Indian Community in British Columbia," GGC, vol. 200, PAC; Adee to Bryce, 7 October 1911, GGC, vol. 201, PAC. The Canadian account said officials told Das that his translations were inadequate, but the version I cite was corroborated by documents reviewed by the immigration committee during hearings in 1926, and Das confirmed it in the hearings; Senate Committee on Immigration, *Ratification and Confirmation of Certain Persons of the Hindu Race*, hearings, 69th Cong., 2d sess., 1926, pp. 25–26.
8. Rodolphe Lemieux to Grey, 15 July 1908, GGC, vol. 209, PAC; clipping from Vancouver *Daily Province*, in GGC, vol. 200, PAC; and W. McLeod to D. I. O., M.D., 10 September 1908, GGC, vol. 200, PAC.
9. McLeod to D. I. O., M.D., 10 September 1908, GGC, vol. 200, PAC.
10. Ronald Spector, "The Vermont Education of Taraknath Das: An Episode in British-American-Indian Relations," *Vermont History* 48 (Spring 1980): 89–

95. Brittain to assistant director of intelligence, 12 December 1908, GGC, vol. 200, PAC.

11. Hopkinson to Cory, 6 November 1909, J. B. Harkin to Cory, 6 October 1909, and Hopkinson to Cory, 9 October 1909, GGC, vol. 200, PAC.

12. Bruce Hay report for assistant director of military intelligence, 17 September 1909, GGC, vol. 200, PAC.

13. Michael to Alvey Adee, 23 June 1910, Adee to G. C. Treadwell, 25 July 1910, Treadwell to Adee, 3 August 1910, all in NA, RG 54.

14. Hopkinson to Cory, 15 November 1908 and 17 January 1910, GGC, vol. 200, PAC.

15. Hopkinson to Cory, 7 March 1910, GGC, vol. 200, PAC.

16. Krishna Kripalani, *Rabindranath Tagore: A Biography* (New York: Grove, 1962), p. 151.

17. "Indian Students Going to America," *Indian Review* 11 (June 1910): 466; Sarangadhar Das, "Information for Indian Students Intending to Come to the Pacific Coast of the United States," *MR* 10 (December 1911): 602–14; and C. B. Walters, "The Treatment of Hindus in America," *MR* 8 (October 1910): 439.

18. "The Life Story of Mohan Singh," 1–4, series A, file 152, and "Contacts of Professor Charles F. Shaw with East Indians," series B, file 123, Smith Collection, UO.

19. Sudhindra Bose, "American Impressions of a Hindu Student," *Forum* 53 (February 1915): 251; Schurr, "Hindus in Los Angeles," series A, file 273, Smith Collection, UO.

20. Das, "Information for Indian Students," p. 602.

21. San Francisco *Examiner*, 28 December 1914, 1:2; San Francisco *Call*, 19 January 1908, 4:4. *Span of Life* 5 (March 1912): in GGC, vol. 202, PAC. An earlier Hindustan association, founded in 1907 by Ram Nath Puri, published the lithographed Urdu periodical *Circular-i-Azadi* (Circular of Freedom) from 1907 to 1908 and had branches in Vancouver and Astoria, but it had either lapsed or had merged with the student group by 1910. Frieda Hauswirth, *A Marriage to India* (New York: Vanguard, 1930), p. 17.

22. Hopkinson to Cory, 26 September 1911, D. O. Malcolm to Cory, 26 September 1911, and Bryce to Knox, 19 September 1911, GGC, vol. 201, PAC.

23. Hopkinson to Cory, 13 October 1911, 23 October 1911, 6 November 1911, and 8 December 1911, GGC, vol. 201, PAC.

24. Hopkinson to Cory, 22 April 1912, Bryce to Arthur Connaught, 22 April 1912, and Connaught to Bryce, 26 April 1912, GGC, vol. 202, PAC. Acting secretary, department of commerce and labor, to Bonaparte, 27 April 1912, file 38–927, NA, RG 60.

25. On 1 March 1912, Hopkinson received a raise to fifteen hundred dollars a year; GGC, vol. 206, PAC.

26. Emily Clara Brown, *Har Dayal: Hindu Revolutionist and Rationalist* (Tucson: University of Arizona Press, 1975), pp. 9–84.

27. San Francisco *Call*, 26 January 1912, 8:1; John D. Barry, "Sidelights of India," copy in GGC, vol. 210, PAC; Brown, *Har Dayal*, pp. 127–28; Har Dayal,

"India in America," *MR* 10 (July 1911): 2; Crewe quoted in H. Verney Lovett, *History of the Indian Nationalist Movement* (London: Murray, 1920), p. 89.

28. Brown, *Har Dayal*, pp. 114–17; Van Wyck Brooks, *Scenes and Portraits* (New York: Dutton, 1954), p. 204.

29. Chandra Chakraberty, *New India* (Calcutta: Vijoyakrishna, 1951), p. 42, claimed that Alice Park had complained; the reasons for his dismissal are in Herrington to Hopkinson, 16 June 1913, GGC, vol. 203, PAC, and in San Francisco *Examiner*, 27 March 1914, GGC, vol. 204, PAC.

30. T. N. Das, "Our Nation Day Celebration in California," *MR* 13 (February 1913): 210–12; Hopkinson to Cory, 6 November 1912 and 16 November 1912, GGC, vol. 200, PAC.

31. Joseph Pope to governor general's secretary, 11 January 1913, GGC, vol. 202, PAC.

32. Hopkinson to Cory, 11 January 1913, GGC, vol. 202, PAC.

33. J. W. Holderness to under secretary of state, colonial office, 22 July 1913, GGC, vol. 203, PAC.

34. Wood, "East Indians in California," p. 4.

35. Ibid., pp. 43–63.

36. Brown, *Har Dayal*, pp. 136–37.

37. Diwakar Prasad Singh, "American Official Attitudes," pp. 192–93.

38. Har Dayal, "India and the World Movement," *MR* 13 (February 1913): 185–88.

39. Ainsworth to Caminetti, 16 July 1913, Hopkinson to Cory, 5 May 1913 and 10 June 1913, Herrington to Hopkinson, 16 June 1913, and Hopkinson to Cory, 18 June 1913, GGC, vol. 203, PAC.

40. Holderness to under secretary of state, colonial office, 22 July 1913, and Hopkinson to Wallinger, 14 August 1913, GGC, vol. 203, PAC.

41. Steele to Hopkinson, August 1913, and Hopkinson to Cory, 26 August 1913, GGC, vol. 203, PAC.

42. Hopkinson to Cory, 14 November 1913, GGC, vol. 203, PAC.

43. Steele to Hopkinson, 22 November 1913, GGC, vol. 203, PAC; Brooks, *Scenes and Portraits*, pp. 204–06.

44. Backus to Caminetti, 6 October 1913, file 52903, NA, RG 85.

45. Weiss to Caminetti, 2 January 1914, file 52903, NA, RG 85.

46. Backus to Caminetti, 23 January 1914, file 52903, NA, RG 85.

47. Hopkinson to Cory, 20 January 1914, and Spring-Rice to Connaught, 6 February 1914, GGC, vol. 204, PAC; Spring-Rice to Connaught, 9 February 1914, in Don K. Dignan, "The Hindu Conspiracy in Anglo-American Relations during World War I," *PHR* 40 (1971): 62; Hopkinson to Wallinger, 16 December 1913, GGC, vol. 203, PAC; Spring-Rice to Moore, 17 February 1914, file 150.456, NA, RG 59.

48. Burjor to Hopkinson, 30 January 1914, GGC, vol. 204, PAC.

49. Hopkinson to Wallinger, 26 January 1914, and Hopkinson to Cory, 4 February 1914, GGC, vol. 204, PAC.

50. Harish K. Puri, *Ghadar Movement: Ideology, Organization and Strategy* (Amritsar: Garu Nanak Dev University, 1983), pp. 104–25, 146–48; and Harish K.

Puri, "Ghadar Movement: An Experiment in New Patterns of Socialization," *Journal of Regional History* 1 (1980): 125–41.

51. Puri, "Ghadar Movement," pp. 127–33.

52. Discussed in Hopkinson to Cory, 27 February 1914, Pandian to Hopkinson, 6 March 1914, GGC, vol. 204, PAC.

53. Brown, *Har Dayal*, pp. 156–59.

54. Ibid., p. 155; New York *Times*, 12 March 1914, 6:5, 27 March 1914, 5:5; San Francisco *Examiner*, 27 March 1914; 28 March 1914; San Francisco *Bulletin*, 27 March 1914, clippings in GGC, vol. 204, PAC; Ligue Droits de l'Homme to Bryan, 31 March 1914, Cama to Bryan, 31 March 1914, Dayal to Bryan, 3 April 1914 and 4 April 1914, file 150.456, NA, RG 59; clipping from Portland *Oregon Journal*, 5 April 1914, GGC, vol. 205, PAC.

55. Secret report, "Indian Agitation in America," continuation of circular no. 12, 1912, GGC, vol. 205, PAC; foreign secretary and Spring-Rice correspondence in Dignan, "Hindu Conspiracy," p. 62.

56. Spring-Rice to Connaught, 7 May 1914, in Dignan, "Hindu Conspiracy," pp. 62–63.

57. Hopkinson to Cory, 3 May 1914, 12 May 1914, 13 May 1914, and C. R. Cleveland note, 11 May 1914, GGC, vol. 205, PAC; state department to S. K. Ratcliffe, 14 May 1914, Henry D. Baker to Bryan, 27 May 1914 and 21 August 1914, and *Pioneer* clipping are in file 150.456, NA, RG 59; Baker to L. Robertson, political secretary to government of Bombay, is in Singh, "American Official Attitudes," pp. 199–203.

58. Criminal intelligence office, Simla, "Indian Agitation in America," April 1914, and C. R. Cleveland, supplementary note, 11 May 1914, both in GGC, vol. 205, PAC.

59. Portland *Telegram* quoted in Singh, *Ghadar 1915*, p. 35; Connaught to Harcourt, 12 August 1914, GGC, vol. 205, PAC; and Hopkinson to Cory, 24 September 1914, GGC, vol. 206, PAC.

60. Barakatullah to Dayal, 24 November 1914, T149, reel 397, GFMA.

61. San Francisco *Chronicle*, 22 October 1914, 4:3; and Puri, *Ghadar Movement*, pp. 136–38, 183. Connaught quoted Steele in a letter to Harcourt, 12 August 1914, GGC, vol. 205, PAC. Hopkinson to Cory, 24 September 1914, GGC, vol. 206, PAC.

62. Hopkinson to Cory, 2 September 1914, GGC, vol. 212, PAC. The dead men were Bela Singh and Harnam Singh; Connaught to Harcourt, 13 October 1914, GGC, vol. 205, PAC; Vancouver *World*, 21 October 1914; Singh, *Ghadar 1915*, p. 39. Tilak Raj Sareen, *Indian Revolutionary Movement Abroad (1905–1921)* (New Delhi: Sterling, 1979), pp. 196–97.

63. Smith, *Nationalism and Reform*, pp. 232–33. For the reception of the *Tosa Maru*, see Michael O'Dwyer, *India As I Knew It, 1885–1925* (London: Constable, 1925), pp. 195–98.

64. Prakash and Vatuk, "Protest Songs," p. 378.

65. Interview with Tuly Singh Johl, 28 May 1975.

66. Ibid. See also 1961 census of India in *Punjab District Census Handbook No. 10, Jullundar District* (Government of Punjab, 1966); Bass, *Language, Religion and Politics in North India*, pp. 311–12. Rural districts in the Punjab Doaba

were later to become strongholds of the Kisan Sabha, the communist front organization that some men from the *Komagata Maru* joined.

Chapter 9

1. *Deutschland—Indiens Hoffnung* (Göttingen, 1914). Copy at HL.
2. Horst Krüger, "Har Dayal in Deutschland," *Mitteilungen des Instituts für Orientforschung* 10 (1964): 141–69, reprints only some of the official German documents. Nirode Kumar Barooah, *India and the Official Germany, 1886–1914* (Frankfurt: Peter Lang, 1977), explores the period up to the outbreak of the war. See also Don Dignan, *New Perspectives on British Far Eastern Policy, 1913–1919* (Brisbane: University of Queensland Press, 1969); and Don Dignan, *The Indian Revolutionary Problem in British Diplomacy, 1914–1919* (New Delhi: Allied Publishers Private Limited, 1983).
3. Llewellyn Woodward, *Great Britain and the War of 1914–1918* (London: Methuen, 1967), p. xiv; Barooah, *India and the Official Germany*, pp. 167–69.
4. Pope to Connaught, 12 December 1914, and Connaught to Hardinge, 28 December 1914, GGC, vol. 212, PAC.
5. Robie L. Reid, "The 'Komagata Maru' and the Central Powers," *British Columbia Historical Quarterly* 6 (1942): 297–99, repeats accusations but offers no concrete evidence. See also articles in GGC, vol. 212, PAC, and Indian Committee of Inquiry into the *Komagata Maru* Affair, *Report* (Calcutta: GPO, 1914).
6. Brown, *Har Dayal*, p. 149, notes that the *Ghadar* made no mention of the German consul in its report of the meeting. Hopkinson to Cory, 20 January 1914, GGC, vol. 204, PAC.
7. Chandra Chakraberty, *New India* (Calcutta: Vijoyakrishna, 1951), p. 52; Warren to Preston, 18 June 1917, file 9–10–3, NA, RG 60; Brooks, *Scenes*, p. 207, says that he knew the Germans were making arrangements for Dayal to go to Constantinople; Wangenheim to GFO, 8 September 1914, T149, reel 397, GFMA; Barooah, *India and the Official Germany*, p. 189.
8. Barooah, *India and the Official Germany*, pp. 170–71.
9. Suggestions from BIC for postwar work, T149, reel 400, GFMA.
10. Regendanz to Langwerth, 20 August 1914, Arthur Zimmermann to German embassy, Constantinople, 28 August 1914, Theobald von Bethmann-Hollweg to German embassy, Constantinople, 4 September 1914, "Questions for Oppenheim," 1 September 1914, Oppenheim to GFO, 9 September 1914, T149, reel 397, GFMA; for more on Oppenheim see New York *Times*, 26 May 1917, 12:6.
11. Wangenheim to GFO, 14 September 1914; Oppenheim memorandum, 16 September 1914, and GFO to Wangenheim, 18 September 1914, T149, reel 397, GFMA.
12. Wangenheim to GFO, 21 September 1914, Bernstorff to GFO, 29 September 1914, and 30 September 1914, Oppenheim to Zimmermann, 17 October 1914, Bernstorff to GFO, 16 October 1914, Von Papen to GFO, 20 October 1914, T149, reel 397, GFMA. See also Majumdar, *History of the Freedom Movement*,

2:411; Agnes Smedley, *Battle Hymn of China* (New York: Knopf, 1943), p. 12, and Janice R. MacKinnon and Stephen R. MacKinnon, *Agnes Smedley* (Berkeley and Los Angeles: University of California Press, 1987). Other biographical details are from C. Sehanavis, "Pioneers Among Indian Revolutionaries in Germany," *Mainstream*, 13, no. 46 (1975): 11–14, and C. Sehanavis, "Indian Revolutionaries Abroad: A Rare Document," *Mainstream*, 13, no. 48 (1975): 22–23. Chatto's older sister, Sarojini Naidu, who had studied in England from 1895 to 1898, was better known than he in India. A suffragist and a supporter of nonviolent resistance, she later became president of the 40th Indian National Congress.

13. For information on Pillai see Mozumdar, *History of Freedom Movement*, 2:411–12.

14. Zimmermann memorandum, 14 October 1914, T137, reel 150, GFMA; Romberg to GFO, 20 October 1914, GFO to Romberg, 23 October 1914, Chatto to Dayal, 24 October 1914, Romberg to GFO, 25 October 1914, and Romberg to GFO, 3 November 1914, T137, reel 397, GFMA.

15. Wangenheim to GFO, 19 May 1915 and 23 June 1915, German embassy, Constantinople, to GFO, 12 August 1915; BIC to Wesendonk, 17 December 1915, T149, reel 398, GFMA; Rai, "India in America," *MR* (May 1916): 525.

16. Correspondence regarding Near Eastern activities is in T149, reel 398, GFMA.

17. Messages from Wangenheim to GFO, 19 May 1915, 23 June 1915, and 12 August 1915, T149, reel 398, GFMA. For information on Berkman see Richard Drinnon, *Rebel in Paradise: A Biography of Emma Goldman* (Chicago: University of Chicago Press, 1961), pp. 206–08.

18. BIC to Wesendonk, 17 December 1915 and 25 December 1915, T149, reel 398, GFMA.

19. BIC to Wesendonk, 4 December 1916, T149, reel 399, GFMA.

20. Brown, *Har Dayal*, pp. 212–13.

21. Bethmann-Hollweg to German embassy, Constantinople, 4 September 1914, Zimmermann Memorandum, 14 October 1914, T137, reel 150, GFMA; Roger Casement to Eoin McNeill, 28 November 1914, in Great Britain, Parliament, *Documents Relative to the Sinn Fein Movement* (London: HMSO, 1921), p. 5; Peter Singleton-gates and Maurice Girodias, *The Black Diaries* (New York: Grove, 1959), p. 368.

22. Bernstorff to GFO, 16 October 1914, von Papen to GFO, 20 October 1914, and 7 December 1914, and copy of discussion with Nadolny, 23 November 1914, T149, reel 397, GFMA.

23. "A Short Summary of the Plan of the Indian Committee in Berlin," undated [early December 1914] T149, reel 397, GFMA. The first two men sent to America were Direndra Kumar Sirkar and N. S. Marathe, according to Sehanavis, "Pioneers," p. 12. The only comment about their activities is in Panchanan Saha, "Indian Revolutionary Movement in Germany," *Mainstream*, 12, no. 6 (1973): 33–36, which says that Arun Chandra Guha met Sirkar in Iowa in the fall of 1914. Sirkar told Guha to return to India to organize secret societies, and Guha then left on a Japanese ship on which some Ghadar Party members also sailed.

24. "Proposals for Work in America," undated [end of December 1914], and addendum to letter of Barakatullah to Dayal, 24 November 1914, T149, reel 397, GFMA. Chatto to Zimmerman, 17 December 1915, Zimmermann to Chatto, 19 December 1915, T149, reel 398, GFMA.

25. BIC to Wesendonk, 9 November 1917, T137, reel 400, GFMA.

26. Gupta's activities are mentioned in BIC communications of 3 February 1915 and in Bernstorff to GFO, 1 March 1915, 3 March 1915, 19 March 1915, 25 March 1915, and 26 March 1915, T149, reel 398, GFMA. The Bernstorff telegram that is often referred to as the first communication directly linking the German diplomats with the Indians in the United States is not in the Indian records of the German archives but is reprinted in Henry Landau, *The Enemy Within* (New York: Putnam, 1937), pp. 29–30; India office to foreign office, 29 December 1914, is quoted in Dignan, "Hindu Conspiracy," p. 63.

27. BIC to Wesendonk, 17 December 1915 and 10 January 1916, T149, reel 398, GFMA; BIC to Wesendonk, 11 December 1916, T149, reel 399, GFMA.

28. Sohan Singh Josh, *Hindustan Gadar Party: A Short History*, 2 vols. (New Delhi: People's Publishing House, 1978), 2:57; Hopkinson to Wallinger, 15 August 1913, GGC, vol. 203, PAC; Chakraberty, *New India*, p. 34.

29. Chakraberty is mentioned in Oppenheim to Wesendonk, 21 September 1914, T149, reel 397, GFMA, and in Bernstorff to GFO, 25 March 1915, unsigned memorandum, 28 March 1915, GFO to Bernstorff, 29 March 1916, BIC memorandum, 24 April 1915, and BIC to Wesendonk, 10 January 1916, T149 reel 398, GFMA.

30. Chakraberty is mentioned in Bernstorff to GFO, 2 May 1916, BIC to Wesendonk, 8 May 1916, and unsigned letter to Chakraberty, 13 July 1916, T149, reel 398, GFMA, and in a report titled "Our Work in America," June-September 1916, T149, reel 399, GFMA.

31. Bernstorff to GFO, 19 January 1917, and BIC to Wesendonk, 17 February 1917, T149, reel 399, GFMA.

32. Accounts of the raid are in Thomas J. Tunney, *Throttled* (Boston: Small, Meynard, 1919), p. 72; New York *Times*, 7 March 1917, 1:1, and 9 March 1917, 2:7; Washington *Post*, 11 March 1917; and Chakraberty, *New India*, p. 38.

33. Josh refers to Chakraberty as "hated most by all the Hindu defendants in the case" but does not condemn Gupta; *Hindustan Gadar Party*, p. 60.

34. Evidence of Gupta's providing information to the British is in report of 26 September 1918, MID file 1054/0722/42, NA, RG 165.

35. Anuradha Sareen, *India and Afghanistan: British Imperialism vs. Afghan Nationalism, 1907–1921* (Delhi: Seems, 1981), pp. 53–101; Bernstorff to GFO, 30 September 1914, and 21 November 1914, and Barakatullah to Dayal, 24 November 1914, T149, reel 397, GFMA.

36. Hopkinson to Wallinger, 12 January 1914, GGC, vol. 204, PAC.

37. Chandra is mentioned in German embassy, San Francisco, to GFO, 22 March 1915, Bernstorff to GFO, 26 March 1915, GFO to Bernstorff, 29 March 1915, Wangenheim to GFO, 19 May 1915, and BIC to Wesendonk, 11 December 1916, T149, reel 398, GFMA. Biographical information is given in Hopkinson to Wallinger, 12 January 1914, GGC, vol. 204, PAC.

38. Josh, *Hindustan Gadar Party*, p. 89. According to Puri, *Ghadar Movement*, pp. 97, 100, Chandra asked Chakraberty for thirty-five thousand dollars, but Chakraberty advised the BIC not to pay it. Puri concludes that, aside from printing propaganda and providing five men with literature to accompany the arms shipment, Chandra did little for the Germans, but does not account for the money Chandra did receive.

39. Datta to Wesendonk, 13 November 1918, T149, reel 400, GFMA.

Chapter 10

This chapter originally appeared, in slightly different form, in *PHR* 48 (1979): 65–83.

1. Giles T. Brown, "The Hindu Conspiracy, 1914–1917," *PHR* 17 (1948): 299–310; Mark Naidis, "Propaganda of the Gadar Party," *PHR* 20 (1951): 251–60. Popular spy accounts are Earl E. Sperry, *German Plots and Intrigues in the United States during the Period of Our Neutrality* (Washington, D.C.: Committee on Public Information, Red, White, and Blue Series, no. 10, July 1918); J. P. Jones and P. M. H. Hollister, *The German Secret Service in America* (Boston: Small, Maynard, 1918); and Tunney, *Throttled*.

2. John W. Spellman, "The International Extensions of Political Conspiracy as Illustrated by the Ghadr Party," *Journal of Indian History* 37 (1959): 23–45; Majumdar, *History of the Freedom Movement*, 2:18–21, 62–64, 469–83; Kalyan Kumar Banerjee, "The Indo-German Conspiracy: Beginning of the End," and "The Gadar Movement and the Hand of Germany," *MR* 118 (1965): 112–119, 381–86; *MR* 116 (1964): 27–30, 335–61, 117 (1965): 97–101, 119 (1966): 26–30, 121 (1967): 99–107.

3. Arun Coomer Bose, "Indian Nationalist Agitators in the U.S.A. and Canada till the Arrival of Har Dayal in 1911," *Journal of Indian History* 43 (1965): 227–39. For more information see Arun Coomer Bose, *Indian Revolutionaries Abroad, 1905–1922* (Patna: Bharat, Bhawan, 1971), and L. P. Mathur, *Indian Revolutionary Movement in the United States of America* (Delhi: Chand, 1970).

4. Dignan, "The Hindu Conspiracy in Anglo-American Relations," pp. 57–77; Rhodri Jeffreys-Jones, *American Espionage: From Secret Service to CIA* (New York: Free Press, 1977), p. 112.

5. Charles G. Fenwick, *The Neutrality Laws of the United States* (Washington, D.C.: Carnegie Endowment for International Peace, 1913), p. 57; New York *Times*, 31 August 1895, 5:4, 24 September 1895, 5:1, 19 November 1895, 5:1, 12 June 1895, 4:7, 23 June 1896, 5:1, and 31 July 1896, 1:5; United States v. Wisborg, 73 Fed. 159 (1896); Ray Emerson Curtis, "The Law of Hostile Military Expeditions as Applied by the United States," *American Journal of International Law* (1914): 249; Lowell L. Blaisdell, *The Desert Revolution: Baja California, 1911* (Madison: University of Wisconsin Press, 1962), pp. 170–71, 189–91; and Lowell L. Blaisdell, "Harry Chandler and the Mexican Border Intrigue, 1914–1917," *PHR* 35 (1966): 385–93. For correspondence on neutrality law enforcement along the Mexican border, see records of the adjutant

general's office, file 1716354 NA, RG 94; United States v. Molina et al., case no. 1564, and United States v. Emilio Vasquez Gomez et al., case no. 2080, Federal Records Center, Fort Worth, Texas; Michael Meyer, *Huerta: A Political Portrait* (Lincoln: University of Nebraska Press, 1972), pp. 221–22, 225; and Raat, *Revoltosos*, pp. 137–67, 231–34.

6. Philip E. Johnson, "The Unnecessary Crime of Conspiracy," *California Law Review* 61 (1975): 1139–40.

7. Francis B. Sayre, "Criminal Conspiracy," *Harvard Law Review* 35 (1922): 383–427; Goldman et al. v. United States, 245 U.S. 474 (1918); Schenck v. United States, 249 U.S. 47 (1919); Dennis v. United States, 341 U.S. 494 (1951); United States v. Spock, 416 F.2d 165 (1969); and United States v. Dellinger, 474 F.2d 340 (1972). The Goldman case was decided on 14 January 1918, before the San Francisco case had been decided but after newspaper publicity had linked Emma Goldman and Alexander Berkman to the "Hindu conspiracy."

8. Brittain to assistant director of intelligence, 5 December 1908, GGC, vol. 200, PAC. Reports from Hopkinson are scattered throughout volumes 200–05 of GGC, PAC. See especially Cory to Hanbury-Williams, 19 January 1909, and Hopkinson to Cory, 7 March 1910 (vol. 200); Hopkinson to Cory, 26 September 1911, 13 October 1911, and 23 October 1911 (vol. 201); Hopkinson to Cory, 3 May 1914, 12 May 1918, and 2 September 1918, and Hopkinson to Wallinger, 30 April 1914 (vol. 205). See also Hopkinson to Zurbrick, 29 June 1914, Zurbrick to Caminetti, 1 July 1914, and Caminetti to acting commissioner of immigration, 8 May 1914, file 52903, NA, RG 85.

9. Connaught to Lewis Harcourt, 12 August 1914, and Hopkinson to Cory, 24 September 1914, GGC, vol. 205, PAC.

10. Spring-Rice to Lansing, 21 December 1916, Gregory to Lansing, 26 February 1917, Spring-Rice to Bryan, 12 May 1915, Spring-Rice to Lansing, 14 June 1915; Bernstorff to Lansing, 2 July 1915, file 9–10–3, NA, RG 60; See also von Papen to foreign office, 31 May 1915, R149, reel 398, GFMA.

11. Spring-Rice transmitted his complaint to the state department on 15 February 1916, file 9–10–3, NA, RG 60; see also Naeem Gul Rathore, "The Indian Nationalist Agitation in the United States: A Study of Lala Lajpat Rai and the Indian Home Rule League of America, 1914–1920" (Ph.D. diss., Columbia University, 1965), p. 88.

12. José de Olivares to state department, 6 May 1916, file 150.456, NA, RG 59, reviews the Lahore trial; see also New York *Times*, 14 June 1915, 4:3; "American-Made Hindu Revolts," *Literary Digest* 51 (10 July 1915): 56; and Dignan, "Hindu Conspiracy," pp. 64–67.

13. Spring-Rice to Lansing, 25 February 1916, file 9–10–3, NA, RG 60.

14. Frank Polk to Charles Warren, 25 February 1916; Warren to Polk, 26 February 1916, file 9–10–3, NA, RG 60.

15. A. B. Law to Connaught, 29 February 1916, GGC, vol. 207, PAC; Norman Thwaites, *Velvet and Vinegar* (London: Grayson & Grayson, 1932), p. 145; Spring-Rice to Polk, 27 March 1916, and Polk to Gregory, 3 April 1916, file 9–10–3, NA, RG 60.

16. Warren to Preston, 13 May 1916, Preston to Gregory, 25 May 1916; Warren

to M. A. Thomas, 3 June 1916, Thomas to Gregory, 9 June 1916, and Gregory to Lansing, 3 June 1916, file 9–10–3, NA, RG 60.

17. Unsigned memorandum for Warren, 25 May 1916, and S. J. Graham to Lansing, 28 June 1916, file 9–10–3, NA, RG 60.

18. Unsigned memorandum for Warren, 14 August 1916, Polk to Gregory, 10 October 1916, and Warren to Lansing, 27 October 1916, Gregory to Lansing, 20 December 1916, and Spring-Rice to Lansing, 21 December 1916, all in file 9–10–3, NA, RG 60.

19. Spring-Rice to Lansing, 15 January 1917, and Lansing to Gregory, 24 January 1917, file 9–10–3, NA, RG 60.

20. Unsigned memorandum for Warren, 15 January 1917, file 9–10–3, NA, RG 60; United States v. Bopp, 230 Fed. 723 (1916).

21. Warren to Preston, 1 February 1917, Preston to Gregory, 13 February 1917, Warren to Preston, 21 February 1917, Gregory to Lansing, 26 February 1917, Lansing to Wilson, 27 February 1917, and Lansing to Gregory, 28 February 1917, file 9–10–3, NA, RG 60; Dignan, "Hindu conspiracy," p. 72; and Lansing memorandum to Spring-Rice, 23 February 1917, file 763.7211, NA, RG 59.

22. Warren to Polk, 8 March 1917, 13 March 1917, and 16 March 1917, Polk to Warren, 14 March 1917 and 15 March 1917, and Warren to Thomas D. McCarthy, 13 March 1917, file 9–10–3, NA, RG 60; Dignan, "Hindu Conspiracy," pp. 73–74; Henry Stockton telegram to Robert Nathan, 23 March 1917, and telegrams to Nathan from agents in Vancouver, 10 April 1917 and 13 April 1917, GGC, vol. 208, PAC; Warren to McCarthy, 26 March 1917, file 9–10–3, NA, RG 60.

23. Warren, "War Notes," Warren Papers, box 5, LC; Preston to Warren, 6 April 1917, file 9–10–3, NA, RG 60.

24. Warren to Preston, 11 April 1917, file 9–10–3, NA, RG 60; Marr telegrams to Nathan, 10 May 1917 and 15 May 1917, and Nathan telegram to Wiseman, 21 May 1917, GGC, vol. 208, PAC.

25. Warren to Charles F. Clyne, 11 April 1917, Preston to Warren, 11 April 1917, and memorandum of conference, 16 June 1917, file 9–10–3, NA, RG 60. The New York indictments were upheld in United States v. Chakraberty et al., 244 Fed. 287 (1917).

26. Jacobsen v. United States, 272 Fed. 399 (1920); an unidentified newspaper clipping describing the charge from the judge is in Warren Papers, box 7, LC; New York *Times*, 19 October 1917, 13:3.

27. Preston to Gregory, 17 November 1917, file 9–10–3, NA, RG 60.

28. For conspiracy trials in general see David B. Filvaroff, "Conspiracy and the First Amendment," *University of Pennsylvania Law Review* 121 (1972): 189; and Johnson, "Unnecessary Crime of Conspiracy," p. 1137.

29. San Francisco *Chronicle*, 18 April 1918, 1:1; San Francisco *Examiner*, 23 November, 1917, 1:1; undated, unsigned history, "The Hindu Conspiracy, the Ghadr Society, and Indian Revolutionary Propaganda," MID file 10560–152, NA, RG 165.

30. Preston to Gregory, 6 August 1918, NA, RG 118; San Francisco *Chronicle*, 24 April 1918, 1:5–8.

34. Smedley to Pacific Coast Hindusthan Association, 31 October 1919, FFI, UCB.
35. Roe to Palmer, 10 September 1919, memorandum to solicitor general, 13 September 1919, memorandum from solicitor general to Palmer, 16 October 1919, and Adams to Palmer, 25 November 1919, file 193424, NA, RG 60; Smedley to Gopal Singh and Ed Gamons, 31 October 1919, FFI, UCB.
36. Johnson, *The Challenge*, p. 154; *Congressional Record*, 66th Cong., 2d Sess., 1920, 59; pt. 4:3569; R. C. Lindsay to Earl Curzon, 6 March 1920, GGC, vol. 208, PAC; *India News Service* 1 (14 February 1920); Eamon DeValera, *India and Ireland* (New York: Friends of Freedom for India, 1920), pp. 13, 20; Smedley to Ed Gamons, 18 March 1919, and Smedley to Bishon Singh, 11 May 1920, FFI, UCB.
37. 41 U.S. 593 (1920); Smedley to Hindusthan Ghadar Party, 6 June 1920, and Smedley to Santokh Singh, 17 August 1920, FFI, UCB.
38. Smedley and Das to Gopel Singh, 31 July 1920, FFI, UCB; and *India News Service* 2 (11 September 1920 and 9 October 1920).
39. For a discussion of Akalis in the Punjab see S. C. Mittal, *Freedom Movement in Punjab (1905–1929)* (Delhi: Concept, 1977), pp. 148–180; Mathur, *Indian Revolutionary Movement*, pp. 131–41; and Fox, *Lions*, pp. 79–104.
40. See *India News Service* 2 (14 August 1920 and 21 August 1920).
41. Lewis Warfield to Harry M. Daugherty, 4 October 1921, Daugherty to Warfield, 10 October 1921, Charles E. Hughes to Daugherty, 20 October 1921, Daugherty to Hughes, 24 October 1921, file 218835, NA, RG 60.
42. M. K. Bunde memorandum to H. Col. Hett, 14 February 1921, and Parker Hitt to Marlborough Churchill, 21 March 1921, MID 9771–B–672 and 709, NA, RG 165.
43. Clippings from Chicago *Daily Tribune*, 26 December 1921, and from *Irish Press*, 1 October 1921 and 4 February 1922, memorandum to Burns, Burns to Foster, 8 February 1922, file 218835, NA, RG 60.
44. "Sympathy of the American Federation of Labour," *MR* 32 Review (September 1922): 406; Sankar Ghose, *Socialism and Communism in India* (Bombay: Allied, 1971), p. 14.
45. Smedley to Santokh Singh, 30 September 1920, FFI, UCB.

Chapter 12

1. For a discussion of naturalization laws in the early nineteenth century see James H. Kettner, *The Development of American Citizenship* (Chapel Hill: University of North Carolina Press, 1978), especially pp. 213–47. The laws about women and children were vague and often changed before 1855, but women were allowed to be naturalized in the early nineteenth century. James Kent, *Commentaries on the American Law*, 4 vols. (New York: Halsted, 1826–1830), 2:72.
2. Kettner, *Development of American Citizenship*, pp. 286–300.
3. Charles J. McClain, Jr., "The Chinese Struggle for Civil Rights in Nineteenth Century America: The First Phase, 1850–1870," *California Law Review* 72

(1984): 529–68; Dudley McGovney, "Our Non-Citizen Nationals: Who Are They?" *California Law Review* 22 (1934): 600; Elk v. Wilkins, 112 U.S. 94 (1884).

4. U.S. Attorney General, *Annual Report* (Washington, D.C.: GPO, 1904), pp. iv–v.

5. William S. Bernard, "The Law, the Mores, and the Oriental," *Rocky Mountain Law Review* 10 (February 1938): 112. According to the 1910 census, 1,368 Chinese had been naturalized and 483 had received their first papers by 1910; Sidney Gulick, *American Democracy and Asiatic Citizenship* (New York: Scribner's, 1918), p. 59.

6. Straus to Bonaparte, 9 January 1907, acting attorney general to Straus, 11 January 1907, Devlin to Bonaparte, 8 August 1907, and Bonaparte to Devlin, 14 August 1907, file 97415, NA, RG 118.

7. "British Indians and Citizenship in White Men's Countries," *Outlook* 87 (7 September 1907): 7–8; Das to Bonaparte, 21 September 1907, Bonaparte to Das, 28 September 1907, W. F. Willcox to Bonaparte, 13 September 1907, Bonaparte to Willcox, 16 September 1907, Willcox to Bonaparte, 24 September 1907, and Bonaparte to Willcox, 27 September 1907, file 97415, NA, RG 118.

8. Willcox to Bonaparte, 13 September 1907, and Das to Bonaparte, 21 September 1907, file 97415, NA, RG 118.

9. United States v. Dolla, 177 Fed. 101 (1910).

10. In re Balsara, 171 Fed. 294 (1909).

11. In re Halladjian et al., 174 Fed. 834 (1909). Abdul Goffor Mondul was admitted to citizenship in Galveston on 9 February 1909. A complete list of the sixty-nine men naturalized is in Senate Committee on Immigration, *Ratification and Confirmation*, p. 1.

12. In re Mudarri, 176 Fed. 465 (1910).

13. United States v. Balsara, 180 Fed. 694 (1910); In re Ellis, 179 Fed. 1002 (1910). 14. United States v. Balsara, 180 Fed. 694 (1910); United States v. Dolla, 177 Fed. 101 (1910).

15. U.S. Department of Commerce, Bureau of the Census, *Thirteenth Census of the United States*, 11 vols. (Washington, D.C.: GPO 1913), 1:125–26. See especially the footnote to table 2.

16. San Francisco *Call*, 29 December 1912, 17:4, 4 May 1913, 50:1.

17. Ex parte Shahid, 205 Fed. 812 (1913).

18. Ex parte Dow, 211 Fed. 486 (1914).

19. In re Dow, 213 Fed. 355 (1914).

20. In re Sadar Bhagwab Singh, 246 Fed. 496 (1917).

21. United States v. Mohan Singh, 257 Fed. 209 (1919); San Francisco *Examiner*, 11 June 1920, 10:5; United States v. Sakharam Ganesh Pandit, 15 F.2d. 285 (1926).

22. For a discussion of aliens and the draft see William S. Bernard, "Arms and the Alien: The Socio-Legal Effects of War Upon Citizenship," *Rocky Mountain Law Review* 11 (April 1939): 181–83, and J. M. O'Brien, "A Current Problem of Naturalization," *Marquette Law Review* 9 (1925): 270–74. Lab Theara Singh died in the American army at Pearl Harbor; *The Hindustanee Student* 2 (September-October 1926): 15. See Toyota v. United States, 268 U.S. 402 (1925),

for the matter of Japanese servicemen and American Protective League to adjutant general, 6 September 1918, NA, RG 94, for a discussion of wartime arrest of a person who refused restaurant service to an Indian serviceman.

23. United States v. Bhagat Singh Thind, 261 U.S. 204 (1922).

24. Takao Ozawa v. United States, 260 U.S. 178 (1922); M. Browning Carrott, "Prejudice Goes to Court: The Japanese and the Supreme Court in the 1920s," *CH* 62 (Summer 1983): 122–38. With the exception of those men covered by special legislation for military service, Chinese, Japanese, Koreans, Filipinos, Hawaiians, and native Americans were excluded, but Mexicans were admitted. The government recognized Mexicans within the naturalization statute because they had been admitted collectively by earlier treaties.

25. United States v. Bhagat Singh Thind, 261 U.S. 204 (1922).

26. D. O. McGovney, "Race Discrimination in Naturalization," *Iowa Law Bulletin* 8 (March 1923): 147; J. B. Scott, "Japanese and Hindu Naturalization," *American Journal of International Law* 17 (April 1923): 330. See also Milton R. Konvitz, *The Alien and the Asiatic in American Law* (Ithaca: Cornell University Press, 1946), p. 88.

27. Newspapers quoted in "Hindus Too Brunette to Vote Here," *Literary Digest* 76 (10 March 1923): 13. For a discussion of race-restrictive convenants in force on residential property and how they applied to Indians and other non-whites see Joan M. Jensen, "Apartheid: Pacific Coast Style," *PHR* 38 (August 1969): 335–40.

28. "Editorial Notes," *Nation* 117 (10 October 1923): 366–67.

29. United States v. Raverat, 222 Fed. 1018 (1915); United States v. Darmer 249 Fed. 989 (1918); U.S. Attorney General, *Annual Report* (Washington, D.C.: GPO, 1918), p. 747; "Recent Trends in Denaturalization in the United States and Abroad," *Columbia Law Review* 44 (September 1944): 742.

30. Das to Palmer, 19 May 1919, Roe to Palmer, 10 September 1919, Post to Palmer, 2 October 1919, and Adams to Palmer, 6 November 1919, file 38–927, NA, RG 60; New York *Times*, 6 December 1920, 16:1; United States v. Kramer, 262 Fed. 395 (1919); United States v. Herberger, 272 Fed. 278 (1919).

31. Post to Palmer, 1 February 1921, senator Joseph E. Ransdell to Palmer, 17 February 1921, Stewart to Silva, 21 February 1921, E. M. Leonard to Daugherty, 2 February 1922, George W. Norris to Daugherty, 3 March 1922, assistant attorney general John W. Crim to Norris, 9 March 1922, file 38–927, NA, RG 60; Tavaknath Das, "An American Attitude to Non-violent Non-co-operation," *MR* 34 (December 1923): 751; United States v. Woerndle, 288 Fed. 47 (1923); William Hayward to Daugherty, 28 February 1923, Adams to U.S. attorney, San Francisco, 21 March 1923, memorandum to Daugherty, 4 May 1923, file 9–19–0, NA, RG 60; Robe White to Daugherty, 1 May 1923, Alma Myers to Daugherty, 11 May 1923, file 38–927, NA, RG 60.

32. United States v. Akhay Kumar Mozumdar, 296 Fed. 173 (1923); Akhay Kumar Mozumdar v. United States, 299 F. 240 (1924); United States v. Ali, 7 F.2d 728 (1925); Marian Schibsby, "Hindus and American Citizenship," *National Conference of Social Work* (1927): 579–81.

33. 42 *U.S. Statutes at Large*, 1021–22 (22 September 1922).

34. Los Angeles *Times*, 18 November 1919, II:1:3; Ray E. Chase and S. G. Pandit,

An Examination of the Opinion of the Supreme Court of the United States Deciding Against the Eligibility of Hindus for Citizenship (1926).

35. Joseph C. Burke to Daugherty, 12 March 1924, Earl J. Davis to Burke, 14 April 1924, Samuel W. McNabb to Harlan Stone, 17 December 1925, White to Stone, 8 January 1926, file 38–524, NA, RG 60.

36. San Francisco *Chronicle*, 13 September 1926, 10:1; Emory R. Buckner to Stone, 18 June 1926, file 38–927, NA, RG 60.

37. San Francisco *Chronicle*, 12 September 1926, 16:1; Gary R. Hess, "The 'Hindu' in America: Immigration and Naturalization Policies and India, 1917–1946" *PHR* 38 (1969): 59–79, discusses India's reactions to the naturalization issue.

38. 69th Cong., 2d sess., 1926, S. Joint Res. 128; O. R. Luhring memorandum, 18 December 1926, file 38–524, NA, RG 60; Reed to Das, 23 December 1926, in Mary K. Das, "True Status of Hindus Regarding American Citizenship," *MR* 41 (April 1927): 464; New York *Times*, 5 May 1927, 9.

39. San Francisco *Chronicle*, 3 November 1926, 15:4; United States v. Sakharam Ganesh Pandit, 15 F.2d. 285 (1926); McNabb to Stone, 9 November 1926, W. W. Husband to Stone, 23 November 1926, and William Donovan to Stone, 4 January 1927, file 38–524, NA, RG 60; "Aliens—Naturalization—Cancellation of Illegally Procured Certificate," *Harvard Law Review* 41 (December 1927): 249.

40. "Exclusion of 'Hindus' from American Citizenship," *MR* 43 (February 1928): 243; Walter N. Nelson to Raymond M. Crist, 7 May 1927, Crist to Nelson, 20 May 1927, and Copeland to White, 21 May 1927, in Das, "Truth," p. 191; United States v. Ali, 7 F.2d. 728 (1925); United States v. Gokhale, 26 F.2d. 360 (1928).

41. Morrison et al. v. California, 291 U.S. 82 (1934).

42. Dudley O. McGovney, "Naturalization of the Mixed-Blood—A Dictum," *California Law Review* 22 (May 1924): 377–91.

43. U. S. Webb to Shepard and Shepard, 9 January 1924, file 225815, NA, RG 118; Surendranath Das Gupta, "Indians in the United States," *MR* 36 (July 1924): 15–19.

44. "Indians Not Eligible for American Citizenship," *MR* 33 (March 1923): 407.

45. "Indian Rights in the United States," *Nation* 117 (17 October 1923): 447; New York *Times*, 11 October 1923, 33.

46. Sudhindra Bose, " 'White' America," *MR* 36 (August 1924): 150–52; San Francisco *Chronicle*, 6 May 1924, 10:4; "Exclusion of Dr. Sudhindra Bose from India," *MR* 36 (December 1924): 745; "Why Dr. Bose Was Not Allowed to Come to India," *MR* 31 (January 1922): 107–08; Gupta, "Indians," p. 15; Carrott, "Prejudice Goes to Court," p. 135, reviews arguments on Japanese landholding.

47. Karen Leonard, "Punjabi Farmers and California's Alien Land Law," *Agricultural History* 59 (October 1985): 549–62. The tradition of Indians using the courts to protect their rights dated back at least to 1919, when rice farmers in Willows, California, sued the Provident Irrigation Syndicate for failure to provide water for their farms; San Francisco *Examiner*, 2 July 1919, 7:7.

48. Karen Leonard, "The Pahkar Singh Murders: A Punjabi Response to California's Alien Land Law," *Amerasia* 11 (1984): 75–87. Complaints of viola-

tions of the law continued, but the government usually took no action. See F. H. Helmer to justice department, 31 October 1927, and B. M. Parmenter, assistant attorney general, to Helmer, 3 December 1927, file 225815, NA, RG 118.

49. Tupper, "American Sentiment," pp. 460–62; San Francisco *Examiner*, 15 April 1924, quoted in Mackett, "Some Aspects," p. 125.

50. H. J. Randall, "Nationality and Naturalization: A Study in the Relativity of Law," *Law Quarterly Review* 40 (January 1924): 28; Helmer to justice department, 31 October 1927, file 225815, NA, RG 60.

51. New York *Times*, 12 June 1924, 16:4, 20 October 1924, 19:6, 26 October 1924, IV:4; A. C., "Anti-Asiatic Fever in America," *MR* (July 1924): 117–18; Bose, " 'White' America," p. 150; New York *Times*, 4 February 1925, 4:4. Das, "True Status," p. 465.

52. Rabindranath Tagore, "East to West," *Atlantic Monthly* 139 (June 1927): 733–34; Province of British Columbia, *Report on Oriental Activities Within the Province* (Victoria: GPO, 1927); A. H. Fenwick, "Far East is East," *MacLean's Magazine*, 15 January 1928, p. 192.

Epilogue

1. For this argument see Michael J. Piore, *Birds of Passage: Migrant Labor and Industrial Societies* (New York: Cambridge University Press, 1979), especially pp. 81–89.

2. Karen Leonard and Bruce La Brack, "Conflict and Compatibility in Punjabi-Mexican Immigrant Families in Rural California, 1916–1965," *Journal of Marriage and the Family* 46 (August 1984): 527–37; and Karen Leonard, "Marriage and Family Life Among Early Asian Indian Immigrants," pp. 67–75.

3. Leonard, "Marriage and Family Life," pp. 67–75; Leonard, "Punjabi Farmers and California's Alien Land Law," pp. 549–62; and Robert Higgs, "Landless by Law: Japanese Immigrants in California Agriculture to 1941," *Journal of Economic History* 38 (March 1978): 205–25.

4. Das, "An American Attitude," p. 751.

5. H. G. Haig to under secretary of state for India, 11 November 1926, GGC, vol. 209, PAC.

6. MacKinnon and MacKinnon, *Agnes Smedley*, pp. 69–81, discuss postwar activities in Germany.

7. There is no good study of the Ghadar Party in the period from 1920 to 1947. Relations with Russia are discussed in Josh, *Hindustan Gadar Party*, 2:214–23. Partial accounts are also in Mahur, *Indian Revolutionary Party*, p. 141, and Naidis, "Propaganda of the Gadar Party," pp. 251–60. None of these accounts is totally reliable.

8. Edwin Irwin telegrams to secretary of state for India, 28 January 1927 and 8 February 1927, GGC, vol. 209, PAC. For information on Russian involvement see David N. Druhe, *Soviet Russia and Indian Communism* (New York: Bantam, 1959), pp. 53–55.

9. Winston Churchill to Lord Julian Byng, 15 August 1921, and Haig to under

secretary of state for India, 11 November 1926, GGC, vol. 209, PAC. Rathore, "Indian Nationalist," pp. 72, 247, discusses Rustomji.

10. Irwin telegrams to secretary of state for India, 28 January 1927 and 8 February 1927, Amery to Freeman Willingdon, 28 February 1927, Ottawa memorandum, 15 March 1927, GGC, vol. 209, PAC.

11. Correspondence regarding the Ghadar Party in the 1930s is in file 845, NA, RG 59. William Roger Lewis, *British Strategy in the Far East, 1919–1939* (Oxford: Clarendon, 1971), pp. 132–35.

12. W. W. Husband to Henry Stimson, 21 December 1931, mentions an 18 December 1931 request for investigation from the British, file 845.00/741, NA, RG 59.

13. C. S. Morrill to Cordell Hull, 12 April 1933, C. S. Morrill to G. H. Austin, 19 August 1931, and Renwick S. McNiece, American consul at Karachi, to Stimson, 23 June 1931, file 211, NA, RG 59.

14. For Morrill's views and other reports see San Francisco *Chronicle*, 27 November 1931, 1:5, 8 December 1931, 5:2, 23 April 1933, 1:7, 25 April 1933, 1:6,and 14 October 1935, 4:1.

15. Josh, *Hindustan Gadar Party*, 2:308–09.

16. For information on Indian immigration during the 1920s, see Norman Buchignani and Doreen M. Indra, *Continuous Journey: A Social History of South Asians in Canada* (Toronto: McClelland and Stewart, 1985), pp. 710–87. For a discussion of continued anti-Asian sentiment in the 1920s, see Province of British Columbia, *Report on Oriental Activities Within the Province* (Victoria: GPO, 1927), pp. 3–4, and MacInnes, *Oriental Occupation of British Columbia*, pp. 140–49.

17. Rathore, "Indian Nationalist Agitation," p. 166.

18. R. Shaplen, "Profiles: One Man Lobby," *New Yorker* 27 (24 March 1951): 35–36.

19. Montague A. Machell, *"Muslim Valley Forge": An Introduction to Mubarek Ali Khan* (Phoenix, Ariz.: privately printed, 1949), pp. i–ii, 28–30.

20. William Roger Louis, *Imperialism at Bay: The United States and the Decolonization of the British Empire, 1941–1945* (New York: Oxford University Press, 1978), pp. 149–50.

21. "Ram Ram, Jad Jao: Yanks in India Master Lingo and Learn How to Get Along," *Newsweek* 21 (4 January 1943): 21; *Ramgarh: "Now It Can Be Told"* (Ranchi: privately printed, n.d.), p. 189; Gary R. Hess, *America Encounters India, 1941–1947* (Baltimore: Johns Hopkins University Press, 1971), pp. 2, 167; and Mackett, "Some Aspects," pp. 438, 442.

22. House Committee on Immigration and Naturalization, *To Grant a Quota to Eastern Hemisphere Indians and to Make Them Racially Eligible for Naturalization*, hearings, 79th Cong., 1st sess., 1945. For a discussion of Roosevelt's action on the bill see Divine, *American Immigration Policy*, p. 153; Roosevelt to Samuel Dickstein, 5 March 1945, quoted in Machell, *"Muslim Valley Forge,"* p. ii; Hess, *American Encounters India*, p. 159.

23. Jawaharlal Nehru, *Visit to America* (New York: John Day, 1950), pp. 3, 79, 115.

24. D. S. Saund, *Congressman from India* (New York: Dutton, 1960), pp. 29–56, 73.

25. For a discussion of the post–1962 immigration see S. Chandrasekhar, ed., *From India to America: Immigration from India to the U.S.* (La Jolla, Calif.: Population Review, 1984), S. Chandrasekhar, ed., *From India to Canada: A Brief History of Immigration; Problems of Discrimination, Admission, and Assimilation* (La Jolla, Calif.: Population Review, 1986), pp. 35–46. Robert W. Gardner, Bryant Robey, and Peter C. Smith, *Asian Americans: Growth, Change, and Diversity* (Washington: Population Reference Bureau, 1985), pp. 2–4, 22–30; and Buchignani and Indra, *Continuous Journey*, pp. 148–204.

26. Joan M. Jensen, "East Indians," in Stephen Thernstrom, ed., *Harvard Encyclopedia of Ethnic Groups* (Cambridge: Harvard University Press, Belknap Press, 1980), pp. 296–301; and Elliott R. Barkan, "Whom Shall We Integrate? A Comparative Analysis of the Immigration and Naturalization Trends of Asians Before and After the 1965 Immigration Act (1951–1978)," *Journal of American Ethnic History* 3 (Fall 1983): 29–57.

27. Richard Ashok Kumar Shankar, "The East Indians of the Greater San Francisco Bay Area of San Francisco," (Ph.D. diss., Boston College, 1977), pp. 148–51, 500–48.

28. Judy Yung, " 'A Bowlful of Tears': Chinese Women Immigrants on Angel Island," *Frontiers* 2, no. 2 (Summer 1977): 52–55.

29. Alexander Saxton, *The Indispensable Enemy: Labor and the Anti-Chinese Movement in California* (Berkeley and Los Angeles: University of California Press, 1971), pp. 258–73.

Selected Bibliography

Articles

Barkan, Elliott. "Whom Shall We Integrate? A Comparative Analysis of the Immigration and Naturalization Trends of Asians Before and After the 1965 Immigration Act (1951–1978)." *Journal of American Ethnic History* 3 (1983): 29–57.

Bose, Arun Coomer. "Indian Nationalist Agitation in the USA and Canada till the Arrival of Har Dayal in 1911." *Journal of Indian History* 93 (April 1965): 227–39.

Buchignani, Norman L. "A Review of the Historical and Sociological Literature on East Indians in Canada." *Canadian Ethnic Studies* 9 (1977): 86–108.

Daniels, Roger. "Westerners From the East: Oriental Immigrants Reappraised." *Pacific Historical Review* 35 (1966): 373–84.

Dignan, Don K. "The Hindu Conspiracy in Anglo-American Relations During World War I." *Pacific Historical Review* 40 (1971): 57–77.

Gordon, Donald C. "Roosevelt's 'Smart Yankee Trick,' " *Pacific Historical Review* 30 (1961): 351–58.

Hennings, Robert. "James D. Phelan and the Woodrow Wilson Anti-Oriental Statement of May 3, 1912." *California Historical Society Quarterly* 42 (December 1963): 291–300.

Hess, Gary R. "The 'Hindu' in America: Immigration and Naturalization Policies and India, 1917–1946." *Pacific Historical Review* 38 (1969): 59–79.

Higgs, R. "Landless by Law: Japanese Immigrants in California Agriculture to 1941." *Journal of Economic History* 38 (1979): 205–25.

Jensen, Joan M. "Apartheid: Pacific Coast Style." *Pacific Historical Review* 38 (1966): 185–201.

———. "East Indians." In *Harvard Encyclopedia of Ethnic Groups*, edited by Stephen Thernstrom, pp. 296–301. Cambridge: Harvard University Press, Belknap Press,1980.

———. "The 'Hindu Conspiracy': A Reevaluation." *Pacific Historical Review* 48 (1979): 65–83.

Krüger, Horst. "Har Dayal in Deutschland." *Mitteilungen des Instituts für Orientforschung* 10 (1964): 141–69.

La Brack, Bruce. "Immigration Law and the Revitalization Process: The Case of the California Sikhs." *Population Review* 25 (1982): 59–66.

———. "Occupational Specialization Among Rural California Sikhs: The Interplay of Culture and Economics." *Amerasia Journal* 9 (1982): 29–56.

Leonard, Karen. "Marriage and Family Life Among Early Asian Indian Immigrants." *Population Review* 125 (1981): 67–75.

———. "The Pahkar Singh Murders: A Punjabi Response to California's Alien Land Law." *Amerasia Journal* 11 (1984): 75–87.

———. "Punjabi Farmers and California's Alien Land Law." *Agricultural History* 59 (1985): 549–62.

Leonard, Karen, and Bruce LaBrack. "Conflict and Compatibility in Punjabi-Mexican Immigrant Families in Rural California: 1915–1965." *Journal of Marriage and the Family* 46 (1984): 527–37.

Le Pore, Herbert P. "Prelude to Prejudice: Hiram Johnson, Woodrow Wilson, and the California Alien Land Law Controversy of 1913." *Southern California Quarterly* 61 (1979): 99–110.

Narayanan, R. "Indian Immigration and the India League of America." *Indian Journal of American Studies* 2, no. 1 (1972): 1–30.

Papademetriou, Demetrios G. "Rethinking International Migration: A Review and Critique." *Comparative Political Studies* 15 (January 1983): 469–98.

Prakash, Ved, and Sylvia Vatuk. "Protest Songs of East Indians on the West Coast, U.S.A." *Folklore* 7 (October 1966): 370–82.

Puri, Harish K. "Ghadar Movement: An Experiment in New Patterns of Socialization." *Journal of Regional History* 1, no. 1 (1980): 120–41.

Raucher, Alan. "American Anti-Imperialists and the Pro-India Movement, 1900–1932." *Pacific Historical Review* 42 (1974): 83–110.

Rockett, Ian R. H. "American Immigration Policy and Ethnic Selection: An Historical Overview." *Journal of Ethnic Studies* 10 (Winter 1983): 1–26.

Saha, Panchanan. "Indian Revolutionary Movement in Germany." *Mainstream* 12, no. 6 (6 October 1973): 33–36.

Sehanavis, C. "Pioneers Among Indian Revolutionaries in Germany." *Mainstream* 13, no. 46 (19 July 1975): 11–14.

Spector, Ronald. "The Vermont Education of Taraknath Das: An Episode in British-American-Indian Relations." *Vermont History* 48 (Spring 1980): 89–95.

Spellman, John W. "The International Extension of Political Conspiracy as Illustrated by the Gadar Party." *Journal of Indian History* 37 (1959): 23–45.

Books

Aurora, G. S. *The New Frontiersmen: A Sociological Study of Indian Immigrants in the United Kingdom*. Bombay: Popular Prakashan, 1967.

Barooah, Nirode Kumar. *India and the Official Germany, 1886–1914*. Frankfurt: Peter Lang, 1977.

Barrier, Norman. *The Punjab Alienation of Land Bill of 1900*. Durham, N.C.: Duke University, 1966.

Bass, Paul. *Language, Religion and Politics in North India*. Cambridge: Cambridge University Press, 1974.

Brown, Emily C. *Har Dayal: Hindu Revolutionalist and Rationalist*. Tucson: University of Arizona Press, 1975.

Buchighani, Norman, and Doreen M. Indra. *Continuous Journey: A Social History of South Asians in Canada*. Toronto: McClelland and Stewart, 1985.

Chadney, James G. *The Sikhs of Vancouver*. New York: AMS Press, 1984.

Chandrasekhar, S., ed. *From India to Canada: A Brief History of Immigration; Problems of Discrimination, Admission and Assimilation*. La Jolla, Calif.: Population Review, 1986.

———. *From India to America: Immigration from India to the U.S.* La Jolla, Calif.: Population Review, 1984.

Cheng, Lucie, and Edna Bonacich. *Labor Immigration Under Capitalism* Berkeley and Los Angeles: University of California Press, 1984.

Daniels, Roger. *The Politics of Prejudice*. Berkeley and Los Angeles: University of California Press, 1962.

Dignan, Don. *The Indian Revolutionary Problem in British Diplomacy, 1914–1919*. New Delhi: Allied Publishers, 1983.

———. *New Perspectives on British Far Eastern Policy, 1913–1919*. Brisbane: University of Queensland Press, 1969.

Fisher, Maxine P. *The Indians of New York City: A Study of Immigrants from India*. Columbia, Mo.: South Asia Books, 1980.

Fox, Richard G. *Lions of the Punjab: Culture in the Making*. Berkeley and Los Angeles: University of California Press, 1985.

Gagai, Leona A. *The East Indians and the Pakastanis in America*. Minneapolis: Lerner, 1972.

Gardner, Robert W., Bryant Robey, and Peter C. Smith. *Asian Americans: Growth, Change and Diversity*. Washington: Population Reference Bureau, 1985.

Hess, Gary R. *America Encounters India, 1941–1947*. Baltimore: Johns Hopkins University Press, 1971.

Huttenback, Robert A. *Racism and Empire: White Settlers and Colored Immigrants in the British Self-Governing Colonies, 1830–1910*. Ithaca: Cornell University Press, 1976.

Jackson, Carl T. *The Oriental Religions and American Thought: Nineteenth Century Explorations*. Westport, Conn.: Greenwood, 1981.

Johnston, Hugh. *The Voyage of the Komagata Maru: The Sikh Challenge to Canada's Colour Bar*. Delhi: Oxford University Press, 1979.

Josh, Sohan Singh. *Hindustan Gadar Party*. 2 vols. New Delhi: People's Publishing, 1977–1978.

———. *Tragedy of Komagata Maru*. New Delhi: People's Publishing, 1975.

Juergensmeyer, Mark, and N. Gerald Barrier, eds. *Sikh Studies, Comparative Perspectives on a Changing Tradition: Working Papers from the Berkeley Conference on Sikh Studies*. Berkeley: Graduate Theological Union, 1979.

Kissinger, Tom G. *Vilyatpur 1848–1968: Social and Economic Change in a North Indian Village*. Berkeley and Los Angeles: University of California Press, 1974.

Louis, William Roger. *Imperialism at Bay: The United States and the Decolonization of the British Empire, 1941–1945*. New York: Oxford University Press, 1978.

Majumdar, R. C. *History of the Freedom Movement in India*. 3 vols. Calcutta: Mukhopadhyay, 1963.

Mathur, L. P. *Indian Revolutionary Movement in the United States*. Delhi: Chand, 1970.

Melendy, H. Brett. *Asians in America: Filipinos, Koreans, and East Indians*. Boston: Twayne, 1977.

Mittal, S. C. *Freedom Movement in Punjab, 1905–1929*. Delhi: Concept Publishing, 1977.

Nagar, Purushottam. *Lala Lajpat Rai: The Man and His Ideas*. New Delhi: Manohar, 1977.

Papademetriou, G., and Mark J. Miller. *The Unavoidable Issue: U.S. Immigration Policy in the 1980s*. Philadelphia: Institute for the Study of Human Issues, 1983.

Piore, Michael J. *Birds of Passage: Migrant Labor and Industrial Societies*. New York: Cambridge University Press, 1979.

Portes, Alejandro, and John Walton. *Labor, Class, and the International System*. New York: Academic Press, 1981.

Price, Charles A. *The Great White Walls Are Built: Restrictive Immigration to North America and Australasia, 1836–1888*. Canberra: Australian National University Press, 1974.

Puri, Harish K. *Ghadar Movement: Ideology, Organization and Strategy*. Amritsar: Garu Nanak Dev University, 1983.

Sareen, Anuradha. *India and Afghanistan: British Imperialism vs. Afghan Nationalism, 1907–1921*. Delhi: Seena Publications, 1981.

Sareen, Tilak Raj. *Indian Revolutionary Movement Abroad (1905–1921)*. New Delhi: Sterling, 1979.

Saund, D. S. *Congressman from India*. New York: Dutton, 1960.

Singh, Diwakar Prasad. *American Attitude Towards Indian Nationalist Movement*. New Delhi: Munshiram Manoharlal, 1974.

Singh, Fauja. *Eminent Freedom Fighters of Punjab*. Patiala: Punjabi University, Department of Punjab Historical Studies, 1972.

Singh, Harnam. *The Indian National Movement and American Opinion*. New Delhi: Central Electric, 1962.

Singh, Kushwant. *A History of the Sikhs*. 2 vols. Princeton: Princeton University Press, 1963–1966.

Tandon, Prakash. *Punjabi Century, 1857–1947*. Berkeley and Los Angeles: University of California Press, 1968.

Tinker, Hugh. *A New System of Slavery: The Export of Indian Labour Overseas, 1830–1920*. London: Oxford University Press, 1974.

Ward, W. Peter. *White Canada Forever: Popular Attitudes and Public Policy Toward Orientals in British Columbia*. Montreal: McGill-Queen's University Press, 1974.

Wolpert, Stanley. *Morley and India, 1906–1910*. Berkeley and Los Angeles: University of California Press, 1967.

———. *Tilak and Gokhale: Revolution and Reform in the Making of Modern India*. Berkeley and Los Angeles: University of California Press, 1962.

Unpublished Sources and Court Cases

In many ways, the Canadian archives are the most valuable because of the reports from undercover agents in the governor general's correspondence. These records, however, relate only to the activities of the West Coast radicals, as does the Ghadar Collection at the University of California at Berkeley. The William C. Smith Documents at the University of Oregon provide the best information on the economic lives of the new immigrants. The activities of the United States government are obviously best studied through the various record groups in the National Archives and the manuscript collections at the Library of Congress. I have also learned much from interviews with Indians and from discussions with other scholars working in the field, particularly from Jan and Steve MacKinnon on the Friends for the Freedom of India and the role of Agnes Smedley in the Indian independence movement, and from Bruce La Brack on the ethnology of the West Coast Sikhs.

Manuscript Collections

California State Library, Sacramento Clipping files
Hoover Library, Stanford University, Palo Alto, California Pamphlets
Library of Congress, Washington, D.C.
    Theodore Roosevelt Papers
    William Howard Taft Papers
    Charles Warren Papers
    Woodrow Wilson Papers
National Archives, Washington, D.C.
    Record Group 59: State Department
    Record Group 60: Justice Department
    Record Group 85: Immigration and Naturalization Service
    Record Group 94: American Protective League
    Record Group 118: United States Attorneys and Marshals
    Record Group 165: Military Intelligence Division
Plumas County Museum, Quincy, California
    Railroad files
Public Archives of Canada, Ottawa, Canada
    Governor General's Correspondence
    Grey of Hardwick Papers
    Mackenzie King Papers
University of California at Berkeley
    Ghadar Collection

University of Oregon at Portland
  William C. Smith Documents
Yale University, New Haven, Connecticut
  E. M. House Papers
  Frank Polk Papers
  William Wiseman Papers

Microfilm

Records of the German Foreign Ministry Archives (Politisches Archiv d. Auswärtige Amt), 1867–1920

Unpublished Papers

Adelson, Roger Dean. "The Formation of British Policy Towards the Middle East, 1914–1918." Ph.D. diss., Washington University in Saint Louis. 1972.

Andracki, Stanislaw. "The Immigration of Orientals into Canada with Special Reference to Chinese." Ph.D. diss., McGill University, 1958.

Bradfield, Helen Haynes. "The East Indians of Yuba City: A Study in Acculturation." M.A. thesis, Sacramento State College, 1971.

Brown, Emily Clara. "Har Dayal: A Portrait of an Indian Intellectual." Ph.D. diss., University of Arizona, 1967.

Carroll, Elizabeth J. "A Study: East Indian (Sikh) Women Students at Yuba College." Education paper, University of Southern California, 1973.

Chakravorti, Robindra C. "The Sikhs of El Centro: A Study in Social Integration." Ph.D. diss., University of Minnesota, 1968.

Crane, Robert I. "The Development of the American View of India, as Seen in Certain Religious Periodicals Published in the U.S., 1897–1931." M.A. thesis, American University, 1943.

Deodhar, Shyama. "The Treatment of India in American Social Studies Textbooks, 1921–1951." Ph.D. diss., University of Michigan, 1954.

Dodd, Balbinder Singh. "Social Change in Two Overseas Sikh Communities." M.A. thesis, University of British Columbia, 1972.

Forth, William Stuart. "Wesley L. Jones: A Political Biography." Ph.D. diss., University of Washington, 1962.

Fuller, Levi Varden. "The Supply of Agricultural Labor as a Factor in the Evolution of Farm Organization in California." Ph.D. diss., University of California at Berkeley, 1939.

Giovinco, Joseph. "The California Career of Anthony Caminetti, Italian American Politician." Ph.D. diss., University of California at Berkeley, 1973.

Hatfield, James R. "California's Migrant Farm Labor Problem and Some Efforts to Deal with It, 1930–1940." M.A. thesis, Sacramento State College, 1968.

Hennings, Robert. "James D. Phelan and the Wilson Progressives of California." Ph.D. diss., University of California at Berkeley, 1961.

Jacoby, Harold S. "Why So Few East Indians: A Study in Social Reticence."

Unpublished paper, Ghadar Party Collection, University of California at Berkeley, n.d.

Khan, Salim. "A Brief History of Pakistanis in the Western United States." M.A. thesis, California State University at Sacramento, 1981.

Khush, Harwant Kaur. "The Social Participation and Attitudes of the Children of East Indian Immigrants." M.A. thesis, Sacramento State College, 1965.

Kshirsager, Shiwaram Krishnarao. "Development of Relations Between India and the United States, 1941–1952." Ph.D. diss., American University, 1957.

La Brack, Bruce Wilfred. "The Sikhs of Northern California: A Sociohistorical Study." Ph.D. diss., Syracuse University, 1980.

Mercer, Dorothy Frederica. "Leaves of Grass and the Bhagavad Gita: A Comparative Study." Ph.D. diss., University of California at Berkeley, 1933.

Miller, Allan P. "An Ethnographic Report on the Sikh (East) Indians of the Sacramento Valley." Unpublished paper, University of California at Berkeley, 1950.

Norman, Dorothy. "The Free World, the U.S.A., and India." Mimeographed paper, Hoover Library, 1954.

Pendleton, Edwin Charles. "History of Labor in Arizona Irrigated Agriculture." Ph.D. diss., University of California at Berkeley, 1950.

Rathore, Naeem Gul. "The Indian Nationalist Agitation in the U.S.: A Study of Lala Lajpat Rai and the Indian Home Rule League of America, 1914–1920." Ph.D. diss., Columbia University, 1965.

Rose, Alice. "The Rise of California Insurgency: Origins of the League of Lincoln-Roosevelt Republican Clubs, 1900–1907." Ph.D. diss., Stanford University, 1942.

Santry, Patricia Josephine. "An Historical Perspective of the Factors Preventing Sikh Assimilation in California, 1906–1946." M.A. thesis, California State University, Fullerton. 1982.

Schmidt, E. R. "American Relations with South Asia, 1900–1940." Ph.D. diss., University of Pennsylvania, 1955.

Schramm, Richard Howard. "The Image of India in Selected American Literary Periodicals, 1870–1900." Ph.D. diss., Duke University, 1964.

Shankar, Richard Ashok. "Integration Goal Definition of East Indian Students in Sutter County." M.A. thesis, Chico State College, 1971.

———. "The East Indians of the Greater San Francisco Bay Area of California: A Study of an Ethnic Status Community." Ph.D. diss., Boston College, 1977.

Singh, Diwakar Prasad. "American Official Attitudes Towards the Indian Nationalist Movement, 1905–1929." Ph.D. diss., University of Hawaii, 1964.

Singh, Harnam. "American Press Opinion About Indian Government and Politics, 1919–1935." Ph.D. diss., Georgetown University, 1949.

Singh, Khushwant. "India's First Armed Revolution: The Ghadr Rebellion of 1915." Mimeographed paper, Asian History Congress, Azad Bhavan, New Delhi, 1961.

Sorich, R. "Fragments in the Biography of M. N. Roy." Typewritten carbon copy dated 23 August 1953, Hoover Library.

Spaeth, Carl B. "The Lucknow Conference: India and the United States." Mimeographed paper, 1950.

Stern, Bernard. "American Views of India and Indians, 1857–1900." Ph.D. diss., University of Pennsylvania, 1956.

Strasser, Marland Keith. "American Neutrality: The Case of Consul-General Bopp." M.A. thesis, University of California at Berkeley, 1939.

Tripathi, Dwijendra. "The United States and India: Economic Links, 1860–1900." Ph.D. diss., University of Wisconsin, 1963.

Tupper, Eleanor, "American Sentiment Toward Japan." Ph.D. diss., Clark University, 1929.

Wu, Charles Ling. "Attitudes Toward Negroes, Jews, and Orientals in the United States." Ph.D. diss., Ohio State University, 1927.

Vyas, P. "The United States Congress and India: A Study in Congressional Attitudes Toward India, 1947–1960." Ph.D. diss., American University, 1961.

Wood, Ann Louise. "East Indians in California: A Study of Their Organizations, 1900–1947." M.A. thesis, University of Wisconsin, 1966.

Wynne, Robert Edward. "Reaction to the Chinese in the Pacific Northwest and British Columbia, 1850 to 1910." Ph.D. diss., University of Washington, 1964.

Interviews

Tuly Singh Johl, 28 May 1975 and 24 August 1975.
Nahn Kaur Singh, 27 May 1975.

Court Cases

Akhay Kumar Mozumdar v. United States, 299 Fed. 240 (1924)
Bessho v. United States, 178 Fed. 245 (1910)
Bhagat Singh v. McGrath, 104 F.2d. 122 (1939)
Channan Singh v. Haff, 103 F.2d. 303 (1939)
Dennis et al. v. United States, 341 U.S. 494 (1951)
Dow v. United States, 226 Fed. 145 (1915)
Elk v. Wilkins, 112 U.S. 94 (1884)
Ex parte Dow, 211 Fed. 486 (1914)
Ex parte Moola Singh et al., 207 Fed. 780 (1913)
Ex parte Shahid, 205 Fed. 812 (1913)
Ex parte Singh, 12 F. Supp. 145 (1935)
Goldman et al. v. United States, 245 U.S. 474 (1918)
In re Akhay Kumar Mozumdar, 207 Fed. 115 (1913)
In re Balsara, 171 Fed. 294 (1909)
In re Bhagat Singh Thind, 268 Fed. 683 (1920)
In re Dow, 213 Fed. 355 (1914)
In re Ellis, 179 Fed. 1002 (1910)
In re Halladjian et al., 174 Fed. 834 (1909)
In re Mohan Singh, 257 Fed. 209 (1919)
In re Mudarri, 176 Fed. 465 (1910)
In re Najour, 174 Fed. 735 (1909)

In re Norian Singh, 18 British Columbia Rep. 506 (1913)
In re Rhagat Singh et al., 209 Fed. 700 (1913)
In re Sadar Bhagwab Singh, 246 Fed. 496 (1917)
Jacobsen v. United States, 272 Fed. 399 (1920)
Kharaiti Ram Samras v. United States, 125 F.2d 879 (1942)
Kishan Singh v. Carr, 88 F.2d. 672 (1937)
Marshall v. Backus, 229 Fed. 1021 (1916)
Mon Singh v. White, 274 Fed. 513 (1921)
Morrison et al. v. California, 291 U.S. 82 (1934)
People v. Hall, 4 Cal. 399 (1854)
Roldan v. Los Angeles County, 129 Cal. App. 268 (1933)
Schenck v. United States, 249 U.S. 47 (1919)
Shermann v. United States, 264 Fed. 917 (1920)
Singh v. District Director of Immigration at San Francisco, 96 F.2d. 969
    (1938)
Singh v. United States, 243 Fed. 557 (1917)
Singh et al. v. United States, 243 Fed. 559 (1917)
Takao Ozawa v. United States, 260 U.S. 178 (1922)
Takuji Yamashita et al. v. Hinkle, 260 U.S. 199 (1922)
Thaman Singh v. Haff, 83 F.2d. 679 (1936)
Toyota v. United States, 268 U.S. 402 (1924)
United States ex. rel. Mazur v. Commissioner of Immigration, 101 F.2d. 707
    (1939)
United States v. Akhay Kumar Mozumdar, 296 Fed. 173 (1923)
United States v. Ali, 7 F.2d. 728 (1925)
United States v. Balsara, 180 Fed. 694 (1910)
United States v. Bhagat Singh Thind, 261 U.S. 204 (1922)
United States v. Bopp, 230 Fed. 723 (1916), 232 Fed. 177 (1916), 237 Fed. 283
    (1916)
United States v. Chakraberty et al., 244 Fed. 287 (1917)
United States v. Darmer, 249 Fed. 989 (1918)
United States v. Dellinger, 474 F.2d. 340 (1972)
United States v. Dolla, 177 Fed. 101 (1910)
United States v. Gokhale, 26 F.2d. 360 (1928)
United States v. Hárt, 78 Fed. 868 (1897)
United States v. Herberger, 272 Fed. 278 (1921)
United States v. Hughes, 75 Fed. 267 (1896)
United States v. Kramer, 262 Fed. 395 (1919)
United States v. Mohan Singh, 257 Fed. 496 (1917)
United States v. Raverat, 222 Fed. 1018 (1915)
United States v. Ruroede et al., 220 Fed. 210 (1915)
United States v. Sakharam Ganesh Pandit, 297 Fed. 529 (1924), 15 F.2d. 285
    (1926)
United States v. Spock, 416 F.2d. 165 (1969)
United States v. Swelgin, 254 Fed. 884 (1918)
United States v. Wiborg et al., 73 Fed. 159 (1896)

United States v. Woerndle, 288 Fed. 47 (1923)
United States v. Wursterbarth, 249 Fed. 908 (1918)
United States v. Ybanez, 53 Fed. 536 (1892)
Wadia v. United States, 101 F.2d. 7 (1939)

Index

Romanet

St. Louis Community College
at Meramec
Library